Understanding psychology and crime

Perspectives on theory and action

CRIME AND JUSTICE
Series editor: Mike Maguire
Cardiff University

Crime and Justice is a series of short introductory texts on central topics in criminology. The books in this series are written for students by internationally renowned authors. Each book tackles a key area within criminology, providing a concise and up-to-date overview of the principal concepts, theories, methods and findings relating to the area. Taken as a whole, the *Crime and Justice* series will cover all the core components of an undergraduate criminology course.

Understanding psychology and crime

Perspectives on theory and action

James McGuire

Open University Press

Open University Press
McGraw-Hill Education
McGraw-Hill House
Shoppenhangers Road
Maidenhead
Berkshire
England
SL6 2QL

email: enquiries@openup.co.uk
world wide web: www.openup.co.uk

and Two Penn Plaza, New York, NY 10121-2289, USA

First published 2004

A catalogue record of this book is available from the British Library

ISBN 0 335 21119 4 (pb)   0 335 21120 8 (hb)

Library of Congress Cataloging-in-Publication Data
CIP data has been applied for

Typeset by RefineCatch Ltd, Bungay, Suffolk
Printed in the UK by Bell & Bain Ltd, Glasgow

Contents

Series editor's foreword

James McGuire's book is the eleventh in the successful *Crime and Justice* series published by Open University Press. The series is now established as a key resource in universities teaching criminology or criminal justice, especially in the UK but increasingly also overseas. The aim from the outset has been to give undergraduates and graduates both a solid grounding in the relevant area and a taste to explore it further. Although aimed primarily at students new to the field, and written as far as possible in plain language, the books are not oversimplified. On the contrary, the authors set out to 'stretch' readers and to encourage them to approach criminological knowledge and theory in a critical and questioning frame of mind.

James McGuire has been a leading figure in the 'What Works' debates that have been increasingly prominent in the criminal justice arena over the last ten years, especially in relation to the development of cognitive-behavioural programmes, which aim to encourage and assist offenders on probation or in prison to understand and address their offending behaviour. Naturally, he covers these issues in this book in considerable depth, but his aims here are much broader. In essence, he sets out to assess the contribution that psychology can make, and has made, to knowledge and practice in the fields of criminology and criminal justice. As he points out, there has been something of a 'divorce' between psychologists and criminologists since the 1970s, when sociological approaches began to dominate academic criminology (in Britain, at least) and psychological approaches were criticized, as part of a major attack on 'positivism', for excessive focus on individual pathology at the expense of attention to broader structural forces in society.

However, as McGuire shows, 'psychology' is an infinitely richer and more complex subject than has been portrayed in many of the cruder attacks on its relevance to the study of crime, and psychologists adopt a wide variety of theoretical approaches which should be of core interest to criminologists. Moreover, psychology has been making a serious 'comeback' in the criminal policy and practice arenas, not just in the 'What Works' developments in prisons and probation, but through major contributions in policing (especially serious crime investigation), criminal evidence to courts, risk assessment, and early interventions with children and families. As a result, many more opportunities are opening up in the criminal justice field for graduates with some knowledge of psychology. This is increasingly being recognized by those running undergraduate and postgraduate degrees in criminology, and more and more modules with a strong psychological slant are being developed. Degrees and courses in forensic psychology, too, are expanding rapidly in universities. This book will be of value to students on all the above.

The book begins with a broad overview of the relationship between psychology and the study of crime, at the same time laying to rest some myths about the assumed philosophical basis of psychology. In Chapters 2, 3 and 4, McGuire argues that the study of individual factors, including cognitive and emotional development, should be seen as one (important) element of a broader understanding of crime, which should include the influences of socialization and peer groups as well as the broader social and economic environment. He also highlights the value of understanding 'pathways' to offending behaviour, and the critical points at which choices are made. Chapters 5 and 6 cover the theoretical and empirical research foundations upon which the identification of 'criminogenic risk factors' has been built, and show how the theory has been turned into practice through the development of offending behaviour programmes. Chapter 7 offers a much broader survey of what psychology has to say about some of the core concepts with which criminologists and penologists have wrestled over the years, including retribution, deterrence and incapacitation. Chapter 8 looks at some of the major practical applications of psychology in policing, prosecution and sentencing. It also raises some of the important ethical and political questions to which they give rise.

Overall, the book offers a rich and wide-ranging – as well as very readable – discussion of the complex relationships between psychology, criminology and criminal justice policy and practice. It demonstrates how important it is to understand practice and policy developments in relation to their theoretical underpinnings, and should be of major interest to practitioners as well as to those engaged in academic study.

Other books previously published in the *Crime and Justice* series – all of whose titles begin with the word 'Understanding' – have covered criminological theory (Sandra Walklate), penal theory (Barbara Hudson), crime data and statistics (Clive Coleman and Jenny Moynihan), youth and crime (Sheila Brown), crime prevention (Gordon Hughes), violent crime (Stephen Jones), community penalties (Peter Raynor and Maurice Vanstone), white collar crime (Hazel Croall), risk and crime (Hazel Kemshall) and social control (Martin Innes). Two are already in second editions and other second editions are planned. Other new books in the pipeline include texts on prisons, policing, criminological research methods, sentencing and criminal justice, drugs and crime, race and crime, and crime and social exclusion. All are major topics in university degree courses on crime and criminal justice, and each book should make an ideal foundation text for a relevant module. As an aid to understanding, clear summaries are provided at regular intervals, and a glossary of key terms and concepts is a feature of every book. In addition, to help students expand their knowledge, recommendations for further reading are given at the end of each chapter.

Mike Maguire
April 2004

Preface

Some years ago, a well-known criminological researcher told me that he 'had never had much use for psychology' in his work and implied he could not see the relevance of it for criminology as a whole. I was at first taken aback by this, mainly on account of its abrupt and all-embracing dismissiveness, and thought it must be an idiosyncratic standpoint. Having become more familiar with the literature of criminology since then, I now realize it is a view that is quite widespread. Writers in criminology have depicted psychology as predominantly positivist in its orientation and have castigated it accordingly (e.g. Roshier 1989). Psychologists themselves have commented on how psychological theory and research have been marginalized and even 'systematically downplayed' in mainstream criminology (e.g. Andrews 1995). Textbooks in the field are evidently much more influenced by other social science disciplines, most prominently sociology. That may account for the 22 out of 564 pages devoted to psychology in the textbook by Conklin (1992), or the even thinner 6 out of 529 pages allotted by Glick (1995).

The rationale for the present book is not to assuage the feelings of hurt and rejection that we poor psychologists may feel in this situation, sensitive though many of us may be! It is instead to examine closely the contribution that psychology is able to make to understanding the activity we call 'crime', and what (if any) practical implications may flow from this. That activity can be studied using many approaches. At least one of them, surely, needs to take into account the observation that whatever other influences may be at play, acts of crime are for the most part committed by individuals. That is certainly the basis on which the law operates: legal decision-making attributes responsibility or guilt for crimes to persons; and while the basis for that may be questioned, there appears little immediate prospect of it being changed in any meaningful way. Even where crimes are committed by corporations or other collective entities, individual decisions are still intimately involved in the process. In a discussion some years after the one mentioned above, another researcher proposed that the recorded increase in crimes of burglary in England and Wales during the years 1980–1982 had been caused by the economic recession of that period. That may indeed have been an important factor. But exactly how did it have its effect? Did the perpetrators of the 200,000 additional burglaries assemble in Hyde Park and jointly decide to embark on a breaking-and-entering spree? Or did their changed circumstances, and their perceptions of and reactions to them, lead to numerous separate decisions to commit a property offence, filtered through each individual's own psychological processes? Why did many other individuals, also afflicted by economic hardship, not resort to burglary during the same period?

There appears to be a widespread assumption that psychology suffers from a number of flaws that make it inapplicable to the study of crime. Its practitioners portray themselves as scientific and adopt the same methods of inquiry as 'hard' scientists, like physicists or biochemists. They talk about behaviour and carry out controlled experiments, at a time when other social studies disciplines have embarked on a search for novel paradigms. Psychology is thought to seek explanations for the things people do more or less exclusively among causes located inside themselves, and to neglect if not actually ignore external, environmental factors such as social conditions or political forces. This has been characterized as an intrinsically conservative stance (Lilly *et al.* 2002). It appears closely allied to biology and medicine, and to the idea of crime as a disease. Psychologists have been known to use rats, pigeons, university students and other exotic species in their research and they make great claims on the basis of some fairly narrowly selected samples and outlandish investigations. In some of their experiments they place people in darkened rooms, make them wear lenses that turn the visual world upside down, or apply electric shocks to them. They employ IQ tests, nonsense syllables, one-way mirrors and aversion therapy. Altogether an odd and unsavoury bunch, with whom it might be better to keep contact to a minimum!

I fully agree: the history of psychology is not entirely wholesome and laudable. It has been littered with some regrettable ideas and unfortunate applications (Gould 1981); though in these respects, it is scarcely unique. I nevertheless am convinced, and hope this book will convince its readers, that psychology contains a great deal that can be useful to criminology in terms of theory, research and application. A recent commentary has noted grounds for a new, potentially more cordial and fruitful relationship between criminology and psychology than has been in evidence for some time (Hollin 2002a). Furthermore, like other disciplines psychology has been steadily evolving, and currently employs a plurality of methodological approaches. Most psychologists recognize that the alleged boundaries between fields of knowledge are subject to shifting and sometimes almost arbitrary definition, and virtually any given problem will require multiple perspectives to be amply understood.

The present volume is offered in that light. It aims as far as possible to project a picture of the psychological elements in crime while identifying as many as possible of the necessary links to other social sciences. This is not to claim that individual, psychological factors are somehow more important than those more regularly studied within criminology. Rather, it is an insistence that if we dismiss or neglect those issues, our ability to comprehend the problem of crime will remain inadequate. Only a combined effort involving theory and evidence from a wide range of sources will help us towards a fuller understanding.

I am very grateful to several people who have had an enormous influence on my understanding of the issues discussed in this book. Foremost is Philip Priestley, to whom I owe an introduction to the field of 'crime and justice' and from whose breadth of knowledge and perspective I benefited enormously. I am very grateful to Mike Maguire for inviting me to be part of the series, and for valuable comments on the manuscript. In discussion at numerous conferences, meetings or advisory panels, I have gained much from being able to pick the brains of some of the most able people in this field. Those who have contributed to the book, in different ways and most often unknowingly, include Don Andrews, Ron Blackburn, Meg Blumsom, Meredith Brown, David Cooke, David Farrington, Paul Gendreau, Clive Hollin, Doug Lipton, Caroline Logan, Friedrich Lösel, Mary McMurran, Frank Porporino, Beverley Rowson, David Thornton and Sheila Vellacott. None of them of course bears blame for any remaining errors or deficiencies.

James McGuire
March 2004

chapter one

Why psychology?

The history and theory texts generally trace the formal study of crime, and the origins of the discipline of criminology, to the first half of the nineteenth century, making it somewhat less than 200 years old. Of course, there is no single documented moment when anyone announced that he or she had just invented a new discipline with such a purpose explicitly in mind. That seems a real pity. The history of ideas would be much more easily written if such moments occurred.

The book you are reading now is devoted to a specific aspect of criminology, or a particular approach within it, informed by psychological theory and research. It is fair to acknowledge from the outset that criminology and psychology have not always had an easy relationship (Hollin 2002a). The pivotal reason for this probably resides in psychologists' perceived over-emphasis on the individual, while many criminologists think of crime as something that can only be understood in terms of social conditions and society-wide trends.

But there are several other aspects to this, which we will explore more fully in this opening chapter. In the remaining chapters of the book, my intention is to outline what, in my view, is the contribution that psychology can make to a number of key questions in criminology. Overall the book is planned as follows. The present chapter is designed to set the scene for the rest. It first of all addresses the question of how crime can be defined. It then provides some background for thinking about the relationship between psychology and criminology, and gives some general information on psychology for readers newly acquainted with it. Chapter 2 considers the relationship between societal, ecological, situational and individual/ psychological factors in helping to explain the occurrence of criminal acts. This involves an excursion into criminological theory, reviewing the principal directions it has taken and the contribution that psychology might make to them. Chapter 3 focuses in more depth on a 'psycho-social' model of individual action and development and how it may be used to understand the emergence, and in some instances the persistence, of patterns of behaviour that are labelled 'criminal'. Chapter 4 will apply this model to provide a more detailed picture of how psychology can contribute to an understanding of the occurrence of four specific kinds of offending behaviour: property crime, personal violence, substance abuse and sexual offending. Chapter 5 takes this one stage further by identifying factors thought to play a part in the development of criminal involvement, nowadays often discussed within what is called a 'risk–needs' framework. Though most people break the law at some time in their lives, a relatively smaller number of them show patterns of repeated offending and are responsible for a fairly large portion of reported crimes. This chapter will also consider what, if any, is the relationship between crime and mental disorder. Chapter 6 turns attention to several kinds of interventions that have been shown to be useful and to have positive outcomes in reducing criminal recidivism. This will entail collating evidence from large-scale reviews of the outcomes of different types of work with offenders. These findings are perhaps one of the main reasons for a recent resurgence of interest in psychology within criminology itself. Chapter 7 addresses the main response society currently makes to offenders: the use of punishment or 'deterrent sanctions'. Despite its widespread use, this appears to be remarkably unsuccessful in achieving its intended goals. Can psychology help us to understand this apparent paradox? Finally, in Chapter 8, we will consider a number of practical applications of psychology, and some ethical and political aspects of a psychologically informed approach to the study of crime. This will include the core question of whether a scientific approach to these and other questions can be compatible with a value-based system grounded in social justice.

Defining crime

Some of the recent debates in criminology have centred on the very definition of crime itself. What exactly is it? On one level this might sound
like an empty, time-wasting question. Surely crime can be easily defined
as any activity publicly proscribed by the written laws of a society. Thus,
specified acts like speeding, criminal damage, theft, fraud and assault
are all defined and prohibited within the statutes of the criminal law. So far
so good: but if you want to study these actions and understand their
patterning, the apparent simplicity of this definition can be very misleading. Criminologists agree that the process of researching crime is made
extremely difficult by the complex relationship that exists between acts
that are formally demarcated in this way, and the information that is generated about them by the activities of citizens, police, courts and the penal
system. The statistics of recorded crime are notoriously difficult to interpret (Walker 1995; Coleman and Moynihan 1996; Maguire 2002), even in
societies where this process has been established in some form for several
hundred years.

Thus there are many uncertainties regarding the overall rate of crime in a
society. Furthermore, conceptions of crime vary between different communities and societies. They also change over time. These differences show
for example even in very straightforward ways, such as the age at which
young people are held to be criminally responsible (and can therefore be
convicted of an offence). Even within the United Kingdom this varies: 8 in
Scotland, 10 in England and Wales. These figures are generally lower than
in other European countries; although it is 7 in Ireland, corresponding ages
elsewhere are 13 in France, 14 in Germany, 15 in Sweden and 16 in Spain.
As a more specific example, within different European countries there
are variations in law regarding the possession of cannabis. In England
and Wales, rates of arrest for this offence have recently shown a decline
(May *et al.* 2002). The reclassification of the drug from Class B to Class C
with effect from January 2004 will have a more marked effect, literally by
changing what then constitutes a 'crime'.

A more serious example is the offence of marital rape. Under English
common law doctrine that had stood since the eighteenth century, it was
presumed that the contract of marriage permitted husbands irrevocable
consent for sexual intercourse with their wives (provided they were living
together), so affording legal immunity from a charge of rape. Following a
judicial ruling in 1992, such behaviour was redefined, a change then
incorporated in the Criminal Justice and Public Order Act of 1994 (Reed
and Seago 1999). This reversed a period of over 200 years during which it
was not deemed to be illegal. Looking farther afield it is possible to find
behaviour with even more drastic consequences. The Mundurucu people
of the South American rainforest regard the birth of twins as a disturbing
indication of regression to an animal state (as species other than ourselves

more often have multiple births). In Mundurucu society, such babies are killed, but no law is broken as a result (Sanday 1981).

Thus, acts that are labelled as crime in some circumstances are not so defined in others: 'there is no behaviour which is always and everywhere criminal' (Phillipson 1971: 5). Contemplating this, we become unsure of what exactly comprises a crime, and whether this can be delineated in any sense 'objectively'. It becomes apparent that crime is a socially constructed phenomenon, in a stronger sense than the one implicit in the idea that it consists of what is written down in codes of law.

In a discussion of this conundrum, Muncie (2001) has identified as many as eleven separate definitions of crime. Some revolve around the familiar idea of criminal law violation, or variations on that theme. Others are couched in the broader context of departures from moral and social codes. Still others locate the sources of definition itself within the power structures of a society, and widen the purpose of criminology to include the study of the processes by which such definitions are manufactured. The most elaborate definitions focus on the doing of harm, and subsume any of a wide range of circumstances in which individuals are denied rights as a result of actions or events within social relationships and systems. Such definitions encompass many types of behaviour not ordinarily considered crimes. They include, for example, disregard of safety standards in the workplace, the marketing of tobacco products in the light of evidence of their harmfulness, deliberate acts of environmental pollution, and covert arms sales to despotic regimes. 'Legal notions of "crime" do seem to provide a peculiarly blinkered vision of the range of misfortunes, dangers, harms, risks and injuries that are a routine part of everyday life' (Muncie 2001: 21). In ideological terms, defining 'crime' in certain ways and directing public attention towards it has the useful benefit of distracting attention from other acts that serve the purposes of powerful interest groups.

These considerations have an important bearing on the status of psychological research and how it is perceived within criminology. For it must be admitted, psychologists have tended to accept broadly traditional and what might be called 'official' notions of what constitutes crime. By and large, therefore, they have concentrated their efforts on the study of acts customarily regarded as unlawful in Western societies, such as offences against persons, violent and sexual assaults, and the illicit use of controlled drugs.

That is arguably, however, not an unreasonable way to proceed, and it is possible to exaggerate the extent of cultural variations in how crime is defined. International surveys suggest there is a sizeable consensus in the unacceptability and condemnation of certain acts. Newman (1976, 1977) carried out a study in which he asked people in six countries whether certain acts should be prohibited by law, and to rate the seriousness of them. The countries were the USA, Italy, Yugoslavia (as it then was), Iran, India and Indonesia. Newman presented respondents with brief vignettes, describing for example actions in which:

- One person forcefully takes money from another, who requires hospitalization as a result.
- A father has sexual relations with his grown-up daughter.
- Someone uses illegal drugs (the named substance varying from one culture to another).
- Managers permit toxic gases to be released from a factory into the atmosphere.

There was a very high level of agreement in terms of how these actions were viewed, in perceptions of them as crimes, and in the ranking of their relative seriousness.

Criminological psychologists have concentrated their efforts on studying crimes defined in these more-or-less conventional terms. To date at least, they have had little or nothing to say about those acts that would be included within Muncie's (2001) widest definitions. There is very little psychological research on corporate crime or money laundering, on the dumping of toxic waste, the traffic in human slaves, the illegal sale of torture equipment, or the theft of plutonium from nuclear plants. Several types of psychological research are potentially relevant to these areas, but to date the connections have not been made. There is psychologically informed work on some crimes that can only be understood in their broader political context, for example on genocide (Staub 1989). Within this book, however, we will focus on the potential usefulness of psychology for making sense of crimes of the more familiar, 'ordinary' type.

Ordinary crime

Arguments regarding the need to think carefully about what we mean when we use the word *crime* are perfectly valid, and very powerful. It remains important, however, not to lose sight of many of the basic actions and events that constitute the stuff of most criminological theorizing and research. Let us therefore begin with a proposal that, whatever may be the sources of error in our various devices for recording and analysing crime, there is an underlying pattern of actual events that genuinely occurred 'out there'. For the purposes of the present book, that means adopting a broadly *realist* approach to this problem. This is grounded in the observation that there are certain things that people sometimes do to others, which are resented by them or by their wider social group. To borrow a distinction from the philosopher John Searle (1995), these are what could be regarded as some of the 'brute facts' of human behaviour. Once they have been codified in a socially constructed set of documents, which cumulatively form what we call the criminal law, they become what Searle calls 'institutional facts'. Undoubtedly, what is subsumed by the latter evolves over time. It shows inter-cultural variations, and often serves the interests of some strata of society more than others. The selection of some types of harm that are then depicted as crime reflects many wider social and political agendas. Hence, it may be impossible for us ever to have a fixed definition of crime, or to have a comprehensive knowledge of its underlying patterns. The different actors involved in any given crime event may have discrepant views of what took place, and we have no reliable way of knowing how frequently or in precisely what pattern such events occurred.

Consider the following examples of what most people would conventionally regard as criminal acts. All were committed and the respective offenders prosecuted under the laws of England and Wales within recent years.

- Paul, aged 15, was arrested a number of times for vehicle theft. On several occasions, this followed high-speed car chases by the police, exceeding 80 miles per hour on ordinary roads, in one of which he received injuries requiring hospital treatment.
- Sheryl, aged 16, was convicted of a series of shop thefts. She had regularly made money by selling bottles of whisky or other spirits she had stolen from supermarkets or smaller stores. On one occasion she walked unchallenged through a checkout with a case of twelve bottles.
- Earl, aged 17, was arrested following an altercation in a mobile phone shop. He made threats to a member of the staff who believed he was in possession of a weapon and called the police.
- Anthony, aged 18, assaulted a youth worker who attempted to intervene in a fight between him and another youth. The intended victim had earlier shouted obscenities at Anthony's younger sister, towards whom he felt very protective.
- Graham, aged 21, was sent to prison for supplying Class A drugs. At the request of a supposed friend, he passed a number of bags of heroin direct to two customers – who, it transpired, were police officers working under cover. He denied knowing what the bags contained.
- Trevor, aged 35, was placed on probation with a requirement that he attend a domestic violence programme, after admitting to and being convicted of a series of assaults on his wife.

You will have noticed that four out of the six people mentioned in the above vignettes are in their mid- to late-teens. It is a familiar finding among the crime statistics in many countries that those years represent the peak age for involvement in law-breaking activities. Five of the six individuals in the list are male; five are white. Criminal activity, at least as recorded in the high-technology nations where criminology is most widely practised, is predominantly (though by no means exclusively) engaged in by young white males. This raises the question of how far any findings obtained about that group, and any theory construction based on them, is applicable to other groups. (Such a criticism has also been levelled, with ample justification, at some of the findings and theories produced within psychology.)

But this pattern of activity is not one that conforms to the picture many people have of crime, if their impressions of it have been gleaned from the daily press, through watching television dramas or reading 'true crime' paperbacks. Felson (2002) has pointed out how the most widely spread perceptions of crime are subject to a number of serious misunderstandings or fallacies. For example, many people picture criminal acts as exciting or dramatic in content and filled with action and suspense. There are probably large amounts of money, jewellery, drugs or maybe even lives at stake. Criminal acts are ingeniously planned, and skilfully and daringly executed. Successful British criminals take up residence in Spain or Brazil where they become even wealthier by running night clubs or casinos.

And, of course, there are criminal acts that are highly organized and likely to yield a better payoff than the ones itemized earlier. Carrabine *et al.* (2002: 96) have compiled a useful table listing some of the more notorious examples of recent years. They include the major scandals surrounding the companies Guinness-Distillers, Barlow-Clowes, Polly Peck and the Bank of Credit and Commerce International (BCCI). In each of them, enormous sums of money were misappropriated, exceeding the total amount stolen in all 'ordinary' thefts and burglaries for the corresponding years (Maguire 2002). In some instances, the perpetrators were never successfully brought to justice.

But while a small proportion of crimes may conform to these descriptions, the vast majority by contrast are ordinary, unspectacular events. They involve little or no prior planning; minimal effort is expended; the stakes are fairly modest. Almost the only aspect of media portrayals of crime that is accurate is that the majority of the actors cast in criminal roles are male.

At the same time, many people are hurt by crime, and many more live in fear of it, whether or not they have directly come into contact with it. To be a victim of a minor crime may cause only limited inconvenience, but is nevertheless an unpleasant and irritating experience. To be verbally threatened or to encounter an intruder in your home can be extremely frightening. Some assaults result in long-term physical and emotional damage. Serious or repeated victimization can cause significant, profound and enduring distress in people's lives. Whatever our definitions of crime, and however much academic debate there may be in relation to them, such events happen. Such reactions to them are not uncommon.

That fallacies like the ones described by Felson (2002) persist, and that the fear of crime bears only an indirect relationship to objectively measurable risks of it (Mirrlees-Black and Allen 1998) is, perhaps, a testimony to the power of the media, or of crime novels, in portraying criminal acts.

Criminology: the case of the missing person

Felson's own principal contribution to criminological thought, *routine activity theory*, manifests some interesting features that are of pointed relevance to the objectives of the present book. Though comparatively recent in origin, it has already become a well-established approach to the study of crime, regarded by some reviewers of the field as a form of 'right realism' (Walklate 1997). Within the theory, crimes against property – *direct contact predatory violations* – are thought likely to occur when there is an intersection in time and space of three vital ingredients: (a) a motivated offender, (b) a suitable target and (c) the absence of capable guardians. While researchers on this topic have expended considerable effort in specifying the features of the latter two variables in detail, the first is deliberately left to one side. In the original version of the theory, 'persons were treated virtually as objects and their motivations were scrupulously avoided as a topic of discussion' (Clarke and Felson 1993: 2).

The present book is an attempt to fill that void: not with respect solely to routine activity theory itself, but more broadly across criminology in general. I hope to show how a balanced, integrative approach to the study of persons, taking account of their histories and of the situations in which they are acting, can help us build a richer, better informed model of what happens when crimes occur.

When hearing of a crime, most people probably assume that the person accused of it had some plausible reason or motivation for acting as he or she did. Media accounts of crime appeal to those assumed motives, though unsurprisingly the type of explanation offered varies according to the nature of the crime. Motivations for property crime may be thought to be self-evidently attributable to acquisitiveness, and whether this is believed to arise from 'greed' or 'need' may depend on the offender's circumstances. A proportion of crimes appears to be driven by strong 'passions', such as anger, hatred, jealousy or vengefulness. Such factors too are comprehensible to most of us; especially if alcohol or other drugs are involved, since they are widely viewed as loosening personal controls. If none of these motives is apparent, people may be puzzled by an act, but still naturally seek to understand it. Crimes might then be ascribed to more vaguely defined causes with no real explanatory value. Some are described as 'mindless', while more serious violent crimes are portrayed as resulting from a larger, malevolent presence or force: the word 'evil' may be applied. But research on common-sense or 'lay' theories of crime suggests that people employ more complex models of causation than is generally presupposed (Furnham 1988). Typically, criminal acts are not viewed as a product of any single motive, and the extent to which the vocabulary of 'motive' is used may depend on the observer's own position in society.

The central argument of this book is that to understand the kinds of events listed earlier, a wide range of influences needs to be taken into account. They include historical and cultural processes, social environment and family background, individual factors, and personal circumstances. There is a constant interplay between them. Their respective roles in relation to any single act of crime may be very difficult to discern. The contributions of these different factors to crime events may also vary from one offence to the next. The relationships between individuals and their social settings need to be understood, using an approach to crime that draws on personal as well as situational and broader societal variables. Criminology needs to be genuinely a 'rendezvous' discipline, an eclectic meeting-point of a variety of approaches (Downes, cited in Rock 2002).

For some time, however, there has been a mutual suspicion between those with fundamentally different approaches to criminological research. In particular, psychological approaches to crime are often viewed as overly deterministic and biologically oriented, and are thought to ignore social and environmental contexts of crime. There are perhaps two particular reasons for this. One is the fairly simple notion, initially propounded by psychologists, of personality typologies; and the viewpoint that there are distinguishing psychological features that underlie tendencies towards criminality. The other is the particular part psychologists have played in the study of violent and sexual crimes. This has led to a perception that criminal behaviour has been 'pathologized' – that is, understood as a manifestation of abnormality or disease, probably with a genetic origin.

The scientific approach

Psychology has fortunately moved considerably beyond these preoccupations. To illustrate its potential role in criminology, the metaphor of a compound microscope might be useful. (This idea will be discussed more fully in Chapter 2, as a way of thinking about levels of explanation in criminological theory.) A compound microscope has lenses of progressively greater power, allowing gradual increases in the visual magnification of organisms too small to be seen by the naked eye. So using our first, but least powerful lens, crime can be studied on a large scale as an aspect of society at an aggregate or 'macro' level. Alternatively, taking our next lens, its relative distribution across different places or times can be explored. Using a psychological approach we are, as it were, deploying the sharpest lens, to look closely at individual acts of crime and the people who have committed them. Inevitably, there are methodological problems involved in proceeding in this way. But if we conduct our research carefully enough, we can take account of at least some of them.

The idea of studying crime in this way is, of course, couched within a particular framework – that of social science. The suggestion that we can study the problem known as crime *scientifically* is in itself a controversial one. Indeed, some writers would challenge the very language I am using here. It implies the notion that crime can be adequately defined, and can be investigated as a phenomenon that 'exists'. This entails the assumption that it is possible to identify 'causes' of crime and, if we succeed in doing this well enough, move on to possible 'remedies'. From what its advocates call a more 'critical' viewpoint, it is asserted that how we go about discussing these questions, and the language and terms we employ to do so, are themselves the fundamental issues to be addressed.

The assumed philosophical basis of psychology

Thus, psychology appears to suffer from several major problems that might arouse misgivings in the mind of a sociologically oriented criminologist. There may be other difficulties as well, but for present purposes let us concentrate on five, cumulatively mortal, sins. (If you do not like *isms*, look away now . . . on second thoughts, you want to understand the rest of this book, so please read on.) These major obstacles are psychology's assumed inclinations towards *positivism, individualism, biologism, determinism* and *reductionism*. In many ways, these ideas are closely interwoven.

Positivism

In its approach to the study of its subject-matter, psychology is often considered to be primarily *positivist* in its orientation. Regrettably, this word is often used in an inaccurate and misleading way. It has become, as Coleman and Moynihan (1996: 6) have said, 'more commonly a term of abuse . . . it more frequently now leads to confusion than enlightenment'. In recent years, modes of thought have arisen within social sciences that are for various reasons suspicious of, if not explicitly hostile to, this approach. Many writers are sceptical regarding the purported 'truth-claims' of the avowedly scientific disciplines. The allegation that psychology is primarily positivistic in its orientation often means it is regarded somewhat cynically, and may even be summarily dismissed, by thinkers who depict themselves as having a more 'critical' outlook. Such a standpoint is now widespread, and is probably traceable to the writings of the 'new criminologists' of the 1970s (Taylor *et al.* 1973).

Set against the dominant trait-psychological approaches of that period and beyond, the criticisms then made may have been amply justified. So, for example, Roshier (1989) envisions a collection of problems that appear enmeshed within positivist criminology, which is where any contribution from psychology would presumptively be located. They include determinism, differentiation, pathology, and diverting attention away from crime and the law, towards individuals. The first two of these features are 'inextricably linked' and entail the view that there are identifiable determinants of crime located within individuals that can serve to differentiate between those disposed to commit crimes and those not so disposed. The success of this approach turns on whether it can 'establish the existence of "types" of human beings (whether in terms of biology, personality, or values) who are crime-prone' (Roshier 1989: 36). The approach further assumes that such proneness towards crime arises within some persons as a result of 'things that are deemed to have "gone wrong" with their biology, psyche or values' (p. 37). Hence the link to pathology which Roshier portrays as essentially a form of moral labelling and nothing more. The focus on individuals and what has allegedly gone awry inside them also diverts attention from larger-scale aspects of the operation of law and the structure of society.

Yet the general thrust of these criticisms is quite misplaced: the situation is a lot more complex than it appears. Halfpenny (1982) has examined the history of the relationship between positivism and sociology and concluded that there are no fewer than twelve different senses of the word *positivism*. Among other things it is a theory of history, a theory of knowledge and a thesis concerning the unity of science. Interestingly, the philosopher Auguste Comte (1798–1857), who developed the basic concepts of positivism, rejected psychology from his scheme for a unified system of sciences, because of its inherent subjectivism (Halfpenny 1982). The word has also been used virtually as a synonym for *empiricism*, the proposition that all knowledge is derived from information gained through sensory experience of the external world. But perhaps the best known manifestation of positivist thinking was in the hands of a group of twentieth-century philosophers known as the Vienna Circle, who founded *logical positivism*. This school of thought concentrated attention on the use of language. Its proponents argued that discussion within science and philosophy should be confined to statements containing elements that can be reducible to direct observation based on sensory experience. All other types of statements, for example about entities or processes that were hypothetical or not directly observable, were held to be empty and pointless.

However, the criticism that psychology owes its primary allegiance to positivism is rather poorly targeted. Very little of contemporary psychology can be described as positivistic in any meaningful sense. Certain radical strands in behavioural psychology, notably what is known as *methodological behaviourism*, are rooted in positivist concepts. For example, Leslie (2002) describes the approach known as *behaviour analysis*, which eschews any use of cognitive or 'mentalistic' concepts or 'hypothetical constructs', as they are not directly observable and in Leslie's view are therefore unscientific and superfluous. According to this argument, psychological phenomena can best be understood by conducting experiments that will enable us to plot relationships between different, observable, patterns of behaviour (though this can also include the study of brain function, and of brain–behaviour relationships).

Most of contemporary psychology can be more accurately described as adopting a *critical realist* perspective on its subject-matter. Critical or scientific realism can take several forms (Chalmers 1999; Searle 1995; Benton and Craib 2001). Common to them all is the assumed existence of an external reality that subsists independently of human minds and of our attempts to make sense of it. To borrow a phrase from Klee (1997), when we investigate the world around us, its reality 'pushes back' against our ideas and hypotheses. While our modes of inquiry and the language we use have an influence on what we find, they alone do not create it. Within this approach, it is explicitly allowed to engage in hypothesis-testing or theory construction invoking events or processes that are not directly observable.

In addition, psychologists also recognize that many of the phenomena they investigate are personal, subjective experiences. Human beings are engaged in a constant process of making sense of the world around them, and what ostensibly appear to be identical circumstances can have entirely different meanings for two participants. This leaves considerable scope for *relativism:* that with regard to many of the areas under exploration, there are no 'objective' facts or findings. Rather, there are solely the perspectives and experiences of participant individuals or groups.

However, a state of affairs in which *some* phenomena can only be described in relative terms is not, by virtue of that situation, one in which it is not possible to discover patterns, or not permissible to make broader generalizations. To insist that all description or inquiry is inevitably confined to a purely relative level, and is constructed wholly by human discourse, is to resort to a form of anti-realism (Norris 1997). That entails an assertion that the perceptible 'external world' is entirely constructed by human ideas, language or culture. This, ultimately, amounts to a denial of the existence of a mind-independent reality.

Overall, in relation to the range of questions they investigate, and depending on the area of research and the nature of any prior findings, psychologists nowadays adopt a combination of critical-realist and social-constructionist perspectives. In psychological research, a spectrum of quantitative and qualitative approaches can be used separately or in combination, in an approach sometimes called *methodological pluralism* (Barker *et al.* 2002).

Individualism

A second apparent problem is that psychology is thought to locate the 'causes' of crime and criminality predominantly if not entirely within individuals. It thereby neglects or ignores social factors. Lilly *et al.* (2002) epitomize this as intrinsically and inevitably a conservative stance: 'By looking inside people for the sources of crime, individualistic theories do not consider what is going on outside of people. There is a tendency to take the existing society as a given and to see crime as the inability of deficient individuals to adjust to that society' (pp. 226–7).

Until recently, some of the most influential theories propounded by psychologists to explain crime were based on the claim that there are differences in *personality* between offenders and non-offenders. This assumes of course that it is possible to find persons who can be neatly divided into those two groups; a questionable assumption at best, since self-report surveys suggest that at some stage almost everyone commits a crime

(Nettler 1984). But let us assume that the claim is restricted to 'habitual criminals', those who have committed many crimes. The most influential exponent of such a view was probably Hans Eysenck (1977), who forwarded a theory of crime based on the idea of personality traits. *Traits* are hypothetical intrapsychic variables that differentiate individuals from each other and on which they can be compared. Traits are defined in quantifiable, dimensional terms and can be measured using self-report personality inventories designed, in the case of Eysenck's theory, to assess such features as a tendency towards neuroticism, extraversion or psychoticism. In Eysenck's model, offenders are expected to score more highly than nonoffenders on those traits. Unfortunately for this theory, as we shall see in Chapter 2, such differences have not been regularly or reliably found. Attempts to achieve the more ambitious objectives of such a project, discovering clear-cut personality correlates of crime, have largely failed.

That is not however to say that in trying to understand patterns of repeated offending there may not be some individual differences that are important, and in Chapter 5 we will encounter some likely candidates for this role. Certain combinations of dimensional differences between individuals do receive empirical support, particularly with reference to those persons for whom a pattern of antisocial activity has become entrenched. But the way in which they are expressed occurs in the context of the situations in which people find themselves, or in some instances create for themselves. If people who enjoy risk-taking have the resources and opportunities to pursue that interest, say through engaging in dangerous sports, they may have their wishes met through such channels. If the only 'sport' around is driving a car at high speed, the only cars around belong to other people, and your only friends have found an obvious solution to this, car theft and 'joyriding' will be the likely result.

Contemporary theories of personality within psychology are based on a recognition that both personality and situational factors are crucial in influencing behaviour – the things people actually do. The interaction between them provides a better account of human activity than either of them considered in isolation. This stance is consequently known as *interactionism* (Mischel 1999; McAdams 2001) and will be discussed at greater length in Chapter 3.

Alongside the finding that most people break the law at some point in their lives, typically committing what are known as 'minor infractions', another pattern prevails. This is that there is a much smaller group of people who more frequently commit offences, and some who are likely to do so in more serious ways (Nettler 1984; Rutter *et al.* 1998). Conversely, successive studies have found that a comparatively small segment of the known offender population, typically in the region of 5–10%, may be responsible for a much higher proportion of all known offences, typically in the region of 50–60%. This type of pattern can be represented by a reverse-J-shaped curve: a large number of people commit only a single crime each, while a small number commit several, and a much smaller number many crimes. This point will be amplified in Chapter 5. The exact shape of the curve varies from one study to another. Estimates regarding the relative ratios vary: 'The exact proportions may be in doubt, but the general conclusion is not' (Rutter *et al.* 1998: 58).

There is evidence that the people to be found in this sub-group, variously defined as 're-offenders', 'repeat', 'persistent', 'prolific' or even 'chronic' offenders, may differ from those who rarely break the law, or who do so in only petty ways. That evidence too will be discussed in some detail in Chapter 5. However, such differences as have been found are not uniformly obtained; and in providing an account of crime they are only one explanatory factor among many, contrary to the core proposition of the earlier personality-based theorists. Furthermore, whether or not those differences will be manifested in a tendency towards more persistent offending is also a function of the life situations, opportunities and other aspects of the environments in which people develop.

Biologism

The origins of positivist criminology are generally traced to the writings of Cesare Lombroso (1835–1909), an Italian physician who became convinced that there was a relationship between bodily characteristics, proneness to disease and tendencies towards violence or other forms of criminality. In the course of his work as a doctor in the Italian army, he was able to measure the body build, slope of the forehead, shape of the ears, presence of tattoos and other characteristics in a sample of more than 3000 soldiers. Given these preoccupations, Lombroso is known as the founder of the 'anthropological school' in criminology, and unanimously regarded as a key exemplar of positivism, having described himself as 'a slave to facts' (Lilly *et al.* 2002: 16). He is also cast by Garland (2002) as having been the instigator of one of the two major strands in criminological thinking over the past 150 years: eponymously entitled the *Lombrosian project*. This is a 'form of inquiry which seeks to develop an etiological, explanatory science, based on the premise that criminals can somehow be scientifically differentiated from non-criminals' (Garland 2002: 8). From the outset of this 'project', some of the determinants of such differentiation were biological.

The other strand, the *governmental project*, is concerned with the large-scale measurement of crime-related information, for the purposes of social management. This will not concern us here, though there will be some discussion of it in Chapter 8. In Garland's view, contemporary criminology has emerged from a convergence of these two distinctive projects. As Lombroso's thinking progressed, he gradually incorporated larger numbers of environmental and social factors into his theorizing, while remaining wedded to some of his initial conceptions. Undoubtedly, the core ideas at the centre of the Lombrosian enterprise have a continuity right down to recent times.

They include the ideas of *physiognomy*, that there is an association between certain body shapes and tendencies towards criminality. This is a specific instance of a presumed association between body typology and personality in general. It is linked to the idea of *heritability*, the expectation that genetic factors play a large part in the development of criminal tendencies, and that the extent of this can be measured through population studies. The latter entails making comparisons, for example, between identical and non-identical twins, or between twins reared by their biological or by adoptive parents (Wilson and Herrnstein 1985; Buikhuisen and Mednick 1988). Personality theorists such as Eysenck (1977) saw the origins of individual differences as being rooted in biology. For example, the personality trait of neuroticism was hypothesized to originate from differences in the arousal level of the nervous system, and the ease with which conditioned reflexes could be established during childhood development.

Given this legacy, it is scarcely surprising that an outsider looking at psychological approaches to crime should gain the impression that they are dominated by biological explanations. Open almost any textbook of criminology theory, and to the extent that psychological theories are represented, they are intimately associated with the tradition descending from Lombroso. But while that strand is certainly still an active one, most current theorizing and research in psychology adopts a much broader, psychosocial orientation. A large-scale review by Walters (1992) revealed only a low correlation between heredity and crime in the best-designed investigations of it. The extent to which heritability is thought to contribute to crime varies among psychologists, but a majority would probably agree with Gottfredson and Hirschi (1990: 61), who assert that its role is 'substantively trivial'. Most would accept instead that by far the bulk of evidence currently available supports the general contention of 'the superiority of social over genetic explanations of delinquency and crime' (Gold 1987: 67; for a fuller discussion, see Joseph 2003).

Determinism

The connections between positivism, individualism and biologism may appear inescapable, as if adoption of one led ineluctably to endorsement of the others. A fourth reason for aversion to psychological accounts of crime arises from psychology's supposed reliance on mechanical, deterministic models of human action. Given psychology's track record of attempting to emulate the 'hard' sciences, and its consequent focus on the measurement of 'variables', the sole objective of inquiry appears to be the building of theories that look like those found in physics, chemistry or biology.

There is no doubt that much psychological research and theory is focused on attempts to identify cause–effect relationships among the phenomena being investigated. There is a fundamental (modernist) scientific assumption that the determinants of events can be traced and eventually mapped out, even if that may remain extraordinarily, and perhaps unsurpassably, difficult in many instances. However, the approach to doing so has shifted significantly from any simple determinist model. There are several distinct strands in this departure.

First, few if any psychologists would anticipate that clear-cut causal pathways could be found for a problem so difficult to define, and so obviously complex, as crime. Rather, any explanations that are found are liable to be *multi-factorial*, with different influences playing different parts and their respective roles themselves varying according to situational, temporal and other variables.

Second, any attempt to understand the occurrence of criminal offences or other complex actions is now much more likely to employ *probabilistic* models. These are used throughout psychology in exploring areas as diverse as child development, cognitive processes and social interaction. Applied to the study of crime, this has led to the emergence of the 'risk factors' approach, in which a number of variables are identified as potential influences, the respective roles of which must be assessed afresh in every individual case. We will look in greater detail at this approach in Chapter 5.

Third, to the extent that psychologists utilize a cause–effect model of relationships between different variables, they do so mainly within a framework known as *reciprocal determinism*. 'In psychological activity, cognitions influence both behaviour and the situation, and these, in turn, influence cognitions' (Bartol and Bartol 1994: 327). Within developmental psychology, it is fully recognized that even before they acquire spoken language, young children engage in a *transactional* process with their caregivers. Most patterns of interaction consist of a series of interchanges involving multiple dynamic processes, where it is virtually impossible to isolate any event as the 'start point' of the sequence.

Fourth, having discarded the positivist dictat that it is unscientific and improper to discuss unobservable events like thoughts and feelings, many forms of psychology make direct reference to such constructs. Within cognitive and social psychology, for example, individuals are seen not as passive products of their environments but as active decision-makers who create meanings in their everyday lives. In almost all forms of psychological therapy, including even behaviourally based approaches, it is vital to gain access to individuals' self-reports on their experiences, to understand their perceptions of events, and their constructions of their circumstances.

A reliance on any form of determinism is sometimes thought to represent a denial that human beings possess 'free will'. This might appear somehow to detract from their humanity. In law, citizens are considered to exercise free will and are therefore held responsible for their own actions, including acts of crime. Much legal discourse and debate focuses on circumstances in which individuals may not have made wholly 'free' choices – that at least is the substance of many defences against criminal charges (Reed and Seago 1999). The philosophical question of the relationship between 'determinism' and 'free will' is far beyond the scope of the present book. From a psychological perspective, we can view human actions as falling along a continuum of relative influence of external, constraining factors and varying levels of voluntary, self-directed decision and choice. Even some of the latter, however, turn out on closer inspection to be in many respects pre-determined through multiple causal paths (Wegner 2002), and this may apply to what are collectively known as the higher mental processes (Bargh and Ferguson 2000).

Determinism is commonly interpreted as the notion that somehow everything must occur in fixed patterns in a mechanical, predetermined universe. Honderich (2002), borrowing a phrase from William James (1842–1910; an eminent pioneer of psychological thought), characterizes this as 'iron-block determinism'. But there are major debates within philosophy concerning the relationship between determinism and free will. Some thinkers have argued against the presumption that the two are irreconcilable. Adopting a more subtle position, Honderich (2002) proposes that while determinism is not compatible with the concept of free will as generally understood (as a faculty of a separate self, or 'origin-ator' of actions), it is nevertheless compatible with the view that some actions can be voluntary. Cognitive or mental self-conscious states can be identifiable agencies of decision and action, while they themselves are 'caused' through other, typically more elaborate pathways.

Reductionism

Associated with the use of positivistic and deterministic models, psych-ology is also often cast as being over-dependent on the use of *reductionist* explanations. Again by supposed analogy with the natural sciences, this implies that the core of any good explanation is that it can be translated into a statement about events at a lower, more elemental level. A table consists of molecules of a complex material called wood, which, in turn, contain atoms of carbon and other substances. Similarly, thoughts are reducible to brain processes such as the firing of neurons, which are a function of the activity of sodium and potassium ions, which is a function of their atomic structure and energy levels in electron shells. And so on, all the way back to the Big Bang.

There may well be such a chain of causality running through natural phenomena, and many psychologists probably accept this as a general principle. Psychology is, therefore, in certain respects a reductionist science. But the meaning of this is often misunderstood, a point succinctly made by Sommerhoff (2000) in discussing the origins of consciousness. It is a mistake to depict reductionism as the view that events at higher levels of complexity in some causal chain are 'nothing but' manifestations of events at lower levels. As Sommerhoff has argued, this criticism is a misrepresen-tation. It appears to imply that any offering of a reductionist explanation 'has destroyed essentials' and 'substitutes a lesser thing for the thing it explains' (p. 91). To suggest that reductionism consists of the view that complex phenomena are merely the product of their more rudimentary units is to ignore the point that such explanations are concerned not only with the components that make up a higher-level structure, but also with understanding their interrelations.

But in addition, the notion of an explanatory chain relating phenomena of different levels of complexity is not always helpful when attempting to understand events at any given point along it. Psychologists spend a great deal of their time arguing instead that although psychological events may be in some manner dependent on physiological or electrochemical processes within the brain, they also need to be understood as phenomena in their own terms. Stating that mental event A is the product of neural events B and C simply does not furnish the best reasons why, for example, thoughts occur as they do, or why they can also have an impact on bodily states; still less why their patterning varies across individuals and situations. While such an explanation might be possible in principle, it would be so forbiddingly complex as to be of little value for any practical purpose.

This accords with a philosophical argument that, although conscious experience and other psychological phenomena may be a product of material substrates, that does not imply that events in the mind consist of nothing more than events in the brain. This invokes the concept of *supervenience*: 'the mental is said to supervene on the physical without being reducible to it' (Guttenplan 1994: 536).

Psychology's task

Overall, in relation to other fields of inquiry adjoining it, psychology is in a unique position in one crucial respect. In a sense, it is an attempt simultaneously to achieve two apparently incompatible goals. One is to study human behaviour and experience in general, to discover patterns within it and arrive at permissible generalizations about it. The other is to gain an understanding of individuals and of what makes each of us unique. Combining these two apparently contradictory objectives presents some formidable challenges, and creates tensions and occasional disputes with respect to what are regarded as acceptable findings.

On a more formal academic level, these two approaches have attracted the technical, and sometimes unfortunately misunderstood terms, *nomothetic* and *idiographic* (we will return to this distinction in Chapter 8). Like other forms of scientific inquiry, psychology consists in part of a search for patterns that are replicable and of findings that can assist in the construction of theories. Complementing that, however, is a focus on the study of individuals, or of group and cultural phenomena, and how they differ from each other. Some kinds of findings obtained from psychological research fall somewhere in between. That is, they have a restricted range of generality, applying to certain combinations of persons and circumstances (Cronbach 1975). Inquiry then focuses on setting the boundaries of the domain within which a particular set of findings is applicable.

Historical roots

Despite sizeable differences in many other respects, criminology and psychology exhibit some striking parallels in their histories. Both were part of a general process, continuous throughout the eighteenth and nineteenth centuries in European thought, through which the study of social issues became emancipated from the study of philosophy; just as in earlier centuries the study of the natural world became separated from religion and magic. Both have subsumed competing 'schools', entertaining a spectrum of theories and ideologies. Both are now at a point where there are major debates concerning whether the traditional scientific paradigm is the most appropriate one to adopt for further genuine advances to be made.

During the eighteenth century, under the influence of Rationalist philosophy, and especially in the period of intellectual ferment commonly known as the European Enlightenment, many established patterns of thinking were re-examined. The balance between ideas that were partly moral, religious or mystical, and partly scientific, shifted in favour of the latter. Newer concepts of human action were enunciated that derived from philosophical reasoning and inquiry into the nature of the human mind, motivation and morality. Thus in the school of thought known as *classical criminology*, proposals were made regarding the likely motives for crime, and what society might do to counteract it. Such investigations were not at that stage, however, based on any attempt at systematic empirical observation.

The first empirically based studies in what is now called criminology were carried out in France and Belgium in the 1820s and 1830s. Although there had been recording of crimes at a local level in a number of countries for several centuries, it was not until 1827 in France that the first national crime statistics were published. Subsequently, in a book that appeared in 1829, André-Michel Guerry (1802–1866) used maps to compare patterns of crime with the distribution of wealth and income, to test the theory that crime was associated with poverty. In another book published in 1831, Adolphe Quetelet (1796–1874), a Belgian astronomer, reported a similar survey covering parts of France, Belgium and Holland (Coleman and Moynihan 1996; Vold *et al.* 1998; Lilly *et al.* 2002). Given the methods these authors used, they are sometimes referred to as the 'cartographic school'. This type of work has been characterized by Garland (2002) as part of the *governmental project*, in which criminology is employed to serve the purposes of large-scale social measurement. (What he has dubbed the *Lombrosian project*, briefly discussed above, did not emerge until the second half of the nineteenth century.)

Psychology can be said to have existed in some form or other in many cultures across many historical epochs. But in the form in which it is now familiar in Western societies, its origins too can be traced to philosophical ideas that emerged during the period of the European Enlightenment. Psychological theorizing developed initially from philosophical inquiry, especially the philosophy of mind, but also from epistemology, the study of how the mind acquires knowledge. In a similar manner to the classical criminologists, European philosophers of the eighteenth century also espoused wide-ranging ideas concerning human motivation in general. It was widely held that mind, regarded in the abstract sense, possessed inherent organizing powers with which it constructed the perceived world. Initially, this thinking was done without direct reference to empirical evidence, beyond the experience and informal observations of the writer in question.

During the nineteenth century, this began to take on the form of empirical investigation and the field of 'psychophysics' developed. Some physiologists considered that conscious experience could be studied by probing into the interrelations of sensation (the external, measurable stimuli impinging on a person) and perception (the internal experience of the subject or observer). This was seen as a purely scientific, experimentally based enterprise for which the laboratory was the obvious setting. The first laboratory explicitly designed to carry out this work was set up by Wilhelm Wundt (1832–1920), a medically trained physiologist, at the University of Leipzig, Germany in 1879. Studies were conducted in which individuals, using a method known as 'experimental self-observation', a controlled form of introspection, reported the contents of consciousness to the researcher under different 'stimulus conditions' (Leahy 1997). Other workers such as Hermann Ebbinghaus (1850–1909), one of the first psychologists to carry out detailed study of memory and forgetting, showed how different segments of a quantity of information were retained or lost over time.

In the years following this, several psychology laboratories were established in the United States of America, at Harvard, Yale, Johns Hopkins and Clark universities. The first doctoral research programme in psychology was announced at Harvard in 1878; the first independent psychology department was established at Clark University in 1887.

The late nineteenth century was a period of rapid growth of interest in the new psychological science. By the 1890s there were numerous academic psychologists working in the USA; many of those who were subsequently to become the most influential in the field obtained their PhD degrees at Leipzig. The American Psychological Association, the world's first professional grouping of psychologists, was founded in 1892. Its first president was G. Stanley Hall, who obtained his PhD at Leipzig and in 1887 founded the *American Journal of Psychology*. The first psychological laboratory or testing centre in the United Kingdom was set up in London in 1885 by Francis Galton, a cousin of Charles Darwin. Although Galton was not trained as a psychologist, it was one of his numerous, varied interests. He also pioneered fingerprinting, developed the study of twins, invented the correlation coefficient, and promoted the Eugenics Movement.

Psychologists are widely associated with the idea of 'mental measurement', employing specially designed tests for assessment of ability and personality. The origins of this may be traced to the first psychological laboratory in France, which was set up in 1885 by Alfred Binet (1857–1911). In 1904 Binet was asked to develop methods of providing educational services to children with learning disabilities. His initial approach, in a method paralleling some of those used by Lombroso, was through the use of *craniometry*; measuring physical characteristics of individuals' heads. He found, however, that this simply did not work. Pursuing an alternative idea, he devised a collection of everyday tasks of progressively increasing difficulty, which could be used to identify learning disabilities; these were formed into a scale published with Theodore Simon in 1908. Binet cautioned against the use of scales of this kind outside the type of setting for which they were devised. These caveats notwithstanding, the Binet-Simon scale was the forerunner of what subsequently came to be developed into *intelligence tests*. It was introduced to the USA and further refined by Lewis Terman at Stanford University in 1916. Its use spread to many other places, such that by 1920 testing the intellectual development of children was a major activity of psychologists.

In the ensuing decades, the use of mental tests became the primary and sometimes the sole focus of the work of many psychologists. They were employed on a massive scale in selection and classification of recruits to the US Army, and in the assessment of immigrants to the USA. Many of the latter deemed not sufficiently intelligent were deported. It has been estimated that several million people were debarred from entry to the United States for this reason (Gould 1981). In the United Kingdom, too, psychology became synonymous with the idea of IQ or ability assessment. The use of psychometric tests now forms only a very small part of the activity of most professional psychologists, and indeed some explicitly disavow their use. It may be that the widespread perception of psychologists as 'mental testers' is a long-term residue of the epoch of mass administration of such scales in the first half of the twentieth century.

The structure of psychology

For any reader unfamiliar with the general nature of psychology as a discipline, let us briefly consider the types of work that it involves. Psychology is traditionally divided into specialist branches and its development in recent years has been such that within them, yet more specialized sub-branches have also evolved. If that were not already confusing enough, there are numerous cross-currents and interconnections between several of the sub-branches. The principal large divisions into which psychology is customarily divided include the following.

- *Physiological or biological psychology* focuses on the biological 'substrates' of behaviour. While most psychologists study human beings, some also carry out research with other animals, on the basis that there are evolutionary links between different species. The latter is also known as *comparative psychology*.
- *Developmental psychology* is the study of the patterns of change that occur between early infancy, through childhood, adolescence and adulthood into old age, and the processes influencing them.
- *Social psychology* is concerned with interaction and group processes, socialization, interpersonal influence, attitudes and social behaviour; overall, with any aspect of the relationships between individuals, groups and society.
- *Cognitive psychology* involves the investigation of internal processes hypothesized to be involved in basic psychological functions such as perception, memory, thinking, reasoning, learning, problem-solving, decision-making and the use of language.
- *Differential psychology*, or the study of individual differences, is more commonly nowadays simply called the psychology of personality. It also includes *abnormal psychology*, the study of unusual experiences, and of mental and behavioural disorders.

In recent years, psychology has played a major role in the emergence of *neuroscience*, an interdisciplinary inquiry also involving contributions from philosophy, physiology and computer science. Nervous systems are considered as organs that have evolved a specialized function for the processing of information about the environment (internal and external) to enable an organism to survive.

In addition to the sub-divisions just described, which could be described as the realm of 'pure' psychology, the discipline also has a number of 'applied' fields. The most highly developed, and in terms of numbers of practitioners numerically the largest, are the following.

- *Clinical psychology*, concerned with psychological factors influencing mental and physical health, the alleviation of distress and disorder, and assessment, intervention and evaluation in healthcare settings.
- *Educational psychology*, which addresses issues arising in learning processes in school and allied settings, and assessment and provision of support for children's learning.
- *Occupational psychology*, the application of psychology to problems in the workplace, including for example staff selection, motivation and team-working, usually in industrial or commercial settings.
- *Forensic psychology*, which is concerned with connections between psychology and the law, the provision of evidence to facilitate legal decision-making, and aspects of the operation of justice.

There are numerous textbooks on all of these areas. For present purposes we will look in greater detail at those areas of psychology that are most closely associated with criminology, and also with the field of law in broader terms.

The relation of psychology to law

The history of psychology applied to law is perhaps less well known than the standard image of the 'mental tester' outlined above. Although this field is now in a state of speedy development, the application of psychology to the study of crime and other areas connected with the operation of law is by no means new. Legal psychology has a significant history in Europe, and across a number of European countries it is possible to trace the study of this area to works written in the middle and late nineteenth century. While early applications were often devoted to exploring 'the criminal mind' and how this might yield an understanding of seemingly inexplicable acts, there were also early studies of how conclusions might be drawn from psychological evidence presented in the courtroom.

For example, the study of eyewitness testimony was instigated in separate research projects by Binet in France and Stern and Munsterberg in Germany, at the start of the twentieth century. Traverso and Manna (1992) have described the origins of criminal psychology among legal academics in Italy as long ago as 1833, and Jakob (1992) has outlined the development of psychological thinking among jurists in nineteenth-century Germany. Treatises on the relationship of psychology to law have been available for many decades in other countries including Spain and Poland.

The 'interface' between psychology, law and criminology is currently an area of considerable and dynamic development. There are several types of interconnections, and the focus on studying crime is only one of them. This can lead to some confusion as a number of different terms may be used to characterize these links. The following three terms are sometimes used interchangeably, though there are important if subtle differences between them with regard to what they are commonly thought to denote.

- *Criminological psychology* is the application of psychology to the study of criminal conduct (Hollin 1989, 2001a; Blackburn 1993; Andrews and Bonta 2003). The prime area of interest here is in the explanation and understanding of offending behaviour, entailing direct research with offender populations in prison, probation, juvenile justice and allied settings. However, this may also draw on longitudinal studies of the development of delinquency and related social problems, or the study of other antisocial acts such as bullying in school. The field has typically, though not exclusively, focused on some types of offending behaviour more than others, with particular emphasis on violence, sexual offending and substance abuse. A portion of this work also involves the study of relationships between crime and mental disorder. The latter is linked with psychiatry and has sometimes been called *clinical criminology*.

- *Legal psychology* is devoted more broadly to psychological factors in the operation of the law itself. This has included, for example, the study of juries and legal decision-making, aspects of criminal responsibility, mistaken convictions, employment and discrimination, family law and child protection, and scientific and ethical aspects of communicating expert evidence in court (Bartol and Bartol 1994; Bull and Carson 1995; Roesch *et al.* 1999; Wrightsman *et al.* 2002).
- *Forensic psychology* is more narrowly concerned with the provision of evidence to facilitate legal decisions (Blackburn 1996). Researchers in this area study such issues as memory for faces or events, witness reliability and credibility, processes of interviewing vulnerable witnesses, and the dependability of children's testimony (Memon *et al.* 1998). In recent years, psychological research on false confession and on suggestibility during police interrogation has had a significant impact on procedure in British courtrooms (Kapardis 1997; Gudjonsson and Hayward 1998; Gudjonsson 2002). Practitioners in this area may carry out direct forensic or clinical assessments of individual defendants or witnesses, for use in diverse settings including criminal courts (youth and adult), mental health tribunals, or for review procedures in cases of alleged miscarriages of justice (Melton *et al.* 1998; Weiner and Hess 2000). In a different vein, forensic psychologists have also contributed to the training of negotiators in hostage-taking situations. In recent years, the term 'forensic psychology' has been broadened to refer to the work of psychologists based in prison, probation, and allied settings.

Newer, yet more specialized fields have also been established, most notably *investigative psychology*, in which psychologists work alongside the police in helping to solve (usually fairly serious) crimes. This involves a range of techniques for analysing patterns among what is left behind after criminal acts (*crime-scene analysis*), and which may reveal psychological characteristics of crime perpetrators and assist the detection process (*offender profiling*) (Canter and Alison 2000; Ainsworth 2001; Holmes and Holmes 2002).

The three main sub-divisions of this field just described have numerous points of contact and overlaps and it is difficult to delineate any firm boundaries between them; so much so that the relationship between them can best be conceptualized as in the Venn diagram in Figure 1.1.

In the final chapter of this book, we will look briefly at some of the activities of psychologists in these areas, and how they are supported by professional bodies and other organizations. In the remaining chapters, my intention is to outline what, in my view, is the contribution that psychology can make to a number of key questions in criminology. Taking these areas in order as discussed earlier, Chapter 2 presents a broader discussion of how psychologically based approaches to understanding crime are related to approaches that originate from other sources inside criminology, and how they may be assembled together in a genuinely integrative account.

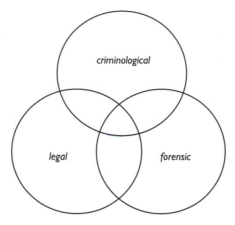

Figure 1.1 Overlapping domains of criminological, legal and forensic psychology

Further reading

There are several texts that provide fuller detail on applications of psychology to the study of crime than is possible to give in a volume of the present size. They include two with the same title: *The Psychology of Criminal Conduct* by Ronald Blackburn (Chichester: Wiley, 1993) and *The Psychology of Criminal Conduct* by Donald A. Andrews and James Bonta (Cincinnati, OH: Anderson, 3rd edn, 2003). For an historical overview of the relationship between psychology and criminology, see Clive R. Hollin (2002), 'Criminological psychology', in *The Oxford Handbook of Criminology* edited by Mike Maguire, Rod Morgan and Robert Reiner (Oxford University Press, 3rd edn, 2002). Further detail on many specific issues can be found in the massive and wide-ranging *Handbook of Offender Assessment and Treatment* edited by Clive R. Hollin (Chichester: Wiley, 2001). If you are looking for a general introduction to psychology itself, there are so many basic texts it is difficult to select just one; but Richard Gross (2001) *Psychology: The Science of Mind and Behaviour* (4th edition, London: Hodder Arnold) is a good example. For more detail on some philosophical aspects of psychology, see William O'Donohue and Richard F. Kitchener (eds., 1996) *The Philosophy of Psychology* (London: Sage Publications). For a broader introduction to the philosophy of science, see Robert Klee (1997) *Introduction to the Philosophy of Science: Cutting Nature at its Seams* (New York: Oxford University Press), and addressing issues in social sciences, Ted Benton and Ian Craib (2001) *Philosophy of Social Science: The Philosophical Foundations of Social Thought* (Basingstoke: Palgrave).

Many books focus more on the legal and forensic rather than the criminological aspects of psychology. To find detail on specific issues, there are two large handbooks available: Ray Bull and David Carson (eds., 1995) *Handbook of Psychology in Legal Contexts* (Chichester: Wiley) focuses more or less exclusively on psycho-legal issues; however, Allen K. Hess and Irving B. Weiner (eds, 1999) *The Handbook of Forensic Psychology* (2nd edn, New York: Wiley) also contains some chapters on psychology and crime. (The Handbook of Psychology in Legal Contexts, edited by David Carson and Ray Bull (2003) has also been issued in a significantly revised second edition, making it virtually a different book (Chichester: Wiley).

Accounting for crime

To grasp the potential contributions of psychology to understanding criminal activity, it will be helpful to begin by locating such explanations alongside others that have been proposed across the field of criminology. For the most part, as outlined in Chapter 1, criminological theory is derived from sociologically informed thinking about large-scale social structures and trends. Even though criminology's relationship with its parent disciplines might now be 'semi-detached', that pattern 'with sociology above all' is likely to continue (Rock 2002: 76). Hence there have been recurrent disputes regarding the usefulness of explanations that appear to make too much of individual, psychological influences. One objective of this chapter, therefore, is to illustrate how such explanations can sit alongside and complement, rather than be compelled to compete with, viewpoints that emphasize political, social or community influences.

As we also saw briefly in Chapter 1, there are sizeable obstacles, both conceptual and empirical, to theory construction in criminology. This chapter will nevertheless proceed on the basis that there is sufficient consensus about what is referred to as 'crime' for there to be a valid task to undertake in attempting to furnish a systematic, empirically based account of it. That is founded, almost by necessity, on an acceptance for working purposes of the official definition of crime reflected in the application of the criminal law. Debates about the limitations of that definition notwithstanding, it remains the one most widely used in textbooks of criminology.

There is in fact a proliferation of theories concerning what gives rise to crime. Even if it is believed to be an inescapable consequence of the emergence of human society, that state of affairs is itself seen as requiring explanation. Open some theory texts and it is not difficult to become confused by the abundance of ideas that have been forwarded in the course of the last century and a half. Different, even mutually incompatible views can each at first sound superficially plausible. Disarmingly often, there is insufficient information available to allow us to decide between them. This may reflect a problem that philosophers of science call the *under-determination of theory* (Klee 1997): the available data are compatible with more than one of the viewpoints on offer.

The chapter is divided into three main sections. In the first, the nature of theoretical explanation in criminology will be briefly characterized, and an account will be given of some of the most influential theoretical approaches arranged in a conceptual scheme according to 'levels of description'. Second, several recently published 'integrative' approaches to explaining crime will be surveyed, and the overall impact of this development evaluated. This material is designed to locate a psychologically based understanding of criminal acts inside a broader criminological framework. Third, some historical background will be provided to explain the origins of the most influential contemporary approach to crime within psychology. That approach, known as *cognitive social learning theory*, will be described more fully in the chapter that follows.

Main concepts in criminological theory

As Garland (2002) has suggested, one of the main 'projects' that has remained central in criminological thinking has been the aetiological one, in which an attempt is made to discover the causes of crime. This has been primarily associated with the proposal that crime results from individual or personal factors. In one version of the approach, the classical school, crimes are construed as outcomes of deliberate, consciously planned actions. Individuals are thought to have weighed up the advantages and disadvantages of different courses of action, and decided on balance in favour of crime. In another, the positivist school, criminality arises from individuals' inherent biological or psychological make-up; in the stronger case determining, and in the weaker case predisposing them, to act in antisocial ways.

However, a search for causal factors is not confined to individually oriented approaches, and it is probably fair to say that the reverse, diametrically opposed perspective is more widely accepted. This is the view that crime is principally a product of social and environmental conditions. There are many variants of this general position and they form the contents of the majority of chapters in most criminology theory textbooks. Many, however, are conjoined with ideas from other approaches, forming hybrid theories that in each case envisage a different sort of balance between selected large-scale, local and individual factors.

Alongside them is yet another view: that crime is a product of an irreconcilable conflict between individual and social forces. Left to pursue their own wishes and desires, most people will act in their own interests without being too concerned over the impact of this on others: 'they will almost certainly break the law if they can' (Rock 2002: 56). This tradition of thought stems initially from the work of the 'social contract' theorists of the Enlightenment, such as Rousseau and Voltaire. Other concepts within it are derived from the work of the French sociologist Emil Durkheim towards the end of the nineteenth century. The resultant ideas have been expressed in a variety of forms, collectively known as *control theories*. For society to remain ordered and coherent it must restrain individuals' tendencies simply to do what they want. The objective of this form of theory is less to explain why certain individuals offend, than to explain why much of the time most people do not.

The foregoing concepts have been central in shaping criminological theory for much of its existence (Vold *et al.* 1998). Despite extensive changes, discernible continuities have remained in some of the concepts from the time of criminology's inception until the present day. Most contemporary theories represent permutations, in one form or another, of these same basic ideas, though with considerable elaboration of detail and search for empirical support (Garland 2002; Rock 2002).

Hence ideas from the classical school of criminology, associated with the writings of Beccaria, Bentham and the utilitarian philosophers of the eighteenth century, can be found in the contemporary model of the 'reasoning criminal'. Here the concept of rational choice has been rejuvenated and has attained considerable influence on the thinking of some criminologists (Clarke and Felson 1993). A second thread is illustrated by the early empirical studies of the cartographic school (Guerry, Quetelet and others), who are sometimes also known as the 'moral statisticians' (Coleman and Moynihan 1996). This was later pursued by the founders of the ecological approach to crime at the University of Chicago from the 1920s onwards, which has played a seminal part in the naissance of a wide spectrum of sociologically oriented approaches.

More recently, since approximately the 1970s, an alternative approach to criminological research and theorizing has been formulated that represents a significant departure from all the viewpoints mentioned so far. Characterized by various names including 'deviance theory' or sometimes simply 'the new criminology', the focus of study within it is the working of the law itself. Its theoretical task is to encompass all the processes by which law is formulated, its edicts acted on, and its consequences felt by everyone involved. In the most radical and 'critical' versions of this approach, there are some thinkers who on epistemological grounds reject the project of 'explaining' crime. They argue that merely to employ the word or discuss how it might be 'caused' is to impose categories on the world around us; the usage of such discourse itself should be the subject of our research. Some post-modernist authors thereby repudiate the notion that there is something in the 'real world' to be explained (Henry and Milovanovic 1991). Others have suggested that this perspective can be combined with a more traditional, 'modernist' one in which it is accepted that causation of crime remains a legitimate subject of inquiry (Schwartz and Friedrichs 1994).

Levels of description

The sheer volume of criminological theorizing makes it necessary to find some organizing scheme within which different approaches can be thematically located. Bernard and Snipes (1996) classify theories into two basic types: 'individual-difference' and 'structure-process' theories. The approach adopted here is to consider models of crime in terms of their descriptive focus and explanatory scope. The apparent disagreement between different criminological theories arises to some extent from the fact that they begin from different *levels of description* when examining the problem of crime.

To simplify this, the field of criminological theory can be characterized as providing approaches to understanding criminal conduct on five discrete but interconnected levels. Broadly speaking, they move from the large-scale, society-wide 'macrocosmic' level to the 'microcosm' of the individual person. To borrow an analogy from biology – which is not to resort to biological theorizing! – they can be thought of as having the features of a compound microscope; representing attempts to view crime through a series of progressively more powerful lenses. This scheme is depicted in Table 2.1. The table shows, for each level, what can be described as the primary 'unit of analysis', the main focus of effort in research and theory construction. The third column specifies the broad objective of theory in that area; the final column lists some illustrative approaches that have their principal roots under each heading in turn.

Table 2.1 A schematic representation of levels of description in criminological theory (adapted from McGuire 2000a)

Level	Descriptive focus (unit of analysis)	Objective	Illustrative theories
1	Society	To understand crime as a large-scale social phenomenon	Conflict theory Strain theory Sociological control theories Feminist theories
2	Localized areas, communities	To account for geo-graphical variations in crime; such as urban–rural differences, or between districts or neighbourhoods	Environmental theories Differential opportunity theory
3	Proximate social groups	To understand the roles of socialization and social influence through family, school or peer group	Sub-cultural delinquency theory Differential association theory Social learning theory
4	Criminal acts and events	To analyse and account for patterns and types of crime events, crime targets and trends over time	Routine activity theory Rational choice theory
5	Individual offenders	To examine patterns of individual behaviour and internal, psychological factors such as thoughts, feelings or attitudes	Neutralization theory Psychological control theories Cognitive social learning theory

Level 1: macro-level accounts

On the first level, crime can be considered to be an unavoidable by-product of the very fact that human beings live together in large social groups. Taking this as a starting point, some theories have been developed in which both crime and the social conditions commonly associated with it, are assumed to be intrinsically bound up with the nature of human society itself.

Several theories can be found at this level. They include *conflict theories* such as those derived from radical political analyses. Here, given the nature of the relationship between competing groups within society, crime is seen as inevitable. Throughout human history there has been and continues to be relentless competition both for limited material resources and for institutionalized power. The dominant class in a society formulates and administers the law in a way that serves its own interests. Crime is created by this general condition and through the application of specific rules devised by the dominant group for the maintenance of social order and the perpetuation of its own power. Although it may constitute a sizeable nuisance, crime also serves a purpose. It furnishes an ongoing, public rationale for the exercise of control over certain segments of the population.

A second illustration is the *strain theory* of the American sociologist Robert Merton. He, too, saw the main objective of industrialized society as the pursuit of material success, with the inevitable results being intense competition and conflict. Since only a selected fraction of the citizenry can acquire the riches promised in this dream, everyone else must somehow adapt to the inexorability of failure, and find a means to cope with the circumstances into which they are placed. In attempting to secure the goals appointed for them by society, some individuals will resort to illegitimate means. Within this framework, Merton delineated several types of *deviant modes of adaptation* that correspond to different forms of criminal activity. Moderate empirical support has been found for a revised form of this theory, which takes account of other factors such as the influence of delinquent peers (Agnew and White 1992).

The emergence of *feminist theories* in criminology can also be placed at this level of description, as the initial concern of such theories was with the overall pattern of crime in society. Possibly the most notable single feature of it is the pronounced male-to-female differential in criminality (the *gender ratio* problem; Daly and Chesney-Lind 1988). Another question consistently asked is whether theories developed on the basis of research with male offenders are applicable to female offenders (the *generalizability* problem). These distortions are evidence of the 'overall masculinist nature' of criminology (Chesney-Lind and Pasko 2004: 2). Other key concerns of researchers in this field have included the disproportionately high levels of victimization of women by men (Heidensohn 2002). These findings, it is held, are inextricably linked to the dominant position of men in society. Even when women commit the crime of embezzlement, for example, their lowlier position in financial organizations is such that their monetary gains are likely to average only one-tenth of that of their male counterparts (Chesney-Lind and Pasko 2004: 102).

A large number of theoretical ideas in criminology can be collected under the heading of *control theories*. In Table 2.1 they are located on two separate levels. On a society-wide level, and through sociological theorizing, their focus is on the occurrence of crime in the community as a whole, and the nature of structures that maintain social order and conformity. On an individual level, the core question is then to discern what (if any) psychological factors, such as differences in personality or levels of self-control, might explain the supposed greater capacity of some people to adhere to the rule of law.

A large volume of empirical research in criminology can be described as focusing on the 'macro-social' level and corresponds closely to what

Garland (2002) has portrayed as the *governmental project*. This includes not only what is nowadays the virtually routine analysis of officially recorded crime rates over time, but also investigation of their association with economic indicators such as rates of unemployment or levels of personal consumption (Field 1990, 1999).

Level 2: locality-based accounts

Apart from the fact that it occurs in all societies, and is much more often committed by males than by females, the most salient feature of crime is that it is unevenly dispersed across different geographical locations *within* societies. This has given rise to a second level of description and theory-building in which the spatial and social distributions of crime are the prime focus of study.

The first systematic attempts to examine this were undertaken in Chicago from the 1920s onwards. The speed of immigration and rapidity of population growth in American cities during the late nineteenth and early twentieth century led sociologists at the University of Chicago to develop a model of how expanding cities change over time. Clifford Shaw, Henry McKay and their colleagues investigated the relationship between urban structure and change on the one hand, and indices of social disruption (including crime rates) on the other. They found that crime was consistently highest in inner-city slum neighbourhoods in which incoming migrants first settled, and which were marred by numerous types of social problems. In some ways this constituted a 'natural experiment': due to migration patterns there was a constant flow of new arrivals to these districts. On gaining some degree of affluence they moved to more salubrious areas of the city where their crime rate then decreased commensurately. The local dynamics of what the Chicago researchers called the *transitional zone* operated in ways that were conducive to delinquency. Crime was claimed to be a function of these processes, which arose independently of any known characteristics of individuals living in the identified areas. These ideas and the studies they generated have attained considerable prominence in the history of criminology. However, Farrington (1993) has questioned whether the evidence supposedly demonstrating the importance of neighbourhood factors is as convincing as has sometimes been alleged. In more recent studies designed to test this, little support has been found for the expectation that socioeconomic differences between neighbourhoods is a good predictor of the onset or rate of serious youth crime (Elliot *et al.* 1996; Wikström and Loeber 2000).

On the basis of this pioneering work, other criminologists developed more elaborate theories to account for the disparate rates of crime in different urban precincts. This has led to an influential strand of research and theory known as *environmental criminology*, which addresses features of the circumstances in which people live, work and play as potential contributors to the occurrence of crime. Another variation on this is *differential opportunity theory*, which combines concepts drawn from strain theory with the notion of 'opportunity structures' in a given local area. The focus here, therefore, is neither on the grand question of why crime occurs in the first place, nor on the question of which individuals (if any) are more likely to commit it. Rather, it is on the fabric of the physical and social environment and how it may influence rates and types of crime at a local level.

Level 3: socialization and group influence processes

We move next to the third lens of the compound microscope and to the third level of description. In this case, our objective is to understand the mechanisms by which even within certain localities or communities some individuals are drawn into crime while others are not. This focuses on variations between smaller 'proximate' units such as families or adolescent peer groups. These are the social networks that are the context for most everyday activity.

Several theoretical models can be found at this level. For example, according to *sub-cultural delinquency theories*, individuals with certain kinds of problems, notably adolescents having difficulties both at school and at home, seek alternative sources of interpersonal affiliation within which they can acquire status in the eyes of their associates. This model has been extensively used in attempts to explain the activity of juvenile gangs.

Other researchers have attempted to provide accounts of the social interaction processes operating in delinquent groups. Sociologist Edwin Sutherland proposed that the process underlying the development of offending behaviour was essentially one of learning, and was a function of the different influences to which individuals are exposed. The central proposal of *differential association theory* is that a person becomes delinquent as a consequence of an excess of definitions 'favourable to violation of law' over definitions unfavourable to it. In other words, the more people you know who argue in favour of shop theft and the fewer you know who argue against it, the likelier it is you will commit an act of shop theft. Generally, involvement in criminal activity is a product of a complex set of learning experiences, in the context of basic life circumstances, but more importantly it is reflected in acquired attitudes and habits of thinking. A key element of Sutherland's theory, of course, is that it is held to be applicable across all strata of society: it is an attempt to explain not only lower-class delinquency in run-down city neighbourhoods, but also 'white-collar crime' (fraud, embezzlement, money laundering, tax evasion) found among professional groups.

As we will see below, the concepts employed in differential association theory, although developed within a sociological framework, are in principle very similar to those of psychological learning theories. They thus provide an invaluable point of contact when seeking an integrative, cross-disciplinary account of offending behaviour.

Level 4: crime events and 'routine activities'

As we saw briefly in Chapter 1, some forms of theory in criminology have focused attention almost exclusively on criminal acts, marginalizing or purposefully ignoring the question of who is the person who committed them. The sole material under study is the criminal event itself. Although it results from the overt behaviour of the offender, any temptation to consider motivations or other individual factors that may have contributed to that action is strenuously avoided (Clarke and Felson 1993).

In this perspective, the focus of inquiry is the patterning of criminal acts across time and space. For example, house burglaries, vehicle thefts and fights are much more common in certain places or at certain hours of the day or night. Criminal acts exhibit patterns that are indicative of the availability of crime opportunities to individuals, as they arise in other cycles of activity they are following in their day-to-day lives. *Routine activity theory*, as this approach to criminology is known, considers the bulk of crime to fit this template and to be explicable through the convergence in space and time of 'motivated offenders, suitable targets, and the absence of capable guardians' (Cohen and Felson 1979: 589).

Some researchers have found a resonance between these ideas and the premises of *rational choice theory*, the origins of which can be traced to the classical view of crime as premeditated, purposeful calculation. In its modern form, however, the approach is applied in a more narrowly circumscribed field, to explain certain types of variation in crime. For example, once an overall decision has been made to commit residential burglary, the would-be burglar considers a range of factors in selecting the best 'target'. The list is likely to include the travelling distance to the target area, ease of access to a dwelling, likelihood of interruption or detection, and anticipated gain (Bennett and Wright 1984).

Ostensibly, the focus of this theory is on cognitive processes within individual offenders, and it could be argued that it belongs in the next level of description considered below. However, only a fraction of the work of rational choice theorists has been directly concerned with offenders' thoughts and decisions. Much more has been devoted to studying likely targets of crime, and drawing indirect inferences about those processes to develop crime prevention strategies such as 'target hardening' and surveillance (Rock 2002). But as the approach has evolved, there has been a growing recognition of the need to ascertain which elements of crime can be regarded as rational and which cannot (Brezina 2002).

Level 5: individual factors

The fifth and final level of description and theory construction in the present conceptual scheme explicitly addresses intra-individual factors. As described in the preceding chapter, most approaches to explaining crime based on the notion of differentiation or individualism do not at present have a very respectable reputation in criminology.

This is probably in many ways a residue of the Lombrosian project and the 'science of causes' that it represented (Garland 2002). At the kernel of most of the specific approaches emanating from this tradition, there is the idea of typologies of people in general and of criminal types in particular. In Lombroso's original version, criminals were divided into four sub-types: born criminals, insane criminals, occasional criminals or 'criminaloids', and criminals of passion. Members of the first group were thought to exhibit atavistic (evolutionarily regressive) characteristics. In a large-scale study in British prisons completed in 1913, Charles Goring failed to find any support for Lombroso's theory of sub-types or any evidence of different physical characteristics between offenders and non-offenders (Garland 2002; Lilly *et al.* 2002). It might have been expected that this would have marked the end of the search for a criminal physique, but other work based on the presupposition of individual correlates or causes of crime continued throughout the twentieth century and until quite recent times. This has taken a number of forms. On a *biological* level, it has included:

- the use of somatotypes by William Sheldon and others based on the proposition that there is an association between body build and propensity towards criminal recidivism (Wilson and Herrnstein 1985);
- the search for a 'criminal gene' (Walters 1992; Rutter *et al.* 1998);
- collection of data from twin studies to establish the strength of a heritability factor for crime (Buikhuisen and Mednick 1988; Brennan *et al.* 1995);
- the use of neuro-imaging techniques to detect hypothesized brain abnormalities in violent men (Raine 1997).

The first two of these possibilities are now wholly discredited, with early claims announced in 1965 of a discovered link between the XYY chromosome pattern and violent behaviour subsequently proving to be statistical artefacts. Concerning the notion of somatotypes, the perseverance of some of these ideas is in many ways remarkable. Goode (1997) has described secret studies that were conducted by Sheldon during the period 1940–1960, when entrants to several American 'Ivy League' universities including Yale and Harvard were photographed naked to record their body posture, in a study of its supposed relationship to intelligence. A number of students who subsequently achieved considerable eminence were photographed in this way, including future President George Bush (Senior), Senator Hillary Clinton and the actor Meryl Streep.

Discussions regarding the possible role of heredity in criminal behaviour have fortunately made some progress since the former days of the crude 'nature–nurture' dispute. Patently, we are all to a certain extent who we are at least in part as a result of some form of genetic transmission. There is no evidence that this contributes in any direct way to a propensity for any form of criminal conduct. However, genetic factors may play indirect roles in establishing vulnerabilities of various sorts, such as a number of features of temperament, which in interaction with adverse environments may then be associated with elevated risks of conduct problems in childhood. For a proportion of children who follow this pathway, a continuation into adolescent and even adult offending may be the result. The ways in which some of these factors might interact are discussed in more detail in Chapters 3 and 5.

Evidence regarding the possible role of brain damage in contributing to crime is tentative at best. For many years there was a widely shared belief that undetected 'minimal brain dysfunction' as a result of obstetric complications at birth was a cause of later impulsivity and risk of delinquency-proneness – until it was realized that such complications are far from uncommon. 'No firm conclusions on the postulated causal role of brain damage deriving from obstetric complications are possible. It is certainly clear that such causation is quite unlikely in most cases of delinquency' (Rutter *et al.* 1998: 140).

On a *psychological* level, most research into the potential role of individual factors was focused on differences in personality, though in the most prominent theories this is proposed to have an identifiable biological basis. While psychologically based accounts of crime-prone personality have originated from several directions, including for example psychoanalytic theory, most criminology theory texts devote little if any attention to them, reserving their criticisms instead for formulations that are most firmly in the Lombrosian tradition.

This type of theory is clearly illustrated by the work of Eysenck (1977), where it is postulated that constitutional factors (individual differences in the functioning of the nervous system, which may be inherited) influence the effectiveness of socialization processes. According to Eysenck, this occurs as a result of individual differences in *conditionability* (the ease with which conditioned responses can be established), which, in turn, has implications for the development of conscience. The combined effects of these factors is associated with differences in measurable personality traits. Three of these (higher extraversion, neuroticism and psychoticism) are held to be correlated with a greater likelihood of involvement in criminality. In essence, while this is a version of *differentiation* as defined by Roshier (1989), it is also a form of *control theory*, since any differences found are thought to determine individual capacities to adhere to society's rules.

Evidence in support of these claims is, however, rather weak. Hollin (1989, 2002a) marshalled findings from a number of research studies comparing offender and non-offender groups on the Eysenck personality scales, yielding somewhat inconsistent results. Possibly the most rigorous test of the theory comes from studies employing the method of cluster analysis, examining the relative proportions of delinquent and non-delinquent samples showing the predicted profile across the three personality scales. In Hollin's (2002a) judgement, the net pattern of results suggests that 'there is empirical evidence in favour of Eysenck's theory' (p. 155), but he also voices some reservations regarding it. Blackburn (1993) also attests that 'while attempts to test it have produced a number of significant findings . . . it must be concluded that Eysenck's theory of criminality is not well supported' (p. 127). The net result is far from convincing and purely personality-based accounts of criminal tendencies using uni-dimensional trait approaches have been all but discarded in favour of more complex, interactional accounts. This point will be discussed more fully in Chapter 3.

Overall, it has proved somewhere between difficult and impossible to isolate any type of personality dimension that can be consistently shown to differentiate between offenders and non-offender comparison groups. The best potential candidate in this respect is thought by Gottfredson and Hirschi (1990) to be *low self-control*. In a large-scale review of the evidence from 21 studies, Pratt and Cullen (2000) found that poor self-control was an important predictor of crime across a broad spectrum of offence types, though it was less well supported by developmental and longitudinal research. Vold *et al.* (1998) place greater emphasis on a different but over-lapping variable, that of *impulsiveness*. Interestingly, Farrington (2002) has suggested that to the extent that Eysenck's theory generated some empirical support, given the structure of the personality inventories used, it is probable that this 'mainly identifies the link between impulsiveness and offending' (p. 665). The evidence that any single dimension can reliably discriminate between offending and non-offending populations is nevertheless scant at best, since the latter groupings are extraordinarily difficult to define and to secure for research purposes. Furthermore, as Farrington (1996) has also suggested, there is surely only a limited prospect of being able to get very far in complex theory construction on the strength of 'only one underlying construct of criminal potential' (p. 79).

Nevertheless, as we shall see in Chapter 5, there is evidence of an association between some individual factors and levels of persistence of criminal offending over time. The variables that appear to have the firmest support are a proneness to experience negative emotions, coupled with a relative absence of personal constraints. The combined action of these two factors may place individuals at higher risk of involvement in offending behaviour (Caspi *et al.* 1994).

Psychological processes in sociological models

The quest for individual factors that would reveal consistent ways in which offenders differed from their law-abiding peers has thus proved largely unsuccessful. It has been widely disparaged by many criminologists as a result; though this was probably as much to do with its underlying assumptions as with its lack of empirical support. Evidence concerning the

presence of certain constellations of personal features among more persistent offenders is somewhat stronger, though the relative importance of these
factors alongside other types of influence remains unclear. Paradoxically,
while individually oriented theories have been a common target of criticism in criminology, psychological factors or processes have been posited
as elements within a number of sociologically based theories of crime.

They include, for example, *containment theory*, which is a variation of
control theory developed by Reckless (1967). This focused on the crucial
question of why, amidst many pressures towards crime, most individuals
(apart from minor lapses) do not become involved in it, and conformity
prevails. This applies even to some boys in high-crime neighbourhoods
who appeared to be 'insulated' from temptations towards delinquency
(Reckless *et al.* 1956). Reckless proposed two sets of factors which he
hypothesized could account for this. *Outer containment* consisted of
external limits placed on children as they developed; for example, the
assigning to them of constructive and meaningful roles, and the availability
of supportive relationships. *Inner containment* resulted from factors such
as a positive self-concept, having a sense of direction in life, ability to
tolerate frustration, and investment in and retention of group norms.

Another illustration of this comes from a different source. In some versions of sub-cultural delinquency theory, it was anticipated that members
of delinquent groups would express 'anti-social' attitudes, involving rejection of the moral values and standards of what may be called 'mainstream'
society. By contrast, research studies more often found that even recidivist
offenders tended to endorse conventional sets of values most of the time.
Neutralization theory (Sykes and Matza 1957) was an attempt to resolve
this discrepancy between hypotheses and research findings. In this model it
is proposed that to enable individuals to tolerate incongruity in their feelings and attitudes related to offending, they employ a series of internal
mechanisms that serve to reduce the incongruity of 'deviant' and 'conform-
ist' values. These self-excusing mechanisms are called *techniques of
neutralization* and consist of the following five processes:

- denial of responsibility: 'It wasn't my fault, I was pushed into doing it'.
- denial of injury: 'They can afford to lose it, they'll claim it on insurance'.
- denial of victim: 'He/she was gay/black/a supporter of the opposing team/scantily dressed'.
- condemning the condemners: 'The police are corrupt, they're just as bad as I am'.
- appeal to higher loyalties: 'You have to stand by your friends in a fight'.

By reacting to their crimes in this way, many offenders can reduce the
dissonance between their professed beliefs and their actual behaviour.
These concepts bear a close resemblance to some of those used within the
cognitive social learning model to be described in Chapter 3. They include
the kinds of self-talk that may precede or be supportive of offending
behaviour, from giving oneself permission to drive while over the legal limit

for alcohol, to the 'cognitive distortions' found among some men who commit sexual offences against children. All of these patterns, if altered, may prove useful in self-management of desistance from crime.

Probably the most notable convergence between sociological and psychological theories of crime, however, occurs in relation to the close conceptual links between differential association theory and ideas drawn from behaviourally based accounts of social learning. In both, crime is viewed as having its origins not in individual predispositions or personality differences, but in group interaction and influence processes.

Akers *et al.* (1979; see also Nietzel 1979) have explicitly elaborated such a model, drawing on extensive findings of research on human learning. They describe this as 'a revision of differential association theory in terms of general behavioural reinforcement theory' (p. 637). (In Chapter 3, we will examine more closely what is meant by reinforcement theory.) These authors posited that crime is learned through processes of imitation and differential reinforcement by which individuals may arrive at evaluative definitions that are supportive of delinquent action. This occurs in the context of social groupings, notably adolescent peer groups. The relative balance of influences within the groups to which individuals are exposed, conceptualized in learning-theory terms, instigates and maintains illicit use of alcohol and other drugs. Akers and his colleagues (1979) initially tested their theory by conducting a self-report survey of involvement in substance abuse among a large sample of teenagers. Significant correlations were found between independent variables (measures of differential association and opportunities for social learning) and dependent variables (levels of substance misuse). Although this study could not explicate the details of the mechanisms involved, it provided preliminary support for the importance of social learning in the onset of some kinds of proscribed behaviour.

A recent large-scale, meta-analytic review of a series of 140 studies by Sellers *et al.* (2000; cited by Lilly *et al.* 2002) has provided substantial support for this model. In a study of offending among young people in Scotland, Jamieson *et al.* (1999) interviewed three groups of young people whom they classed as *resisters* (those who had never offended), *desisters* (those who had previously offended but stopped) and *persisters* (those who continued for some time in offending). Their respondents reported patterns of family offending, and of rates of offending among their friends, that closely fitted the model. As Lilly *et al.* (2002) point out and as we shall see more fully in Chapters 5 and 6, additional support for this perspective can be gained from two other sources. One is the series of findings obtained through large-scale review of predictive factors for criminal re-offending by Andrews and Bonta (2003) among others; the other is evidence concerning the types of interventions that are most consistently associated with reductions in offender recidivism.

The crossover that is found in the foregoing theories between sociological and psychological concepts demonstrates the potential for theoretical integration, and opens up the possibility of this incorporating yet more variables from other perspectives or levels of analysis. In the next section, I will briefly survey some of the more fruitful attempts that have been made in this direction to date.

Theory integration

Earlier, we noted the abundance of theoretical models in criminology and the possibility that there has even been some over-provision. Considering the diversity of models to be found, some authors have called for a simplification of the field, or for a rapprochement between viewpoints and conceptual integration of different models. 'Unfortunately, the theoretical insights and empirical findings derived from these different approaches remain largely disconnected. Consequently, deviance and crime are understood only in piecemeal fashion, and the various approaches adopted to study these topics are badly in need of some attempt at unification' (Cohen and Machalek 1988: 466). Furthermore, given the marked tendency of researchers to advocate models based on one class of variables only, it has been contended that 'criminological theories need to be more wide-ranging and need to include all these different types of variables' (Farrington 1993: 30).

Bernard (1990) surveyed the progress of criminological theory over a 20-year period, and expressed dismay concerning its status. He suggested that there had been no meaningful advance, as nothing could be subjected to the philosophical principle of *falsification*; that is, subjected to empirical test in which whatever is 'out there' can be given an opportunity to 'push back' against our thinking (Klee 1997). There appeared to be little to choose between so many competing, equally plausible standpoints. But reviewing the position even within only a few years, Bernard and Snipes (1996) were able to feel more optimistic concerning the prospects. One ingredient in this transformation was the emergence of theories of progressively increasing breadth in terms of explanatory power. Over recent years, several genuinely integrative theories have appeared regarding the causation and maintenance of crime, even although some authors have remained pessimistic concerning the likely value of this effort (Leavitt 1999).

Some early integrative work was done drawing on a number of theoretical perspectives by Elliott *et al.* (1979). Their model combines elements of strain theory, control theory and social learning theory. Individuals experience strain as a result of being unable to achieve success (in terms defined by the culture to which they belong). In conditions of social disorganization they will also be subject to relatively weak controls and attachment to conventional norms. Social learning processes operate in such a way that the balance of their attachments shifts towards delinquent attitudes, with criminal behaviour as the result. This early attempt at conceptual integration was vigorously rebutted by Hirschi (1979), who averred that exercises along such lines were pointless and urged that they be abandoned. Despite this reprimand, during the period since then attempts to unite theoretical models with one another have continued apace. Arguments for the relative merits of theory integration versus theory elaboration or 'oppositional' theory-building are debated in the volumes edited by Messner *et al.* (1989) and by Barak (1998).

The importance of integration and the need to draw upon constructs from different realms is illustrated in a large-scale, cross-national study carried out in four countries (the Netherlands, Switzerland, Hungary and the United States). A substantial sample (7,000–8,000) of young people aged 15–19 years took part in this research (Vazsonyi *et al.* 2001, 2002). These researchers found that different portions of the variance in self-reported offending were associated with separate predictor variables. Patterns of everyday routine activities explained 16–18% of the variation in offending among sample members. Similarly, individual differences in self-control explained between 16 and 20% of the variance. To build a realistic model of offending behaviour, both of these variables, and several others besides, would need to be assembled into a coherent framework. (These findings emerged consistently across the samples regardless of national context.) In what follows, some of the most notable attempts to amalgamate theoretical concepts in criminology will be briefly outlined.

Integrative developmental models

In attempting to develop coherent theories, most criminological researchers would consider it essential to provide some account of the transitional years from middle childhood into adolescence, as the period when troubled behaviour is first likely to emerge. As we will see in the following chapters, the extensive findings from a number of longitudinal studies carried out in different parts of the world have been an invaluable asset in taking this agenda forward.

Thornberry (1987) has delineated an *interactional* theory of delinquency that combines explanatory concepts from the model of Elliott *et al.* (1979) just cited with other ideas from control theory and social learning theory. The model seeks to explain the net outcome of two processes: how constraints over behaviour may become progressively weakened, and equally how 'the resulting freedom is channeled into delinquent patterns' (Thornberry 1987: 865). The model contains six key interactive variables predictive of delinquency: attachment to parents, to school and to conventional attitudes; and associations with delinquent peers, adoption of their values and delinquent behaviour itself. However, these factors are not conceived as somehow taking fixed values such that, for example, the developing child's level of parental bonding becomes a static independent variable. Rather, the central tenet of the theory is that it is patterns of interaction over time that must be understood to give an account of the onset of delinquency. In addition, Thornberry places great emphasis on the inclusion in the model of reciprocal processes, and insists that a reliance on the concept of uni-directional causal effects must be discarded. Hence, just as the young person's detachment from parents may lead to gradual immersion in anti-social values, so the latter will also have consequences for the former. The developmental interplay of factors conducive to criminality can be depicted as occurring in an 'amplifying causal loop'. In a final layer of complexity, the pattern of interaction of the variables is expected to vary between early, middle and later adolescence.

In a later paper, Thornberry (1996) adduced a sizeable volume of evidence, collated from 17 separate studies, providing support for the operation of bi-directional causal effects. The studies reported on relationships between a number of variables in his initial model (parental and school attachment, deviant beliefs and attitudes, delinquent associates) and a variety of offence behaviours (minor and serious 'generalist' delinquency, theft, vandalism, shoplifting, drug abuse and interpersonal violence). Two other large-scale studies published since that time (Matsueda and Anderson 1998; Wright *et al.* 2001) have provided further support for the theory, which has also been extensively tested in the findings of the Rochester Youth Development Study (Thornberry *et al.* 2003).

An analogous perspective was adopted by Catalano and Hawkins (1996), whose model synthesizes control theory, social learning theory and differential association theory, though in a balance somewhat different from Thornberry's. These authors saw it as essential to incorporate a developmental dimension and in order to do so constructed a general model, together with four age-specific 'sub-models'. Developmental processes are 'transactional' in the sense that not only is there mutual influence between variables, but this generates qualitatively different outcomes at successive stages. Three primary external factors set the context for development in general: the individual's position in the social structure (socio-economic class, gender, race and age); constitutional/temperamental factors; and other external environmental constraints. Four constructs are considered as central in influencing the direction of development: (a) perceived opportunities for involvement in interactions with others, (b) the degree of involvement in those, (c) possession of the skills to participate in these activities, and (d) the anticipated reinforcement that accrues from doing so. When these factors work cohesively, a social bond develops, which may then have separate, independent influence in producing (or failing to produce) controls on later behaviour. The combination of pro-social and anti-social behaviours so learned, and the balance between the two, will decide whether children proceed along different 'pathways'. The causal elements in the model yield a number of indicators for points of intervention, which Catalano and Hawkins illustrate.

Introducing another theme into these discussions, Laub and Sampson (1993) have reminded criminologists that while there are some continuities in criminal careers, there are also turning points. Some are due to changes occurring naturally over time, others result from the impact of life events. Patterns of crime and potential causal or contributory factors are not necessarily stable across different phases of the lifespan. Hence a model which proves applicable to offending by young people may not explain adult criminality. Participation, maintenance, escalation and desistance might each be a function of separate variables, or of similar variables interacting in different ways. Theorists should accept 'the futility of an invariant or deterministic conception of human development' (Laub and Sampson 1993: 310). Even once involved in crime, there is evidence that individuals' motivations for such relatively high-frequency offences as shop theft, vehicle taking and some forms of drug use mutate during the years between early adolescence, the later teens and adulthood (McGuire 1997a, 2001a; Jamieson *et al.* 1999).

Several other theorists have offered variants of the theme developed here, in which factors contributing to crime are postulated as operating on several levels. Martens (1993) introduces concepts from a perspective based in studies of child development into an ecological frame of reference. The growing child is located in a complex network of associations on four levels: the *microsystem* (the child and his or her immediate surroundings); the *mesosystem* (significant others at home, school and play); the *exosystem* (the socioeconomic position of the parents, the neighbourhood environment); and the *macrosystem* (wider structural and sociocultural influences). Martens examines the dynamic interplay between various factors at each of these system levels, introducing the additional dimension of change over time.

LeBlanc's (1993) 'multi-layered' perspective is more complex still and comprises several stages of theory construction. This rests first on a distinction between delinquent acts, delinquent actors and delinquency as a social phenomenon. Each of these is itself seen as a product of several interacting variables, and LeBlanc presents a model of principal causal pathways in relation to each. The resultant sub-systems are then superimposed to construct a three-layered 'isomorphic model' integrating a total of 18 interdependent variables. In essence, its complexity notwithstanding, this is a form of control theory, as the fundamental orientation is towards understanding factors that either strengthen or weaken the individual's bonding to conventional norms, or provide inducements to engage in delinquency. Thus, LeBlanc enters into the equation three kinds of factors that respectively:

- operate to constrain delinquent acts (such as the presence of capable guardians versus crime opportunities);
- produce internal constraints in would-be offenders (such as attachments to others, especially pro-social models versus criminal associates); or
- moderate the level of crime in the community as a whole (legitimate opportunity structures, law enforcement agencies and criminal sanctions versus social disorganization and anomie).

Evolutionary frameworks

In an innovative departure, a fresh element was introduced into criminological theorizing by Cohen and Machalek (1988). These authors developed an approach to crime which adopts ideas from evolutionary theory and behavioural ecology. This was applied first to *expropriative* crime, meaning acts of theft or other property offences. It is proposed that, in common with other species, human beings have through evolutionary history developed a range of methods for securing both material and symbolic resources. Expropriation is viewed as simply one type of behaviour strategy for acquisition of resources; many animals as well as humans engage in it. Such a strategy is likely to be most efficient in certain circumstances and has specific interrelations with types of strategies employed by other members of the population. Adopting this approach, it proves possible to integrate ideas emanating from a number of criminological theories. The normality of crime; its higher frequency in some sub-cultures or in disorganized communities; differential association, social learning and control processes; and dimensions of individual differences, can all be fused together within a single, coherent theoretical framework. It should be noted that the model presented is not a repackaged form of sociobiology in which a range of behaviour patterns is attributed to genetically driven tactics for maximizing reproductive success. Cohen and Machalek explicitly distance themselves from that orientation.

Possibly the most comprehensive model provided to date is the integrative paradigm forwarded by Vila. This builds upon and extends the evolutionary ecological approach of Cohen and Machalek (1988) to make it applicable to a wider range of criminal acts. Vila (1994) first classifies crimes as falling into four major types, claiming this to be an 'arguably exhaustive categorization' (p. 315). Crimes may be one of the following:

- *expropriative* (e.g. theft, fraud, embezzlement): the object of which is to obtain material resources such as property from another person without his or her knowledge or cooperation;
- *expressive* (e.g. sexual assault, illicit drug use): to obtain hedonistic resources that increase pleasurable feelings or decrease unpleasant feelings;
- *economic* (e.g. drug-trafficking, prostitution): to obtain monetary resources through profitable illegal cooperative activities;
- *political* (e.g. terrorism, election-rigging): to obtain political resources by using a wide variety of tactics.

In common with some of the models already outlined, Vila also describes three levels of analysis of multiple connections between contributory factors: *ecological* (interactions between persons and their physical environment), *macro-level* (interactions between social groups) and *micro-level* (factors affecting the motivations of individuals). The three levels in turn are considered to interact synergistically; and the entire system of relationships is placed in a developmental context in which it also evolves dynamically over time.

If they are going to do the job they are designed for, integrative theories such as these must have several features. Obviously, they need to take into account a large number of variables. They should also address variables from different levels (e.g. individual, family, community, society) and make statements concerning the interrelations of those levels. They must be dynamic, taking into account both developmental change and environmental change. Given this degree of complexity, as adumbrated in Chapter 1 such models are probabilistic rather than deterministic. Their component variables can be interpreted as having causal relations but their interactions may take place in multiple directions, and are context-dependent, such that while the pattern as a whole can be described, the outcome for any one individual cannot be predicted with certainty. To quote Vila (1994) again, the outcome of his attempt at integration is an 'emphatically nondeterministic paradigm' (p. 311).

A second important feature of successful integrative theories is that they should address both *structural* and *process* variables. For example, statements concerning the varying prevalence of crime across localities, even if firmly supported by data, are unsatisfactory in themselves unless they also explain the sequence of events through which such differences come about. Some of the integrated theories meet both of these demands and identify plausible interconnections between the two categories of variables. However, it could still be regarded as a significant failing that none of them focuses attention on the behaviour of the law itself as an integral dimension. The present review of attempts at integration has itself paid scant attention to this, and while acknowledging it as an all-embracing contextual factor, we have focused instead on the orthodox position that certain aspects of criminal acts and actors can in themselves be a legitimate subject of inquiry.

To circumvent this criticism, Vold *et al.* (1998) have proposed a *unified conflict theory* of crime that attempts to meet all of these criteria. Their model is designed to address both structure and process while simultaneously taking into account variations in the operation of the law. Much work remains to be done in refining and validating an approach such as this, but it is important that these authors have demonstrated the possibility in principle of constructing a theory that will meet those requirements. Given the ambitious nature of the project, it may be unlikely that a consensus will be reached regarding unified criminological theory in the near future. In any case, Bernard and Snipes (1996) point out that the level of generality in such a theory could be so great as to render it impossible to test.

Another individual-level variable has received little recognition among the various models discussed so far. This is the thinking or *cognition* of individuals as they pursue everyday activities, interact with each other, solve problems and make decisions. Recently, informed partly by findings from within psychology, there has been a growing appreciation within criminology of the significant role played by cognitive processes in the genesis of criminal acts. This is exemplified in a paper by Foglia (2000), who examines several dimensions of the skills involved in solving everyday personal and social problems, and explicates the inclusion of cognitive variables in sociological theories that is often assumed at an implicit level. Such a departure accords with viewpoints expressed by psychologists seeking a rapprochement between psychological and sociological models of criminal conduct (e.g. Andrews and Bonta 2003).

Within the framework of the present book, the above review of proposals for integrative theory construction in criminology is designed to highlight the crucial need to address some individual, personal, psychological factors alongside developmental, familial, situational, community, and large-scale structural and political processes. An integrative model of this type has been developed over a number of years by Farrington (2003) to account for 'offending and antisocial behaviour by working-class males' (p. 165). This incorporates biological, psychological, family, community and social factors. There is a distinction between 'energizing' and 'inhibiting' processes leading towards or away from criminal acts; and between long-term/developmental and short-term situational or internal processes and external events. There are some potentially unwarranted assumptions embedded in the model regarding the supposed differential valuation of excitement, and of short-term versus long-term goals, in different social classes. This may be a particular obstacle given the indirect and relatively weak association between socioeconomic status and criminality (Gendreau et al. 1996; Wright et al. 1999; Dunawayk et al. 2000; Andrews and Bonta 2003). Nevertheless, the model is genuinely integrative and draws on variables that are found at all five levels of the conceptual scheme introduced earlier. The interrelations of the main components of this model are depicted in Figure 2.1.

Dodge and Pettit (2003) have forwarded a general model not dissimilar to this, focused on the development of conduct problems in adolescence. Some researchers consider the latter to be an antecedent of serious or persistent offending likely to last into adulthood. The major categories of variables composing the model are biological predispositions, parenting influences, peer influences, mental processes and the sociocultural context.

All of the attempts at theory integration that have been discussed in this section have deployed some kinds of individual-level variables. To do so does not entail a reassertion of the concepts of individuality and differentiation as they were subsumed under earlier typological models. Equally, the processes that are identified in these approaches are held to be universal – in the sense that they apply equally to both offenders and non-offenders (however defined). Within the current limits of generalizability of each theory in turn, this does not involve recourse to simplistic notions of categorization or pathology.

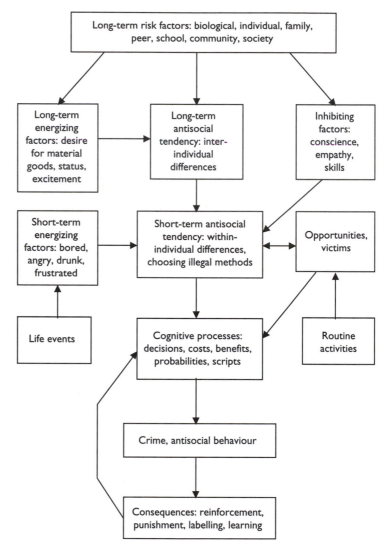

Figure 2.1 Farrington's integrative theory (Farrington 2003)

Origins of (cognitive) social learning theory

In the next chapter, we will look in more detail at some of the psychological processes that have the strongest support as candidates for inclusion in a genuinely integrative theory of crime. This will entail presenting a theoretical framework known as *cognitive social learning theory*. This was originally known simply as *social learning theory* and the word *cognitive* is a more recently added optional extra; mainly as a way of emphasizing that aspect of the core idea. The theory has the potential to plug, or to insert richer detail into, what could be called some of the gaps in the integrative criminological models outlined in the previous section. It elaborates, in other words, on the kinds of processes occurring within and between people, which particularly during childhood and adolescence shape them as persons. This appears, to the present author at least, to be a seminal task for illustrating how psychology can contribute to understanding crime.

Historically speaking, this theory is still relatively new. It is itself the product of a process of integration of ideas that were formerly unrelated (because the people who held them were simply focusing on different things) or were considered incongruent (because of philosophical assumptions about what could be meaningfully discussed). To conclude the present chapter, it will be useful to sketch the historical background that led to the emergence of this model.

Social learning theory was first clearly articulated during the 1970s as the result of a convergence between two previously separate strands of research and theorizing. One was *behaviourism*, which was rooted in the idea of making psychology an objective science by focusing only on what could be directly observed, measured and recorded, and within which there were explicitly positivist trends. The other was *cognitive psychology*, which began as a direct approach to studying certain, usually 'formal', mental processes such as logical reasoning or abstract problem-solving. Since approximately the 1960s, it has been heavily influenced by concepts from artificial intelligence and the development of computer science.

In the period after it was first established as an independent discipline, psychology as you might expect reflected the current thinking of the epoch. In the late nineteenth century, the translation of the Darwinian outlook into psychology took the form of assuming that most kinds of human action were the result of biologically innate urges or drives: the instincts. That such patterns might be part of our natural endowment seems perfectly reasonable with reference to the origins of hunger, thirst or sexuality. But aggression, competition, accumulation of wealth, leadership and artistic creativity were also alleged to be traceable to inherited and instinctively motivated forces.

Elsewhere, in the immensely influential work of Wundt and his associates, much effort was focused on the search for links between sensory and perceptual experience. The principal method of data-gathering used in their work was that of systematic self-observation or *introspection*. This required individuals taking part in experiments to describe their thoughts and inner experiences. (This kind of data would now be called 'verbal report' or 'self-report'.) These ideas and practices were called into question in 1913 when John B. Watson (1878–1958), an American psychologist, insisted that if psychology were to emulate other sciences, it should collect information only about events that could be directly observed. What was observable about human beings and other animals was their behaviour: any talk of internal, mental processes was purely speculative and unscientific. Watson called this radical suggestion *behaviourism*, and argued it should supplant the dominant *mentalism* of the period. Allied to this basic epistemological stance, Watson also asserted the need to recognize that a large proportion of human behaviour is learned. To indicate how psychologists might study this, he drew on the work of the eminent Russian physiologist, Ivan Pavlov. As we will see in Chapter 3, Pavlov had reported the discovery of some basic mechanisms of learning that could be investigated on a purely behavioural level.

In the ensuing decades, behaviourism became one of the major schools of psychological thought. Given the proposal that mechanisms of learning could be studied in carefully controlled experiments, and were common across species, much early behavioural research was conducted with animals in laboratory settings. A central principle informing such work was that of moving from the simple to the more complex, in gradual stages, as had been powerfully and emotionally advocated by Pavlov (Morison 1960). Hence the behaviourists' painstaking (and regrettably, sometimes pain-inflicting) studies of learning processes in experiments using rats, mice and pigeons. The near-ubiquitous white rat, used in psychological research since 1901, has been a subject of much controversy inside and outside psychology, but is defended on the grounds of having played the same role as sweet peas or *Drosophila* (fruit flies) in genetics (Barker 1994).

The study of cognitive development

However, the behaviourist 'revolution' just described did not entirely halt the direct investigation of thinking and other cognitive processes. Throughout the middle decades of the twentieth century, some psychologists continued to carry out research on memory, perception and allied areas. Probably the most influential was a Swiss psychologist, Jean Piaget (1896–1970), who studied the learning and progressive problem-solving of children from the very earliest stages of life. Piaget's starting point was the notion that the mind had certain inherent capacities for making sense of its surroundings, and that during the process of maturation these unfolded in much the same way as did physical growth. For example, just as – given favourable circumstances – most children will learn to walk, so Piaget thought they also learned such concepts as the constancy of objects, conservation of mass or volume, and causality. By the 1960s, many research findings had accumulated on the development of children's thinking, and also on memory, reasoning, the role of language in thought, and other aspects of cognition in adults. The growth of cognitive psychology accelerated with the ready availability of computers from the 1960s onwards, catalysed by the concepts of artificial intelligence. This held out the prospect of being able to investigate human cognitive processes by designing software that simulated them in electronic form. In turn, that led to widespread use of the concept of information processing as a model for understanding what occurred inside the human mind or brain.

Throughout the half-century up to the 1970s, there was little meaningful contact between psychologists who described themselves as 'behaviourists' and those who called themselves 'cognitive psychologists'. Findings of behavioural research, however, had begun to indicate that the mechanism of conditioning that was postulated as the fundamental unit of learning was not able to carry the explanatory weight that until then had been loaded on to it.

Several crucial developments within behaviourism itself led to a broadening of perspective and an acceptance that events that were not directly observable, but were indirectly inferred or reported, could nevertheless be important factors in explaining learning and other forms of behavioural change. The first was the advent of *behaviour therapy* during the 1950s through the work of Joseph Wolpe, a psychiatrist, and the psychologist Hans Eysenck (whose later work on crime and personality was discussed above). During the 1920s Rosalie Rayner, a postgraduate student supervised by John Watson, had demonstrated how harmless objects could come to be feared through a process of conditioned learning. If most human behaviour is learned, this should apply also to the acquisition of problems such as irrational fears or *phobias*. Wolpe and Eysenck extended this principle and developed a range of psychological therapies based on learning theory. Using this it was possible to show that individuals could learn, in step-by-step fashion, to replace the fear they felt for a phobic object with a different form of emotional response such as relaxation. The technique Wolpe devised for achieving this, *systematic desensitization*, has been one of the most widely used in behaviour therapy for the reduction of anxiety problems.

A second influential development was the accumulation of a sizeable body of research findings on the process of *self-regulation* of behaviour by means of language. The acquisition of such control depends initially on speech. During early childhood, children's behaviour is considerably influenced by things their parents and other adults say to them. As they acquire language, children begin to repeat these things to themselves; initially aloud, later more inwardly or covertly. Later still, they lose all awareness of saying them. Actions are governed by cognitive events that occur automatically, without deliberate reflection and outside conscious awareness. These observations by behavioural researchers were in close concordance with those made by cognitively oriented developmental psychologists. The central idea can be summed up in a statement made by Farber (1963: 196): 'the things people say to themselves determine the rest of the things they do'.

The fusion of these and other ideas led to the formulation by psychologist Albert Bandura (1977) of *social learning theory*. This was also influenced by another set of findings Bandura and his colleagues had obtained from behavioural research. For an animal to learn, it did not need to have direct experience of rewards and punishments, as earlier behaviourists had supposed. It could learn indirectly, by observing outcomes of behaviour for other members of its species. Researchers hypothesized that such *obser-vational learning* must rely on internal mechanisms that could not be accounted for by direct conditioning alone. Bandura amassed a large quantity of evidence on the importance of learning from 'models' in human development. Social learning theory posits both direct conditioning and observational learning from models as basic processes in development. Bandura identified three separate classes of models that were powerful in learning: family members, particularly parents or other caregivers; other immediate associates such as members of a peer group; and symbolic models, encountered through the media.

These developments represented crucial departures in the way behaviourally based ideas were applied to learning and change. For example, in learning to overcome a phobia, individuals can imagine progressively more threatening situations in which they would usually become highly anxious, and use the method of desensitization to reduce their level of fear. A therapist working with them pays attention to, and makes use of, their self-observations and verbal reports. In social learning theory, observation of models and subsequent learning are dependent on the proposition that internal, cognitive processes are indispensable for such learning to take place. In both these approaches, in other words, there is a reliance on cognition as an explanatory tool in the account of learning that is given. Having made these assumptions, behavioural psychology was open to some form of 'merger' with ideas from cognitive science.

The cognitive–social learning synthesis

Within a short period during the mid-1970s a number of books and articles were published that combined, with different emphases but in broadly the same vein, ideas from the behavioural, social-learning and cognitive strands within psychology (e.g. Mahoney 1974; Meichenbaum 1977). This was closely associated with the emergence of a family of intervention methods, used initially in work in mental health settings, and collectively known as *cognitive-behavioural therapies*. The influence of behaviourism on this was reflected in an emphasis on the role of the environment in learning, alongside the idea of breaking complex actions into simple, more comprehensible units, creating the possibility of behaviour change in gradual, clearly defined steps. There was also a recognition of the universal importance of individuals' monitoring and evaluation of their actions from the outset to the completion of the process, including follow-up to examine maintenance of change.

The impact of what had been learned from cognitive research was reflected in complementary principles. They included an acceptance of the value of self-reports; attention to the crucial part played by language and of people's self-referent 'inner speech' in the regulation of action; and also in the genesis, maintenance and reduction of disorder and distress. Assembled into a coherent framework, these concepts provided a powerful new approach to understanding the complex dynamic relationships between thoughts, feelings and behaviour.

The conceptual framework of cognitive social learning theory continues to evolve. Its application to progressively more areas is intimately associated with the cognitive-behavioural interventions for which it provides the underpinning theoretical model. According to Meichenbaum (1995), there have been three principal stages in the evolution of these ideas, which he portrays as a succession of core metaphors: *conditioning, information processing* and *constructive narrative*. When behaviourism was first formulated, all change was conceptualized in terms of alterations in learning mechanisms in the nervous system. (Even cognitive events were originally viewed by behaviourists as covert forms of conditioning.) While this gave rise to some valuable findings, the concepts were too rigid to encompass the range of individual differences that were observed and the complexity of the factors that were operating. As these inadequacies became more apparent, cognitive events were recognized as crucial mediators of action, and the idea of 'information processing' came to the centre of theory construction. Cognitive social learning theory was a product of this synthesis. However, it has retained the behaviourists' practice of routinely analysing individuals' reports on their experiences into smaller segments. More recently, an appreciation has developed of how individuals generate more complex sets of cognitive patterns, which can loosely be called 'stories', through which they understand, express and create their own lives. At this stage in the development of cognitive-behavioural approaches, this view of individuals as architects of their own individual existences is gaining ascendancy and being actively researched. The guiding metaphor within this is that of 'constructive narrative'. This is the idea of understanding individuals, and where appropriate assisting them in personal change, by entering into the sets of meanings they have created in their lives. Practitioners become collaborators in the rearrangement of such narratives to enable individuals to resolve difficulties and create new images of themselves (Maruna 2001).

Further reading

There are several well-known textbooks on criminological theories. The ones on which I have drawn most often are George B. Vold, Thomas J. Bernard and Jeffrey B. Snipes (1998) *Theoretical Criminology* (4th edn, New York: Oxford University Press) and J. Robert Lilly, Francis T. Cullen and Richard A. Ball (2002) *Criminological Theory: Context and Consequences* (3rd edn, Thousand Oaks, CA: Sage Publications). There are also several valuable collections of key papers. From the perspective of theory integration the most important is Gregg Barak (ed., 1998) *Integrative Criminology* (Aldershot: Ashgate). Other useful readings are provided in the books by Peter Cordella and Larry Siegel (eds., 1996) *Readings in Contemporary Criminological Theory* (Boston, MA: Northeastern University Press) and Stuart Henry and Werner Einstadter (eds., 1998) *The Criminology Theory Reader* (New York: New York University Press).

Psychologically based theories are dealt with in greater depth in Donald A. Andrews and James Bonta (2003) *The Psychology of Criminal Conduct* (3rd edn, Cincinnati, OH: Anderson) and Ronald Blackburn (1993) *The Psychology of Criminal Conduct* (Chichester: Wiley). These books also cover psychoanalytic and other theoretical perspectives not discussed in the present volume. See also Clive R. Hollin (1992) *Criminal Behaviour* (London: Falmer Press).

Psychological processes in crime

The joint objective of this chapter and the two that follow is to provide a more detailed account of the contribution psychology can make to understanding acts and patterns of crime. From the brief critique in Chapter 2, we saw that the traditional personality-based approach to crime, centred on the notion of dimensional constructs called *traits*, has not been very firmly supported by research findings. To some extent this has brought further discredit upon the 'individual difference' framework, which many criminologists already regarded with hesitation, given its traditional links with the positivist, determinist, biologically oriented 'Lombrosian project'.

To assert that criminal actions are entirely a product of social environments or political forces, however, appears a similarly myopic perspective. To locate the causes of crime exclusively in factors external to individuals is simply to adopt a different but equally unworkable form of crude determinism. This denies any role for agency and individuality in human action. It runs counter to the immediate experiences people have as they live their lives and observe other people around them, as well as being plainly at odds with the evidence. It would be a fairly drastic step, therefore, to propose that crime can be understood on that basis alone.

Even the most doctrinaire environmental determinist would surely agree, given that most criminal acts are committed by individuals, that there must be some internal processes at work within the protagonists. Surely, also, they are not identical in every case: people are not, well at least not yet, clones of each other. These key issues form the substance of this chapter and the next two. In the present one, we will focus on the kinds of psychological events and processes that are likely to be involved in the occurrence and, for some individuals, the maintenance of offending behaviour. Those processes are essentially the same ones that we can use to explain any of a wide variety of things that people do, and cut across any dividing line that might be thought to exist between the 'normal' and the 'abnormal' when thinking about human activity. In Chapter 4, we will apply this to some selected types of offending behaviour and draw upon evidence that illustrates the application of the general model to specific classes of criminal acts. Given that these processes may take a similar but never exactly the same direction in two different people, in Chapter 5 we will then consider what role there might be for factors arising from individual differences that influence levels of involvement in crime.

Basic processes

The model to be presented here, then, is driven by the core assumption that there is a role for psychological factors in helping us to understand the causation of crime. Specifically, the way in which those factors operate will be described in terms of an approach known as *cognitive social learning theory*, the origins of which were briefly described in Chapter 2. Such a theory can enable us to comprehend not only the kinds of actions that frequently attract the label 'crime', but a whole array of other types of behaviour in addition. They may range from everyday, ordinary, mundane activities all the way to behaviour that is extremely unusual. For this reason, a sizeable tract of the chapter will appear not to be about crime at all, as we will be considering a general psychological theory applicable to a wide range of human actions.

Such an approach offers a psychologically based outlook on offending behaviour that is free of the tendency to 'pathologize'. This theoretical formulation is additionally valuable in that it provides the conceptual underpinnings for a group of interventions that have yielded positive outcomes in attempts to reduce the frequency of re-offending; this is an area that will be addressed more fully in Chapter 6. To provide an account of this theory, I would like first to outline some key concepts, then present fuller detail 'from the ground up'. This will involve outlining the theory's three core elements in reverse order – *learning, social, cognition* – as that both reflects the level of complexity of the processes involved and also coincides with the way it was developed.

Learning. Like several of the theories discussed in Chapter 2, one starting point of this model is that most kinds of behaviour manifested by human beings are to a very large extent learned. That may be obvious in the case of activities like ice skating, driving heavy goods vehicles, or providing simultaneous translations at the UN. It is perhaps less so in relation to apparently simple actions, such as sitting upright, walking or bowel control. But those too are learned. All are influenced, engendered or constrained by our biological make-up. As living organisms we share some essential characteristics with other species, most notably those processes that are connected with survival and procreation. Many other developmental patterns are the result of a combination of biological maturation and learning processes. For example, human infants take steps – figuratively and literally – and start to learn to walk without being prompted to do so. Physical growth engenders behavioural change, with ensuing trial and error, practice and feedback honing the child's skills. Learning can be understood partly on a biological level, as it entails changes in our nervous systems. A learning theory approach enables us to recognize these links to our biological inheritance and our status as products of an evolutionary process.

Social. Human development and learning, however, have a vitally important feature: they take place in a social context. Our attainment, relative to most other species, of such a high degree of control over our environments is largely a result of our ability to cooperate with each other. From the moment they are born, human infants are socialized by parents or other caregivers, and that setting channels the direction of the learning processes referred to previously. The development of our brains has been influenced, to a degree far beyond that of other creatures, by our preference for living in groups, our need to communicate, and consequent development of a facility for use of complex language. That, in turn, has enabled us to develop the elaborate communal phenomenon we call culture.

Cognition. The feature of human beings that is most frequently highlighted as distinguishing us from other species is our possession of large and complex brains, giving us the highest ratio of brain-to-body weight in the animal world. Particularly important is the part of that organ known as the *cerebral cortex*, which creates the space for holding and managing an extraordinary quantity of information about the external and internal environments. The human brain consists of a bewilderingly intricate network of specialized cells called *neurons*. Brains contain, on average, one hundred billion ($100,000,000,000$ or 10^{11}) of these cells. Each one has connections with as many as 1,000 of its neighbours (Kandel *et al.* 2000). Our brains are the residence of consciousness and other inner experience, 'the engine of reason, the seat of the soul' (Churchland 1995). (Perhaps that is an unwarranted claim, but no other part of the body has been put forward as a plausible alternative candidate.) The many processes that are associated with such experience – attention, perception, remembering, understanding, reasoning, planning, problem-solving, imagining, dreaming – are nowadays collectively known by the general term *cognition*.

Theory 'from the ground up'

Learning theory emanates from behavioural psychology; indeed, it is sometimes perceived as synonymous with it. The processes that behaviourists say are responsible for learning happen at a very basic level within the nervous system. This specialized network of organs helps to ensure our survival by processing information about the environment. It is also a system with an in-built capacity for change.

The forerunner of behavioural learning theory is a famous series of experiments conducted at the start of the twentieth century by the Russian physiologist Ivan Pavlov (1849–1936), as part of his research on the digestive system of dogs, for which he received the Nobel Prize in 1906. As part of this he undertook a number of studies of reflex actions. Reflexes are patterns of responding (e.g. salivation, startle, knee-jerk, sweating, goose-pimples, vomiting) that occur automatically following presentation of a stimulus (a tasty morsel, a loud bang, a blow just below the knee, a steep rise in temperature, ingestion of Marmite), and are 'hard wired' into the working of the system itself.

Pavlov's key discovery was that such reflexes could be modified by experience. When dogs were presented with food, they salivated – an unconditioned or naturally occurring reflex. After a series of trials in which presentation of food was accompanied by the ringing of a bell, the dogs salivated following the ringing of the bell alone. Pavlov called this process *conditioning*. There are many complexities in it that need not detain us here; but essentially, a change in the response pattern of the nervous system was brought about by a change in the environment. This type of change is sometimes known as *classical* or *Pavlovian* conditioning. The mechanisms underlying it are beginning to be understood at a molecular level, and involve a number of processes, including one that neuroscientists call *long-term potentiation* (Kandel *et al.* 2000).

Another form of conditioning occurs when a response is influenced by the consequences that follow it. This applies to actions that are voluntary (as opposed to reflexive) and is called *instrumental conditioning*. It is used more specifically to describe particular responses called *operants*, which act or 'operate on' the environment. Here, the focus of interest is on the strength of the relationship between behavioural responses and their consequences, such as rewards and punishments. This paradigm is known as *operant conditioning*. It was extensively researched by Burrhus F. Skinner (1904–1990), who investigated the relationships between patterns of behaviour and the *reinforcement contingencies* – schedules or rates of positive and negative consequences – which influence the likelihood of occurrence of different behaviours.

The *cognitive social learning* model (Bandura 1977, 2001) builds upon the understanding of behaviour gained from studies of conditioning. However, it also adds a vital new element: a focus on intervening processes – what goes on between the stimulus and the response. That, of course, is

not directly observable and so is ruled out of court by the more method-
ologically pure among behaviourists. But the difficulty with both of the
conditioned learning models (classical and operant) is that an anticipated
link between stimuli, responses and consequences does not always appear
in a way that would be predicted by the regularities of conditioning alone.
Something crucial was left out of the initial learning model: the organism
itself and what is going on inside it. Depending on how internal processes
such as attention, perception and memory operate, and on the meaning of
events within them, different organisms or different people presented with
the same stimulus do not always emit the same response. These internal
processes are, moreover, intrinsically interesting in their own right.

In terms of the notation sometimes used to denote models in psychology,
the cognitive social learning model can be represented as S-O-R-C, where

S = stimulus: the external event or conditions impinging on the person
O = organism: the internal state of the individual, including current
   representations of the external world, and their history
R = response: the behavioural or motor reaction
C = consequences: the pattern of reinforcers or punishers which follow

The level of abstraction at which this is stated is too high to be of any
real value in explicating its various components. In essence, it is simply a
mnemonic for reminding us of the need to take into account all four sets
of variables.

Interrelationships of thoughts, feelings and behaviour

In most applications of cognitive social learning theory, it is customary to
consider an individual's activity as having three modalities: behaviour,
emotion and cognition. They are in themselves constructs and there is
a certain element of artificiality in segmenting experience in this way.
That granted, these concepts can be remarkably useful and they can be
concretely anchored in systematic observation and experiential report.

In this conceptual scheme, 'behaviour' is externally observable action,
the things people overtly, visibly or audibly do. So it is usually taken to
refer to the movements of the motor or muscular system, including 'verbal
behaviour' or speech. The word 'emotion' is more difficult to define, as it is
used to depict physiological or somatic expression of feeling (as in arousal,
when we feel tense, and our heart rate and blood pressure increase). It is
also, however, used to refer to cognitive aspects of a bodily state. 'Cognition' refers to mental events which each of us directly experiences, but
which we cannot directly observe in others. We nevertheless assume that
others experience them, through a process of inference and analogy with
our own internal self-observations (Searle 1995). Whatever the precise
coverage of the terms used, the key principle is that these three aspects of
action are in reality indivisible. An account of human functioning with
one of them left out would be absurd. They are not only interlinked but

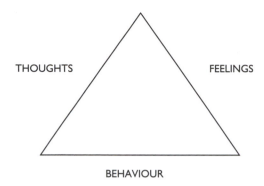

Figure 3.1 Interdependence of thoughts, feelings and behaviour

interlocked. For this reason it can be a helpful reminder to represent them in the form of a triangle as shown in Figure 3.1. This is simply a metaphorical way of representing the inseparable relationship between the three categories of events.

Cognition, emotion and behaviour are sometimes referred to as three 'systems' and sometimes as three 'domains'.

Information processing

In exploring the relationships between thoughts, feelings and behaviour, it is important not to lose sight of the fact that the locus of most of this activity is the human brain. Cognitive psychology has made significant advances over the past few decades through the use of models of brain function based on the concept of information processing. The brain is considered to be a specialized organ for collecting, integrating and analysing information about the external and internal environment. Of special relevance here is a key distinction that has emerged from this work, and which is supported by large amounts of empirical evidence: between *automatic* and *controlled* processing of information and of sequences of action.

A very large proportion of the things we do each day relies on *automatic processing*. Washing, dressing, eating breakfast and many similar activities are run as highly 'routinized' programmes, which, apart from when they are first being learned, require minimal purposeful thought for their execution. Our capacity for learning routines and programmes of this kind is very impressive. A large number of them can operate in parallel at any one time.

Controlled processing differs from this. Its activities must be run serially, we are usually aware of doing it, and it calls for attention and effort. This is the type of cognitive activity called upon when we face novel situations, think hard, make decisions or solve problems. It also coordinates our automatic processing. If a routine 'automatic' sequence of activities is interrupted, or becomes pointless, controlled processing may make the switch to a different routine.

Controlled processing also performs a self-regulatory function. In infancy, much of our behaviour is regulated externally, by parents and others. Learning and socialization not only modify our behavioural repertoires, they also help us acquire the skills of monitoring and managing ourselves. A large proportion of this is done through the medium of language.

Although our capacity to store automatic programmes is large, there are much more limited capacities for making use of the information in controlled processes. Language facilitates this to some extent. The developing infant learns to self-regulate with the assistance of language. This is at first overt: the child speaks words aloud, as if repeating instructions. Later this becomes covert: the link between the words and actions becomes automatic and disappears from awareness. Such self-regulation then takes the form of internalized instructions concerning a given sequence of action. This is the foundation of the important part played by cognitive processes in the self-management of feelings and behaviour. A similar process is reproduced, at later stages, when we try to learn a new skill, such as driving a car or playing a musical instrument. We use self-instructions to guide our actions and prompt ourselves to do things, even speaking them aloud. With repetition, practice and feedback, this develops into a self-regulatory, unconscious routine. Once patterns of this kind have been established, an individual becomes much less dependent on the environment, or on external sources of stimulation for the direction of behaviour. Over time, individuals also develop awareness of their capacity to influence different outcomes in their lives, a process they keep subject to constant monitoring and review. This generalized set of expectations regarding personal effectiveness is known as *self-efficacy* (Bandura 1997).

You will have noticed I just used the word 'unconscious'. For many years, that word was banned from the vocabulary of large numbers of psychologists. In social learning theory, however, there is no taboo against it, though it does not refer to the same virtual entity as discussed for example in psychoanalysis. According to cognitive-social-learning theory, cognitive events can be classed as occurring under four conditions (Meichenbaum and Gilmore 1984). They are:

- Sequences of thought that are present when we are consciously learning something, but that through practice become automatic and fade from awareness. This also applies to messages we absorb through socialization.
- Ideas and feelings we may have, but have not consciously articulated until it becomes necessary, for example in order to make a choice or a judgement of some kind. This might involve a process of internal search or reflection.
- 'Troubleshooting' and problem-solving: as when plans are interrupted or a course of action goes wrong, and we mentally review what has occurred.

- Recall of information about a past event or scene: a large amount of material may be retained that has left our awareness. It may include memories of our feelings at the time of the event.

'Each of the four conditions described ... whereby cognitive events can become objects of conscious scrutiny and report, illuminates a corresponding condition in which cognitions are latent and/or unobserved' (Meichenbaum and Gilmore 1984: 275).

Sometimes we do things for which the reasons are not obvious to us at the time. When trying to understand this, perhaps because we want to act differently next time round, it can be useful to explore cognitive events that were initially outside awareness. Work of this kind forms part of some of the cognitive-behavioural interventions that will be discussed in Chapter 6.

Interactionism

In social learning approaches, it is assumed that we can only understand the things people do if we combine information about them as individuals with information about the circumstances in which they are acting. Put more technically, this means that both *personal* variables, and *situational* and other environmental variables, are viewed as important. The latter can be either *proximal*, meaning they are comparatively close by in space or time; or *distal*, in that they are far-off or long-term influences. The core proposal, then, is that the best explanation of human behaviour will come from an analysis of the interaction between the two, although factors in the immediate situation often have the most powerful effect. But this is likely to be moderated by a combination of many attributes of all the factors involved.

Research studies in psychology have repeatedly supported the proposal that the best prediction of behaviour comes not from information concerning either personal or situational factors, but from the combined effects of the two. This was lucidly demonstrated in a review by Bowers (1973) of the accuracy of predictions based on information concerning personality traits as compared with information about situations. In every instance studied, the *interaction effect* – the combination of the two kinds of influences – accounted for more of the variance in outcomes than either of the two 'independent variables' considered alone.

This stance is known as *interactionism*. It is closely interconnected with the idea of *reciprocal determinism*. Human action is the product of a complex, dynamic interplay between personal and situational factors. In the cognitive-social-learning framework, however, the person is described not purely in terms of the 'traits' of traditional personality theories, but in terms of relationships between cognitive, affective and behavioural factors (Mischel 1999, 2004). Of course, some patterns among the latter may remain relatively stable over time, and could still be conceptualized as dimensional traits. Alternatively, they could be considered to consist of relative continuities in 'processing dynamics', or recurring patterns in the ways in which individuals perceive and respond to situations. This is the essence of the cognitive-social-learning approach to understanding personality (Cervone and Shoda 1999). People manifest both stability and variability in their interactions with their surroundings (Mischel and Shoda 1998). From a theoretical standpoint, this might sound like 'having your cake and eating it'. Let us look in more detail at what it means.

Environmental variables include an enormous range of events, encompassing anything from a bright flash which leads to the pupil of your eye to constrict, to the complex sequence of experiences involved in the socialization of a child within a disadvantaged family in an economically deprived neighbourhood. In different circumstances, the relative importance of the two sets of factors, personal and situational, may vary. This point is depicted schematically in Figure 3.2.

This might at first seem like an unexpected and counter-intuitive finding. Our own experience of ourselves is of having an enduring identity. Even if our sense of it evolves slowly over time, we feel we are the same people doing the same things across a variety of situations. That applies equally when we look around at others: we observe patterns that are relatively reliable and consistent across situations and through the passage of time. If people changed with great abruptness or rapidity, relationships would be extremely difficult (of course, a few of them are, for exactly that reason). The core problem here has been called the 'personality paradox' (Bem and Allen 1974). We think of personality as being stable. Yet research evidence shows relatively low levels of constancy from one situation to another (Mischel 1968).

The interactionist approach is one step towards resolving the paradox. Within this framework, we anticipate that both personal and situational factors will be necessary to understand how someone will behave. But the ways in which they interact will themselves vary from one context to another, as the conceptual scheme shown in Figure 3.2 indicates. Epstein and O'Brien (1985) argued that if we expect personal factors such as traits

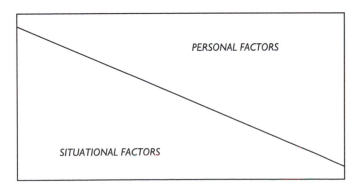

Figure 3.2 Person–situation interactionism and reciprocal determinism

to yield a prediction of how someone will act in any specific situation, we are asking too much; maybe expecting the impossible. But across a range of situations, some stable patterns will emerge and the larger the number of situations we 'sample', the higher that stability will be. They therefore argued that personality variables have an *aggregate* importance for helping us to understand someone, even if that does not mean we can be sure what he or she will do or how he or she will feel in any given set of circumstances.

The debate between 'trait' and 'situational' approaches to understanding people's actions has continued, sometimes acerbically, for many years. But there are signs that it is on the brink of being resolved (Funder 2001; Mischel 2004). In one sense, the two points of view are sharply polarized. From another perspective, they are mainly differences of emphasis.

One important contribution to resolving the 'personality paradox' has come from the work of Shoda *et al.* 1994; Mischel 1999; McAdams 2001. Based on intensive observations of the actions of a large group of 10-year-old children with problem behaviour at a summer camp, they re-conceptualized the study of personality–situation interactions as a search for a series of conditional, '*If . . . then . . .*' statements. In this study, the specific responses of each child were studied in a set of five specific situations, such as being approached or teased by peers, or praised or warned by adults. Each child exhibited a unique 'personal signature' in which he or she showed a uniform type of response across certain situations, but acted differently in other situations. There was, in other words, consistency within the variability. For example, some children would repeatedly show verbal aggression in certain circumstances, but very little in others. That is, they were not perpetually hostile as individuals; so assessing some presumed trait of hostility with a personality questionnaire would not have given us a very accurate picture of them. Yet they did react in this way with a high degree of predictability under some conditions. Perhaps inevitably, the overall amount of variability was higher for some children than for others. Nevertheless, this study and others have shown the ways in which person–situation interactions occur, and themselves vary, but in orderly ways. These patterns give us a much fuller understanding of individuals' reactions than would either of the factors considered alone.

This kind of interaction has been studied in criminology using a slightly different term, that of *interdependence*. It can be illustrated using data from the Dunedin Multidisciplinary Health and Developmental Study, a longitudinal project following the progress of a cohort of children born in New Zealand in 1972–1973 up to the age of 21. Wright *et al.* (2001) have reported on the interrelations of individual and social-circumstances factors on the self-reported and officially recorded crime rates for a sample of 956 study participants. Members of this sample were interviewed concerning their educational achievements, employment patterns, family ties, numbers of delinquent associates, and rates of offending in the 12 months prior to age 21. Researchers also assessed sample members' levels of self-control during childhood and adolescence, obtaining information from participants themselves, from parents, teachers, peers and trained observers. This covered such factors as 'impulsivity, hyperactivity, inattention, physical response to conflict, and risk-taking' (Wright *et al.* 2001: 329). When members of the sample were divided into sub-groups according to levels of self-control (low versus high), those with habitually low self-control had higher rates of offending. However, this was moderated by several other variables. Figure 3.3 shows some key interaction effects found. For persons with low self-control, level of educational achievement was an important factor influencing extent of involvement in crime. Where this too was low (relative to the sample as a whole), numbers of self-reported crimes were higher. For the high self-control group, these differences were much less marked.

With respect to numbers of delinquent peers, again for the low self-control group this was a crucial influence on self-reported offending: those with many such associates reported considerably higher rates. By contrast for the high self-control group, the trend was comparatively much weaker. In summary, then, rates of self-reported offending among this sample were a product of an interdependence between personal factors, such as levels of self-control, and social or situational factors, such as numbers of peers involved in delinquency.

'Ordinary' behaviour

To recapitulate a point made earlier, the model described here is intended to be a general account of human action. It is applicable to the full

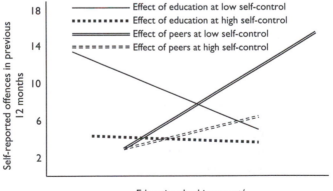

Figure 3.3 Interaction effects: interdependence of levels of self-control, and education versus delinquent peers on self-reported rates of offending (based on Wright *et al.* 2001)

spectrum of activities we engage in: from ostensibly healthy, well-adjusted individuals doing ordinary everyday things, to occurrences such as extreme aggression, repeated self-harm, or delusional beliefs that might at first seem incomprehensible. Although the phenomena observed and the experiences reported at opposite ends of this continuum are very different, the same explanatory principles are used to make sense of both. In other words, there is no clear line of demarcation between so-called 'normality' and 'abnormality'. These words can be interpreted with reference to statistical frequency only. But they are far more often employed in a way that is value-laden and carries messages about cultural or moral desirability.

Everyday habits and routines

On a daily basis, in average circumstances, most people's lives are fairly orderly. The vast majority of us wake around the same time every morning. We engage in organized work, domestic or leisure activities within approximately the same time-bands through the course of most days. The pattern may change now and then and we might get bored if it did not. But by and large, we can describe a lot of our behaviour as following routines. It occurs in sequences that are more or less fixed, obeying certain rules – to the extent that unplanned departures from it can sometimes feel quite stressful (though they can also be very liberating).

Behaviourism has supplied a theoretical account for understanding the establishment and continual recurrence of these regularities. This begins from the fundamental principle that such behaviour is learned. The physical and social environment provides patterns of reinforcement to which individuals are conditioned according to complex learning schedules. Many patterns of activity can be viewed in these terms: they are initiated, maintained and then brought to a halt by external events that impinge upon us and have direct relationships to even quite complex responses we make.

Some specific behaviour chains can be thought of as 'automatic' in a different sense. When we set out to perform an everyday task like making a hot drink or having a shower, the sequence of behaviours involved, once learned, becomes more or less fixed. We do it virtually without any requirement for conscious, controlled thought. That's one reason why we can sometimes carry out an action without realizing we have done so. If you regularly drive a car, in a typical journey you are unlikely to be conscious of changing gears or looking in the rear-view mirror. You will probably have your attention focused on something else: listening to news or music, conversing with your passenger, thinking about next weekend. Only when interrupted or distracted during the execution of routines like these do we become conscious of the minutiae of what we are doing.

A lot of the time, much behaviour follows this type of pattern. 'People routinize their habits of thought and action through repeated use to the point where they execute them with little accompanying awareness. This routinization is achieved through several different processes, all of which involve transfer of control to nonconscious regulatory systems ... As a result, people often react with fixed ways of thinking unreflectively and with habitual ways of behaving unthinkingly' (Bandura 1997: 341).

Such everyday, regularly repeated, highly routinized patterns are said to exhibit the feature of *automaticity* (Bargh 1997). But it does not stop there. On top of the cyclic formations we call habits, automaticity characterizes several other types of behaviour; in fact, it is present in a surprisingly high proportion of the things that we do. The idea 'that most of a person's everyday life is determined not by their conscious intentions and deliberate choices but by mental processes that are put into motion by features of the environment and that operate outside of conscious awareness and guidance – is a very difficult one for people to accept' (Bargh and Chartrand 1999: 462). Yet a large volume of evidence from the field of social cognition strongly suggests that this is a faithful picture of what happens.

Most people would readily agree that some obviously non-conscious, high-speed internal processes, even very complex ones, are automatic. That applies, for example, to mental assembly of different perceptual elements to form an object (which psychologists call *figural synthesis*). It applies to storing, organization and retrieval of information; and implementing procedural memories, for example in the enactment of a skill. What is less obvious and perhaps less palatable to us is that several types of action sequences that we think of as consciously decided, goal-directed or 'willed' can also be directly activated by external events, and executed all the way to completion without entering awareness. Our responses to various situations; the way we form impressions of other people; our reactions to them; even our pursuit of goals and other behaviours we call 'purposive' can be instigated and carried out in ways that make them not very different from actions that we usually regard as occurring without conscious thought. What appears to be intentional, goal-directed behaviour can be initiated without conscious decision-making (Aarts and Dijksterhuis 2000). What we call our intentions are directly influenced and can be predicted by patterns of past behaviour (Ouellette and Wood 1998).

Findings like these have come from research in the field of social cognition, using several different experimental situations including one known as *priming*. Participants are first asked to carry out a task in which, for example, they are subtly presented with particular ideas. For example, they may be asked to form sentences out of scrambles of words containing specific adjectives (rude/polite, friendly/hostile). The pre-selected words are hypothesized to activate certain internal sequences of non-conscious processing, that will predispose individuals to think or act in certain ways. They are then invited to take part in an apparently quite unrelated task, in which they might work with other people and then be asked to describe them afterwards. The descriptions they subsequently produce have been shown to reflect, with remarkable consistency, the sets of adjectives with which they were 'primed' in the earlier, and seemingly unrelated, phase of the study (Bargh and Ferguson 2000). Once an idea is in your head, without your awareness it may later guide your actions, even unfolding what to all intents and purposes appear to be goal-directed endeavours.

A related aspect of this, and one that may help to explain some acts of crime, consists of what is known as *acrasic* (or *akrasic*) behaviour. This kind of behaviour (more commonly called *acrasia* according to the *Oxford English Dictionary*, which somewhat judgmentally defines it as weakness or incontinence of the will) occurs when a person has a choice between two courses of action. On one level, both are equally desirable. But one is perceived as generally preferable in more global terms, leading to the best overall outcome. Despite this, however, it is often the other that is chosen (Trasler 1993; Brezina 2002).

A common example of this is where, having had several drinks in a bar, a person is deciding whether or not to have one more. He or she may have already decided that it would be best, overall, not to do so – but nevertheless does! The same apparent dilemma arises with reference to eating cream cakes or chocolate, smoking, doing some difficult task now or putting it off to another day. You may name your habitual vice at this point and check whether this applies. A similar pattern probably occurs in some kinds of offending. Certainly, we can view this as a failure of will-power, but in learning-theory terms it is a result of the greater influence of proximal (immediate) than distal reinforcers over behaviour.

Self-regulation: functional and dysfunctional

We can understand complex learned behaviours more readily still if we examine the cognitive processes that have played a vital role in their establishment and execution. Our habitual activities are supported and governed by a standard set of 'self-instructions'. Preparing to go out in the morning and noticing the clock, we speed up or slow down according to how close we are to a prearranged schedule. A cognitive event, telling ourselves that time is short and we might miss the bus, makes us accelerate our standard routines, skip sub-routines, or cancel an entire sequence. The bulk of the time, such internal self-regulatory processes have a function in achieving goals we have previously set.

Self-regulation is thus a crucial concept in understanding goal-directed behaviour. Some pre-programmed routine behaviour sequences can be run automatically without its intervention. But decisions concerning which routines to execute, or what to do if they are subject to any kind of interference, are made at a self-regulatory level, which is likely to be conscious and reflective. This recalls the important distinction made earlier between automatic and controlled processing. The former entails many 'programmes' that do not enter conscious awareness. The second intervenes when decisions have to be made concerning which 'programme' to run, or how to achieve the goal of a programme if its progress is blocked in any way.

Most of the daily routines people follow, and the internal processes that are linked to them, serve what can be called a 'purpose'. We can describe activities as *functional* in relation to goals an individual is attempting to achieve. However, in some circumstances they can become *dysfunctional*. These words are very difficult to define clearly. They can only be made meaningful on the basis of an understanding of the context in which they are being applied. Over time, some kinds of behaviour that are usually rewarding can become harmful; but despite this they may have developed sufficient strength as habits to make them very difficult to alter. For instance, a person's alcohol consumption may steadily rise to a level that is clearly threatening to health. But it may be impossible to decide at what point it began to constitute a problem. Cognitive processes can also be described as functional or dysfunctional for an individual. In each case, a great deal of information will be needed to ascertain whether any given pattern can be placed under either of these headings.

The example of anger

What, you may be asking, does all this have to do with crime? The foregoing discussion might seem remote from the problem that is the central subject-matter of this book. It may be useful to look at an example of a specific model based on social learning theory, to illustrate how a number of processes are interconnected and may be functional in some circumstances, but dysfunctional in others.

Most discussions of aggression begin with a key distinction between two forms of it: *instrumental* and *expressive*. In the first, the motive is not aggression itself but some other goal or incentive; injury to a victim facilitates achievement of non-aggressive goals, as for example in street robbery. This form of aggression is seen as a means to committing an offence rather than a prime motive and even though it may have serious effects, it has received comparatively less attention in research. Anderson and Bushman (2002), however, have distinguished between the immediate or *proximate* goals and the eventual or *ultimate* goals of aggression, and contend that the distinction just described applies more clearly with reference to the latter.

In expressive or hostile aggression, 'harm or injury to the victim reduces an aversive emotional state' (Blackburn 1993: 211). This has been studied extensively. Novaco (1975) developed a model of anger for the purpose of devising a treatment programme to help reduce its frequency and intensity. Novaco explains that anger is a normal, adaptive response to certain events, which motivates coping strategies. In certain circumstances, then, it can be *functional*. Showing anger at certain times is an indicator of perfectly good psychological health. There is even evidence that a proportion of angry exchanges can strengthen close relationships! Furthermore, research by Kassinove and Tafrate (2002) suggests that only 10% of angry incidents are followed by actual aggression. (One implication of the foregoing points is that it is important not to assume that all offenders who commit assaults are driven by anger.)

Novaco's model includes environmental, cognitive, physiological and behavioural (motor) components, as shown in Figure 3.4. Note that the ingredients of the model parallel the elements of the general cognitive-social-learning (S-O-R-C) framework described earlier. The cognitive appraisal process is of crucial importance in the model. Environmental events are not in themselves provocative. They only become so when filtered through the cognitive apparatus of a perceiver. Thereafter, the familiar triad of cognition, behaviour and affect are called into play in interrelated ways.

Anger can become *dysfunctional* when it is inappropriate in terms of the interpersonal context or prevailing value system; or when it is out of control, producing a response that is disproportionate relative to the provoking agent. It may then give rise to other problems including offences of violence.

As an extension of the model, Novaco developed an intervention known as *anger control training*. This can enable individuals to understand, and then learn to regulate, their degree of physical arousal and related anger behaviour. A first step in this is to explain the model to the person concerned: to provide him or her with an understanding of anger and of how the components of it interact. The intervention combines relaxation training (which helps to reduce tension) and cognitive self-instructions (to counteract thoughts that make anger escalate).

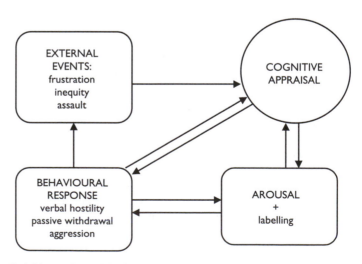

Figure 3.4 Novaco's model of anger arousal

Psychological processes and individual differences

The preceding discussion began with a general outline of cognitive social learning theory. From this I hope there are visible links between the social learning model and a number of proposals forwarded for theoretical integration in criminology, for example those of Akers *et al.* (1979), Thornberry (1987, 1996), Cohen and Machalek (1988) and Vila (1994). Next there followed a more detailed exposition of the processes that underlie social learning. Then, we contemplated how those processes operate with reference to normal, everyday, well-adjusted, harm-free functioning (. . . if any lifestyle can be found to fit that description).

We can consider the application of psychology to understanding crime in two principal ways, focused on *processes* and on *individual differences*, respectively. First, some internal, psychological events are involved in all crimes – just as they are in any other form of behaviour. That is, crime events consist of, or are the result of, individual acts linked to other activities such as thoughts, feelings, attitudes or interpersonal exchanges. These patterns can be viewed similarly to any other kind of behaviour in which people engage on an ordinary, everyday basis.

Second, various types of crime can be placed along a continuum according to the extent to which individual differences have contributed to them. At one end of the continuum, some kinds of offences are described as 'normal'. They are the most common and widespread types of offence, committed mainly against property (such as theft and criminal damage). Psychology can contribute to an understanding of them, but mainly to the extent that it provides a general account of action and the processes underlying it. Attempts to discover reliable personal differences between persons who have or who have not offended in minor ways, or in a purely sporadic manner, are unlikely to meet with much success. But when we move from more common or less serious types of offence to ones that are graver or more unusual – or from a pattern of isolated, occasional law-breaking to more repetitive offending – then the individual-difference dimension of psychology is gradually called more into play. As crimes become rarer or their patterning appears more idiosyncratic, psychological factors and individuality can take on cardinal importance. This essentially replicates a dynamic, interactional process that can be found with reference to many other areas of human functioning (Mischel and Shoda 1998).

This in a sense is an application of the person–situation interaction diagram shown earlier (Figure 3.2). The most frequent types of crime have a strong situational component; personal factors may account for very little of the variance among them. Social-psychological analysis of situations may furnish helpful explanatory concepts and findings applicable to such events. The more a crime represents a departure from societal norms, the likelier it is that personal, psychological factors will be important in explaining it. Bear in mind that there are no circumstances in which situational or personal factors alone will account for all the variations observed.

Both the 'process' and the 'individual difference' dimensions of psychological factors can help to bridge the gap between environmental and social variables and the acts that we call crime. This can be illustrated with reference to research on the relationships between socioeconomic status and crime. In many well-established sociological theories, this relationship is taken as central to understanding variations in the patterning of crime. Where such a relationship is found, however, it may have more to do with the activity of the criminal justice system in response to 'official' delinquency and known offenders than with the underlying pattern of behaviours. For example, it may reflect the differential attention of the police to some sectors of society rather than others. In more recent studies, therefore, when the presumed association between socioeconomic status and self-reported crime has been carefully examined, it has been found to be fairly weak (Dunawayk *et al.* 2000). The largest integrative review of this field to date, described by Andrews and Bonta (2003), included 97 studies of the relationships between social class of origin and self-reported crime. The rather low average correlation that they found led these authors to draw the scathing conclusion that: 'the theoreticism of mainstream sociological criminology in regard to social class may well become one of the intellectual scandals of science' (p. 74).

Yet to the extent that there may be some underlying relationship between socioeconomic status and crime, to understand it we may need to draw on psychological variables. This emerges from the work of Wright *et al.* (1999) using data from the Dunedin study described earlier in this chapter. Wright and his colleagues used self-report data from their sample ($n = 956$) at the age of 21. 'Delinquency' was measured in terms of the variety of offences reported across a range of 48 types (rather than the more commonly used measure of frequency of offending). The overall correlation between socioeconomic status and crime was just below zero (-0.02), but this masked some important variations. For individuals with lower and higher socioeconomic status, respectively, different factors operated to make delinquency more or less likely in each group. At the lower end of the socioeconomic status range, financial strain, alienation and aggression were positively associated with delinquency, and educational and occupational aspirations negatively associated. At the higher end, an inclination towards risk-taking and sense of personal power were positively associated with delinquency, and dismissal of conventional values negatively associated. The flowchart shown in Figure 3.5 illustrates some of these patterns. The analysis was repeated using different methods of measuring each of the variables. While the correlations in some instances were relatively low, they were statistically significant and the findings overall were fairly robust given the complexity of this research.

The key point for emphasis here is that psychological factors – variables from level 5 in the conceptual scheme outlined in Chapter 2 – mediate the

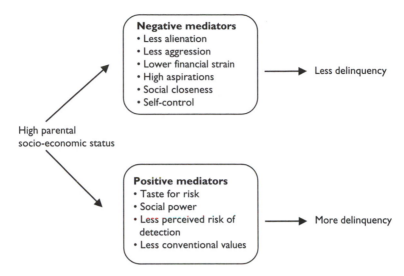

Figure 3.5 Variables mediating the relationship between socioeconomic status and crime (adapted from Wright et al. 1999)

relationship between socioeconomic status and the occurrence of delinquency. A picture of that relationship will be vague and incomplete unless it incorporates those factors. We will encounter other examples of such mediating processes in the following chapter.

In Chapter 4, we will explore the roles of social learning and cognition within the processes at work in four types of criminal behaviour: property offences, interpersonal violence, substance abuse and sexual assault. So the model presented above will be applied to contribute to an understanding of how some of the acts we call 'crime' occur. This will provide us with some 'snapshots' of offending behaviour and its occurrence at particular points in time, looking mainly at the event itself and the period just preceding it. But acts of this kind can be better understood if we place them in a longer-term, developmental, 'lifespan' context. The number of influences that act in concert to shape human development is very large. The number of separate pathways that individuals might take through the developmental maze is potentially infinite. In Chapter 5, we will consider factors affecting individuals' journeys along some pathways rather than others, towards or away from involvement in crime.

Further reading

Albert Bandura (1977) provides an extensive presentation of the social learning model in his book *Social Learning Theory* (New York: Prentice-Hall), with a modified version taking account of self-efficacy given in Albert Bandura (1997) *Self-efficacy: The Exercise of Control* (New York:

W. H. Freeman & Co.). For a thorough coverage of the interactional, cognitive-social-learning approach to personality, among several other approaches, see Walter Mischel (1999) *Introduction to Personality* (6th edn, Forth Worth, TX: Harcourt Brace). An updated account of that perspective is given by Walter Mischel (2004) 'Toward an integrative science of the person', *Annual Review of Psychology*, 55, 1–22. Another valuable text covering a range of approaches to personality theory and research is Daniel P. McAdams (2001) *The Person: An Integrated Introduction to Personality Psychology* (3rd edn, Fort Worth, TX: Harcourt Brace). If you would like a fuller account of cognitive psychology, again there are many books to choose from, but see Kathleen M. Galotti (1994) *Cognitive Psychology In and Out of the Laboratory* (Pacific Grove, CA: Brooks/ Cole).

Pathways to offending behaviour

Some criminologists are dismissive of the idea that there might be specific aspects of individuals that influence them to commit certain crimes rather than others. Thus Gottfredson and Hirschi (1990) propose that there is a fundamental psychological feature to be found in offenders: low self-control, which they portray as 'the only enduring personality characteristic predictive of criminal (and related) behavior' (p. 111). But they criticize 'positivist research' for conflating crime and criminality, and for being mesmerized by the idea that because there are different categories of crime, there must be discoverable differences between the types of people who commit them. Such a view is contradicted, for example, by the finding that the majority of offenders are versatile 'non-specialists' who commit several types of offence. Variations in types of crimes are therefore held to be merely a function of opportunity structures.

That is, however, an empirical question. Whether there are different specific learning or motivational processes contributing to involvement in different sorts of offence is worthy of some further investigation. In this chapter, while the overall objective is to apply the model presented in Chapter 3 to selected patterns of criminal offending, we will also search for specific ways in which psychology can illuminate the factors that influence such events. This will be done with reference to four major groupings of officially recorded crime: property offences, personal violence, substance misuse and sexual assault.

Property offences

Property offences constitute by far the majority of both recorded crimes and unrecorded crime incidents recounted in self-report studies and victim surveys. In the year 2000 in England and Wales, of the 100 or so categories of notifiable offences, thefts and burglary accounted for well over half of recorded crimes (58%). When fraud and criminal damage are added the proportion rises to 83% (Maguire 2002). The motives for theft, fraud and burglary are considered to be primarily acquisitive, and this is borne out by several lines of evidence. They range from long-term analysis of the relationship between property crime and economic indicators, to in-depth interviews with offenders. Given such motives, the basis of which looks almost self-evident, further attempts at explanation are sometimes regarded as redundant.

It is here more than anywhere else that psychology has usually been perceived as having little to offer, and it is true that psychologists have had much less to say about these actions than about crimes against the person. There is still relatively little psychological research on this type of offend-ing, by comparison with the amount of it devoted to violent and sexual assault. As we have noted before, the available evidence suggests that at some point in their lives most people commit a crime; it is most likely to be an offence against property. The role of psychological factors in such offences, more than any other types of crime, may appear marginal, even irrelevant. On the other hand, if 'crime is normal', then most of psycho-logy, which is about people generally considered 'normal', is potentially relevant to an understanding of it!

Given the volume of crime that consists of theft and burglary, some research in criminology has focused on modelling trends within it as a function of macroeconomic factors such as the rate of unemployment and the general level of consumer expenditure. Field (1990) analysed patterns within this for England and Wales for the period between 1945 and the late 1980s. As consumption rose and fell, this was reflected in changes in the rate of burglary and theft. Rising unemployment and reduced spending during periods of recession were associated with increases in these crimes. A similar pattern was found in France, the United States and Japan. In a later, more elaborate version of the model, Field (1999) included other variables, notably the availability of crime opportunities (the numbers of 'stealable goods') in the economy, and the proportion of young males aged 15–20 in the population. Note that this approach focuses exclusively on aggregate crime and in conceptual terms it belongs on level 1 of the framework presented in Chapter 2. It has nothing to say about environmental, community, familial or individual influences.

However, taking a specific type of property offence, theft from shops, it is hardly surprising that psychological research on the motives for it suggests they are pre-eminently economic. This has emerged from cross-sectional studies of persons convicted of shoplifting and also community-based surveys utilizing self-reports, using the method of cluster analysis. However, this is by no means the whole story. Findings suggest that there are disparate motives for engaging in shop theft. They appear to include a mixture of other factors such as excitement, peer influence and emotional dysphoria (low or unsettled mood). Furthermore, the balance among these factors appears to change between adolescence, adulthood and middle age (McGuire 1997a).

Gottfredson and Hirschi (1990) have commented that by and large 'ordinary crime requires little in the way of effort, planning, preparation or skill' (p. 17). This statement probably applies most aptly to property offences. Many are opportunistic, committed against readily available targets rather than ones that would require careful preparation or the travelling of any great distance. They occur in a geographical space that is within easy reach in terms of the usual lifestyle of the offender. They might even be incorporated into something else he or she was already going to do. More crimes are attempted than are successfully completed. The average loss in most property crime is small, often so trivial as not to be reported by victims. Overall, offenders gain relatively little, and the majority do not repeat the criminal act.

There are several aspects of the processes involved in committing property offences that can be accounted for in terms of social learning theory, but given the scarcity of available research they can be suggested in only the most general terms. To make sense of the theoretical concepts outlined here, they should be combined with the other levels of explanation that we used in the wider framework presented in Chapter 2.

In most societies there is a general pressure towards acquisitiveness. It may even have an evolutionary source. That is what is posited in some of the theories examined earlier, like those of Cohen and Machalek (1988) and Vila (1994). Without apparently having any explicit rules regarding property, as we humans do, many other species nevertheless appear to have a sense of ownership, and individuals expropriate items from each other: most commonly food, building materials or territory. Competition over scarce resources is proposed in a number of theories as a general background factor creating the basic conditions for crime.

Such pressures may be felt more keenly in some sectors of the community. The most important factors affecting this are socioeconomic inequalities, disadvantage and deprivation, and these are major influences on the emergence of high-crime neighbourhoods. In a large-scale British study of social disadvantage, the Newcastle Thousand Family Study, Kolvin *et al.* (1988) found that there was a strong association between multiple deprivation in childhood and later criminal conduct. *Multiple deprivation* was defined as a cluster of factors, including overcrowding, economic dependency, marital instability and poor parental care. Levels of deprivation in families were associated with numbers of convictions among young people, particularly in the mid-teenage years.

Thus there are clear links between social circumstances and crime, though they are not quite so strong as is often supposed. The result just mentioned notwithstanding, by no means all of those who grow up in adverse circumstances later break the law. For example, just under 50% of those designated 'multiply-deprived' in the Newcastle study were *not* later recorded in the criminal statistics.

To account for these findings we need to turn to another set of factors, taking us to the third level of explanation as set out in Chapter 2. Low incomes and associated economic difficulties place all communities and families under stress, but there are sizeable differences in how this affects the socialization of children. A range of factors is probably called into play. They include the presence of criminal models; the quality of parenting; availability of opportunities to learn different methods of coping (or approaches to solving problems); acquisition of 'pro-social' values and norms; and the differential impact of attitudes expressed within a family. Many sociological theories of crime, such as *containment theory* (Reckless 1967) outlined briefly in Chapter 2, have developed these kinds of ideas. They posit variables such as norm retention or frustration tolerance as important operating factors affecting the potential for development of delinquency.

Socialization, attitude formation, the instillation of norms and of rule-following behaviour are all forms of social influence. Using the terminology cited earlier, they could be described as *distal* in that they are long-term, formative influences on the life-span development of individuals. Acts of crime occur in specific situations where there may also be more *proximal* influences. The most widely researched of these is the effect of the peer group and the pressure this may exert towards experimentation, rule-breaking and other manifestations of growing independence, particularly in the early teenage years in Western societies.

Interpersonal contexts of property offending

Many offences, particularly among young people, are committed in a group setting. Baldwin *et al.* (1976) found a clear age trend for this in their study of crime in Sheffield. Whereas 61.5% of males and 67.7% of females aged 10–14 years committed offences in pairs or larger groups, among 17- to 20-year-olds the corresponding figures were 18.6 and 48%, and among 30- to 44-year-olds, 8.8 and 10%. There are several possible explanations for peer generation effects, some of which have to do with the quest for affiliation and status in the face of rejection by (or of) adult society. In a survey of more than 800 young offenders in Canada,

Brownfield and Thompson (1991) found a strong association between self-reported offending and peer involvement in delinquency. Many other studies have noted a close relationship between self-reported levels of offending and numbers of known delinquent peers or 'criminal associates' (Matsueda and Anderson 1998).

Another plausible reason for this commonly discovered link resides in patterns of social interaction inside such groupings. Individuals may apply pressure to each other in a diffuse manner, or to specific individuals who are seen as acquiescent or easily led. Alternatively, group members may excite or escalate each other's interest in law-breaking activities. Working in a Bristol housing estate, Light *et al.* (1993) interviewed young people and adults aged 14–35 with histories of vehicle-taking. The influence of friends was named as the single most frequent motive for involvement in offending. Most were taught basic driving skills by an older offender with more experience. Some considered themselves to be better drivers than the police. Interactions within groups almost certainly reinforce sets of attitudes supportive of or conducive to the commission of offences.

According to social learning and differential association theories, the interactive sequences inside such groups, and also within larger social networks, play a major role in leading individuals towards or away from offence behaviour. Modelling and observational learning play a direct part in the establishment of patterns of delinquent behaviour; while symbolic learning and values-acquisition occur alongside them and further absorb individuals into the acceptance of or willingness to engage in offending. For some young people whose preference would be to avoid being drawn into offences, pressures towards involvement can prove overwhelming. They may lack the personal resources for resisting group norms, or for defying the arguments, and perhaps threats, of dominant individuals. There is evidence that direct behavioural learning through modelling and imitation (as social learning theory would suggest) is a more potent factor in group influence than exposure to and assimilation of offence-supportive attitudes (as differential association theory would suggest). Warr and Stafford (1991) analysed data from a sample of 1,726 respondents to the US National Youth Survey, concerning participation in three types of illicit behaviour: theft, cheating in exams and using marijuana. The *behaviour* of friends was a stronger predictor of individuals' own actions than either their friends' or even their own expressed attitudes.

Research findings provide support for the suggestion that these patterns of social influence are an important factor in delinquent involvement. Observational studies of groups of young offenders in institutional settings showed that there is a high level of positive reinforcement, much of it communicated non-verbally, for rule-breaking, criticism of adults and adult rules, and aggression (Buehler *et al.* 1966). Conversely, there were displays of disapproval when an individual broke with 'delinquent norms'. Worryingly, staff reactions were unsystematic and indiscriminate, providing no effective counter-weight to the peer-group ethos.

However, it is important to retain the standpoint that these influence processes have a reciprocal relationship to pre-existing tendencies that are manifested at the individual level. Matsueda and Anderson (1998) studied levels of property offences (minor theft, more serious theft, and burglary from a building or vehicle) in a large representative sample ($n = 1,494$) of young people in the US National Youth Survey, followed up at three time-points each two years apart. This study was designed to test the relative strength of two competing views of the relationships between patterns of involvement in offending and membership of delinquent peer groups. One is the view that individuals prone to offend will selectively associate with each other ('birds of a feather flock together'). The other is the view that offending is largely a product of social influence in small groups. Using a very detailed statistical analysis designed to eliminate methodological arte-facts and other sources of error in their findings, Matsueda and Anderson found that both numbers of delinquent peers, and individual predisposi-tions, were associated with observed rates of offending. However, of the two, the latter had the more significant effect. 'Delinquent peers and delin-quency are reciprocally related in a dynamic process' (Matsueda and Anderson 1998: 301). This accords with other findings discussed in Chapter 3, showing that levels of self-reported offending and official convictions can best be predicted taking account of the interdependence between fac-tors such as peer influence and personal propensities (Wright *et al.* 2001).

Similar processes appear to be at work when offender groups congeal into the formations we call gangs. But here mutual influence and inter-personal learning may become marginally more important. Esbensen *et al.* (2001) surveyed a large sample ($n = 5,935$) of young people in the age range 13–15 from 42 high schools in eleven American cities. Using a loose defi-nition of gang participation – whether someone had ever been in a gang, allowing respondents to construe this as they wished – 16.8% of the sample reported that they had. With a stricter definition entailing current core membership of an organized, delinquent gang, only 2.3% emerged as members. Collecting a wide range of data from this sample, Esbensen and his colleagues concluded that prediction of gang membership was best achieved by a combination of personal/demographic and social-influence variables. However, 'the theoretical predictors from social learning theory (especially association with delinquent peers, perceptions of guilt, and neutralizations for fighting) supersede the importance of demographic characteristics' (Esbensen *et al.* 2001: 124). Interestingly, ongoing core membership of a gang increased the likelihood of having committed a property crime by a factor of six over the rate for non-gang members. This ratio was similar to that obtained for personal (violent) offences; but involvement in drug sales was increased by a factor of 22.

Although as we saw earlier a large share of offending by young people is committed in groups, the influence of peers is not simply a matter of co-offending. In a longitudinal study in the city of Denver, Colorado, Huizinga *et al.* (2003) found that the higher the level of involvement youths reported with delinquent peers, the greater the likelihood that they would also commit crimes alone (this applied in particular to offences of assault). This may be the result of social learning or differential association processes, but could also be an effect of the combination of personal and situational factors noted in other studies described above.

Moods, cognitions and crime

Finally, there are momentary changes in mood and in self-regard that have been shown to have effects on behaviour and on the chances that someone will break a rule, including one they have previously obeyed. Short-term changes in how people feel about themselves – their *self-esteem* – may predispose them to adhere to or violate social prohibitions. This has been shown in experiments in which a brief decline in self-esteem is induced, for example by giving someone (false) negative feedback about their performance on a test. Adults are then more likely to cheat at cards; children are more likely to play with a toy belonging to someone else (Aronson and Mettee 1968; Graf 1971; Fry 1975). Admittedly, this is laboratory evidence; it may lack what researchers call 'ecological validity', and may not correspond to what happens in real-life settings. But other kinds of evidence, which we will examine more fully in later chapters, suggests that among repeat offenders, new offences are often associated with periods when individuals are experiencing strong negative feelings about themselves and their lives (Zamble and Quinsey 1997).

In places where there are opportunities to offend, people's pattern of thoughts may be a crucial influence on their subsequent actions. Carroll and Weaver (1986) placed an advertisement in a Chicago newspaper inviting regular shoplifters to take part in a research study. Participants admitted to having committed thefts on an average of 100 previous occasions. Each volunteer was given a tape recorder and a lapel microphone, and asked to speak aloud his or her thoughts for one hour, while walking through department stores accompanied by a researcher. This 'expert' group was compared with a cohort of 'novices', would-be shoplifters who despite self-confessed urges had never crossed the legal barrier and stolen anything. The verbalizations of the two groups were remarkably different in content. While the experienced group analysed the situation for opportunities to steal and escape undetected, the novices were constantly perturbed by thoughts of being caught, arrested and punished. In effect, they deterred themselves from stealing.

Earlier criminological research has illustrated that the kinds of things people say to themselves are important influences on their ability to cope with having committed criminal offences. This is the essence of *neutralization theory* (Sykes and Matza 1957), which we encountered cursorily in Chapter 2. Neutralization techniques are strategies people may use to dispel negative feelings that arise from having acted in ways that run counter to their own value systems. Making inner statements that reduce responsibility, locate blame elsewhere and distance oneself from victims can be a helpful way of reassuring and maintaining an otherwise fragile self, or simply of excusing departures from what a person proclaims to be his or her basic beliefs (Agnew 1994; see below).

Other types of property offences have received even less attention in research than theft. There is some work on psychological factors in criminal damage or vandalism, primarily focused on discerning the different motivations for it. Several attempts have been made to develop typologies. A portion of it may be plainly acquisitive or instrumental: some objects are damaged in an attempt to obtain others. At other times it may be done for sheer enjoyment or even aesthetic reasons, a response to a challenge or a display of skill, as in graffiti-writing and 'tagging' commuter trains. Sometimes destruction can be intrinsically rewarding. Some of it can be classified as aggressive or sparked by feelings of anger, and a portion of this might result from perceived inequity, with individuals damaging objects as a form of asserting control (Goldstein 1996). These are potentially useful speculations, but require considerable research if they are to illuminate the problem more clearly.

Personal violence

After the numerous types of offence that are collected under the generic heading of 'property crime', the next most frequent type of offending is that of interpersonal violence. In most countries, this typically constitutes a far smaller fraction of all crimes than theft or burglary. For example, in England and Wales in 2001 it formed 15% of recorded crime (Simmons and colleagues 2002), though its crude rate varies hugely from one country to another (Newman *et al.* 2001). This much lower proportion notwithstanding, the personal and emotional damage done by such offending is enormous, and is generally much more far-reaching and longer-lasting than for property crimes. Even given that the amount of violent crime in England and Wales fell for several years after 1997, as was estimated by the British Crime Survey, in 2001–2002 there were still nearly 2.9 million violent incidents (Simmons and colleagues 2002).

Surveying data on a global scale, the World Health Organization has estimated that in the year 2000, there were approximately 1.66 million deaths due to violence (Krug *et al.* 2002). Of these, just under half (815,000) were suicides, approximately one-third (510,000) were homicides and about one-fifth (310,000) were war-related. More than 90% of violence-related deaths occurred in low- and middle-income countries. Males accounted for 77% of all homicides.

There is probably more psychologically based research on aggression and violence than on any other type of anti-social behaviour. Whereas many people may at some stage steal something, the numbers who are likely to cause physical harm to others is considerably lower. In trying to account for the development of a pattern of emerging aggressiveness, some key environmental and socialization factors play major roles. *Aggressiveness* is conceptualized as 'a relatively persistent readiness to become aggressive in a variety of different situations' (Berkowitz 1993: 21). Where an individual manifests a habitual pattern of resorting to violence, this is usually the result of a lengthy period of development and adaptation, with a number of influences interacting in fairly complex ways.

There is evidence of relative stability or continuity in patterns of aggressiveness between infancy, middle childhood, adolescence and adulthood. Olweus (1979, 1988) reported a review of 16 longitudinal studies examining levels of consistency in aggressive behaviour over periods ranging from one to 21 years. The average size of samples in these studies was 111. The dependent variables in the studies were not self-reports, but nominations or ratings of aggressiveness by peers, teachers or other observers. From this Olweus extracted a total of 24 correlation coefficients and plotted their interrelationships on a regression line. The results showed a striking degree of consistency over time, though inevitably the correlations decreased with increasing intervals. For example, mean correlations across one year were 0.76; two years, 0.69; but in one 21-year follow-up, 0.36. In a subsequent review, Zumkley (1994) analysed a further ten studies, with an average sample size of 159, producing a further 34 'stability coefficients'. This confirmed the pattern found by Olweus. Their findings are shown in Figure 4.1.

For intermediate periods of say ten years or so, childhood aggressiveness seems to be indicative of likely future problems. For example, the presence

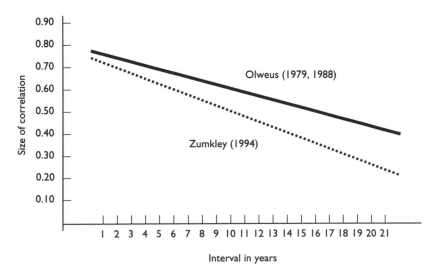

Figure 4.1 Stability of aggression: regression lines combining the results from 26 studies (Olweus 1979, 1988; Zumkley 1994)

of aggressive classroom behaviour at an early age has been shown to be a good predictor of delinquency in the teenage years (Spivack and Cianci 1987). Across a more limited time-span of five or six years, studies have shown that aggressive behaviour in middle childhood is strongly predictive of conduct problems in adolescence (Loeber and Stouthamer-Loeber 1987; Farrington and West 1993). Such problems are exacerbated if a child's aggressiveness leads to social isolation, due to being rejected by peers (Coie *et al.* 1992).

Given that there is a sizeable degree of stability in aggressiveness, the question has often arisen as to whether such patterns are inherited. As we saw in Chapter 1, most criminologists are not convinced by accounts that place too much emphasis on those factors, and see a much larger role for environmental influences. Findings such as those of Olweus (1979) are probably best explained as resulting from a complex interplay between inherited and environmental factors, as follows.

There is no evidence to the effect that genes play any direct causal part in the development of criminality (Joseph 2003). But there may be a distant role for inherited factors, in the form of a set of dispositions that are collectively called *temperament*. This refers to a number of fairly global features of the typical behavioural and emotional reactions of young children. It includes general activity level, attentiveness, adaptiveness to new situations, quality and intensity of mood expression, relative proneness to distress, and distractibility (Chess and Thomas 1990; Rothbart *et al.* 1994). Individual differences in some of these variables appear very soon after birth and before any significant learning experiences. There is evidence that they are maintained into the first few months and perhaps first few years of life; though regarding their long-term consistency, even using a relatively broad 'easy–difficult' continuum, findings are less cohesive and convincing (Chess and Thomas 1990). Nevertheless, longitudinal studies have uncovered some noteworthy consistencies in temperament variables over very lengthy periods. In one study of this kind, Caspi and his colleagues (Caspi *et al.* 1995; Caspi and Silva 1995) compared observations of children when aged 3 with independent descriptions of them at age 15, and their descriptions of themselves at age 18. Three-year-olds described as 'undercontrolled' and who manifested irritability and impulsiveness, as rated by observers, were more likely to be described as having 'externalizing' problems when aged 15. This pattern held for both girls and boys. When aged 18 they were more likely than others to describe themselves as reckless, careless and rebellious, and more prepared to cause discomfort or harm to others. In a separate study, parallel findings were obtained for the age range 20–30 years, with significant associations emerging in features labelled *negative emotionality* and *constraint* at these two points ten years apart in adulthood (McGue *et al.* 1993).

For such differences to remain consistent and have implications at a later developmental stage, environmental factors almost certainly play a decisive role. For example, the cluster of features grouped together as 'difficult temperament', in conjunction with some kinds of parenting, is associated with poor school attainment and troublesome behaviour in later childhood and early adolescence. Thus, for example, if a physically very active, easily distressed, emotionally needy child is born to anxious, inattentive, easily irritated parents, the overlay of their socialization style on the child's temperament may set the scene for increasing and perhaps lasting difficulty. In one long-term study, links were found between the presence of temper tantrums in early childhood and employment status nearly 40 years later (Caspi *et al.* 1990).

Family interactions

A great deal of research now links observed patterns of continuity in aggressiveness to socialization experiences within families (Rutter *et al.* 1998). The predominant factors at work in this context, and which contribute to the development of longer-term aggressiveness and the risk of violence, are found in child-rearing and parenting processes (Snyder and Patterson 1987; Farrington 1995, 1996; Gulbenkian Foundation 1995). In general terms, the larger the number of these factors present earlier in life, the greater the likelihood that a young person will later become involved in offending. (Note, however, that the precise ways in which these influences combine is unlikely to be uniformly additive. More often, they probably interact with each other in complex ways that are as yet poorly understood.)

Problems of this kind are more likely to accumulate in adverse circumstances entailing social deprivation, low incomes and poor housing, which place families under significant stress. This, in turn, affects the enduring mood and demeanour of parents or other caregivers, their interactions with each other, and the manner in which they respond to children. Some studies have illuminated the intermediate links in a chain of processes through which economic hardship may be associated with problem behaviour and in due course 'official' delinquency.

Dodge *et al.* (1994) studied a set of 585 children over a four-year period between the ages of 4 and 7. Information was also obtained from their parents concerning economic circumstances, socialization practices and other conditions in the family home, and from teachers and classmates concerning the children's behaviour in school. The latter was described mainly in terms of the presence or absence of *externalizing* problems, which included the extent to which a child was involved in fighting, or threatening other people. The best prediction of the level of a child's externalizing or aggressive problems came not from direct socioeconomic indicators, but from a set of pathways involving intermediate events: patterns of interaction within the family. They included harshness of discipline, exposure to violence, maternal support, maternal warmth, maternal endorsement of aggressive values, having only transient contacts with people outside the family, and level of cognitive stimulation. Thus the association between family hardship and the child's behaviour could be

best understood through a model that included a set of interactional processes inside the family as mediating variables.

Working with an older, early adolescent age group, Conger *et al.* (1994)
tested a similar model of mediating processes between financial privation
and young people's antisocial behaviour. This is depicted in Figure 4.2 and
was tested in a study involving 378 families living in varying degrees of
adverse economic conditions. This study focused in particular on levels of
conflict within families – both between mothers and fathers, and parents
and children – over the issue of money itself. When families are under
stress, the quality of these interactions often deteriorates, and the data
collected by Conger and his colleagues (1994) provided good support for
their model.

Given the nature and time-scale of individual development, the accumulating impact of these processes may not become manifest until a number
of years later when children have reached adolescence or early adulthood.
James (1995) has forwarded a complex model linking the United
Kingdom's economic hardships of the early 1980s, a consequence of government policies of that period, with the rise in violent offending by young
people ten years later in the early 1990s.

However, recall that, as we saw earlier in relation to property offences,
adverse circumstances alone are not sufficient to account for their occurrence. This applies also to offences of violence. Data from the Newcastle
Thousand Family Study (Kolvin *et al.* 1988), mentioned above, showed that
even within the most disadvantaged group – those with the largest number
of social deprivation indicators – the rate of violent offending was only 3%.

Several specific dimensions of interpersonal and socialization process
have been associated with the development of the tendency to use aggression (Anderson and Bushman 2002). The first includes the presence of

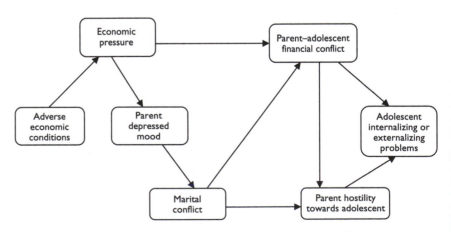

Figure 4.2 Theoretical model linking family economic stress, conflict and adolescent
problems (Conger *et al.* 1994)

criminal parents and of siblings (brothers and sisters) with behaviour problems. These features may themselves be causally linked. The second relates to the everyday behaviour of the parents or caregivers. Parental conflict, poor or inconsistent supervision, and physical or emotional neglect are associated in general terms with later overall risks for delinquency. Evidence suggests that these factors are as significant as familial disruption and 'broken homes' (Juby and Farrington 2001). With reference more specifically to aggression, there is evidence that within intact families, some parents provide little reinforcement of children's 'pro-social' behaviours, while at the same time giving direct reinforcement of 'coercive' behaviours. This has been shown in numerous studies carried out over a 40-year period in the Oregon Social Learning Center (OSLC). Patterson (1982) has reviewed early studies showing the extent to which parents inadvertently reward their children for acting in unpleasant ways. He describes aspects of this as a 'reinforcement trap', in the sense that parental reactions that reduce the likelihood of an aversive behaviour (such as aggression) in the short term can serve to increase its likelihood in the long term. Reid *et al.* (2002) have provided a detailed account of the voluminous output of the OSLC.

Thus children can progressively learn that their own belligerent behaviour 'works', either in securing attention of parents or in terminating unwanted intrusions by them (Patterson and Yoerger 1993). This also helps to explain why adolescents who regularly assault others have been found to have significantly lower rates of positive communication with their families than do other young people their age (Blaske *et al.* 1989).

Patterns of socialization and adult–child interaction of these kinds are associated with the gradual development of aggression as a habitual way of dealing with others. There are other features of upbringing expressly associated with more pronounced aggressiveness. They include cruel and authoritarian discipline; use of physical methods of control; and shaming and emotional degradation of children. Findings collated by the Gulbenkian Foundation (1995) are virtually unanimous with respect to this: research 'emphatically confirms that harsh and humiliating discipline are implicated in the development of anti-social and violent behaviour' (p. 134). These findings are concordant with others concerning the long-term impact upon young people of childhood maltreatment, and the extent to which there is inter-generational continuity in patterns of physical and sexual abuse. While the results of some studies have been equivocal concerning these connections, the balance of available findings suggests that 'a childhood history of severe abuse and of witnessing family violence is significantly associated with ongoing violent behaviors in adulthood' (Widom 1989: 710; Widom and Maxfield 2001).

Farrington (2002) has reviewed a number of long-term studies, including the Cambridge-Somerville Youth Study, the Rochester Youth Development Study and the work of Widom in Indianapolis, with follow-up periods of up to 30 years. Clear links have been found between child abuse, neglect and the later emergence of delinquency in general, and of violent offending in particular. This emerged even when other factors including gender, race and socioeconomic status were controlled.

All of the above findings are consistent with a social learning model, which posits a combination of direct experiences and observational learning processes as fundamental in the growth of tendencies towards anti-social, and especially aggressive, attitudes and behaviour. The family is the most powerful single agent of socialization in individuals' lives. As Loeber (1990: 17) has stated, 'factors in the family are among the best predictors of later delinquency in offspring'. Other important influences come from adolescent peer groups and the media, but neither of these comes close to family environment in the strength of its effects.

The role of the media in relation to violence has been a hotly debated topic for many years. Social learning theory was influential in placing this on the agenda as an object of study, through Bandura's early studies on modelling and imitation. However, disagreements have continued as to whether viewing television violence arouses aggressive feelings and thereby catalyses violent acts, or conversely it is the result of choices made by those who would probably be prone to violence anyway. A recent study by Huesmann *et al.* (2003) is interesting in that it was possible to examine the strength of the former with the effects of the latter taken into account. Huesmann and his colleagues re-interviewed a group of 557 participants in a TV-viewing study they had originally begun in 1977. At that stage members of their sample were in the age ranges 6–7 and 8–9 years; at the time of follow-up they were young adults with mean ages of 21 and 23 years, respectively. Data were collected on background characteristics; educational level; evidence of aggressiveness as children; perceived realism of violence in TV programmes; and extent of identification with characters seen in programmes containing violence.

The results suggest strongly that television is an agent of socialization for developing children that may influence their likelihood of being violent as adults. 'For both male and female participants, more childhood exposure to TV violence, greater childhood identification with same-sex aggressive TV characters, and a stronger childhood belief that violent shows tell about life "just like it is" predicted more adult aggression regardless of how aggressive participants were as children' (Huesmann *et al.* 2003: 216). Huesmann and his associates also cite evidence from studies of the television marketing industry to the effect that 'prime time' violent programmes are on average cheaper to produce than non-violent ones. Each violent act in a TV drama reduced its production cost by US$1,500, and the chances of a programme being exported increased by 16% if it contained violence.

Situational factors and social signals

The research findings discussed so far demonstrate the existence of some kind of continuity in socialization which is linked to the appearance of aggression and violence in young people. To obtain a fuller understanding of this behaviour, we have to supplement this background with information on the immediate precursors of aggression. This has come from laboratory and field research in social psychology (Berkowitz 1993). That work shows that there is an enormous range of situational influences on aggression. They include basic stimulus conditions like levels of heat and noise, a wide array of personal frustrations and stresses, as well as defining events like provocations or threats.

Other factors superimposed on these include audience or self-image enhancement effects, group norms concerning aggression, and wider cultural values promoting violence, for example through glamorization of a 'macho' image. As noted earlier, a number of criminologists have expressed scepticism concerning research on some of these issues, which is often drawn from controlled experiments conducted in laboratory settings. They argue that it is futile to attempt to distinguish a propensity to aggression from other forms of criminality (Gottfredson and Hirschi 1993).

But certain kinds of events do appear to be potential precursors of aggressive acts. They may be subtle exchanges of looks, glances, facial expressions or other non-verbal signals that convey hostility, or are simply interpreted as hostile by perceivers. Aggressive signals usually instil fear and escape reactions in others. This was shown, for example, in a somewhat risky field study by Ellsworth *et al.* (1972). Researchers waited by traffic lights, either sitting on a scooter or standing on the street corner. When motorists or pedestrians stopped at red lights, the experimenters either stared straight at them, or looked at them but without staring. They then measured the time taken to cross the intersection when the lights changed to green. Those who were stared at sped off significantly faster. The stare constituted a 'stimulus to flight'. Perhaps the authors did not know that for some individuals a stare is interpreted differently, with a threat being experienced as a challenge, so leading to escalation of aggression. Whether this occurred is not reported in the paper, and the researchers (well the ones whose names we have) clearly survived to the publication stage.

Cognition and violence

On a separate front, several other researchers have drawn attention to the importance of *social information processing* in contributing to the likelihood of aggression. According to this proposal, the emergence or maintenance of aggressive behaviour depends on cognitive appraisal and other internal processes (Dodge and Schwartz 1997).

Few external events lead uniformly to aggression. The *meaning* an individual attributes to an event is a prime determinant of his or her subsequent behavioural response. The components of this process were elaborated by Crick and Dodge (1994) in an information-processing model of social maladjustment and aggression proneness. In this model, reactions to an external event are analysed in terms of a sequence of cognitive events, comprising six stages: encoding, representation, goal clarification, response construction, response decision and enactment. Akhtar and Bradley (1991) and Kendall (1993) have reviewed research comparing frequently aggressive children with non-aggressive control groups. The following differences have been found. Frequently aggressive children:

- encode a narrower range of environmental cues or sources of information;
- selectively attend to aggressive cues;
- attribute hostile intent to others, especially in ambiguous situations;
- more readily label internal states of arousal as anger;
- generate fewer potential alternative solutions to problems;
- select action-oriented rather than reflective solutions;
- possess a more limited range of interactive skills;
- manifest an 'egocentric' perspective in social problem-solving.

The patterning of these differences varies between individuals. It is highly unlikely that all of the above tendencies will be present in any one person. The key point, as we saw earlier with reference to anger, is that whatever the environmental or stimulus conditions, it is what is going on inside someone's head that often matters most: the things people say to themselves. This also includes expected outcomes of aggression. Young people in their early teens say they are more likely to act aggressively if they think this will be seen positively by peers. Aggression is also more likely if they do not think it will make them feel bad; and if they do not care about making a victim feel bad (Hall *et al.* 1998).

Further evidence for a role of cognition in aggressive behaviour comes from a review of 41 studies (total sample size: 6,017) of the relationship between it and the hostile attribution of intent: that is, the tendancy to infer that others have a hostile attidue or are about to act in a malign way towards you (Orobrio de Castro *et al.* 2002). Paralleling this, a review of seven studies found evidence that violent offending is significantly correlated with low cognitive empathy (Jolliffe and Farrington 2003); though the possibility that this may have been a function of intelligence and SES could not be ruled out.

Related to this, there is evidence that the process of neutralization is also important in permitting engagement in violent behaviour or in enabling individuals to excuse it afterwards. Agnew (1994) analysed data concerning this from the National Youth Survey in the United States, conducted in annual waves in the late 1970s with a large representative sample (1,600+) of young people in the age range 11–17. Agnew found first that the overwhelming majority (93%) of respondents stated that it is wrong to hit people; only 0.5% took the view that it was not wrong at all. Even those who admitted to having acted violently in the previous year expressed disapproval of hitting. However, more than half (54%) of the sample accepted one or more of a series of statements justifying the use of violence.

Endorsement of these statements was a significant predictor of involvement in violence cross-sectionally (at a specific moment in time) and also longitudinally (one year later). Neutralizations were equivalent in their effects to the influence of delinquent peers, and considerably more so than attitudes generally approving of violence.

Some of these cognitive processes also possess the feature of *automaticity* we encountered in Chapter 3. There are several channels through which an individual's non-conscious mental activity might be 'primed' with constructs associated with aggression. Todorov and Bargh (2002) have reviewed evidence pertaining to this. For example, if individuals are subliminally exposed to aggressive words – that is, they are shown the words on a screen for such a brief period that they cannot enter consciousness – they subsequently describe another person as more aggressive than individuals similarly exposed to neutral words. In other studies priming was shown to automatically predispose individuals to express more hostility when interacting with others, even where there was no immediate situational source of tension. With repeated use, aggression-related constructs may become 'chronically accessible', perhaps disposing individuals to pre-emptive aggression in the absence of any provocative event. The probability of aggression will be further heightened if the protagonist has been engaging in repeated rumination, possibly centred on themes of resentment or retaliation, perhaps even mentally rehearsing scenes of revenge (Caprara 1986; Collins and Bell 1997).

Overall, we have arrived at a view of violent offending that has a wide range of components. There may well be evolutionary predispositions to aggression in some interpersonal circumstances, for which we all carry the potential. There are also individual differences in temperament at birth that may be a product of inheritance. Socialization influences, notably parenting skills and styles, interact with these tendencies to affect the course of development in the early years. The level of economic stress and adversity to which parents or other caregivers are subjected will significantly influence the environment they create for their children. Basic learning processes are overlaid with the transmission of attitudes and expectations that growing children absorb, which, in turn, shapes their own perceptions of their surroundings and their styles and habits when interpreting the actions of others. All these factors will influence the way someone deals with interpersonal conflict. Within each category of events, it is possible to identify specific patterns that are associated with tendencies to respond with aggression, and ultimately physical violence, in conflict situations. Anderson and Bushman (2002) have forwarded an integrative *general aggression model* of how the foregoing variables interact.

Interpersonal aggression takes many forms and some have been researched in greater depth. In the case of specific types of violence, such as male non-sexual violence towards women, certain additional factors also contribute. They include men's culturally transmitted beliefs about the position and roles of women, and in the use of physical coercion as a form of power (Russell 1995, 2002; Harway and O'Neil 1999). O'Neil and Harway (1999) have forwarded a complex, multivariate model of a wide range of factors shown to contribute to battering of women by men. Their model comprises six levels of variables:

- *Macro-societal*: for example, historical patterns supporting male aggression; patriarchal, sexist and other ingrained attitudes.
- *Biological*: for example, evolutionary processes and events at a hormonal or neuro-anatomical level.
- *Socialization/gender-role*: developmental and contextual influences on male and female role development and pressures towards different patterns of play, social interaction, and beliefs regarding gender.
- *Psychological*: differences in experience (e.g. exposure to observing violence) and individual differences, for example, in modes of expression, self-esteem, ability to empathize, or skill in solving problems.
- *Psychosocial*: for example, age, employment and income, poverty, social status, alcohol or drug use.
- *Relational*: for example, patterns of interaction, use of power, communication difficulties, relationship stability, family dynamics.

Thus a wide range of elements contributes to the occurrence of domestic violence if it is not specifically sexual in nature. With reference to sexual aggression, as we will see later in the present chapter, yet other factors appear to be involved.

Substance use and social learning

There are numerous types of drug-related offences, including some that in all probability are essentially economic in motivation (Dorn *et al.* 1992). That is, as for other acquisitive crimes, the primary objective of the perpetrator is to make money. This probably applies alike to primary producers, international traffickers and smugglers, and local drug dealers. It is estimated that this industry rivals some legitimate sectors of world trade in its scale.

The focus here, however, is on the direct consumption of illegal or controlled substances. Based on the 2001–2002 British Crime Survey, Aust *et al.* (2002) estimated that in England and Wales, approximately four million people aged between 16 and 59 used some illicit drug, with around one million having used a Class A drug. Roughly 34% of those in the 16–59 age group have used an illegal drug at some time in their lives. For young people in particular, drugs are relatively easy to access. For those in the age group 16–24, the proportions reporting that drugs were 'very or fairly easy' to obtain were: for cannabis, 68%; amphetamines, 45%; cocaine, 33%; and heroin, 20%.

On a worldwide scale, there appears to be a gradual upward trend in the use of illicit substances. A survey of 92 countries by the United Nations Office on Drugs and Crime (UNODC 2003) showed that while some countries reported decreased levels, the majority found levels of usage had risen in 2001 compared with previous years. This survey yielded global figures for the use of various illegal drugs as follows: cannabis, an estimated 162.8 million users; amphetamines, 34.3 million; opiates 14.9 million (of which 9.5 million used heroin); cocaine 14.1 million; and ecstasy, 7.7 million users.

In most Western societies, the generally accepted position on these issues contains some sharp internal contradictions. Two very powerful drugs, alcohol and tobacco, are widely available for legal consumption, though laws restrict their sale to varying extents in different countries. Some recent curbs notwithstanding, they are extensively advertised both in direct marketing terms and more subtle yet pervasive ways throughout many media. Both are associated with major health problems, and cause large numbers of preventable deaths. Other drugs that are used for medical purposes but which also have desirable psychotropic effects are more strictly controlled, but nevertheless widely abused. Still other drugs are entirely illegal and their sale or use can result in imprisonment.

It is still widely believed that regular consumption of certain chemicals such as alcohol, initially for pleasurable purposes, leads to a bodily reaction that in due course can become an addiction. In this 'medical model', the site of this addiction is thought to be a physiological one. This presupposes that there is an interaction between the substance and other chemical events in the body, such that the user finds it intolerable to be without the drug, or even to let its concentration in the blood fall below a certain level. A more radical version of this theory is what is known as the *disease theory* of alcoholism. This holds that inside some individuals there is a state of susceptibility or vulnerability, caused by a chemical already present in the body, which makes them more prone to become addicted to alcohol. It has been argued that this is under the control of genes; that there is literally a gene for alcoholism.

It is difficult to test a theory of this kind. But it is worth noting that, while there may be some genetic contribution to individuals' responses to alcohol (Cook and Gurling 2001), no substances meeting the requirements of the disease or gene theory have ever been isolated. Obviously, there is a wide range of substances ingestion which leads to dramatic bodily changes, sometimes in the long run causing severe damage to vital organs. However, there is an alternative explanation of the observed phenomena of the 'addictive' behaviours, which locates the mechanisms of habitual use on a psychological rather than a physiological level (Davies 1992).

The traditional behavioural model of addiction portrayed it, as with other acquired habits, as a form of learned behaviour due to conditioning. Over recent years, more elaborate models have been assembled, which identify the modulating effects of substances on levels of mood arousal as the principal factor in the maintenance of substance dependence. The user needs the substance not because of the inherent physiological reaction it produces, but because of the cycle of mood changes that is experienced as a result (Brown 1997; McMurran 2002). This conception accords well with a social learning approach to the understanding of self-damaging behaviour. Coincidentally, it has been found that symptoms of dependence can occur in relation to activities other than substance use. They include gambling (Peck 1986) physical exercise (De Coverley Veale 1987) and even shopping (Glatt and Cook 1987). The last authors described a 24-year-old woman with a six-year history of 'pathological spending'. During this period she accumulated debts to retailers or credit card companies totalling £55,000. She felt compelled to buy numerous items she did not need and including some she already possessed. There was evidence of tolerance, in that over time she spent progressively larger sums of money; and continued to do so in the face of mounting complications, including criminal proceedings and acute personal distress. There also appear to be compulsive elements not unlike addiction in some types of sexual offending, and possibly also in a small proportion of property offences, such as joyriding (Kilpatrick 1987) and shop theft (McGuire 1997a), though such patterns are probably extremely rare.

Many potentially 'addictive' substances can be used in modest quantities without leading to habit formation and dependence. For the use of a substance or the involvement in some activity to be considered 'addictive' or to have resulted in dependence, there is a consensus that the following features should be present:

- *Salience*: frequency of the problem and its dominance over other spheres of life including many aspects of thoughts, feelings and behaviour.
- *Conflict*: gradually increasing awareness of the negative consequences alongside difficulties in addressing them.
- *Tolerance*: the need for increasing levels of the substance or activity to produce the same desired effects.
- *Withdrawals*: marked discomfort, distress and other aversive feelings during periods when the activity is discontinued.
- *Craving and relief*: longing for the activity in its absence and rapid reduction in negative feelings after re-commencement.
- *Relapse*: reinstatement of the problem behaviour after attempts to desist, after periods of cessation, even when these periods may have been lengthy.

The salience of illegal substance use when it takes hold of people's lives is illustrated by the finding that often, individuals will resort to other types of crime to finance a drug habit. For example, in their work with frequent heroin users, Jarvis and Parker (1989) found that acquisitive crime was the principal means of securing funds to buy the drug. Of the 61 people interviewed, 87% admitted to property offences committed for this reason; within this shop theft was the most common type of offence, though in other studies cited by these authors burglary was more frequently reported.

The fundamental point to emphasize here is that to understand the development of a pattern of illegal drug use by an individual, we need to take several types of factors into account. For alcohol, they include aspects of the social context in which drinking occurs, of the drinker's personal history, and of psychological processes that influence the interplay between them (Collins and Bradizza 2001). Such social and cognitive processes may be essentially the same whether we are focusing on dependence on legal substances like alcohol, or controlled drugs such as heroin. In as far as either of these may for some individuals be associated with committing offences, either in terms of possession of the proscribed substance itself, or of other actions taken to procure it, the role of psychological factors is an indispensable component of any satisfactory explanatory model.

Most of the above comments refer to those kinds of offences in which the use of a substance constitutes an offence in itself (as with controlled drugs), or is defined by the context (as with driving while intoxicated). There are many circumstances, of course, where substance misuse is related to other types of crimes. This connection arises most frequently with alcohol, which is implicated in a wide range of offences. For example, a large proportion of recorded personal violence occurs following consumption of alcohol. The links between alcohol and crime are very complex. Graham and West (2001) have reviewed evidence concerning this, and outlined a model of interactions between four main categories of variables. These are the cultural context, situational factors, personal characteristics and the effects of alcohol itself. Walters (1998) has described how frequent substance abuse and offending, in the context of person–situation interactions and in combination with other behavioural, cognitive and attitudinal parameters, may become the core of an entrenched lifestyle.

The model proposed by Graham and West (2001) depicts, in a manner not dissimilar to the scheme outlined in Chapter 2, a set of interconnections between society-wide, situational and individual processes, in helping to explain links between alcohol and crime. 'How much people drink, how they behave when they drink, the frequency of crime, and the forms of social control over both drinking and crime, all vary across cultures' (Graham and West 2001: 446). Thus people learn to drink alcohol and follow a pattern of its use as practised in the groupings to which they belong. But also, 'characteristics of the individual, such as attitudes and personality, are directly relevant to the relationship between alcohol and crime' (p. 446, italics in original). The substance itself is just one type of influence and even where alcohol is involved, criminal acts cannot be understood in terms of this alone (unless that constitutes the definition of the crime, as in public drunkenness).

With specific reference to the relationship between alcohol and violent offending, McMurran (2002) has synthesized evidence from research on the various factors likely to contribute to the establishment of an interconnected pattern of aggression, drinking and intoxicated violence. They include difficult temperament in childhood; impulsivity and restlessness;

aspects of parenting, including both poor management of troublesome childhood behaviour, and modelling of acceptance of heavy drinking; low commitment to school and consequent poor educational attainment; delinquent peer associations; and hostile attributional biases. These interact with the effects of inebriation (there are several mechanisms by which alcohol and other drugs can increase the likelihood of aggression); and with outcome expectancies concerning the effects of drinking alcohol, particularly in the social contexts in which heavy drinking occurs. McMurran provides an account of the developmental processes involved, and sets out an integrative model of the major pathways through which they interact.

Sexual offending

Though they are a constant focus of media attention, sexual offences constitute a fairly small proportion of crime as a whole: only 5% of the violent crimes and 0.7% of all crimes recorded by the police for England and Wales in 2001 (Simmons and colleagues 2002). The concern to which these offences give rise is a result of the physical and emotional damage that they cause, but is probably also influenced by society's general difficulties in addressing a whole series of issues connected with sexuality, from adolescent pregnancy or birth control to sexual diversity among adults. For example, there is a recurrent focus on the dangers posed by those offenders labelled as 'paedophiles'. In 2001, a British newspaper caused considerable sensation and controversy by publishing photographs of men with convictions for serious sexual offences. The legal, ethical and social implications of such publicity are in themselves exceedingly complex. But the disproportionate focus on this specific problem can also be highly misleading.

First, most people who commit sexual offences against children, even including indecent assaults, cannot be accurately described as paedophilic. The latter is a diagnostic category within psychiatry, requiring the presence of certain characteristics found in only a proportion, probably somewhere between 25 and 40%, of offenders against children (Grubin 1998). Second, most sexual assaults and even murders of children are committed by people known to them. The latter sometimes includes close family members, even parents. To put it simply, children are more at risk in their own homes than from random molestation by a stranger in the street. About 80% of assaults take place in the home of the victim or the offender (Grubin 1998). It is extremely difficult to gain an accurate picture of the extent of sexual abuse of children, as different sources of information produce widely discrepant estimates. Using different data sets, Grubin (1998) calculated that the number of children abused in England and Wales lies 'somewhere between 3,500 and 72,600 individuals each year' (p. 11).

As with other types of crime, to obtain the fullest picture of sexual offending we need to draw on factors from different levels of the explanatory

framework introduced in Chapter 2, including some that illustrate important roles for social learning and cognition. Individual variations in the
patterning of this occur within a wider cultural context in which, contrary
to society's officially proclaimed stance on these matters, there are many
pressures towards sexually coercive behaviour. While rape occurs in almost
all societies, there are reported exceptions. Sanday (2003) has described its
almost complete absence among the Minangkabau people of Western
Sumatra, which she ascribes to the pattern in that society of symmetrical
male–female status and relationships. In other societies, by contrast, certain forms of sexual violence are officially condoned. That was the case
until recently in England and Wales with regard to marital rape, and it
remains so in many other countries. For example in Bangladesh, a survey
has shown that 26.8% of women reported having been victims of sexual
violence by their husbands in the previous year. 'Not only is forced sex
within marriage tolerated . . . but also the sociocultural contexts shape and
support such sexual coercion' (Hadi 2000: 790).

In an American study, Baron *et al.* (1988) tested a *cultural spillover*
theory of the relationship between society-wide attitudes concerning sexual
aggression and the rates of serious sexual crimes. They developed a composite measure, the Legitimate Violence Index, that combined various indicators of the extent to which it could be inferred that there was social
approval of violence. The measure included the level of violent content
on television programmes; rates of readership of magazines with a high
violence content; existence of laws permitting corporal punishment in
schools; numbers of hunting licences issued; levels of National Guard
enrolment; and the numbers of lynchings per million population in the
period 1882–1927. Combining these data, the level of support for violence
was assessed in 50 US states.

Scores on the index were then compared with recorded rates of rape
in each state. Broadly speaking, mountain and central states such as
Wyoming, Montana, Mississippi, Utah and Idaho had high scores on
the index. Eastern and north-eastern states such as Rhode Island,
Massachusetts, New Jersey, Maryland and New York came at the bottom
of the scale. There was sizeable variability in the rate of rape between
the states: differences between the lowest and highest varied by a factor
of eight. A method known as *path analysis* was used to examine the
data. Several types of demographic information were also entered into
this analysis: each state's level of urbanization; degree of income inequality; age distribution; and numbers of single and divorced males in the
population.

A parallel analysis was conducted using another measure, the Violence
Approval Index, based on an attitude survey in which citizens were asked
their views regarding the use of violence in certain situations. For example,
would it be permissible to punch an adult male stranger under certain
circumstances, such as a man who was drunk and bumped into you in the
street?

In both analyses, demographic variables, including the level of urbanization and percentage of divorced males in the population, were strong predictors of the rate of rape. But so also were the Legitimate Violence Index and the Violence Approval Index; the former highly significant, the second significant but less markedly. It is remarkable that these findings emerged from such a complex analysis, providing support for the authors' conclusion that 'the social approval of nonsexual and noncriminal violence has a significant relationship to rape, independently of those effects contributed by the control variables' (Baron *et al.* 1988: 95).

In Western societies, sexually aggressive or coercive behaviour is almost certainly much more widespread than official statistics suggest. Surveys of adult women show that as many as 50% of them report some form of sexual victimization at some point after the age of 14, while comparatively few, less than 10%, report assaults to the police (Marshall 2001). Other survey studies have shown that a sizeable portion of men hold attitudes supportive of sexually coercive behaviour, though this appears to be modified by age, by levels of contact with women, and other factors (Bell *et al.* 1992; Dean and Malamuth 1997; Aromaeki *et al.* 2002). This calls into question the view that 'sexual violence is a psychopathologically isolated, idiosyncratic act limited to a few "sick" men' (Scully 1990: 161). Scully advocates instead the feminist perspective, and 'the assumption that sexual violence is sociocultural in origin: men learn to rape' (p. 162). The route through which culturally embedded values and attitudes are implanted in individuals involves social learning and cognitive processes. This occurs both through socialization by caregivers during childhood, and through the influence of images of women conveyed through the media and advertising (Lanis and Covell 1995). However, there are also important individual differences, and serious sexual offences are committed by only a minority of males, and a tiny minority of females.

Several other processes are thought to occur in leading towards the committing of a sexual assault. While there are important overlaps, different sets of factors are thought to affect the occurrence of adult rape, sexual abuse of children and sexual offending by adolescents, respectively. With reference to the first of these, the following factors are thought to be involved (Prentky 1995; Marshall 2001).

- *Social interaction difficulties.* Many research studies have shown that adults who repeatedly sexually offend have difficulties in interacting with, or forming close and lasting relationships with, others. This may be partly a result of a lack of confidence or skill in ordinary social interaction. Alternatively (or additionally), the individual may manifest problems of intimacy or attachment, seeking inappropriate and ultimately futile ways of achieving these goals: perhaps by the exercise of power over others; by habitually confusing sexual contact as a means to fulfil intimacy needs; or by forming romantic attachments to children. These patterns are thought to arise from the individual's own socialization experiences, during which there may have been limited opportunities to acquire skills, or impairments in the formation of secure attachments.

- *Empathy.* The absence of feelings of empathy for a victim can be a 'powerful disinhibitor' for any type of violence (Prentky 1995: 161), and this has been thought to be a key operative factor in sexual aggression. However, empathy is extremely difficult to assess and recent work has suggested that sex offenders may not, as has been widely supposed, lack general capacity in this respect. Rather, they do not empathize with their victims. For example, they may show as much empathy for a female victim of an accident as non-offending comparison groups, but considerably less for victims of their own actions. It may instead be that 'empathy deficits in sexual offenders are inextricably linked to cognitive distortions' (Marshall *et al.* 1999: 84).

- *Cognitive distortions.* This term refers to patterns of thinking which are self-serving for offenders in that they create conditions in which illegal sexual acts become permissible; or they are enabled to distance themselves from the negative aspects of their impact. For example, sexual motivation may be wrongly attributed to victims, or their emotional reactions to force misinterpreted. Men may entertain 'rape myths' such as the view that women secretly want to have sex forced upon them. Following the offence, perpetrators may deny responsibility for their actions, or seek to minimize the level of harm they have done. Marshall *et al.* (1999) list several types of distortion found in their research with men who have committed serious sexual assaults. The concept of 'cognitive distortion' shares parallel features with that of 'neutralization', discussed above and in Chapter 2.

- *Sexual preferences and deviant arousal.* We might expect that this would be a pivotal factor in differentiating persons who commit sexual offences from those who do not. While most adults show a preference for consenting sexual contact with other adults (of the opposite or same sex), some have preferences for children and others for sexual contact that is coerced. This is generally thought to be the result of a learning process. Frequently, assaultive males maintain their sexual interests by engaging in fantasy, reinforced by masturbation in a cyclical process.

- *Self-esteem and anger.* As with other types of offending, it has not proved possible to find consistent differences in personality between those who commit sexual offences and those who do not. However, several other features have been noted to characterize sexual recidivists, including low self-esteem and poor control over feelings of anger. These patterns are not invariant and are more likely to be found among those whose record of offending is more serious or persistent.

There are several advantages of this type of model. One is that, though doing so may be difficult, it can be empirically tested, since each of the above factors can be separately defined. Another is that it prescribes a framework for assessment of the individual. The exact patterning of factors will vary from person to person, so this is not based on any presumption that individuals who commit specific offences are necessarily of one 'personality type'. But an individual's functioning in the above areas may influence his or her level of risk of future offending, a process that will be illustrated in Chapter 5. The third related advantage is that the model can then also act as a guide for the design of interventions to reduce those risks, a point to which we will return more fully in Chapter 6.

The model just outlined was developed with reference to serious sexual assaults committed by adult males and may not be applicable to other groups. For example, as many as one-third of sexual assaults are committed by young people in the age range 12–17 (Grubin 1998). Again, an overwhelming majority of such perpetrators are male. A different set of factors needs to be invoked to understand this category of offending. An explanatory model of sexual aggression by this age group was forwarded by Becker and Kaplan (1988). This proposes that the teenager who engages in acts of sexual coercion or assault is characterized by a number of other emotional or developmental difficulties. He or she may feel socially isolated and lonely, be lacking in assertiveness, be experiencing family problems, be doing badly at school, have low self-esteem, be depressed, show cognitive distortions, have problems in the management or channelling of anger and, in some instances, concomitant problems of substance abuse. Such a young person may also be at risk of developing into a sexually exploitative or aggressive adult. To date, however, only a few attempts to test this model have been reported (e.g. Shields and Jordan 1995; and see Becker 1998), and have furnished only partial support. Overall, the volume of research in this area is limited and the key questions remain 'critically under-explored' (Hudson and Ward 2001: 367).

Further reading

Models of psychological factors and the roles they play in different types of offence are presented by several of the contributors to the *Handbook of Offender Assessment and Treatment* edited by Clive R. Hollin (Chichester: Wiley, 2001). There are chapters devoted to specific types of criminal activity in books such as those by Ronald Blackburn (1993) *The Psychology of Criminal Conduct* (Chichester: Wiley) and James McGuire (ed., 2002) *Offender Rehabilitation and Treatment: Effective Programmes and Policies to Reduce Re-Offending* (Chichester: Wiley).

chapter five

Individual factors in crime

For some criminologists, the search for differences between offenders and non-offenders, supposing we could meaningfully identify such groups, in some elusive quality called 'personality' epitomizes everything that is wrong with a psychologically based approach to crime. Attempts to account for crime in terms of individual differences of the kind usually denoted by that word have not met with much empirical support. Critics of the assumptions on which such an approach is based might well feel vindicated by that result. For the criminal statistics alone show that around one-third of us will have been arrested at least once by the time we are 30. An even larger fraction of the population admits to breaking the law at some stage of their lives. On the face of it, the expectation that 'offenders' are in any way different from anyone else looks somewhat misguided.

On the other hand, the idea that such differences might exist is not in principle an unreasonable one. There are undoubtedly some features of people that remain stable over time. Ordinary human interaction would be quite perplexing if things were otherwise! We base our everyday dealings with one other on the recognition and use of such consistencies. Even if people are moody or changeable, there is enough regularity within the variation to make their individuality recognizable. Were that not the case, communal living would be unremittingly hazardous.

Perhaps it would not be too big a shock then to find that some personal characteristics are associated with the tendency to act without thinking; to be easily angered; to develop dependence on substances; or to have a habit of disregarding or devaluing others. That, at least, is the hypothesis of some psychological approaches to studying crime.

Yet it remains true that these differences have proved highly elusive when comparisons have been made between groups designated as offenders and non-offenders, respectively. Perhaps the critical theorists are right in saying that such a division is spurious, and what matters much more is the way these supposed definitions are constructed. Alternatively, maybe there are genuine differences between those who mainly do, or who intermittently do not, conform to society's rules, but we have not yet discovered what such qualities are, or any valid way to assess and record them.

These suggestions are plausible, but a third possibility seems distinctly more likely. Amongst those who have been convicted of crimes, another finding is obtained with a high degree of reliability. Individuals who break the law do so with varying frequency. *Ergo*, at one end of the distribution, there are people who do so more often than the rest. Could there be some psychological factors that differentiate them from those who commit offences with only moderate, or low, or very low frequency?

Numerous studies have confirmed the finding that a small segment of the known offending population – so comprising only a small minority of the population as a whole – is responsible for committing a disproportionately large number of crimes. Evidence in support of this comes from many sources. For example:

- In England and Wales, data submitted to the House of Commons Home Affairs Committee (1993) demonstrated that there were small numbers of young offenders who committed sizeable numbers of crimes. Among 17-year-olds, a mere 1% of those born in 1973 was responsible for 60% of crimes committed by their age group.
- Parallel results were found in the Youth Lifestyles Survey, a study of 4,000 people aged 12–30 conducted in the late 1990s. Roughly 10% of those with previous convictions were responsible for nearly 50% of offences. They represented approximately 2% of males and 1% of females in the sample as a whole (East and Campbell 2000).
- In the Philadelphia birth cohorts, two long-term studies carried out across different generations, individuals with at least five police contacts

(designated 'chronic offenders'), though constituting only 6 and 7.5% respectively of the samples, were responsible for 63 and 61% of the recorded offences (Tracy *et al.* 1985).

- In a comparable study in Stockholm, 'repeat offenders', those with two or more convictions, forming only 20% of the sample, accounted for 88% of recorded crimes (Guttridge *et al.* 1983).
- In another study in Copenhagen, males with convictions for two or more violent offences, though forming only 0.6% of the sample, accounted for 43% of the violent assaults committed by the entire male cohort (Janson 1983).

Andrews and Bonta (2003) and Rutter *et al.* (1998) have collated other data pertaining to this point. As we noted in Chapter 1, the exact proportions and ratios vary from study to study. But the general pattern can be summarized in the form of a 'reverse-J' shaped curve of the kind shown in Figure 5.1.

What applies to individuals may, at least in this instance, also apply to their families. In the Pittsburgh Youth Study, a large sample of 1,517 boys, detailed information was sought concerning the criminal convictions of relatives of the study group (Farrington *et al.* 2001). The researchers found that small numbers of families accounted for a disproportionate number of offences: 'Four families (1% of families), containing 33 persons, totalled 448 convictions (18% of all convictions)' (p. 580). Half of all the recorded convictions were accounted for by 23 families (6% of the sample). Nearly two-thirds (64%) of all convictions were accounted for by 10% of the sample.

At the same time, a note of caution should be sounded. The consequences of attaching pejorative labels such as violent, serious, persistent or chronic to individuals who have broken the law are well known. Could there, furthermore, be a risk that we might overestimate the percentage of

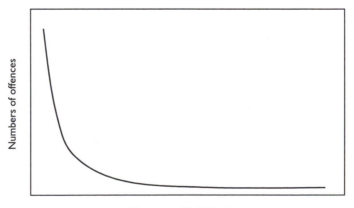

Figure 5.1 A reverse J-curve

total crime that is attributable to a recidivistic minority? A study in Britain by Hagell and Newburn (1994) highlighted some of the difficulties. These authors examined a sample of 531 young 're-offenders' arrested three or more times during 1992, and attempted to identify the most 'persistent'. Three separate definitions of the latter were used: (a) simple frequency of arrests over a one-year period; (b) frequency of known and alleged offending over a single three-month period; and (c) individuals aged 12–14 who had committed three imprisonable offences, one of them while under supervision. Focusing on 193 young people from a Midlands-based sample, comparisons were made for the extent of overlap between definitions. While 36 young offenders were 'persistent' according to one or other of the criteria, only three were common to all the definitions.

How can this apparent conundrum be resolved? On the basis of many sets of official statistics, and numerous research studies, it appears as if a small sub-set of offenders commits many more crimes and manifests a pattern of repetitive law-breaking. Yet when we look more closely for them, they all but disappear. The problem here may be partly one of belief in 'the law of small numbers': the assumption that the pattern evident in a large sample will be reproduced in any small sub-sample drawn from it. In terms of the crime statistics, Hagell and Newburn's (1994) sample size was quite small, and the young people constituting it did commit proportionately more offences than most other young people their age. The evidence that some individuals are responsible for a high portion of recorded crimes appears incontrovertible.

Loeber *et al.* (1998) attempted to produce more clarity in this area by defining the words 'serious' and 'violent' in strict legally based terms, while recognizing that labels such as 'chronic' and 'persistent' generate controversy due to varying, sometimes almost arbitrary, cut-off points. Loeber and his colleagues also noted that any definitions adopted in this field need to be different for female and male offenders.

To investigate whether distinctions between serious, violent and persistent/chronic young offenders could be empirically based, Snyder (1998) analysed criminal history data for Maricopa County, Arizona for the period 1980–1995. With a population of 2.4 million, Maricopa (which includes the city of Phoenix) was then the sixth largest county in the USA, and had rates of property and of violent crime 75 and 12% above the national average, respectively.

Snyder classified offence patterns into several sub-groups. First, young people who came into contact with the police for reasons such as running away from home, truancy from school, underage drinking, curfew violations or traffic offences were excluded from the analysis. In the UK and many other countries, many of these behaviours would not warrant police attention. In the United States, they are called 'status offences'. Exclusion of these cases resulted in a figure of 151,209 young people aged under 18 who were referred to the juvenile court for delinquent offences during the study period. Offences were grouped as follows:

- Violent offences included murder and manslaughter, kidnapping, violent sexual assault, robbery and aggravated assault.
- Serious non-violent offences included burglary, serious theft, vehicle-taking, arson, possessing weapons and drug-trafficking.
- Non-serious offences included minor thefts, minor assaults, possessing drugs, disorderly conduct, vandalism and non-violent sexual assault.
- Chronic offenders were defined as those with four or more referrals to the juvenile court (before their eighteenth birthdays).

The majority of the sample (85.4%) was classed as 'non-chronic'. That is, they were the subject of fewer than four referrals, though some had committed serious offences. Members of that group were referred for an average of 1.39 offences. The remainder, whose offence pattern was defined as 'chronic', were by contrast referred for an averaged of 6.56 offences. Of the latter group, 7.9% had committed at least one serious non-violent offence, 0.9% had committed at least one violent offence and 3.3% had committed at least one offence of each type. A final smaller group (2.5%) though also classed as 'chronic' had not committed any serious offences. Cumulatively, the 14.6% of the sample defined as 'chronic' accounted for 44.6% of all the referrals for sample as a whole, and for 58.2% of the serious and 60.0% of the violent crimes. More frequent offending was associated with a greater likelihood of committing a serious offence. The greater the length of a young person's 'officially recognized offending career', the higher the likelihood of referral for a violent offence. The relationship between the various categories as defined by Snyder is shown diagrammatically in Figure 5.2.

Combining different studies, the bulk of the evidence suggests overall that those who commit more than five serious offences while juveniles may be a distinctive group. Going one step further, it is plausible that such repeated offending may be associated with other features of individuals that are relatively stable over time. This might be at least partly a function of their personalities – what sorts of people they are. But it could also be that previous definitions or concepts of this have been too narrow, focused on constructs such as traits that can be measured by self-report questionnaires.

Employing a broader framework, it is more likely that there is a cluster of interconnected features that includes personality as traditionally conceived, alongside other characteristics like daily habits, lifestyles, attitudes, and typical modes of thinking or reacting when faced with problems. A central idea of social learning theory is that, through development, people acquire behavioural and cognitive routines, habitual modes of functioning, that are a net product of their temperaments and of the social environments in which their learning took place. Through cumulative experience they cultivate a mixture of skills, showing relative strengths in some areas, while having recurrent difficulties in others.

Evidence that there are configurations of this kind comes from several sources. For convenience we can consider it under three headings:

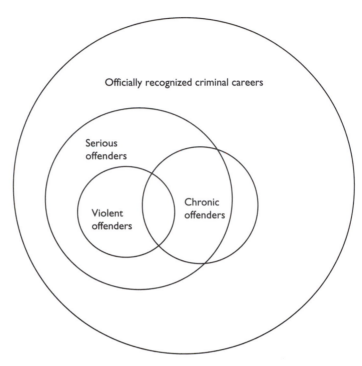

Figure 5.2 Definitions of serious, violent and chronic offenders (from Snyder 1998)

- The principal one is a collection of *longitudinal* studies, conducted at a number of locations in several different countries across roughly the last three-quarters of a century. In research of this kind, cohorts of children or adolescents are followed for varying lengths of time, sometimes all the way from birth to adulthood. This is usually regarded as the most powerful kind of evidence available, as it provides a picture of the *temporal sequence* of cause and effect. Although discerning such links is far from easy, without studying the life-course in this way any conclusions would remain on much shakier ground.
- Another source consists of *cross-sectional* studies. Here, comparisons are made between known offender samples and non-offending control samples at a single point in time. The groups have to be equivalent ('matched') on some variables to eliminate their effects, while researchers investigate differences in other variables.
- A third source is *evaluation research* on the outcomes of attempts to reduce recidivism rates by addressing some aspect of offenders' functioning. If we compare projects that succeed in doing this with ones that fail, this can furnish evidence concerning what kinds of factors make a difference to the outcome. While this approach in some ways is less direct, it can provide supplementary evidence for an idea gained from the first two types of studies.

In recent years, studies of all these kinds have been scrutinized more thoroughly than before employing the method of *statistical review* or *meta-analysis*. Because this method is now of vital importance for interpreting data and trying to draw conclusions from it, we will devote some space below to describing what it entails.

Longitudinal studies

One of the earliest examples of a longitudinal project focused on the development and temporal patterning of problem behaviour was a study of referrals to a child guidance clinic in St Louis, Missouri, in the late 1920s (Robins 1974). A series of 524 children formed the sample; they ranged in age from under 6 to 17 years (with a median of 13). Data were also collected on a matched non-clinical comparison sample of 100 schoolchildren. Over 30 years later, in the years 1955–1960, Robins was able to interview 82% of the original clinic sample. Subsequently, a second cohort comprising 235 African-American boys from a primary (elementary) school was also followed up over a 30-year period. Robins (1974) describes earlier research along similar lines, conducted in Germany, Norway and Sweden, involving children born as long ago as 1903.

Since then, projects of this kind, known as *birth cohort studies* or *panel designs*, have been carried out at a number of sites around the world: in the United Kingdom, the Netherlands, Denmark, Sweden, Finland, the United States, Canada and New Zealand (Loeber and Farrington 1997; Andrews and Bonta 2003; Thornberry and Krohn 2003). Early studies of this kind were *retrospective*; that is, information concerning the participants was collected by working backwards from a later time-point. An important feature of the majority of the more recent studies is that data collection is *prospective*; that is, planned in advance and directly recorded at pre-arranged time-points as individuals develop. This produces more reliable, higher-quality information than retrospective data collection. In some studies, both approaches have been employed.

All such projects have multiple objectives. Researchers typically investigate a wide range of areas, including child health, family functioning, education, employment, income and lifestyle, as well as contacts with the criminal justice system. Most also draw on several sources of information, including participants themselves, parents, siblings, peers, teachers and other professionals. They use varied methods of data collection such as: interviews; school, health or criminal records; psychometric assessments; or behavioural observations. Inevitably given the passage of time and the occurrence of life-events (and in some cases death), there is attrition in the sample sizes. In a review of nine long-term studies, Capaldi and Patterson (1987) found an average retention rate of 53% for studies up to ten years in duration; probably not surprising if a study spans that period of time.

However, other studies have done remarkably well in keeping sample loss to a minimum and have achieved follow-up contact rates of 85% or better even over lengthy periods.

Table 5.1 lists some of the best known studies of this genre (including all the ones cited anywhere in the present book) with information on the age ranges covered and key background sources. Several of the projects listed are still ongoing. While the basic design of these studies is essentially similar, there are also some notable differences between them. In some, a single cohort was followed from the beginning to the last data-point of the study period (e.g. the Cambridge study). In others, several overlapping subgroups, each a different mean age at the outset, were followed in parallel for the same number of years (the Denver and Pittsburgh studies). That format is known as an *accelerated longitudinal design*. In still others, data have been collected from two or three successive generations of families (the Houston and St Louis studies).

The projects also differ in the 'unit of analysis'. While in most cases this is the individual, in some (the Iowa study) it is the family. Most samples contain both males and females in roughly equal numbers, though some used stratified sampling so that males were over-represented (the Rochester study), and a few focused on males only. Many, in particular those conducted in the USA, include a variety of ethnic groups, with some samples having a majority of African-American youth and sizeable numbers of Hispanic or Mexican-American origin. The Kauai study consisted predominantly of Japanese, Hawaiian and Filipino children.

Among these studies it has been consistently found that a relatively small proportion of youths or adults is responsible for a comparatively larger proportion of criminal offences. This has led to an emphasis on those variables most regularly found to be associated with the 'criminal career': an individual's extended involvement in criminality for a significant episode of the life-span. Such an approach is called *developmental criminology* (Loeber and LeBlanc 1990; Farrington 2002).

Developmental pathways

On the basis of this accumulated evidence, it is possible to construct an inventory of the factors within individual development that contribute to the emergence and, where it occurs, the persistence of offending behaviour. Farrington (1996) has catalogued the major classes of variables shown to be important in influencing the pathways developing children follow in this respect. They are:

- Prenatal and perinatal factors: child health and influences on it before and during birth.
- Hyperactivity and impulsivity, elements of 'difficult temperament' that pose a challenge to parents.
- Parental supervision, discipline and attitudes to child-rearing.

Table 5.1 Selected longitudinal studies of the development of offending

Project	Initial sample, n	Age ranges (years)	Illustrative source
London and Isle of Wight studies (UK)	1,689 1,279	10–25 10–14	Rutter (1981)
Newcastle Thousand Family Study (UK)	1,142	0–22	Kolvin et al. (1988)
Cambridge Study of Delinquent Development (UK)	411	8/9–40	Farrington (2003)
Copenhagen Birth Cohort (Denmark)	28,879	0–30	Guttridge et al. (1983)
Stockholm Project Metropolitan (Sweden)	15,117	0–30	Wikström (1990)
Finnish Longitudinal Study (Finland)	369	8/9–26	Hämäläinen and Pulkinnen (1995)
Montreal Birth Cohort (Canada)	3,142 934	0–23	LeBlanc and Girard (1997)
Montreal Longitudinal and Experimental Study (Canada)	1,161	6–22	Tremblay et al. (2003)
Christchurch Child Development Study (New Zealand)	1,265	0–18	Fergusson et al. (2000)
Dunedin Multidisciplinary Health and Development Study (New Zealand)	1,661	0–21	Moffitt et al. (2001)
St Louis Child Guidance Clinic (USA)	624 235	0–30+ 0–35	Robins (1974)
Philadelphia Birth Cohorts (USA) (1945) (1958)	9,945 27,160	0–30 0–18	Tracy et al. (1985)
Kauai Longitudinal Study (Hawaii, USA)	698	0–32	Werner (1987)
National Youth Survey (USA)	1,725	11–17	Matsueda and Anderson (1998)
Nashville-Knoxville-Bloomington Study (USA)	585	4–7	Dodge et al. (1994)
Iowa Youth and Families Project (USA)	378	12–14	Conger et al. (1994, 1995)
National Institute of Justice (USA)	1,575	<11–18/40	Widom and Maxfield (2001)

Table 5.1 – contd

Project	Initial sample, n	Age ranges (years)	Illustrative source
Oregon Youth Study (USA)	206	10–18	Reid et al. (2002)
Denver Youth Survey (USA)	1,527	7–18 9–20 11–22 13–24 15–26	Huizinga et al. (2003)
Houston Longitudinal Study (USA)	7,618 6,414	12–40+ 12–15	Kaplan (2003)
Pittsburgh Youth Study (USA)	503 508 506	5–14 8–17 12–19	Loeber et al. (2003)
Rochester Youth Development Study (USA)	1,000	13–22	Thornberry et al. (2003)
Seattle Social Development Survey (USA)	808	10–24	Hawkins et al. (2003)

- Broken homes, where this is associated with marked emotional distress, especially if prolonged.
- Parental criminality, most frequently of fathers but in some instances of both parents or of older siblings; also of grandparents, uncles and aunts.
- Large family size, which reduces parental attention for each child and may increase conflict.
- Socioeconomic deprivation and the internal pressures this exerts upon families.
- Below-average intelligence and educational attainment, which reduces the chances of success defined conventionally in terms of employment and income.
- Peer influences, including both attitudes and behaviour, as we saw in Chapter 4.
- School influences, most importantly the way a school is run and the ethos created within it.
- Community influences, including crime opportunities and neighbourhood environments.
- Situational variables, for example the combinations of people present and the interactions between them.

Risk and protective factors

The type of empirically driven approach favoured by Farrington (1995, 1996, 2002) and many others has led, as with the integrative models surveyed in Chapter 2, to a conceptualization of crime in which theories are not expressed in terms of direct causal determinants. Instead, crime is viewed as an outcome of an interaction or combination of a range of risk and protective factors.

Risk factors are individual or environmental variables, such as those in the above list, which have been shown to be associated with greater likelihood of involvement in criminal activity (Blackburn 1993). The presence of such factors seems to have a cumulative and interactive effect, though the nature of this may not be simply additive. Risks almost certainly interplay with each other in ways that are not yet fully understood. Several researchers, including Patterson and Yoerger (1993), have proposed integrative models of such processes. They postulated that the causal patterns detected in the longitudinal studies have a developmental impact on the child's cognitive appraisals, social-cognitive skills, and typical modes of construing and problem-solving in personal relationships.

By contrast, working in the opposite direction, *protective factors* are those which 'enhance the resilience of those exposed to high levels of risk and protect them from undesirable outcomes' (Catalano and Hawkins 1996: 153). Thus even in unfavourable circumstances, a portion of those individuals exposed to risk factors do not resort to antisocial behaviour. Important protective factors identified in longitudinal studies have included being first-born, coming from a small family, a high IQ, a high level of caretaker attention and good maternal health. However, protective factors are not always simply the inverse of risk factors, and the interactions between the two can be quite complex (Lösel and Bender 2003). For example, social isolation may be a protective factor against some forms of offending, by reducing the influence of peer groups. But it may not safeguard a young person against other kinds of dysfunction such as emotional or mental health problems (Farrington 1995). Furthermore, the route from risk factors to the actual occurrence of antisocial acts may not be a uni-directional one: reversals can occur along the pathway (Rutter 1989; Lösel and Bliesener 1994).

Research by Wikström and Loeber (2000) has shown that there are complex interactions between risk and protective factors and attributes of neighbourhoods. At high levels of risk factors, young people were likely to become involved in offending regardless of neighbourhood context. Protective factors such as good parental supervision, motivation at school and experience of guilt reduced the likelihood of early onset of delinquency, again regardless of context. However, in adverse neighbourhood conditions, the risk of delinquency increased sharply with time, even for 'well-adjusted' children. (This is an example of an interaction between personal and situational variables of the kind outlined in Chapter 3.) Overall, however, both Wikström and Loeber (2000) and Elliott *et al.* (1996) concluded that individual risk and protective factors are better predictors of involvement in delinquency than characteristics of communities.

Another important outcome from longitudinal studies is a clearer understanding of patterns of continuity and discontinuity within different kinds of behaviour. In the overwhelming majority of cases, the acts that come to be labelled as 'criminal' are linked to other patterns that existed beforehand. Where offending becomes persistent, a focus on official statistics alone tells only one part of the story. Frequent adolescent and adult crime usually has its precursors in violence in families, school bullying or serious conduct disorders. Thus Farrington (1994) has argued for examining officially recorded delinquency alongside other forms of troublesome behaviour among the young.

Synthesizing research findings

The volume of data generated by the projects just described, and in this field more generally, is enormous. Making sense of it all is a formidable task. How can we discern patterns, if there are any, across potentially hundreds of pieces of research, themselves differing in numerous ways? During recent years, a particular approach to this problem has become widely applied throughout the social sciences and is now regarded virtually as standard.

The process of building knowledge through research involves several stages. Its building blocks are individual projects or *primary studies*. As findings on a given topic accumulate, researchers periodically draw them together to discover whether any distinct trend has emerged. This activity, known as *research review*, takes two main forms. The traditional version has a *narrative* format: the reviewer reads all the accessible literature relating to a given question, and summarizes it in a review article. Well-executed narrative reviews are very useful. But when the number of primary studies is large, it can be difficult to extract a clear picture from them. To overcome this, an alternative approach has been devised, in which the reviewer collectively analyses the statistical results across all the individual studies. That process is called *meta-analysis* (to distinguish it from *primary analysis*, the management of data within individual projects; and *secondary analysis*, where data are re-analysed to check them or extract other information from them).

Although meta-analysis is not new, it only came into more frequent use during the late 1970s (Glass 1976). For example, Glass *et al.* (1981) used the method to resolve the long-standing question of whether there is a relationship between class size (or more accurately, the pupil–teacher ratio) and the educational attainment of young people. Glass and his colleagues used meta-analytic techniques to review 300 studies published over a 70-year period, containing data from 12 countries, with a total sample of 900,000 participants. Their review showed unequivocally that, with other variables controlled, there is a clear relationship between class size and educational performance. For example, a reduction in class size from 40 to 15 is associated with a 20% average improvement in exam results.

In any field of research, the available primary studies will vary in many ways. The following are some of the differences typically found:

- their country and language of origin;
- their date of completion;
- whether they are published or unpublished;
- size and composition of the samples involved;
- the amounts of descriptive information provided on participants;
- the type of study design and its methodological quality;
- the level of detail given on procedures used;
- types of outcome measure employed;
- methods of data analysis.

It is hardly surprising that it is difficult to make sense of a batch of studies when there can be so many variations between them. And sometimes, of course, there just is no discernible trend among the findings. More commonly, there is a detectable trend that is concealed by the sheer volume of studies and the other differences between them.

The findings of meta-analyses are usually reported in the form of a general outcome variable called the *effect size*. As this is the whole object of the enterprise, effect size matters. We will see in Chapter 6 that there are several different effect size measures and numerous formats for reporting them. The most commonly used statistic when examining the relationships between variables is the *correlation coefficient*. This can be calculated in several ways, but all yield a statistic that tells us how close the association is between two variables. For example, we might ask whether there is a relationship between numbers of previous convictions up to a given time-point, and likelihood of a further re-conviction in the next two years; or whether endorsement of hostile statements on an attitude scale is associated with aggression towards others. If these correlations have been computed in a number of studies, by examining their averages we may be able to arrive at systematic conclusions about the relative strengths of different patterns of association.

Discovering risk factors through meta-analysis

The meta-analytic approach has now been extensively applied in efforts to discover relationships between individual, family, social and other variables, and subsequent involvement in criminal or other antisocial behaviour, especially where it has become repetitive or entrenched. For example, Lipsey and Derzon (1998) used it to amalgamate findings from a number of longitudinal studies. Their primary interest was in which variables would best predict serious or violent offending between the ages of 15 and 25. They combined data from 34 independent studies, each with a sample of between 200 and 500 participants, yielding a total of 155 effect sizes. The search for predictors was carried out based on two prior age ranges: 6–11 and 12–14 years. The attrition rate, the reduction in the samples between the prediction and outcome points, was less than 5% in each of the studies found. In any attempt to fuse primary research findings together in this way, a portion of the variation in the results will be due to methodological differences between the studies. It is therefore important firstly to examine the extent of this and take account of it in the analysis.

Once this had been done, Lipsey and Derzon found that slightly different factors served best as predictors from the two initial age ranges. For prediction from 6–11 to 15–25, the best predictors were a history of any type of offending, substance use, male gender, family socioeconomic status and having parents who themselves had a history of criminal behaviour. For prediction from 12–14, the best predictors were a lack of social ties, involvement with antisocial peers and a history of previous offences.

Three other meta-analyses have been reported of predictors of re-offending by young people. Simourd and Andrews (1994) reviewed research, published and unpublished, conducted in the 30 years before 1994. They located 60 studies, conjointly producing a total of 464 correlations between a wide range of factors and involvement in delinquency (but excluding criminal history variables). The most potent predictors were antisocial peers and attitudes (unfortunately, the authors did not test the separate effects of these two factors); temperament and misconduct problems; poor educational performance; and difficulties in parent–child relationships. Other factors such as socioeconomic status and self-reported personal distress were not associated with offending. A main objective of the review by Simourd and Andrews was to determine whether there were differences between the sexes in factors predictive of recidivism. However, no such differences were found: patterns of predictive power across various factors were very similar for both males and females.

Cottle *et al.* (2001) reviewed 25 studies published between 1983 and 2000, comprising 22 independent samples with a combined total of 15,265 participants. Whereas a youth's age on first commitment to court and age at first contact with the law were the two strongest predictors of recidivism, the number of previous commitments was only a moderately good predictor, and number of previous arrests a comparatively poor predictor. Presence of delinquent peers was a relatively strong predictor; by contrast, socioeconomic status was a fairly weak one. Cottle and her colleagues did not directly examine attitudinal, cognitive or personality variables.

Hubbard and Pratt (2002) analysed predictors of delinquency among girls. They surveyed all published studies of predictors of female delinquency; they do not give the number of studies but they contained 97 effect size estimates from a combined sample of 5,981. Like Simourd and Andrews, they found similar factors operating as for young males. These included antisocial peers (effect size 0.53); prior history of antisocial behaviour (0.48), antisocial personality (0.21), attitudes and beliefs (0.18). However, some additional factors also emerged, including school relationships (0.25), history of physical or sexual victimization (0.21), and family relationships (0.17). As in most other reviews, socioeconomic status was a poor predictor (effect size 0.03).

For adults, the strongest predictors of offending have been elucidated in a meta-analysis by Gendreau *et al.* (1996). This drew on a total of 131 studies published between 1970 and 1994, with an aggregate sample size of just under 700,000, and yielding a total of 1,141 correlations between predictor variables and recidivism. The review surveyed 18 'predictor domains' embracing demographic, family background, criminal history and personal functioning variables. The most robust predictors were: having a network of companions or associates themselves involved in offending; expressing antisocial attitudes or cognitions; antisocial personality assessed by one of several psychometric scales or structured interviews; and criminal history as an adult or adolescent.

A study by Simourd and Olver (2002) of 381 adult male Canadian prisoners has underlined the importance of attitudes towards crime and criminality, and illustrated aspects of their structure. The men in their sample ranged in age from 19 to 60, represented several different ethnic groups and had an average of over 13 previous convictions. They were asked to complete a modified version of the Criminal Sentiments Scale, a self-report questionnaire of attitudes, beliefs and values concerning the law and crime. The results supported earlier findings that there are several components of attitudes conducive to committing crimes. One aspect of this was the individual's general view of the law and its enforcement. Another was belief in or tolerance of law-breaking as a means to get what one wants. A third element was identification with 'criminal others'. These aspects of attitudes exhibited modest but statistically significant relationships to several separate indicators of criminal activity (e.g. re-arrest, violent re-arrest, violating supervision arrangements, reconviction and re-incarceration).

Identifying risk factors through evaluation of outcomes

Another approach to testing the importance of different variables is to compare the relative impact of interventions, focused on different aspects of individuals' functioning, on their risk of re-offending. Table 5.2 shows the results of a series of meta-analyses reported by Dowden and Andrews (2000) on factors associated with re-offending by young people. The items are listed in descending order according to the mean effect size obtained. The number of studies contributing to each calculation is shown in the right-hand column. The topmost item in the table (*criminogenic needs*) refers to a cluster of factors combining criminal peers and antisocial attitudes, which as we have seen emerged strongly from other reviews outlined above.

The core proposition tested in this kind of work is that 'individuals varying in their criminal past (as documented by cross-sectional studies)

Table 5.2 Criminogenic dynamic risk factors (adapted from Dowden and Andrews 2000)

Variable	Mean effect size (r)	Number of tests
General criminogenic needs	+0.36	47
Family: supervision	+0.35	17
Family: affection	+0.33	24
Barriers to treatment	+0.30	12
Self-control	+0.29	40
Anger/antisocial feelings	+0.28	41
Vocational skills + job	+0.26	9
Academic	+0.23	51
Pro-social model	+0.19	19
Antisocial attitudes	+0.13	17
Reduce antisocial peers	+0.11	8
Vocational skills	+0.09	17
Relapse prevention	+0.07	7
Substances abuse treatment (any)	+0.04	11

and their criminal future (as documented in longitudinal studies) may be differentiated at levels well above chance on a number of situational, circumstantial, personal, interpersonal, familial and structural/cultural/economic factors' (Andrews 1995: 36). Support for this proposition comes from an integrative evidence base of 372 studies of variables associated with offending (Andrews and Bonta 2003). Andrews and his associates have analysed these studies both in combination and in separate groupings defined by moderator variables such as gender, age and ethnicity; and research variables including the specific way in which 'crime' was measured and the type of research design employed. The net conclusion from these reviews is that the major factors with demonstrable links to risks of crime are as follows:

- Antisocial or pro-criminal attitudes, beliefs and cognitive-emotional states.
- Association with pro-criminal peers.
- A number of temperamental and personality factors, including impulsivity, restless aggressive energy, egocentrism, and poor problem-solving and self-regulation skills.
- A varied history of antisocial behaviour.
- Family history of criminality, evidence of poor parental supervision and discipline.
- Low levels of personal, educational, vocational or financial achievement.

Standing back for a moment to survey the assembly of reviews just outlined, we can see that there are some disparities among the findings obtained. That is not surprising given the complexity of the influences that are operating, and the mixture of studies done. All of this represents work in progress, and there is a need for more research both to check and to amplify the results obtained.

Nevertheless, the degree of consistency across the findings is sizeable with regard to those factors that appear to differentiate young people or adults at risk of involvement in a pattern of offending; especially one that is more serious or protracted. Where criminal history variables are included in an analysis, they emerge as strong predictors of future offending. That is important information for prognostic purposes, but in itself it carries little explanatory value. Studies and reviews that discriminate other factors, such as aspects of social networks, lifestyles, attitudes, values or reported problems, arguably take us beneath the surface of the criminal and demo-graphic statistics and reveal more about discrete pathways towards or away from offending.

In summary, there is now a sizeable body of information in this field. The findings we have collected emerge from cross-sectional studies com-paring individuals who have different levels of contact with the criminal justice system. Other findings, from longitudinal studies within which it is possible to capture the developmental sequences of events, highlight the same sets of variables. Evidence that rehabilitative efforts focused on the same factors can lead to reductions in re-offending further confirms their influence. Together, these results build a strong case for the importance of certain factors in the origins and maintenance of criminal conduct at the individual level.

Static and dynamic

A useful distinction that emerges from analyses of this kind is between *static* and *dynamic* risk predictors. The former generally consist of demo-graphic or criminal-history variables, which at any given moment are fixed or determined beforehand (by prior events). They include, for example, gender, age when first convicted of an offence, having a parent with a criminal record, present age, types of offences committed and total number of previous convictions. Dynamic risk factors by contrast fluctuate more rapidly over time, and reflect internal states or temporary circumstances of the individual. They include, for example, attitudes and cognitions, every-day companions or associates, impulsivity, self-management and control (or its absence), and the pattern or extent of substance misuse. Research suggests these play a pivotal role in the recurrence of offending (Zamble and Quinsey 1997). When Gendreau *et al.* (1996) grouped together various factors of this type in the meta-analysis cited earlier, they found they were on average more closely correlated with recidivism than were demographic and criminal history variables.

Criminogenic and non-criminogenic

Another distinction that is widely used is between *criminogenic* and *non-criminogenic* needs. This terminology comes from the work of Andrews,

Bonta, Gendreau and their co-workers. It refers to the difference between those aspects of an individual's functioning, which, if modified, will have an impact on the likelihood of re-offending; as opposed to other attributes that have been shown to be unrelated to that outcome. For example, if it proves possible to alter an individual's attitudes, or numbers of peer associates involved in offending, this increases the chances of a reduction in recidivism. Such established dynamic risk factors are then called *criminogenic needs*. It is necessary to make them targets of change if we wish to reduce risk levels. Conversely, certain other targets are less promising as the focus of change in efforts to reduce offending behaviour. They include diffuse or vaguely defined emotional or personal problems, such as feelings of anxiety or low mood; or an individual's level of self-esteem. As we will see in Chapter 6, when the latter have been made targets of intervention programmes, in some cases this has led to *increases* in recidivism (Andrews 2001).

This is not meant to imply that we should disregard needs of the latter kind, in some obstinate, single-minded drive to do what is most likely to tackle offending behaviour and nothing more. Individuals are entitled to have such needs met regardless of whether they have broken the law. The argument on which this distinction turns is simply that in the light of the evidence to hand, addressing these needs will not by itself be sufficient to bring about adjustments in offending behaviour. This overturns what was for many years a widespread assumption in working with offenders and trying to 'rehabilitate' them. The distinction might also raise important questions about what should be the role of criminal justice agencies in meeting offenders' needs, an issue to which we will return in Chapter 8.

Specific risk factors?

None of the studies we have discussed so far permits us to draw clear conclusions regarding whether there are particular developmental risk factors associated with any single type of offence as compared to others. Most individuals who are repeatedly convicted of crimes are non-specialists in that they commit an assortment of offences. In the Cambridge Study of Delinquent Development, for example, 'the causes of aggression and violence were essentially the same as the causes of persistent and extreme antisocial, delinquent and criminal behaviour' (Farrington 1995: 945). This point has been further emphasized by Andrews and Bonta (2003), who have reviewed sets of risk factors for general, violent and sexual offending, as well as offending by persons suffering from mental disorders. By and large, only minor variations are found in the sets of factors that can be identified, although there are likely to be different processes at work, as we saw in Chapter 4.

However, efforts have been made, and continue to be made, to isolate risk factors for specific forms of offending. The research literature pertaining to this is voluminous, though very unevenly spread across different offence types. Perhaps not surprisingly there is a tendency to focus on various manifestations of violence. Three examples serve to illustrate the kinds of work carried out.

Sexual offending by adolescents

Many studies have focused on adolescents who commit sexual assaults. Cross-sectional comparisons appear to indicate that they may have experienced more violence from parents than other groups of aggressive juveniles (Ford and Linney 1995). They are also described as being more isolated and having poor social relationships with both family members and peers (Vizard et al. 1995), a picture quite different from that seen in the meta-analyses for general offending where peer influence is a major factor. Hudson and Ward (2001) have forwarded an account of this specific form of assault by adolescents.

Worling and Långström (2003) reviewed the research on risk of recidivism and concluded that several factors are quite firmly supported by the work that has been done: deviant sexual interests; previous sanctions for sexual assault; having two or more previous victims; selecting a stranger as victim; social isolation; and incomplete participation in treatment programmes. Other factors were thought to be promising as predictors: problematic relationships with parents, and attitudes supportive of sexual offending. Several other variables were thought to be possible risk factors but are not yet sufficiently supported by empirical findings. Contrary to what is widely believed, there is no clear relationship between experience of childhood sexual victimization and sexual assault recidivism in either adolescence or adulthood. Similarly, denial of sexual offending, frequently assumed to be an indicator of higher risk, is associated with lower subsequent rates of re-offending (Worling and Långström 2003).

Gang involvement

Being a member of a delinquent gang is associated with committing more serious offences, including violence. Hill et al. (1999) used data from the Seattle Social Development Project, one of the longitudinal studies listed earlier, to investigate risk factors for involvement in a gang. Hill and his colleagues searched for predictors from ages 10–12 of joining a gang between the ages of 13 and 18. In their sample of 808 young people from diverse ethnic backgrounds, roughly one in six reported having belonged to a gang at some point. Several risk factors emerged as predictive of gang membership. They included the number of young people in trouble in a neighbourhood and the local availability of marijuana. Living in any arrangement other than with both parents was associated with elevated risk, as was doing poorly at school. At an individual level, young people prone to externalizing behaviours, who reported having been violent before the age of 12, who had tried marijuana by the age of 12, and who rejected conventional beliefs, were more likely to be in gangs. There was a strong association between the numbers of risk factors at work and the likelihood of being in a gang. Those exposed to seven or more risk factors were over 13 times more likely to be gang members than those exposed to none or just one.

Multiple murder in schools

There has even been an attempt to determine whether there are any specific risk characteristics for 'school shooters', given the disturbing numbers of multiple killings by schoolchildren in the USA. The Federal Bureau of Investigation has published a 'threat assessment' document based on in-depth examination of a series of 18 of these incidents by a multidisciplinary expert group (O'Toole 2001). The objective of this study was to provide senior educators and parents with a guide to interpreting any warning signs that a student might be about to unleash such devastating violence.

This resulted in a 'four-pronged assessment model' requiring analysis of the personality of the student, family dynamics, school dynamics and social or community dynamics. No fewer than 28 features were identified as possible indicators at the individual level. Where individuals have made threats, some attributes of them can be taken more seriously as indicating the threats are real, for example where they are 'direct, specific as to the victim, motivation, weapon, place and time' (O'Toole 2001: 9). It is difficult to evaluate the status of specific items in the lists generated. For example, one perpetrator, who was taking a home economics class, baked a cake in the shape of a gun. By itself that might be indicative of a fertile if slightly macabre imagination, or wacky sense of humour. The school writings and other work of youth in question showed recurrent themes of violence. Hence the report emphasizes the importance of looking across the totality of the indicators, to avoid any risk of unfairly labelling a young person.

Two patterns of offending?

Drawing together the evidence found so far, there is sufficient consistency to justify several conclusions. There are large individual differences in the likelihood of criminal offending. While many – perhaps most – of us break the law at some stage (usually in adolescence, and in minor ways), there are some individuals with a far higher level of criminal activity. That array of differences shows a sizeable amount of stability over time. Thus a person's past record of crime provides a reasonably sound basis for predicting the likelihood of similar activity in the future. Individual differences in psychological or psychosocial variables provide an equally viable, even superior, basis for predicting the extent of future offending.

Thus it appears fair to say *both* that there are many people who commit offences just once or twice in their lives, *and* that there is a small group who do so much more often. The latter group may, to recall the terminology used by Shoda *et al.* (1994: see Chapter 3), have particular psychological 'signatures' with respect to the ways in which they habitually respond to certain situations.

In an attempt to make sense of the apparent lopsidedness of these findings, Moffitt (1993) has offered a model of differential pathways in development. The key to this is a distinction between two types of delinquency each with its own characteristics and causes:

- *Adolescence-limited*. This refers to the bulk of offending, for which the peak incidence occurs in the mid-to-late teenage years but which wanes in frequency thereafter. 'Actual rates of illegal behavior soar so high during adolescence that participation in delinquency appears to be a normal part of teen life' (Moffitt 1993: 675). The roots of this are in the differential rates at which young people mature physically, emotionally and socially, and in the conflict between them and adults as they strive for autonomy. It occurs in this way because 'a secular change in the duration of adolescence has generated an age-dependent motivational state' (p. 689). The sheer volume of this type of offending increased considerably from the early part of the twentieth century onwards in the world's richer nations.
- *Life course persistent*. This refers to problem behaviour that is of earlier onset, is usually more serious, and which continues on into adulthood. Moffitt suggested that those manifesting this pattern might sometimes serve as role models for the first group. She also estimated that they form approximately 5% of the male population. In Moffitt's view and that of several other researchers, the behaviour of this group is probably indicative of psychopathology. For example, she adduced evidence that it may be due to some underlying neuropsychological difference between them and the 'time-limited' majority.

The key proposal here, then, is that there are two forms of delinquent activity that have dissimilar origins and require separate explanations. However, it remains unclear whether the 'persistent' group is genuinely distinct. There may be a sub-group within it that is characterized by features such as neuropsychological damage, or other pervasive problems including personality disorders (a possibility we will consider below). But it may be more accurate to think of the generally observed pattern as a continuum, rather than a typology, as has been suggested, for example, by Thornberry *et al.* (2003). Brezina (2002) has forwarded several possible reasons other than psychopathology why there may be individuals whose illegal behaviour becomes more persistent. They include patterns of socialization such as those discussed in the preceding two chapters of the present book.

Offenders with mental disorders

Models such as the one proposed by Moffitt (1993) implicate psycho-pathology as a likely cause of repetitive offending. Even criminologists who are critical of psychology (e.g. Roshier 1989) acknowledge some association, albeit extremely limited, between crime and mental disorder, though also maintaining that the usage of any of these categories is problematic. The fundamental mistake attributed to psychology arises from a perceived overstatement of the role of pathology in crime. This brings us to the keenly disputed question of the extent to which, or whether, there is a relationship of this kind. Can mental disorder be considered criminogenic in the sense defined earlier?

This area is one in which myths and misconceptions abound, unfortunately as enduring as they are pervasive. Labelling and stigmatization remain common and individuals who experience particular combinations of mental health problems are still widely regarded as 'dangerous'. Incidents in which people suffering from mental disorders commit serious crimes are sensationalized, and lurid portrayals of such possibilities in many media give a distorted picture of the personal experience and consequences of mental distress.

A more systematic scrutiny of the evidence does not support the view that people suffering from mental disorder pose a significant threat to others. Taylor and Gunn (1999) have charted the numbers of homicides in England and Wales committed by persons with serious mental disorders over a 38-year period. Such incidents consistently form only a small proportion of homicides overall, and their annual rate has steadily *declined* since the 1950s. The frequency of other kinds of violence was monitored in the MacArthur Violence Risk Assessment Study, a follow-up of a large sample ($n = 1,136$) of patients discharged from psychiatric hospitals into the community in three US cities. Data were collected at ten-week intervals for a period of 12 months. The authors found that the rate of violence for study groups was no higher than that for non-clinical comparison samples in the same neighbourhoods (Steadman *et al.* 1998).

Problems of definition

As we saw in Chapter 1, the question of how to define crime is notoriously difficult. No consensus has ever emerged concerning it; some writers query the legitimacy of the whole exercise. Before discussing whether there is a relationship between crime and mental disorder, it is important to clarify the terms on which any such discussion is based. Sadly for those of us who would prefer a simple life, definitions in the study of mental disorder are if anything even more elusive and controversial.

The dominant approach to this is in the province of psychiatry, which is a branch of medicine. As such it is founded upon the concept and everyday application of the process of *diagnosis*. This serves four main purposes (Eastman 2000):

- description and classification of the observed phenomena;
- aetiology – provision of a causal model for understanding a disorder and its origins;
- prognosis, or the prediction of the likely progress and outcome of a problem;
- decision-making with regard to therapeutic interventions.

To accomplish these goals, elaborate taxonomic systems have been created for mental disorder syndromes. The two most widely used are the Diagnostic and Statistical Manual of Mental Disorders (DSM-IV; American Psychiatric Association 2000) and the International Classification of Mental and Behavioural Disorders (ICD-10; World Health Organization 1992).

Some types of mental disorder have a clear underlying neural pathology, even if its exact nature has not yet been ascertained. They include degenerative brain diseases such as Alzheimer's, seizure disorders such as epilepsy, and traumatic brain injury caused by traffic accidents or assaults (Lishman 1997).

However, for the overwhelming majority of mental health problems, there is no known organic cause (Pilgrim and Rogers 1993; Mechanic 1999). Indeed, for most, it is unlikely that any direct physical substratum will be found. In the absence of known aetiology, some researchers question the very use of diagnostic frameworks for mental health problems. This has led to disagreements among psychiatrists themselves; and as in criminology there is a 'critical' tendency within the profession (Szasz 1961; Breggin 1991). Similar disagreements also arise between psychiatry and other professions including psychology and sociology. The use of diagnosis is fraught with technical problems (Clark *et al.* 1995) and it has been argued that its basis is more political than scientific (Kutchins and Kirk 1997). These reservations notwithstanding, most research on the links between crime and mental disorder is conducted with reference to diagnostic systems and categories.

Mental health problems in offenders

Individuals who have broken the law face personal problems of various sorts, and a proportion may also experience symptoms of mental disorder. Where that arises, it of course represents a healthcare issue in its own right. It might partly explain the disturbingly high incidence of suicide and self-harm in penal institutions. Surveys have been conducted to investigate the prevalence of mental disorders among prisoners in several countries. For example:

- *United Kingdom.* In a survey for the Office of National Statistics, Singleton *et al.* (1998) interviewed 3142 prisoners. They found that 7% of male sentenced prisoners, 10% of males on remand and 14% of female prisoners met criteria for diagnosis of psychotic illness. The corresponding figures for antisocial personality disorder were 49, 63 and 31%, and for neurotic disorders 40, 59 and 76%. Levels of harmful or hazardous alcohol and drug use were very high. Overall, fewer than one in ten prisoners showed no evidence of the major diagnostic categories examined in the survey.

• *United States.* Steadman *et al.* (1989) conducted a survey of 3,332 prison inmates in New York State. They found that 8% suffered from severe psychiatric disorders, with an additional 16% being found to suffer from disorders which, though less severe, nevertheless required treatment. Among a random sample of 728 male admissions to a US county jail, Teplin (1990) found that 6.4% met diagnostic criteria for major mental disorders such as schizophrenia, mania or clinical depression. An analogous study with female prisoners showed an even higher rate of 15% (Teplin *et al.* 1996).

• *Canada.* Among Canadian penitentiary inmates, both Hodgins and Côté (1990) and Motiuk and Porporino (1991) found significant proportions of prisoners suffering from major mental disorders. In Ontario, for example, proportions of those fulfilling diagnostic criteria for various disorders were: psychosis, 8.6%; major depression, 11.9%; generalized anxiety disorder, 27.9%; drug dependence, 36.7%; antisocial personality disorder, 59.0%; and alcohol dependence, 69.1%.

Reviewing the North American literature, Lamb and Weinberger (1998) concluded that the proportion of prisoners suffering from severe mental disorders in local city and county jails in the USA ranged from 6 to 15%, and in state prisons from 10 to 15%. Extrapolating from official statistics for England and Wales, Peay (2002) estimated that in mid-2001 there were likely to have been 4,648 prisoners suffering from some form of psychosis, and who were in need of transfer to hospital. On the basis of a large-scale, integrative review of 62 survey-based studies from 12 countries, Fazel and Danesh (2002) deduced that, globally, the number of prisoners suffering from mental disorders is likely to run into several millions.

Mental disorder and risk of offending

These data collectively suggest that there is a significant unmet need for mental health services within the prison population. However, the presence of serious mental health problems in imprisoned offenders does not in itself demonstrate that they constitute a risk factor for criminal behaviour. For that to be shown, we would need detailed information on the patterning of symptoms and of offending for each individual. An alternative way to approach this, coming from the opposite direction as it were, is to study criminal offending in people diagnosed as suffering from mental disorders.

Several types of evidence converge to suggest two broad conclusions that

Table 5.3 Predictors of recidivism among mentally disordered offenders (Bonta et al. 1998)

Category of predictor	General recidivism	Violent recidivism
Demographic	0.12	0.12
Criminal history	0.08	0.15
Deviant lifestyle	0.07	0.08
Clinical	−0.02	−0.03

can be drawn at present. First, contrary to a widely held stereotype, people diagnosed with even relatively severe mental disorders are on balance no more likely, and perhaps slightly less likely, to commit criminal offences than the population as a whole. Second, some recent research has focused on the question of whether there may be certain exceptions to this, associated with particular types of symptoms, or mental and emotional states.

Employing meta-analysis, Bonta et al. (1998) reviewed a series of long-term follow-up studies to establish which factors were the best predictors of criminal and violent recidivism among offenders with serious mental disorders. The set of studies they compiled incorporated 68 independent samples (a total sample size of 15,245). Predictors were classed into four sets: *demographic, criminal history, deviant lifestyle* and *clinical*. The last included psychiatric diagnosis. As Table 5.3 shows, the most accurate predictors were demographic and criminal history variables; indeed, the overall pattern obtained was a close parallel to that typically found with non-mentally disordered offender populations. The weakest predictors of recidivism were clinical variables. Most notably, although a diagnosis of antisocial personality disorder (a category used within the DSM) was associated with a greater risk of future criminality, no other diagnostic category emerged as significant. Psychosis was in fact negatively correlated with future recidivism.

Long-term follow-up research of the kind reviewed by Bonta and his colleagues has been carried out in a number of countries, including the UK, USA, Canada, Sweden and Italy (McGuire 2001b). For example, Buchanan (1998) has described a 10½-year community follow-up of 425 patients discharged from high-security hospitals in England. Broadly consistent patterns of results have emerged from these studies. Factors associated with greater likelihood of re-conviction include being younger, male, unmarried and having a diagnosis of personality disorder, most importantly antisocial or psychopathic disorder. It has been consistently found that the risk of violence is elevated when a diagnosis of major mental disorder is conjoined with substance abuse (Swanson et al. 1997).

With reference to clinical variables, probably the best interpretation of these findings that can be offered at present is that diagnosis by itself is too rudimentary a description to provide much information concerning risk factors. When specific symptoms are examined more closely, some interesting patterns emerge. However, as yet the picture obtained remains unclear due to some ambiguities within them.

Important evidence bearing on this came from the Epidemiological Catchment Area (ECA) study, a large-scale survey of psychiatric morbidity in a community sample of 10,059 respondents from three American cities (Swanson *et al.* 1990; Swanson 1994). Data collection included questions concerning whether respondents had engaged in any act of violence in the preceding 12 months. The rates reported by different sub-groups varied considerably by diagnosis. For those not diagnosed with any disorder the rate was 2.1%; for those diagnosed as suffering from schizophrenia it was 12.7%, and for those with drug dependence 34.7%.

More detailed examination of these findings showed that almost all the difference in rates of violence between patient and non-patient samples could be accounted for by certain psychotic symptoms (Link *et al.* 1992; Link and Stueve 1994). The specific symptoms most closely associated with violent acts were paranoid delusions, especially those in which individuals felt threatened because their own self-controls are being invaded by external forces. Link and Stueve (1994) called these patterns *threat/control-override* (TCO) symptoms. Other research has shown that depending upon their content, and on aspects of the situation, *command hallucinations* may also be associated with the occurrence of acts of violence (McNiel 1994). Here, individuals may hear voices issuing commands, in some instances directly to themselves ordering them to commit assaults.

However, in the most sophisticated study of its kind to date, the pattern of results obtained differed somewhat from this. The MacArthur Violence Risk Assessment Study employed complex statistical techniques to disentangle the relative effects of different risk factors on the occurrence of violent behaviour (Monahan *et al.* 2001). Some factors that emerged were familiar: the impact of prior criminality, father's criminality and substance abuse, and the individual's own history of drug and alcohol abuse. Others that emerged as significant were engagement in violent fantasy and the behavioural expression of anger. But there was no evidence that schizophrenia was a risk factor for violence, and contrary to the ECA findings neither paranoid delusions nor command hallucinations were predictive of it.

Our focus here and throughout this chapter has been on individual attributes associated with a repetitive involvement in offending. However, it is vital to reiterate that these links are moderated by social and contextual factors: a further example of interaction between the person and the situation described in Chapter 3. In the MacArthur study, neighbourhoods at different levels of affluence also differed in rates of violence, and this was an important predictor of violence rates in combination with individual variables in an interactional model.

Personality disorder

Probably the psychiatric category most consistently associated with repetitive involvement in crime is that of personality disorder, which in the two diagnostic systems mentioned earlier is further divided into various subtypes (see McMurran 2001 for a side-by-side comparison). From a psychiatric standpoint, persistent offending may be attributable to the presence of underlying personality disorder. As defined in DSM-IV, the type most often found among male offenders is *antisocial personality disorder*, which is also the most frequently studied, and in 12 separate reports was found to have a median community prevalence of 1.2% (Mattia and Zimmerman 2001). In diagnostic terms, personality disorder is conceptualized as 'an enduring pattern of inner experience and behaviour that deviates markedly from the expectations of the individual's culture' (American Psychiatric Association 2000: 689), manifested in cognition, emotional responding, interpersonal functioning, or impulse control. Antisocial personality disorder is characterized by a pattern of disregarding the rights of others, which shows itself in such features as repetitive involvement in criminal behaviour, deceitfulness, impulsiveness, irritability and aggressiveness, irresponsibility and lack of remorse. The argument here is susceptible to the charge of circularity: if a psychiatric disorder is partly defined by specified kinds of behaviour, then it is scarcely surprising if it is found to correlate with that behaviour described in other ways. There are more conceptual confusions, if not contortions, in this area, especially revolving round the related word *psychopath*. This term has a curious history, from its original German usage to mean a psychologically damaged person to later, recurrent interpretative disputes regarding its clinical and scientific status (Blackburn 1992, 1993). It is not part of any diagnostic system, although it continued in use as a legal category in the 1983 Mental Health Act of England and Wales, and in research on the prediction of violence.

Individual differences: practical implications

Discussing the evidence from longitudinal research, Laub and Sampson (1993) pointed out that theoretical models in criminology are typically based on aggregate samples, and so fail to take adequate account of the heterogeneity of individuals. Consequently, there sometimes appears to be an unbridgeable gap between theory construction and the more ordinary task of making sense of particular offences or of the people who have committed them.

The findings reviewed in this chapter arguably constitute a sizeable advance in our understanding of the development and maintenance of involvement in crime at the individual level. With respect to both the accumulation of knowledge and the refinement of theory, they have brought us a long way. They have established the existence of fairly robust individual differences in the likelihood of persistent offending. The importance of many of the variables is confirmed by their concurrent validation through studies that used different methodological perspectives. It is only a short step from this set of findings to the proposal that the information so produced is potentially useful for purposes of assessment and prediction within criminal justice. If we find that certain aspects of individuals' development or their functioning are convincingly associated with their chances of re-offending, it should be possible to discover some method of combining this information that will enable us to forecast that event (Andrews 1989; Andrews *et al.* 1990a).

The crucial question of course is the accuracy with which this can be done. The success of any approach in foretelling the likelihood of involvement in further offending is called its *predictive validity*. For any given method this should be rigorously tested in follow-up research and be shown to achieve satisfactory levels before we apply it in practical settings.

An advantage of this approach, if it can be shown to work, is that it holds out the prospect of helping to solve the problem posed by Laub and Sampson (1993) of making links between large-scale theory and single cases. While a general consensus on an integrative theoretical model may continue to be elusive, employing a risk-assessment framework could greatly facilitate the everyday practical task of understanding individual offence patterns.

Risk assessment

This has led to the assembly, testing and dissemination of a number – some would say a plethora – of risk assessment instruments. Strategies for undertaking this have traditionally been classified into two principal types:

- *Clinical* approaches evolved from the accumulation of everyday experience of practitioners working with individual cases, and so are founded on subjective judgements drawing on recollection of previous examples. The word 'clinical' here does not refer exclusively to medical practitioners such as psychiatrists, but may include psychologists, social workers, probation officers, parole officers, case managers in youth justice services, or psychiatric nurses.
- *Actuarial* approaches by contrast are empirically driven in the sense that they involve systematic measurement of a specified set of factors derived from a research database, which is then statistically analysed, yielding a formula that will allow usage of the information to provide risk-level scores. A steady stream of research has clearly demonstrated the superior accuracy of this approach over clinical prediction.

If our focus is simply on prediction of average re-offence rates among selected offender populations, a reasonably high level of predictive accuracy can be attained on the basis of static risk factors alone (Lloyd *et al.*

1994). In the United Kingdom, this led to development of the Offender Group Reconviction Scale (OGRS; Copas and Marshall 1998). This employs seven pieces of information to generate a risk score: gender, present age, age at first conviction, number of previous offences, number of previous custodial sentences, presence or absence of a custodial sentence as a youth, and type of current offence. Combining these data using a computerized procedure yields a score representing the percentage of offenders with any given set of characteristics likely to be re-convicted within the next two years. Later research investigated whether social background factors are as closely associated with re-conviction as criminal history variables, but found that 'their effect in improving prediction is only slight' (May 1999: ix). The revised version of the scale (OGRS-2) has become a standard assessment in offender management in prison and probation services in England and Wales.

In recent years, the 'risk factors' framework has been used to construct a number of more complex, in-depth assessment instruments for the prediction of future involvement in crime. Several scales now exist for combined assessment of static and dynamic risk factors. Probably the best-known example is the Level of Service Inventory-Revised (LSI-R; Bonta 1996; Andrews and Bonta 1995). However, there are now numerous specialized methods of carrying out this work (for a valuable review of them, see Hollin 2002b). This type of approach, based on amalgamation of variables, is widely perceived as having more practical value than any single theoretical model, though the contents of such scales may be derived from formal theoretical precepts. The content areas of the LSI-R are listed in Table 5.4.

Other scales have been developed for the prediction of specific types of offence, though primarily those of a violent nature as they give rise to greatest concern. Thus there are frameworks for prediction of the risk of general violence, sexual violence against adults, sexual violence against children, and domestic violence. There are also specialized approaches for assessment of younger offenders (Hoge and Andrews 1996; Hoge 2002).

To the two long-standing approaches (clinical and actuarial) outlined above, Melton *et al.* (1998) have suggested adding a third, entitled *anamnestic* risk assessment. This entails compilation of a checklist of risk factors on an actuarial basis, supplemented by clinical judgement. That

Table 5.4 Content areas of the Level of Service Inventory-Revised (Andrews and Bonta 1995)

Criminal history (10 items)	Leisure/recreation (2 items)
Education/employment (10 items)	Companions (5 items)
Financial (2 items)	Alcohol/drug problems (9 items)
Family/marital (4 items)	Emotional/personal (5 items)
Accommodation (3 items)	Attitudes/orientation (4 items)

information is then combined with other material concerning the offender's environment. This entails the compilation of an inventory of situations in which he or she may be at risk of re-offending, accompanied by a series of estimates of the probabilities that such circumstances will occur.

Risk assessment and mental disorder

Assessing the risk that someone will re-offend is fraught with difficulty, but nowhere more so than in regard to offenders with serious mental disorders and a history of violence. Errors made in this area may have considerable social cost. Although as we saw earlier a diagnosis of mental disorder is not in itself associated with increased risk of antisocial behaviour, some permutations of symptoms appear to heighten the possibility. In the United Kingdom, several notorious instances during the 1990s in which discharged patients committed homicides generated considerable public concern and media attention, and resulted in a statutory requirement that there should be an official inquiry following such events (Reith 1998).

It is conventional to describe the history of the risk assessment enterprise with this population as having travelled through several phases or 'generations' of activity. The first was based upon naturalistic follow-up studies of patients discharged from secure hospitals, and clinical judgements concerning them. The second entailed the use of more structured and shorter-term predictions, and clearer specification of outcomes. A more loosely defined third phase is roughly identified with the advent of the more highly systematized approaches currently in use (Monahan and Steadman 1994; Gendreau et al. 1996). All methods, unfortunately, produce an unacceptably high rate of 'false-positives': that is, persons who were expected to re-offend but did not. Nevertheless, this proportion has been reducing as the prediction process has become more refined. Blackburn (2000a) provides a clear introduction to the research background and the technicalities of risk prediction.

Several methods predominate in risk assessments in this field. Given the firm link between some kinds of personality disorder and interpersonal aggression, the most widely used is the Psychopathy Check List-Revised (PCL-R; see Hare 1996). An individual's score on this is derived from a semi-structured interview for which special training is required, though the information can also be extracted from case files. The PCL-R takes account of both criminal history and lifestyle variables, and personal and psychological factors. While this implement is widely regarded as the best currently available for the prediction of serious violence, Gendreau et al. (2002b) have adduced evidence that the LSI-R achieves greater accuracy for that purpose.

An individual's score on the PCL-R can be entered into a more elaborate system, the HCR-20 (Webster et al. 1997), so called because it requires the combination of 20 areas of information: ten *Historical*, five *Clinical* and five referring to *Risk management* issues. Items that are assessed and which

Table 5.5 Content areas of the HCR-20 (Webster *et al.* 1997)

Historical (past)		Clinical (present)		Risk management (future)	
H1	Previous violence	C1	Lack of insight	R1	Plans lack feasibility
H2	Young age at first violent incident	C2	Negative attitudes	R2	Exposure to destabilizers
H3	Relationship instability	C3	Active symptoms of major mental illness	R3	Lack of personal support
H4	Employment problems	C4	Impulsivity	R4	Non-compliance with remediation attempts
H5	Substance use problems	C5	Unresponsiveness to treatment	R5	Stress
H6	Major mental illness				
H7	Psychopathy				
H8	Early maladjustment				
H9	Personality disorder				
H10	Prior supervision failure				

form the basis of risk predictions within this scheme are listed in Table 5.5. The additional value of methods such as the LSI-R and HCR-20 resides in their usefulness for specifying intervention targets with individual offenders, which may help to reduce the chances that antisocial behaviour will recur.

The context of risk assessment

Professional judgement is still widely thought to have an indispensable contribution to make to risk assessment (Monahan 1997). Integrating the findings in this area, Monahan and his colleagues (2001) have urged that risk assessment be carried out within an explicit, structured framework. This should be informed by the use of well-tested actuarial instruments, allocating factors that appear to affect judgements of an individual's risk level in a stepwise, systematic method which they call a *classification tree*. They further advocate that when this is done it should be repeated several times using a slightly different approach each time. Only when there is sufficient agreement between assessments carried out in different ways can confidence be felt in the predictions made (Monahan *et al.* 2001).

The background to this cautious approach is the heavy burden of expectation placed on the outcomes of risk assessment. Though improvements in predictive accuracy have been quite impressive, whatever advances are still to be made and however sophisticated any approaches may eventually become, they are unlikely ever to be error-free. Such empirical findings have then to be placed in the wider context of the ethical issues raised by behavioural prediction. Risk assessment intrinsically involves attempting to strike a balance between the rights and interests of persons being assessed and of the community's need for safety. We will consider the challenges arising from this more fully in Chapter 8.

A framework for crime prevention

The findings reviewed in this chapter have a second practical application in helping to inform direct work with offenders: the attempt to reduce rates of crime. The identification of risk factors can enable practitioners to choose between more and less effective methods of working, and to design and deliver services accordingly. There is now a growing number of evidence-based approaches to that task. The wealth of them is such that we need a framework for organizing them. There are several schemes for doing this (see, for example, MacKenzie 1997; Farrington 2002). The most straightforward, adapted from Guerra *et al.* (1994), classifies crime prevention approaches into three principal types: *primary, secondary* and *tertiary*.

Primary prevention is an attempt to stop crimes from being committed. One version of it, influenced mainly by criminological research, includes situational or community-oriented initiatives, designed to remove criminal opportunities or protect likely targets (Eck 2002; Pease 2002). These interventions are often based on the rational choice model of offending behaviour and a detailed exposition of them is beyond the scope of this book. Much of this is done through environmental or policing measures (better street lighting, CCTV cameras, anti-theft locks, security coding) or by heightening community awareness (neighbourhood watch, publicity campaigns). In a different form, primary prevention also includes various forms of long-term *developmental prevention*. Here, additional services are provided on a population-wide basis for children and families in potentially criminogenic environments, such as impoverished urban neighbourhoods (Schweinhart *et al.* 1993; Yoshikawa 1994; Farrington and Welsh 2002; Farrington and Coid 2003).

Secondary prevention has received much less attention in the research literature. It entails provision of services to children or adolescents who are manifesting other problems thought to place them at risk of involvement in delinquency, for example because of truancy from school. It may also involve educational or community-based initiatives to tackle problems like bullying or vandalism, by addressing them while at a low level before they escalate to greater seriousness (Goldstein 1996, 2002).

Tertiary prevention denotes efforts to reduce recidivism among adjudicated offenders: those already convicted of crimes and being managed by the penal system (Gendreau and Andrews 1990). Crime prevention efforts at this level are the central theme of the next chapter.

Further reading

A general review of concepts and background research on developmental studies of criminal offending is given by David P. Farrington (2002) in his chapter 'Developmental criminology and risk-focused prevention', in *The Oxford Handbook of Criminology* edited by Mike Maguire, Rod Morgan and Robert Reiner (2002, 3rd edn. Oxford: Oxford University Press). See also the edited volume by Terence P. Thornberry and Marvin D. Krohn (eds., 2003) *Taking Stock of Delinquency: An Overview of Findings from Contemporary Longitudinal Studies* (New York: Kluver Academic/Plenum Publishers). A useful general text which focuses particular attention on developmental issues is Michael Rutter, Henri Giller and Ann Hagell (1998) *Antisocial Behaviour by Young People* (Cambridge: Cambridge University Press). For an introduction to meta-analysis, see Mark W. Lipsey and David B. Wilson (2001) *Practical Meta-Analysis* (Thousand Oaks, CA: Sage Publications).

chapter six

Preventing and reducing crime

For most of the last three decades, the possibility of reducing crime by working directly with those who have committed it was regarded as an elusive and probably unrealistic goal. In recent years, that position has been quite dramatically reversed. There is currently a widespread, though by no means unanimous view that 'offender rehabilitation' can be practical, achievable and cost-effective. For many years, research findings pertaining to this were the subject of spirited and sometimes acrimonious debate. Borrowing the title of a very influential article that helped to set it in motion, this controversy is sometimes encapsulated in the phrase 'what works'. While the exact points at issue have changed over time, the debate is still going on and seems likely to continue.

In this chapter, we will consider the kinds of methods used to generate the evidence entered into that dispute. Next, we will survey the evidence itself: particularly the conclusion that recidivism rates can be reduced, even among firmly entrenched offenders. The chapter will continue with some illustrations of the kinds of methods used to achieve these outcomes, for young and adult offenders and for specific types of offence.

Background to the debate

The research literature relevant to evaluating the comparative outcome of various forms of intervention with offenders was comprehensively reviewed during the 1970s on both sides of the Atlantic. In the United States, the government of New York State commissioned a report on the effectiveness of rehabilitation with offenders. Although this work began in 1968, its final version incorporating the findings of 231 studies was not published in book form until the mid-1970s (Lipton *et al.* 1975). At approximately the same time, the Home Office in the United Kingdom undertook a similar project to review the outcome of 100 studies on the effectiveness of sentencing (Brody 1976).

The authors of these reports found the field to be characterized by relatively poor-quality research from which, in the main, no clear conclusions could be drawn. The most frequently cited overview is a journal paper by Robert Martinson (1974), which was an early by-product of the US-based review and is the origin of the phrase 'what works'. Its pessimistic conclusions regarding the ineffectiveness of rehabilitation are considered to have had a significant impact on penology since that time. According to Martinson, the results 'give us very little reason to hope that we have in fact found a sure way of reducing recidivism through rehabilitation'. He surmised that 'education at its best, or psychotherapy at its best, cannot overcome, or even appreciably reduce, the powerful tendency for offenders to continue in criminal behavior' (p. 49).

The publication of Martinson's article has been described as 'a watershed event. In many ways, it ended a 150-year-old era of optimism about the possibilities of reforming the offender' (Gaes 1998: 713). Its conclusions were vigorously rebutted by a number of researchers (e.g. Palmer 1975), mainly on the grounds that positive evidence had been ignored, though others accepted the original conclusions (e.g. Plattner 1976). At a later stage, Gendreau and Ross (1980) published a paper pointedly entitled 'bibliotherapy for cynics', and edited a volume containing a collection of research studies with more favourable outcomes.

By that time, however, Martinson (1979) had already re-analysed some of the data on which he had earlier worked. This led him to overturn his initial negative conclusions: 'I have often said that treatment added to the networks of criminal justice is "impotent", and I withdraw this characterization' (p. 254). Reaching for an account that would be 'more adequate to the facts at hand' (p. 252), Martinson concluded instead that some interventions were beneficial, others not, and some were downright harmful: 'The critical fact seems to be the *conditions* under which the program is delivered' (p. 254, emphasis in original).

The extent to which subsequent changes in penal policy and practice, mainly towards more punitive sentencing, really can be attributed to the impact of Martinson's first paper, or were the manifestation of a trend that would have occurred in any case, is difficult to discern. In the United States, a report of the Committee for the Study of Incarceration (von Hirsch 1976), which was dismissive of treatment and advocated a justice policy based on desert and deterrence, may have been influential. But that report also strongly recommended 'stringent limitations' on the use of imprisonment. Whatever its origin, there was a widening endorsement of the 'death of treatment'. In the United Kingdom, for example, probation officers were urged to demote it in their list of working priorities (Bottoms and McWilliams 1979).

The ensuing period in criminal justice has been colloquially dubbed the era of 'nothing works'. It was not until the mounting volume of review evidence of the 1980s and 1990s achieved some critical mass of persuasiveness that, to repeat a widely used metaphor, the pendulum began to swing back again in the direction of thinking that offender rehabilitation was possible. Before we look more closely at the character of that evidence itself, it will be useful to outline the methods by which it was obtained.

Discovering 'what works' through meta-analysis

In the previous chapter, we encountered the method of *meta-analysis* as an important tool for synthesizing research findings and making sense of data from a range of sources. In the material described there, meta-analysis was used to clarify the relationships between variables across a large number of studies. In asking 'what works?', the objective is slightly different. The focus is on comparing outcomes. The main question of interest is whether there are any methods that will serve to 'rehabilitate' or reduce the recidivism of offenders.

In summarizing the trends that are found, the variable of prime interest is once again the effect size. In intervention studies, it indicates the relative impact of the experimental (treatment) and comparison (no treatment) conditions on the dependent variable. In work with offenders, the most frequently reported outcome is the rate of recidivism in the two groups, though of course there could be other outcomes as well. If at the end of an experimental study the effect size were zero, that would mean the two groups did not differ in recidivism rates: the experimental intervention made no difference. Where experimental group effects are superior to those for the controls, it is conventional to express the effect size in numerically positive terms. If you are unfortunate enough to find the experimental group has fared worse than the controls (meaning in this case, they have committed more crimes), the effect size will be numerically negative. As its name implies, the mean effect size is simply an average of the effects found across all the studies included in a review, or across some sub-set of them selected for a particular purpose.

There are several different effect size estimates. In reviews of outcome research in criminal justice, three main types have been used (Lipsey and Wilson 2001; Wilson 2001):

- The *correlation coefficient*. There are several forms of this, the most widely used being Pearson's r, used to compute a correlation between two continuous variables, such as hours of contact and subsequent rates of recidivism. If the variables are dichotomous (i.e. assigned to two categories such as success versus failure, or improvement versus no improvement), another version of this statistic, called the *phi* coefficient (φ), is used instead. Correlation coefficients will be positive if the experimental group has done better than the controls (in this instance, has lower recidivism), negative if the reverse transpires and zero if there is no effect (nothing works).
- The *standardized mean difference* (known in slightly differing forms by various names including Cohen's d, Hedges's g). This is probably the most easily interpreted way of grasping what a meta-analysis has found. It compares changes in the respective means of experimental and control samples from pre-test to post-test. So it will allow a conclusion to be drawn such as 'the re-conviction rate of the experimental group was 15% lower than that of the controls'.
- The *odds ratio* expresses the chances of one of two outcomes (such as whether or not a person has been re-convicted) for the two study groups (experimental and comparison) relative to each other. This, too, is intuitively appealing, as it conveys a sense of the extent to which one group out-performed the other (or not, as the case may be), and membership of it increased the chances or odds of a successful outcome.

There are formulae for converting one type of effect size into another, so that different studies or reviews can be compared in terms of a 'common metric'. One particularly useful tool is a tabular format known as the *binomial effect size display* or BESD (Rosenthal and Rubin 1982), which provides a kind of instant picture of the size of an effect. Both standardized mean differences and correlation coefficients can easily be converted into a 2 × 2 table showing respective outcomes for the experimental and comparison groups. This *success rate differential* gives a straightforward representation of the scale of an effect. Table 6.1 shows examples, using imaginary but plausible data, for three arbitrarily

Table 6.1 Binomial effect size display for three measured effect sizes

	No recidivism	Recidivism	Total
Experimental	52.5	47.5	100
Comparison	47.5	52.5	100
Total	100.0	100.0	200

Effect size (a): standardized mean difference = 0.10
correlation coefficient = 0.05
percent reduction in offending
(experimental relative to comparison) = 9.5% (5/52.5)

	No recidivism	Recidivism	Total
Experimental	55.0	45.0	100
Comparison	45.0	55.0	100
Total	100.0	100.0	200

Effect size (b): standardized mean difference = 0.20
correlation coefficient = 0.10
percent reduction in offending
(experimental relative to comparison) = 18.2% (10/55)

	No recidivism	Recidivism	Total
Experimental	62.0	38.0	100
Comparison	38.0	62.0	100
Total	100.0	100.0	200

Effect size (c): standardized mean difference = 0.50
correlation coefficient = 0.24
percent reduction in offending
(experimental relative to comparison) = 38.7% (24/62)

chosen effect sizes ranging from unabashedly small to disarmingly moderate.

Meta-analysis has now been so widely employed as an approach to integrating the results of outcome studies in social science that even by the beginning of the 1990s there were over 300 such reviews in the behavioural sciences literature alone (Lipsey and Wilson 1993). Petrosino (2000) has compiled an annotated listing of meta-analyses in criminology and allied disciplines including others addressing primary and secondary prevention, and which focus on a wider range of outcome variables such as drug use, school vandalism and sexual abuse.

Main features of the reviews

The first meta-analytic review to focus on offenders was published in 1985. Between then and approximately mid-2003, a total of 42 such reviews appeared. Let us now look at some of their key features:

- *Sources*. The majority of them, and the bulk of the primary research on which they are based, originate from North America – although data from many countries are encompassed within them, and several have been conducted in Europe. Most are published in the English language, but in the largest review so far conducted (Pearson *et al.* 1997), contacts were made with 14 non-English-speaking countries and more than 300 reports obtained in languages other than English.

- *Gender.* The overwhelming majority of the primary studies deals with male offenders. In one of the largest meta-analyses, carried out by Lipsey (1992, 1995), only 3% of published studies focused solely on samples of female offenders. A later review by Dowden and Andrews (1999a) was specifically designed to counterbalance this, and explored whether similar patterns of effects as found with men would be obtained from studies with women offenders.

- *Age.* About two-thirds of the reviews focus on interventions with adolescent or young adult offenders in the age range 14–21. This covers the peak age for offending in most countries. Several of the remainder are concerned exclusively with adults, but a few include offenders across a wide range of ages.

- *Ethnicity.* While many primary studies provide data on the proportions of offenders from different ethnic groups, the pattern of this is variable and it is not consistently recorded in the analyses. However, particularly given the over-representation of African-Americans and members of other minority communities under criminal justice jurisdiction in the USA, and similar configurations in the UK and other countries, these findings are based on populations containing a broad admixture in terms of ethnicity. One review has focused explicitly on the question of whether there are differences in outcome effects with different ethnic groups (Wilson *et al.* 2003).

- *Authorship.* Research in this area is a genuinely multidisciplinary enterprise. Some reviewers have coded the professional backgrounds of those who undertook the primary studies. For example, Lipsey and Wilson (1998) reviewed 200 reports on the outcomes of work with serious and violent young offenders. Of these studies, they found that 29% of the senior authors were from psychology and 19% from criminology. Other backgrounds represented included sociology (8%), education (7%), psychiatry (4%), political science (3%) and social work (2%), though for a further 28% of the studies no main discipline was identifiable.

Ground covered

Table 6.2 lists the reviews, ordered chronologically according to date of publication, showing the number of findings analysed and mean effect sizes where available. To provide an overview of all this work at a glance as it were, the following is a list of the areas covered in the reviews showing the number carried out under various headings. (Note, however, that most reviews include a range of studies and the principal focus could be defined in different ways.)

- Young offenders 9
- Sex offenders 5
- Deterrence/sanctions 5
- Cognitive/non-cognitive focus 1
- Violence 2
- Drink-drive 1
- Substance-abuse 1
- European studies 3
- CDATE 1
- Educational/vocational 1

- Therapeutic communities 2
- Family-based interventions 2
- Cognitive-behavioural methods 2
- 'Principles of human service' 1
- Restorative justice 1
- School-based interventions 1
- Gender effects 1
- Ethnicity effects 1
- Age effects 1
- Personality disorder 1

Table 6.2 Meta-analyses of outcome studies

Author(s) and date of publication	Focus of review	Number of tests	Mean effect size reported
Garrett 1985	Young offenders in residential placements	121	+0.18
Gensheimer et al. 1986	Diversion schemes for young offenders	31	+0.26
Mayer et al. 1986	Social learning-based interventions	17	+0.33
Gottschalk et al. 1987a	Community-based interventions	61	+0.22
Gottschalk et al. 1987b	Behavioural interventions	14	+0.25
Lösel and Koferl 1989	Sociotherapeutic prison regimes in Germany	16	+0.12
Whitehead and Lab 1989	Young offenders: general	50	+0.13
Andrews et al. 1990b	Test of model of 'human service principles'	154	+0.10
Izzo and Ross 1990	Cognitive versus non-cognitive interventions	46	2.5/1
Roberts and Camasso 1991	Young offenders: general	46	NA
Lipsey 1992, 1995, 1999	Offenders aged 12–21	397	+0.10
Hall 1995	Sexual offending	12	+0.12
Wells-Parker et al. 1995	Drink-driving offences	215	8–9%
Gendreau and Goggin 1996	Deterrence and intermediate punishment	138	0.00
Cleland et al. 1997	Impact of age as moderator variable	659	NA
Pearson et al. 1997	CDATE Project: comprehensive review	846	NA
Redondo et al. 1997	European programmes	57	+0.12

Author(s) and date of publication	Focus of review	Number of tests	Mean effect size reported
Lipsey and Wilson 1998	Serious violent and sexual offending by youth	83, 117	+0.10, +0.14
Alexander 1999	Sexual offending	79	+0.10
Dowden and Andrews 1999a	Programmes for women offenders	24	NA
Dowden and Andrews 1999b	Young offenders: general	229	+0.09
Gallagher et al. 1999	Sexual offending	25	d = +0.43
Pearson and Lipton 1999	Substance abuse treatment and offending	30	NA
Polizzi et al. 1999	Sexual offending	13	NA
Redondo et al. 1999	European programmes	32	+0.12
Dowden and Andrews 2000	Interventions for violent offenders	52	+0.07
Petrosino et al. 2000	Scared straight programmes	9	−0.01
Wilson et al. 2000	Educational and vocational programmes, adults	53	OR = 1.52
Wilson and Lipsey 2000	Wilderness challenge programmes	22	+0.18
Gendreau et al. 2001	Intermediate punishment	140	0.00
Lipsey et al. 2001	Cognitive-behavioural interventions	14	OR = 0.66
MacKenzie et al. 2001	Correctional boot camps	44	OR = 1.02
Wilson et al. 2001	School-based interventions	40	d = +0.04
Hanson et al. 2002	Sexual offending	43	OR = 0.81, 0.56
Lipton et al. 2002a	Therapeutic communities	35	+0.14
Lipton et al. 2002b	Cognitive-behavioural interventions	68	+0.12
Redondo et al. 2002	European programmes	23	+0.21
Salekin 2002	Personality disorders	5	NA
Woolfenden et al. 2002	Family-based interventions	5	OR = 0.66
Andrews and Bonta 2003	Restorative justice	44	+0.03
Farrington and Welsh 2003	Family-based interventions	40	+0.32
Wilson et al. 2003	Impact of ethnicity as moderator variable	305	NA

The first published meta-analysis of work with offenders was an evaluation of the impact of institutionally based interventions for juvenile offenders (Garrett 1985). Garrett surveyed 111 studies conducted in the period 1960–1984, describing residential treatment programmes. Altogether, 13,055 individuals with a mean age of 15.8 years were involved in the studies. Since then, another eight meta-analyses have been conducted covering a wide range of interventions with young offenders. Some authors limited themselves to the earlier adolescent age range (Whitehead and Lab 1989; Roberts and Camasso 1991), while others covered up to age 21 and so included young adults (Lipsey 1992, 1995; Dowden and Andrews 1999b). In addition, there have been reviews of community-based interventions with young offenders (Gottschalk *et al.* 1987a). The latter research group have also evaluated behavioural or social learning based interventions (Mayer *et al.* 1986; Gottschalk *et al.* 1987b) and the impact of diversion schemes (Gensheimer *et al.* 1986).

Turning to offence types or offender classifications, five reviews have been published on interventions with sex offenders, including both adolescents and adults (Hall 1995; Alexander 1999; Gallagher *et al.* 1999; Polizzi *et al.* 1999; Hanson *et al.* 2002; see also Marshall and McGuire 2003). There is one meta-analysis on violent offenders (Dowden and Andrews 2000) and one on young offenders convicted of violent, sexual or other serious crimes (Lipsey and Wilson 1998). The remaining specific offence-focused review is of interventions for drink-driving offenders (Wells-Parker *et al.* 1995). Finally, one review focused on offenders categorized as having personality disorders (Salekin 2002).

Several reviews have focused on different types of punitive sanctions. This includes two, though with many overlapping studies, on 'intermediate punishment' (Gendreau and Goggin 1996; Gendreau *et al.* 2001). Another dealt with 'scared straight' interventions (Petrosino *et al.* 2000), one with correctional boot camps (MacKenzie *et al.* 2001) and one with outdoor-pursuit, 'wilderness challenge' schemes (Wilson and Lipsey 2000). Bear in mind, of course, that several other meta-analyses also included studies evaluating punishment or deterrence-based procedures.

With regard to specific types of intervention, in addition to those for young offenders already mentioned, one review is available on educational and vocational programmes for adults (Wilson *et al.* 2000). There is one review of the impact of specially designed socio-therapeutic prison regimes in Germany (Lösel and Koferl 1989); its findings were also incorporated in a later, wider-ranging review of therapeutic communities (Lipton *et al.* 2002a). There are two meta-analyses of the effectiveness of cognitive-behavioural programmes, one using fairly liberal inclusion criteria and subsuming 68 studies (Lipton *et al.* 2002b), the other applying much stricter inclusion criteria, containing only 14 studies (Lipsey *et al.* 2001). There are two reviews of family-based interventions (Woolfenden *et al.* 2002; Farrington and Welsh 2003), one of school-based interventions (Wilson *et al.* 2001; see also Gottfredson *et al.* 2002) and one of the impact on recidivism of substance-abuse treatment (Pearson and Lipton 1999). Meta-analysis has also been used to synthesize findings from evaluations of restorative justice (Andrews and Bonta 2003).

The largest review of this kind so far attempted is known as the Correctional Drug Abuse Treatment Evaluation (CDATE) Project, carried out by National Development and Research Institutes (NDRI) in the USA. This project ran for a four-year period and in the course of it reports were collected from many countries. Altogether, researchers collected more than 10,000 documents. Approximately 1,600 of them were reports of intervention experiments that included recidivism as an outcome measure. Sections of the data were analysed and presented at conferences (Lipton *et al.* 1997; Pearson *et al.* 1997). However, this precious collection of documents was stored in NDRI's headquarters office, located in the World Trade Center in New York City. It was lost in its entirety when the twin towers were attacked and destroyed on 11 September 2001.

Several reviews have been designed to test specific hypotheses. Given that, as previously mentioned, most of the studies and reviews are North American in origin, three successive reviews using a gradually expanding database have evaluated studies conducted in Europe (Redondo *et al.* 1997, 1999, 2002). As also previously mentioned, given the preponderance of studies with male offenders, one review has been undertaken to determine whether similar patterns of effects would be observed with females (Dowden and Andrews 1999a). Another tested whether 'mainstream' forms of intervention used with white offenders are equally effective with ethnic minorities (Wilson *et al.* 2003). Using a sub-set of the CDATE collection of studies, another review tested whether effect sizes differ according to the age group of study participants (Cleland *et al.* 1997). A review by Izzo and Ross (1990) was designed to evaluate whether structured programmes containing 'cognitive training' activities achieved higher effect sizes than those without such elements.

Finally, possibly one of the most influential reviews (Andrews *et al.* 1990b) tested the hypothesis that interventions adhering to certain principles (allocating offenders according to risk levels and factors, and employing selected methods of working), would yield higher effect sizes than other types of work. The thinking behind this developed in three stages. First, on the basis of criminological and psychological literature, Andrews and his colleagues generated a theoretical model of risk factors for offending behaviour. Second, they then used the model heuristically to formulate a set of hypotheses regarding elements of interventions that were most likely to contribute to reducing recidivism. Third, a set of 154 outcome studies was sub-divided into four groups according to the extent to which they possessed those elements. These groups were designated *appropriate service, unspecified service, inappropriate service* and *criminal sanctions*, respectively. The observed effect sizes differed systematically in the order predicted by the model. These findings provided a powerful demonstration of the possibility of delineating a cluster of factors that could be shown to increase the likelihood of success in reducing recidivism (Andrews *et al.* 1990a).

Limitations of the reviews

Meta-analysis has been subjected to some severe criticism, on a variety of grounds. If the quality of the original research is poor, it will not really be permissible to draw any neat conclusions, even from the most carefully conducted review of it (the phrase 'garbage in, garbage out' comes to mind). Adjudicated offenders – those who have appeared in court, been convicted of a crime and sentenced – are managed by criminal justice agencies. Given the circumstances in which most research of this kind takes place, there are limitations on the design of evaluation studies. It can be difficult to use random allocation to experimental and comparison samples, and the members of these groups are often not well matched, as researchers may have little control over who is placed under what conditions. There is all too often a comparatively short period of follow-up: six months is by no means uncommon, though there are plenty of studies with one-year or two-year follow-ups, and a few where data have been collected for as long as four or five years. Sometimes sample sizes are small at the start of a study, and the problem of drop-out (technically known as 'attrition') makes them even smaller at the end. It has also been alleged that positive outcomes are purely a product of selection effects: if offenders participating in whatever is called the 'treatment' change, it is mainly because they were motivated to do so (Simon 1998). The widely cited review by Andrews and his colleagues (1990b) has been attacked on the grounds that it is based on a circular or tautological argument (Logan and Gaes 1993). That is, it entails identifying features that contribute to positive outcomes, labelling them as 'appropriate treatment', and then pretending to test a hypothesis that interventions with the identified features are the ones most likely to work.

Another problem is known as 'publication bias': the possibility that those research studies that appear in print are unrepresentative of the research actually done. It is well known that studies finding nil effects (statistically non-significant findings) are less likely to see the light of day. So resting our conclusions on the ones that do may give a very distorted picture. Finally, when attempting to review studies, anything other than the most 'broad brush' conclusions can be difficult to draw. Although the volume of research output in this field is quite large, approaching 2,000 separate primary studies, when looked at more closely the number in any given category (or 'cell') might be fairly small (Lösel 2001).

Many of these factors can be corrected in meta-analysis, though there are limits to how much it is possible to compensate for badly done primary research. But studies with larger samples can be given more weight, and well-designed and poorly designed experiments can be evaluated separately to see if they obtain broadly similar effects. Also, while the reviewers of the 1970s understandably deplored the dismal quality of much research conducted before then, there is evidence that there have been sizeable improvements in the research done in more recent years.

Publication bias cannot be eradicated, but it can be minimized by making every possible effort to locate unpublished studies. It can also be taken account of by computing what is known as the *file-drawer number* (also called the *fail-safe number*). Imagine that you have conducted a review of this kind and obtained a positive mean effect size. You suspect there may be unpublished studies that have found zero or negative effects. The file-drawer *n* is the number of unpublished studies with zero or negative effect sizes that would be needed to annul your observed effect size. If the latter is very large or your cache of studies is very large (or both), there would have to be many unpublished zero-effect sizes to undermine it. You are entitled to feel more confident that the finding is 'real'. If, on the other hand, you have located few studies and your effect size though positive is rather weak, there could easily be enough studies out there to negate it. So calculating the fail-safe *n* allows researchers to express their findings with greater or lesser assurance, depending on the strength of the different factors involved.

The comments by Logan and Gaes (1993) on the meta-analysis by Andrews and others (1990b) appear to be based on a misunderstanding of the logic of that review. Extracting a pattern from a sub-set of data (in one study or a set of studies) and then using it to test associated hypotheses across the whole data array is an accepted confirmatory principle in research. The criticisms also miss the point that there were independent theoretical grounds for predicting the pattern that was observed. In any case, the sheer weight of findings accumulated since 1990 undermines the allegation that the findings were somehow manufactured by sleight of hand.

General impact

What a journalist might call the front-page banner headline, scanning results across all meta-analyses, is that the impact of intervention is on average positive. That is, it is associated with a net reduction in recidivism in experimental relative to comparison samples. This sharply contradicts the commonly repeated assertion that 'nothing works' (Hollin 1999, 2001a; Lösel 2001; McGuire 2002a).

However, the average effect taken across a broad spectrum of different types of treatment or intervention is relatively modest. Expressed as a correlation coefficient, it is estimated on average to be approximately 0.10 (Lösel 1995). This can be represented in a different form using the *binomial effect size display* described above. A correlation of 0.10 translates to an average difference of 10 percentage points between experimental and control groups across all the intervention studies. The BESD compares outcomes for the two groups against a hypothetical situation where the expected rate of recidivism across all groups is 50%. The average finding obtained from the meta-analyses corresponds to recidivism rates of 45% for the experimental groups and 55% for the control groups, respectively. That situation is shown in the central section of Table 6.1. Cohen (1988) has proposed a broad classification of effect sizes, suggesting that those in the region of 0.20 or less are small, those in the region of 0.50 are moderate and those in the region of 0.80 and above are large. While this is a very rough-and-ready guide, many researchers refer to it as a useful yardstick. According to Cohen's scheme, then, this is a relatively small effect.

Remember, however, that the effect we are discussing here is averaged across all types of intervention. The experimental 'treatments' studied in this research can consist of a huge variety of approaches. They include criminal sanctions (punishment), which as we will see in more detail in Chapter 7, have often been found to have zero and sometimes even negative effect sizes. If such effects were excluded from the overall calculation, the average for the remaining treatments would be higher than 0.10.

But given that its overall scale is apparently unremarkable, the question inevitably arises as to whether this finding tells us anything meaningful in practical or policy terms. One way of putting this in perspective is to consider the distinction between what Rosenthal (1994) has called *statistical* and *practical* significance. The mean effect size obtained here, although small, is statistically significant and compares reasonably well with those found in other fields (Lipsey 1995). Some healthcare interventions that are generally regarded as producing worthwhile benefits have lower mean effect sizes. Others with mean effects only marginally higher are in receipt of considerable public investment (Lipsey and Wilson 1993). McGuire (2002a) tabulated a series of effect sizes from various sources and found the following. For the impact of aspirin in reducing the risk of myocardial infarction (a type of heart attack), the effect size was 0.034; for chemotherapy reducing the risk of recurrence of breast cancer, 0.08; for bypass surgery reducing the risk of coronary heart disease, 0.15.

But in any case, like all averages, the figure just discussed simplifies the picture. As the old joke goes, it is possible to drown in a pool of water averaging only six inches deep. Within various sub-groups of the studies that have been reviewed, there are quite large differences in effect sizes. As we will see below, the patterning of this has proved to be much more informative than the grand mean. There are, of course, many sources of the observed variation between studies, but when artefacts such as the study design and other methodological influences have been discounted, some consistent trends still emerge. In the following section, we will examine some of the details within these trends.

Patterns in effect sizes

Not surprisingly given the complexity of the research we are discussing, even when methodological influences have been allowed for, there are still many factors at work. The scale of effects is moderated by several variables; some of the most important include the following:

- *Age differences*. On average, effect sizes are larger for adolescent and for adult offenders than for those in what is usually called the 'young adult' age range. Cleland *et al.* (1997) analysed age trends in effect sizes across a set of 659 studies, with a cumulative sample size of 157,038. All the effect sizes obtained were positive and significant – that is, interventions led to a net overall reduction in recidivism. The mean effect size for offender samples below 15 years of age was 0.09, for those aged 15–18 it was 0.04 and for adults it was 0.05. When values for 'appropriate treatment' were computed, defining this along the guidelines proposed by Andrews *et al.* (1990b), the corresponding mean effect sizes for the three age groups were 0.16, 0.11 and 0.17, respectively. The largest single effect sizes reported to date have been with intensive, multi-faceted interventions for serious young offenders (see below).

- *Institution versus community*. While the prison is often accorded central place in many images of the dispensation of justice, several reviews indicate that, on balance, community-based interventions have larger effect sizes than those delivered in institutions (e.g. Andrews *et al.* 1990b; Redondo *et al.* 1997; Lipsey and Wilson 1998). When similar programmes have been compared in their relative effects in institutional or community settings, the latter out-performed the former in terms of reduced recidivism. The ratio of relative effect sizes obtained has ranged from approximately 1.33 : 1 to as high as 1.75 : 1. But there are some complex interactions between settings in which interventions are provided, the types of methods used, and the 'quality of delivery' or the way in which the work is done. The best-designed services are of greatest benefit when provided in a non-custodial setting. By contrast, badly designed, inappropriate forms of intervention will probably be ineffective regardless of the context (e.g. institution versus community). But even well-designed intervention programmes may have zero and possibly even negative effects if the quality of delivery is poor.

- *Offence type*. Another trend noted in some meta-analyses is that effect sizes for property offences (theft, burglary, robbery) or for drug-related offences are typically lower than those obtained for personal (violent and sexual) offences (e.g. Redondo *et al.* 1999). The number of studies for which this kind of comparison can be made is, however, relatively small. Were this finding consistently replicated, we might speculate that it is partly a function of the potentially larger role played by social and environmental factors in the occurrence of property crimes. That issue was discussed to some extent in Chapter 3. More research is needed before it can be resolved (McGuire 2001a).

Factors contributing to effectiveness

We have seen that the average effect size across all interventions is not especially large. That may leave us feeling disappointed – though the situation is not dissimilar to one found in several other fields. But we noted, too, that some rather poor outcomes deflate the observed mean effect. This points to potentially the most striking aspect of the findings, and in some respects the most revealing one: the *heterogeneity* among the effect sizes obtained. There are many sources of this variability. Meta-analysts have expended considerable energy in attempting to detach those parts of it that are due to methodological attributes of the primary studies, from those which tell us something about the area we are investigating.

Once discrete sources of error and other types of variation between studies have been accounted for, the remaining effect size patterns should enable us to draw conclusions about different aspects of interventions themselves. What can then be described as the most effective kinds of intervention are those which achieve the largest effect sizes with the greatest consistency.

There is now a broad consensus that it is possible to maximize effect sizes by combining a number of elements in offender programmes (Andrews 1995, 2001; Gendreau 1996a; Hollin 1999). Effective interventions are thought to possess certain common features, which Andrews and his colleagues (1990b) called 'principles of human service'. Taking this a step further, if we can empirically identify those features from past outcome studies, it should be possible to design interventions that can be tested in future studies. If the results conform to the same pattern as found before, this provides confirmation of the value of the approach, and builds up confidence both in the methods being employed and in the theoretical model underpinning them. When Andrews and his associates pinpointed those features that contributed separately to enhancing effect size, they found that the combination of them produced an additive effect, corresponding to a reduction in recidivism rates of 53%. That figure, alongside a selection of others illustrating the range of findings in the meta-analyses, is displayed graphically in Figure 6.1.

First the down side

But before we examine more positive findings, the meta-analyses also provide some useful indications regarding interventions that seem not to work. Counter to the expectations of many people, one of them is punishment or deterrence, an issue we will probe more fully in the next chapter. There are some other approaches, too, that receive little or no support as effective methods of working. The main types include:

Category of intervention

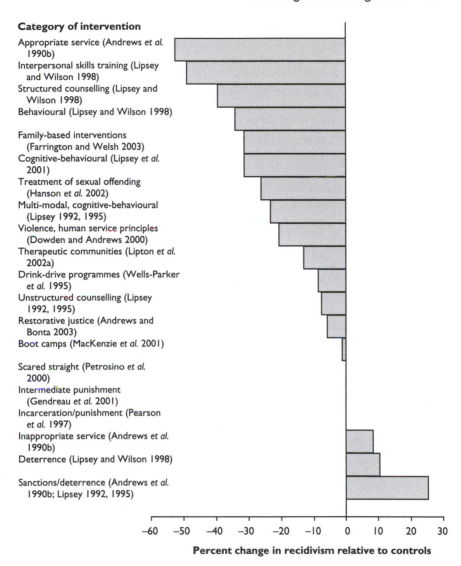

Appropriate service (Andrews *et al.*
    1990b)
Interpersonal skills training (Lipsey
    and Wilson 1998)
Structured counselling (Lipsey and
    Wilson 1998)
Behavioural (Lipsey and Wilson 1998)

Family-based interventions
    (Farrington and Welsh 2003)
Cognitive-behavioural (Lipsey *et al.*
    2001)
Treatment of sexual offending
    (Hanson *et al.* 2002)
Multi-modal, cognitive-behavioural
    (Lipsey 1992, 1995)
Violence, human service principles
    (Dowden and Andrews 2000)
Therapeutic communities (Lipton *et al.*
    2002a)
Drink-drive programmes (Wells-Parker
    et al. 1995)
Unstructured counselling (Lipsey
    1992, 1995)
Restorative justice (Andrews and
    Bonta 2003)
Boot camps (MacKenzie *et al.* 2001)

Scared straight (Petrosino *et al.*
    2000)
Intermediate punishment
    (Gendreau *et al.* 2001)
Incarceration/punishment (Pearson
    et al. 1997)
Inappropriate service (Andrews *et al.*
    1990b)
Deterrence (Lipsey and Wilson 1998)

Sanctions/deterrence (Andrews *et al.*
    1990b; Lipsey 1992, 1995)

−60 −50 −40 −30 −20 −10   0   10   20   30

Percent change in recidivism relative to controls

Figure 6.1 Illustrative variations in effect sizes

- Vocational training activities that do not lead to genuine prospects of employment. In other words, people are prepared for employment, or shown how to look for a job, including interview practice and so on, but there are no real jobs available for them at the end. This appears to result in increased recidivism (Lipsey 1992, 1995; Lipsey and Wilson 1998), though the number of studies pertaining to it is fairly small.
- Outdoor pursuit or 'wilderness challenge' programmes. These have yielded mainly weak or non-existent effects, unless they are accom-

panied by sessions of high-quality training or therapeutic elements (Lipsey 1992, 1995; Lipsey and Wilson 1998; Wilson and Lipsey 2000).
- So-called 'scared straight' programmes. Here, youthful or novice offenders are taken to meet serious 'heavy-end' criminals in high-security prisons. On average, these lead to a slight increase in recidivism (Gendreau *et al.* 2001) and some researchers have declared them to be potentially damaging (Petrosino *et al.* 2000).
- There is very little evidence that interventions based on psychodynamic approaches or allied models, unstructured counselling, milieu therapy, or other methods based on the assumed promotion of insight, lead to positive effects on the reduction of re-offending. Each of them may be valuable for other therapeutic purposes. But in terms of leading to reductions in offending behaviour, they receive very little support.

Finally, given the well-established linkage between drug abuse and crime, we might expect that treatment for substance abuse problems would have an indirect effect on the rate of recidivism. Not so: evidence in support of substance abuse treatment or drug abstinence programmes as a means of reducing recidivism among young offenders is unexpectedly weak. Two meta-analyses have addressed this point. The effects obtained were only slightly positive and not significantly different from zero (Lipsey and Wilson 1998; Dowden and Andrews 1999b).

Structured programmes

Returning to the more positive findings of the reviews, probably the most widely disseminated innovation flowing from the above findings has been the synthesis of methods and materials into a number of prearranged formats known as *programmes*. This word sounds sinister to some people. Perhaps it conjures up images of a rigid and highly prescriptive method of working, or carries undertones of authoritarian, Orwellian interference in people's lives, tampering with their thinking to keep them under control.

To dispel these suspicions, it may help to note first that the word 'programme' has several interrelated meanings. McGuire (2001c) has distinguished three. In the first, strictest sense, a programme can be defined simply as consisting of *a planned sequence of learning opportunities*. Used in criminal justice settings, its general objective is to reduce participants' subsequent criminal recidivism. Within that context, the typical programme is a circumscribed set of activities, with an appointed objective, and consisting of a number of elements interconnected according to a planned design. The closest parallel to it in other settings is that of a *curriculum* in a college or school. In essence, this is a psycho-educational or training enterprise, with an emphasis on change through positive reinforcement rather than punishment. Gendreau (1996b), for example, has indicated that in a criminal justice programme, positive reinforcers should out-number punishers in a ratio of not less than 4 : 1.

However, in criminal justice the word 'programme' is also used in a second, broader and more flexible sense. For example, mentoring schemes for young offenders, or therapeutic communities for substance-abusing offenders, are also referred to as programmes. In the core sense of the preceding definition, the term is here a misnomer. Yet it is possible to specify the objectives of both these processes and to define operationally what is intended to happen within them.

Taking a still broader perspective, MacKenzie (1997) conceptualized all criminal justice interventions as programmes, consisting of six overlapping groups: incapacitation; deterrence; rehabilitation; community restraints; structure; discipline and challenge; and combined rehabilitation and restraint. This constitutes, potentially, a third definition of the word 'programme', encompassing the full range of responses society makes to those who have broken the law.

The largest single part played by psychology has been in designing structured programmes that conform to the first of these definitions. Most such programmes currently extant in the criminal justice system use methods derived from cognitive social learning theory (one reason for its central place in this book). Programmes originating from this source carry the label *cognitive-behavioural*. While this is by no means the only theoretical option available, to date it has proven particularly valuable in shaping intervention designs. Programmes of this type are usually supported by a manual. This provides details of the methods to be used and the contents of sessions.

Features of 'likely to succeed' services

Regarding the impact of programmes, some informative and reassuringly reliable patterns have emerged from the meta-analyses concerning the approaches with the largest effect sizes in reducing offending. The most influential interpretation of the findings is probably that forwarded by the Carleton/New Brunswick group of researchers, whose work we first encountered in the preceding chapter (Andrews *et al.* 1990a,b; Gendreau and Andrews 1990; Andrews 2001; Gendreau *et al.* 2002a; Andrews and Bonta 2003). A second major influence has been the work of a group of researchers based at the universities of Maryland in the USA and Cambridge in the UK (Sherman *et al.* 1997, 2002). Segments of the latter work were commissioned by the US National Institute of Justice. Conclusions of the meta-analyses or illustrative accounts of primary studies have been presented and discussed in detail in a number of other volumes (McGuire 1995a, 2002b; Ross *et al.* 1995; Harland 1996; Bernfeld *et al.* 2001; Crow 2001; Hollin 2001b).

The principal conclusion drawn, on which there is a reasonable consensus, is that there are certain features of criminal justice interventions that maximize the likelihood of securing a practical, meaningful impact in terms of reduced re-offending. The major findings include the following:

- *Theory and evidence base*. Intervention efforts are more likely to succeed if they are based on a theory of criminal behaviour that is conceptually sound and has firm empirical support. This provides a rationale for the methods that are used and the 'vehicle of change' hypothesized to be at work when an individual participates in the programme. For example, will this be accomplished by learning new skills, changing attitudes, improving ability to communicate, increasing self-knowledge, solving problems, overcoming bad feelings?
- *Risk level*. It is widely regarded as good practice to assess risk levels and allocate individuals to different levels of service accordingly. Risk assessment is usually based on information about an individual's criminal history, using methods of the kind described in the previous chapter that assess 'static risk factors'. The most intensive types of intervention should be reserved for those offenders assessed as posing the highest risk of re-offending; those at a much lower risk level should not be allotted to such services. This has been called the *risk principle* (Andrews and Bonta 2003) and it appears to apply equally well to young and adult offenders. But while most of the data runs in this direction, the pattern has not emerged unfailingly from all reviews (Antonowicz and Ross 1994).
- *Risk factors as targets of change*. In the previous chapter we saw that certain patterns of social interaction, social or cognitive skills, attitudes and other factors are associated with an elevated risk of involvement in crime. If work with offenders is to make a difference to their prospects of re-offending, it is best focused on those factors, many of which are amenable to change. They are therefore called *dynamic risk factors* and there are clear reasons for prioritizing them in rehabilitation services. Such factors are also known as *criminogenic needs*, meaning that changing them is a prerequisite of broader behavioural change. (As we shall see in Chapter 8, interpretation of this point has been the subject of some dispute.) In our intervention efforts, then, these facets become the intermediate 'targets' of change that will contribute to bringing about the longer-term change of reduced re-offending.
- *Breadth*. Given the multiplicity of factors known to contribute to criminal activity, there is virtual unanimity among researchers that more effective interventions will comprise a number of ingredients, addressed at a range of the aforementioned risks. Interventions that successfully do this are called *multimodal*. For example, working with a group of young people might involve training in social skills, learning self-control of impulses, and providing support for these changes through a mentoring scheme. Palmer (1992) called this idea the 'breadth principle'.
- *Responsivity*. This refers to the finding that there are certain methods or approaches that have a superior track record in engaging, motivating and helping participants in criminal justice interventions to change (Gendreau and Andrews 1990; Andrews 2001). There are two aspects of this. One is *general* responsivity. Rehabilitative efforts will work better if they have clear, concrete objectives, their contents are structured,

and there is a focus on activity and the acquisition of skills (as, for example, in a training course to learn an occupational skill or a foreign language). Personnel involved in providing this should possess high-quality interpersonal skills and foster warm, collaborative relationships within clearly explained boundaries. The other is *specific* responsivity. This refers to adapting intervention strategies to accommodate difference and diversity among participants (with respect to age, gender, ethnicity, sexuality, language, learning styles).

- *Integrity*. Lipsey (1995) and other meta-analysts have noted that intervention services appear to work better when they are 'researcher monitored'. There is a cynical view that this happens because said researchers have manipulated the results. Having discounted this scurrilous imputation, the best interpretation of the finding is that regular collection of data on how an intervention is delivered sustains its clarity of purpose and adherence to the methods it was intended to deploy. This feature is called *integrity* or *fidelity* of an intervention (Hollin 1995; Bernfeld 2001). It is sometimes divided into two sub-types. *Programme integrity* is preserved when, in providing rehabilitative services, managers of an agency ensure that adequate resources are available; including appropriately trained staff, who have access to suitable accommodation, sufficient time, supervision and other supports. *Treatment integrity* refers to the quality of delivery of the programme sessions or other direct contacts between staff and offenders, proper application of the theoretical model, and exercise of interpersonal skills according to the specifications set out by the designers.

- *Community base*. Building on the frequently obtained finding that community-based interventions have higher effect sizes, Andrews (2001) and others recommend the use of community-based services where possible, in natural settings such as the family. Where custodial settings are required for other reasons, primarily to restrain those thought to pose a danger to others, they should be as community-oriented as possible.

To optimize the delivery of the above kinds of services, many other ingredients should be in place. All of the assessments carried out, and procedures for integrating their results, should be founded on the best-validated methods currently available. This applies equally to processes for monitoring integrity and continuity of provision, and evaluating outcomes. It applies also at a strategic level, in the management and coordination of the portfolio of programmes and allied services that a criminal justice agency seeks to provide (Andrews 2001).

Methods of working

The remainder of this chapter is devoted to examining in a little more detail some of the methods that have been shown to reduce rates of further criminal acts. Where possible this is based on the results of meta-analyses, but in some instances details of primary studies will be given to illustrate the kinds of work done. Here and there, in the absence of large-scale systematic evaluations, we will draw on findings of smaller-scale studies and occasionally single case reports. We will look briefly at the contents, and also the results, of some of the most promising programmes.

Many studies in the field of offender rehabilitation report on mixed samples, in the sense that programme participants have typically committed a range of offences. The focus on overall recidivism as an outcome variable often precludes more detailed reporting of the relative recurrence of different types of offence. This may also reflect the finding, obtained from longitudinal studies, to the effect that most offenders are 'versatile', or 'generalists' who commit a variety of different types of offence (Farrington 1996). For example, even among those found guilty of assaults, the majority have only one conviction of this type; the remainder of their criminal record consists of various other offences (Levi and Maguire 2002). Similarly, among 1,087 offenders attending specially designed car crime projects, 75% had previous convictions for theft, 60% for burglary and 30% for violence against the person (Sugg 1998).

The volume and variety of material is such that this could be organized in a number of ways. Let us first take a broad brush look at the most effective work documented to date with young and adult offenders, respectively. After that we will look a little more closely at outcomes for specific types of offence: property, driving-related, violence, drug abuse and sexual assault. To conclude the chapter, attention will turn to address the problems of offenders with mental disorders.

Young offenders

For young offenders who have committed serious violent or sexual offences, interventions in the 'most consistently effective' category have been shown to have an average impact in reducing recidivism of 40% in community settings and 30% in custodial settings (Lipsey and Wilson 1998). Lipsey (1995) recommended that intervention programmes for more serious young offenders generally need to be provided for a period of not less than six months, with contact at least twice weekly.

Successful programmes in this category for the most part employ the following types of methods (Lipsey and Wilson 1998; Dowden and Andrews 1999b):

- *Interpersonal skills training*. This consists of a series of exercises designed to improve participants' skills in interacting with others.

Working in a small group, individuals identify situations in which they are not sure how to act or sometimes mishandle, for example giving into pressure applied by others. Suitable ways of behaving in the situation are discussed, then practised using role-play, plus practice and feedback.

- *Behavioural interventions.* A wide range of methods can be grouped under this heading (McGuire 2000b). In work with offenders, this has included contingency contracts, where individual offenders and their supervisors compose a list of problem behaviours and a system of rewards for progress in modifying them. Behavioural training procedures such as modelling and graduated practice form part of many other types of interventions.

- *Cognitive skills training.* There are several programmes of this type. Most consist of a series of structured sessions, each containing exercises designed to help participants acquire or develop their abilities in the domain of thinking about and solving everyday (usually interpersonal) problems. Typical material includes work on putting a problem into words, gathering information, generating ideas, linking means and ends, anticipating consequences, perspective-taking and decision-making. While this sounds very abstract, materials and methods are usually directed towards tackling real-life, concrete problems faced by those taking part.

- *Structured individual counselling.* Counselling takes numerous forms and is used in many settings, including education, employment, healthcare and personal development. In what is probably its most familiar format, it is a relatively unstructured activity, in which the counsellor acts in a person-centred, non-directive manner, allowing the client to take the lead. While this can be invaluable for a number of purposes, as we saw earlier it has not emerged as an effective means of reducing offender recidivism. For it to work in that context, research suggests it needs to be more directive and structured, and based on a 'reality therapy' or 'problem-solving' framework.

- *Teaching family homes.* These are residential units or group homes in which specially trained adults work in pairs as 'teaching parents'. Their role is to develop positive working alliances with residents, impart a range of interactional or self-management skills, and provide counselling and advocacy services. Young people can continue to attend school and return to their homes-of-origin at weekends.

A more comprehensive list of the kinds of interventions found by Lipsey and Wilson to be most effective, together with reported effect sizes, is shown in Table 6.3. With particular reference to youth violence, an extensive report by the United States Department of Health and Human Services presents a wide range of evidence bearing on the most effective methods for its reduction (Surgeon General 2001).

One of the earliest examples of a study using a structured programme of skills training is the work of Chandler (1973), who examined the

Table 6.3 Summary of effect size patterns for non-institutionalized and institutionalized serious young offenders (Lipsey and Wilson 1998)

Non-institutionalized offenders (117 studies)		Institutionalized offenders (83 studies)	
Treatment type	Midpoint of estimated effect sizes	Treatment type	Midpoint of estimated effect sizes
Positive effects, consistent evidence			
Individual counselling	0.46	Interpersonal skills	0.39
Interpersonal skills	0.44		
Behavioural programmes	0.42	Teaching family home	0.34
Positive effects, less consistent evidence			
Multiple services	0.29	Behavioural programmes	0.33
Restitution, probation/ parole	0.15	Community residential	0.28
		Multiple services	0.20

social-cognitive skill of *perspective-taking* in a group of persistent young offenders aged 11–13 years. Using specially designed role-playing and story-telling techniques, he found first that the young offender group was significantly more 'egocentric'. That is, they appeared less able to adopt other people's perspectives than a comparison group of non-offenders. Forty-five youths were then randomly assigned to one of three conditions. The 'experimental' group undertook a series of training sessions involving videotaped role-reversal and perspective-taking exercises. The 'attention placebo' group used video cameras to make tapes of other activities, while the 'no-treatment' group had neither intervention nor attention. On completion of the sessions, evaluation showed that the treated group improved significantly in their role-playing and perspective-taking abilities. Moreover, an 18-month follow-up showed a significant reduction in the recidivism rate of the experimental group alone.

Chandler provided a very clear account of the intervention methods that he used. Other interventions are more difficult to define but have been shown to be moderately effective. In work with young offenders, there is support for a range of activities loosely described as *multiple services* or service brokerage, though their effect sizes are not as high or consistently found as for the approaches mentioned above. In these programmes, project managers assemble an array of different types of provision or access to community services designed according to young people's individual needs. This might include a wide range of opportunities, including academic, employment, behavioural, therapeutic or other ingredients (Lipsey and Wilson 1998).

Some studies have found *mentoring* to be a valuable and beneficial form of intervention. Mentors are volunteers assigned to work individually with young people, and to provide support, advice or practical help in obtaining other community services. It is important that there is careful matching of young people and mentors on key background variables. Positive outcomes from this are, however, not always easy to interpret for two reasons. First, the term 'mentoring' is very broadly defined and is applied to a quite diverse range of activities and roles on the part of the mentor (Thornton *et al.* 2000). Second, as a process mentoring is often the main aspect of intervention, but occasionally it is combined with some other ingredient. As an accompaniment to participation in structured programmes, it can have considerable 'added value' in reducing recidivism.

The interpersonal context

The primary objective of the foregoing kinds of interventions is to address aspects of offenders' difficulties with reference to attitudes, peer influences, behavioural or cognitive skills, or attainment in terms of education or employment. All of this sounds very *individualistic* in its flavour; and as we have seen, that is one of the points of keenest disagreement between psychology and criminology. The use of interventions based on such models makes it appear as if persons have somehow been extracted from their natural environments; and all the factors that influence their offending have been located within them.

This issue has been addressed in a number of more complex models of intervention. While this conclusion is not derived from any single meta-analysis, there is a general trend in which as services touch on more areas of an individual's life, so the possibility of securing and maintaining change increases commensurately.

An initial way to achieve this is to involve a *significant other* person in the young offender's life in working alongside him or her; that person also attends any individual programmes of the types cited above that are being provided. The third party may be a close relative with whom they have a positive relationship, or a mentor who is also familiar with the nature of the programme. This innovation improves the effect size over that obtained from attendance at the programme alone (Goldstein *et al.* 1994; Goldstein and Glick 2001).

Effect sizes reaching 60% reduction in recidivism have been obtained from *functional family therapy, parenting wisely*, family empowerment and affiliated therapeutic approaches that involve working with young offenders and their families. For the most part, such programmes have been provided for young people who have committed fairly serious offences. Some have been followed up for lengthy periods (Gordon *et al.* 1995; Dembo *et al.* 2000; Gordon 2002). For functional family therapy, reductions in delinquency were found not only among participating youths themselves, but also for their siblings, in follow-up periods of between 2½ and 3½ years after the therapy (Klein *et al.* 1977). Positive effects have also been obtained from studies evaluating the usefulness of *multidimensional treatment foster care* with high-risk young offenders (Chamberlain and Reid 1998; Chamberlain 2003).

Effective programmes involving young offenders and their families usually entail a specific focus on selected aspects of the family's functioning. Notably, they address areas such as parental supervision, training in negotiation and conflict resolution skills, and affectional bonds (Dowden and Andrews 1999b). There are strong indications that services of this kind will not be effective if they simply revolve around the provision of general family support. Approaches that involve diffuse, poorly defined work with families have been associated with increased recidivism (Dowden and Andrews 1999b).

Meta-analytic reviews have found that family, parenting and related interventions produce positive and significant effects. Woolfenden *et al.* (2002) confined their review to randomized controlled trials of interventions for 10- to 17-year-olds. Farrington and Welsh (2003) integrated findings from 40 well-designed studies, 30 of which involved random allocation. Some of these studies focused on very young children where the objective was to reduce behavioural problems rather than re-offending. For the latter, the mean overall effect found was equivalent to a recidivism rate for the experimental group of 34% as opposed to 50% for controls.

The family is, of course, not the only social context of young people's lives. Encouraging results have also been obtained in direct work with offender peer groups. This was done in a specially devised programme called Equipping Youth to Help One Another, or EQUIP (Leeman *et al.* 1993). First, staff members of one residential unit in a young offender institution were trained to foster an ethos of mutual support, 'positive peer culture'. In addition, residents attended a 30-session programme, *aggression replacement training*, consisting of intercalated modules on social skills, self-control and moral reasoning. The respective recidivism rates for EQUIP participants and comparison groups were 15% and 40.5%, respectively, at a one-year follow-up.

As multi-faceted programmes reach out into different spheres of young offenders' lives, still higher effect sizes can be obtained. Possibly the most notable to date has come from evaluation of *multi-systemic therapy* (MST), which comprises work with the young person, his or her family, and school staff (Borduin *et al.* 1995; Henggeler *et al.* 1998). A reduction in serious/violent recidivism of 72% was obtained at a four-year follow-up, though this effect has not been matched when the programme was replicated elsewhere. Understandably, services of this type are comparatively resource-intensive. As we shall see in Chapter 8, however, the comparatively heavy investment that a programme like this requires can be more than compensated for by savings that result later, from crimes prevented and consequent reduced costs to criminal justice, health and social services.

Adults

For adult offenders, as we saw earlier, average effect sizes are generally lower than for those of younger age groups. Nevertheless, results are meaningful in practice, and comparable patterns emerge with respect to the types of intervention most likely to work. With this age group, interventions involving families are (understandably) less likely to be used. At an individual level, the methods most frequently associated with the highest reductions in recidivism include the following:

- Structured cognitive-behavioural programmes focused on risk factors for criminal recidivism (Andrews *et al.* 1990a; Lipsey *et al.* 2001; Lipton *et al.* 2002b). Variants of the approach have been well validated primarily for individuals with patterns of violent, sexual and substance-related offending (Hollin 2001b; Motiuk and Serin 2001; McGuire 2002b).
- Specially designed programmes with additional components have been developed for adults who have committed violent offences. This may include a focus on anger control, modulation of moods, and recognition and self-management of risk. For men who have committed domestic violence offences, further sessions are included examining perceptions of male and female roles, responsibility for actions, or concepts of masculinity (Russell 1995, 2002; Dobash and Dobash 2000).
- Still further ingredients are added in work with individuals who have committed sexual offences, the vast majority of whom are male. In addition to cognitive and social skills training and similar activities, these interventions usually also include a focus on deviant sexual arousal, cognitive distortions, empathy training and other sessions designed to address the established risk factors for this kind of offence. The precise contents may vary further according to specific types of offence, differentiated mainly by whether victims are children or adult women (Marshall *et al.* 1999; Marshall 2001).
- For offenders with lengthy histories of substance abuse, therapeutic communities have been shown to be beneficial. These may be located in institutions or in the wider community and there are several different models on which they can be based (Lipton *et al.* 2002a).
- Education and vocational training is also associated with positive outcomes. Wilson *et al.* (2000) reported a meta-analysis of 33 studies yielding 53 tests of the impact of education, vocational training and allied programmes with adult offenders. The mean effects size expressed as an odds ratio (OR) was 1.52, with the highest effect sizes for post-secondary education programmes (OR = 1.74), corresponding to recidivism rates for intervention and comparison groups of 37%

and 50%, respectively. Effect sizes were lowest for a mixed group of multi-component studies (OR = 1.33).

In what could be described as the 'prototype' of the kinds of programmes now in widespread use, Platt *et al.* (1980) described results of the Wharton Tract Program, based in a 45-bed, open-door prison satellite unit. Residents of the unit were in transition from prison to the community; all participants were adult male offenders with lengthy histories of criminal behaviour and of heroin use. Platt and his colleagues combined two elements in a structured group intervention programme. The first was a form of *guided group interaction*, a specified pattern of activity in which the group leader took an active role to emphasize the development of the group and to create a supportive atmosphere. Members were enjoined to think of themselves as agents of change for others. The second was a focus on the learning of a series of communication and problem-solving skills. These included recognizing problems, generating alternative ideas, consequential thinking, means–end thinking, decision-making and perspective-taking. At the end of a two-year follow-up period, group participants were reported by parole officers to be significantly better adjusted than the comparison sample. They had a significantly lower re-arrest rate (49% versus 66%), and if re-convicted had a lower rate of re-commitment to institutions, implying their re-offences were of a less serious nature. Also, if they were re-arrested, this occurred after a longer average arrest-free period (238 versus 168 days) than for the control group members.

Driving offences

There is one meta-analysis of remedial interventions for offenders convicted of driving while intoxicated (Wells-Parker *et al.* 1995). This incorporated findings from 215 studies and reported an average reduction in recidivism of 8–9%. Multimodal interventions combining education with psychotherapy or counselling, and probation follow-up, had the most positive effects in reducing drink-drive recidivism and alcohol-related accidents. On the other hand, some single modalities (psychotherapy and attendance at Alcoholics Anonymous) when used alone had negative effect sizes, though the number of studies under those headings was very small.

Research has also been reported on interventions for other motoring offences, for example driving while disqualified. Bakker *et al.* (2000) described the evaluation of a multimodal cognitive-behavioural package (The Driving Offender Treatment Program; see Bakker *et al.* 1997) provided in a New Zealand prison. Participants (*n* = 144) were followed for up to three years after discharge and compared with a matched control group. There was a significant reduction in licence revocation misdemeanours and in general offending, but no difference in drink-driving convictions.

Property offences

Available research devoted exclusively to property offending is rather limited in scope and design. Much of it is small-scale or based on single cases; although as a means of informing practitioners, such research can be very useful. There are several studies of individual young offenders, or case series employing methods such as contingency contracts, training parents in behaviour modification, and self-control training (Stumphauzer 1976; Reid and Patterson 1977; Hollin 1990). Henderson (1981) summarized work with ten children who were provided with individually adapted combinations of self-control methods, coupled with the involvement of a significant adult. A follow-up of between two and five years showed that only two of the children had resumed stealing.

There is slightly more research on shoplifting by adults, though much of it has been done with first-time offenders, or where there was a compulsive element in offending. As with stealing by children, most interventions have entailed the use of behaviourally based methods such as contingency contracts, activity schedules or desensitization (Marzagao 1972; Guidry 1975; Gauthier and Pellegrin 1982; Glover 1985; Aust 1987). All of these studies used single-case designs and, in every instance, successful outcomes were obtained. But in addition, other studies have been carried out using variations on cognitive therapy, or semi-structured counselling, provided in group settings (Edwards and Roundtree 1982; Solomon and Ray 1984; MacDevitt and Kedzierzawski 1990; Kolman and Wasserman 1991). Two studies have evaluated diversion programmes for first-offence shoplifters (Casey and Shulman 1979; Royse and Buck 1991). The outcomes of all of these studies are again positive; but design limitations would rule out their inclusion in a meta-analysis.

Turning to vehicle theft, again very little evaluative work has been done, and the pattern of outcomes is very uneven. During the early 1990s, several evaluations appeared that suggested specially constructed 'motor projects' resulted in reduced re-offending among individuals with histories of repeated vehicle-taking. For example, while 80% of those sent to prison for car theft re-offended within two years, the corresponding figure for participants in motor projects who continued to attend for a three-month period was 30% (McGillivray 1993). Offenders completing such projects run by probation services in the West Midlands were compared with non-completers, yielding re-conviction rates of 54% and 100%, respectively; the corresponding re-conviction rates specifically for motoring offences were 27% and 61%, respectively (Davies 1993). However, none of these studies included properly matched comparison samples. A subsequent review of 42 such projects by the Home Office concluded that they were ineffective, with the poorest results for those that consisted of activities such as 'banger' racing (Sugg 1998).

Slightly stronger evidence came from evaluation of the Ilderton Motor Project, based in London, where a follow-up evaluation demonstrated significant reductions in re-offending (Wilkinson 1997). Over a three-year follow-up period, the re-offence rate among programme participants was 62%, while that among a comparison sample was 100%. There was also a significant difference in the proportions receiving custodial sentences (15% versus 46%), though the sample sizes were relatively small.

Substance abuse

Therapeutic communities for offenders have been used primarily with two somewhat loosely identified groups: (a) offenders with lengthy histories of substance-abuse; (b) offenders assessed as 'high-risk' and typically con-victed of serious crimes and serving lengthy sentences. For offenders with substance abuse problems, a number of well-designed studies have shown positive effects of prison-based therapeutic communities on both sub-sequent substance abuse and criminal recidivism (MacKenzie 2002). Benefits are further enhanced by continuation of treatment and support efforts into the community.

Using studies from the CDATE meta-analysis, Lipton *et al.* (2002a; Pear-son and Lipton 1999) conducted a meta-analytic review of 42 therapeutic community interventions with offenders; 35 with adults and 7 with juven-iles. The effect sizes obtained were positive, and although not large (10–18% reduction in recidivism) it is worth remembering that these ser-vices are directed predominantly at persistent, high-risk offenders with concomitant substance-abuse problems, a group whom many people regard as intransigent.

From a separate batch of CDATE studies, Lipton and his colleagues (2002b) have also adduced evidence of the value of the cognitive-behavioural approach for relapse prevention in substance abuse treatment. A combination of these interventions with adaptations of interviewing designed to increase individuals' motivation to change could prove particu-larly valuable, given emerging evidence concerning the effectiveness of the latter in reducing alcohol and drug misuse (Burke *et al.* 2002). Springer *et al.* (2002) provide practical details on a range of other individual, family and group interventions for substance-abusing offenders.

Misuse of controlled drugs is by definition a legal problem. But in most respects, and especially in its consequences, it is primarily a healthcare one. Effective interventions in this area are likely to entail a combination of medical and psychosocial approaches (J. Brown 2001). This has been shown, for example, in the National Treatment Outcome Research Study in the United Kingdom, in which a sample of 418 users of a range of drugs including heroin, non-prescribed methadone, cocaine and benzodiazepines was followed up for an average of 4.4 years (Gossop *et al.* 2003). Residential and community rehabilitation services that were evaluated within this had an impact not only in terms of reduced substance use, most notably of heroin, but also on rates of acquisitive crime, reducing it to averages of 36% and 23%, respectively, of the levels found at intake.

Violent offences

Two meta-analyses have helped to narrow down the features likely to contribute to success in reducing violent re-offending. One is the review by
Lipsey and Wilson (1998) of interventions for serious and persistent young
offenders, discussed in some detail above. The other is a review by Dowden
and Andrews (2000), who integrated a series of 34 evaluations of interventions to reduce violence, yielding 52 effect-size tests. The target offence
behaviours included general violence, sexual and domestic assaults. Most
(70%) of the studies that were included focused primarily on work with
adults. The overall mean effect size was +0.07, though again there was
enormous heterogeneity with effect sizes ranging from a low of −0.22 to a
high of +0.63. The effect size for interventions based on punishment was
just below zero (−0.01). By contrast, the corresponding figure for 'human
service interventions', based on combining the principles defined by Gendreau and Andrews (1990), was +0.12. Using the BESD, this corresponds
to recidivism rates of 44% for experimental and 56% for control groups.

Anger management

Novaco's model of anger, outlined in Chapter 3, or variations of it have
been applied with a wide range of groups, not solely in criminal justice
settings. It has been used with adolescent offenders and psychiatric patients
(Feindler and Ecton 1986), and with adult offenders (Howells *et al.* 1997;
Novaco 1997).

Tafrate (1995) reviewed a series of 30 studies using different approaches
to anger management. Very positive effects were found with most methods;
however, most of the studies cited did not use offender samples. In a more
detailed review, and taking fuller account of methodological differences,
Edmondson and Conger (1996) carried out a synthesis of 18 studies. Most
had small samples and the total time (session length multiplied by number
of sessions) was fairly limited, usually six to eight hours of contact. The
effect sizes were remarkably high, though they varied according to the
outcome target. The authors suggested that the choice of anger treatment
should depend on the specific types of anger problems experienced by
participants. More recently, DiGuiseppe and Tafrate (2003) have reported
a meta-analysis of 50 studies (total sample, 1,841 participants) and found
positive effects of interventions on both expression of anger and on aggressive behaviour; and the maintenance of gains over time. Two other reviews
by Sukhodolsky *et al* (2004) and Del Vecchio and O'Leary (2004) have
found similarly encouraging results for children, adolescents and adults
respectively.

In penal settings, one of the most extensive applications of anger control
programmes has been carried out in Canadian prisons. The programme
consisted of 25 two-hour sessions, offered between two and five times per
week, for groups varying between four and ten prisoners. Dowden *et al.*
(1999) reported a three-year follow-up of 110 programme participants and

matched controls. For lower-risk cases, there was no impact on levels of re-offending. For high-risk cases, however, there was a 69% reduction in general (non-violent) recidivism and an 86% reduction in violent re-offending. Hollenhorst (1998) has discussed usage of the approach in US correctional services, and Serin and Preston (2000) have reviewed other studies showing positive outcomes from the use of specially developed programmes for violent prisoners in Canada.

Not all the evaluations in this area have proved to be successful, however; and in some instances treatment gains have been very small. Howells *et al* (2002) carried out a large-scale evaluation of anger management programmes in several prisons in Australia. On the basis of their results, the authors made a number of recommendations. They proposed that anger management interventions should be continued, but advocated moving away from 'blanket delivery' of programmes. The same authors have also drawn attention to the importance of 'readiness for change' in assigning prisoners to anger control sessions (Howells and Day 2003).

Cognitive skills programmes

'Cognitive skills' programmes are so called because their objectives and the methods they employ are directed towards helping participants to acquire new capacities for thinking about and solving their problems, particularly in the interpersonal domain. They draw on earlier work such as that of Chandler (1973) and Platt *et al.* (1980) discussed above.

Programmes of this type are derived from the *cognitive model of offender rehabilitation* proposed by Ross and Fabiano (1985), a variant of social learning theory with a particular accent on cognitive skills. Solving real-life problems requires a set of particular skills or habits of thinking (McGuire 2002c). They include, for example, the capacity, when faced with a personal difficulty, to:

- identify and tell yourself exactly what the problem is;
- control the impulse to act on the first idea that comes into your head;
- generate alternative solutions – consider other things you could do;
- think in a flexible rather than a rigid way about the problem;
- look ahead and anticipate the possible consequences of your actions;
- understand the perspective of other people affected by the problem.

Acquiring skills of this kind usually occurs naturally during development (Spivack *et al.* 1976). It takes place not through direct instruction (as happens, even though in an informal way, when we learn to swim or ride a bike), but through implicit social learning. But unless individuals are exposed to opportunities to observe and assimilate such skills, they are unlikely to acquire them. They may even learn to act in ways that cause problems, such as resorting to the use of force. Ross and Fabiano suggested that individuals who lack or do not apply problem-solving skills are at risk of involvement in crime, using it as a means of resolving everyday difficulties with which they are faced. Some of the processes by which this happens were described in Chapters 3 and 4. Such skill 'deficits' are not in themselves direct causes of criminality. However, they may interact with other risk factors and with opportunities in the environment to increase the likelihood of criminal acts.

Probably the most widely disseminated programme based upon this, Reasoning and Rehabilitation, consists of a series of 36 two-hour sessions delivered on a group basis and led by specially trained tutors. Its constituent materials are organized into a sequence of interlinked modules focusing on problem-solving, social interaction, self-management, negotiation and conflict resolution, critical thinking, and related kinds of skill. The programme was first piloted in probation services, with very positive short-term outcomes (Ross *et al.* 1988).

In a large-scale evaluation for Correctional Services Canada, with a sizeable sample of federally sentenced prisoners ($n = 1,444$), there was a reduction in recidivism of 36.4% among those completing the programme as compared with controls (Robinson 1995; Robinson and Porporino 2001). Effects were moderated, however, by offence type: prisoners with records of violent, sexual and substance-related offending were less likely to be re-convicted than those with histories of property crimes. Since then the programme has been applied extensively in both prison and probation settings in the United Kingdom and other countries (McGuire 1995b; Williams 1995; Raynor and Vanstone 1996). However, results of three recent evaluations of its delivery in prisons in England and Wales have been mixed, and predominantly negative (Friendship *et al.* 2002; Cann *et al.* 2003; Falshaw *et al.* 2003).

Other multi-modal cognitive skills group programmes that have demonstrated success in reducing violence include the Montgomery House Violence Prevention Project in New Zealand (Polaschek and Reynolds 2001), and the Controlling Aggression Programme run by probation staff in the UK (McGuire *et al.* submitted).

Cognitive self-change
Cognitive skills programmes are designed to impart to their participants a series of cognitive, interpersonal and self-management skills, limitations or deficits in which are thought to have contributed to the occurrence of acts of crime. An alternative approach is to consider such acts as arising from *cognitive distortions* held by the offender: beliefs or assumptions that are directly conducive to antisocial acts.

A programme of this type was developed within an adult prison establishment in the Vermont Department of Corrections, USA. Bush (1995) has described the rationale for the programme and its mode of delivery. Sessions were run within a separate unit inside the prison; groups of between five and ten prisoners met three to five times per week. In each session, one prisoner was asked to describe an incident in which he had been involved, and to furnish a *thinking report*. This is a detailed record of thoughts and feelings before, during and after an offence incident. Groups collaborated in identifying criminogenic thought patterns and generating new thoughts, or practising skills that would make a criminal act less likely.

Henning and Frueh (1996) have reported a two-year follow-up of 55 prisoners who attended this programme for an average of 9.8 months, compared with an appropriately matched sample of 141 non-attenders. There was a significant difference in the respective recidivism rates of the two groups (50% versus 71%). Follow-up analysis also showed that members of the experimental group survived significantly longer in the community before committing new offences.

Specific patterns of thinking concerning relationships, power and responsibility have been associated with acts of domestic violence, and there are positive reports of group-based interventions designed to reduce rates of it using a combination of methods. A central element of this includes addressing abusive beliefs. Dobash *et al.* (1996) describe the work of the Change programme and the Lothian Domestic Violence Project in Scotland. In a one-year follow-up, partners of men who took part in these projects reported further violent incidents at a much lower rate than those of men subject to other criminal justice disposals (7% versus 37%).

Sexual offences

There are numerous designs for intervention programmes for those (over-whelmingly male) offenders who have committed sexual offences, with different emphases according to the exact type of offence, age of offender and age of the victim. Concerning sexual abuse of children, Ward *et al.* (2001) suggest the main components of intervention should include norm-building; understanding offending through cognitive restructuring; arousal reconditioning (a behaviourally based approach for modification of sexual preferences); understanding victim impact and developing empathy; mood management; training in relationship skills; and 'breaking the chain' of offending through relapse prevention. For offenders against adult women, broadly similar ingredients are recommended: Marshall (2001) includes among the necessary targets of treatment the enhancement of self-esteem; reducing cognitive distortions and rationalizations; improving social skills with particular focus on empathy and intimacy; modifying deviant sexuality; and relapse prevention. However, as new findings emerge there is continuing debate concerning the exact components required in these interventions. For example, Marshall *et al.* (1999) questioned whether altering sexual predilection is an essential ingredient of treatment programmes for men who have committed rape.

Although there have been no fewer than five meta-analyses of this area, some have been criticized for poor methodology (see Marshall and McGuire 2003). The most thorough is the review by Hanson *et al.* (2002); in Table 6.2, two effect sizes from that work are given, for sexual recidivism and general recidivism, respectively. Hanson and his colleagues found that cognitive-behavioural methods yielded reductions in sexual recidivism from 17.4% to 9.9% and general recidivism from 51% to 32%. Several UK studies have reported positive long-term benefits of sex offender treatment programmes in both prison (Friendship *et al.* 2003) and probation settings (Beech *et al.* 2001); though effects were much less marked with offenders assessed as high-risk and showing higher levels of sexual deviance. Beech and Mann (2002) consider some of the issues arising from the pattern of findings obtained in this area.

Treatment approaches for offenders with mental disorders

The predominant form of treatment for persons diagnosed with serious mental health problems is medical. This consists of pharmacological therapy: for example, the administration of drugs such as neuroleptics for those diagnosed with psychoses, or of anti-androgens to reduce sexual libido (Hodgins and Müller-Isberner 2000). However, psychosocial methods have also been used and have met with a fair measure of success. Often, individuals prefer them as they do not have unwanted side-effects, avoid the risk of dependence and involve a more collaborative ethos. However, for the majority of offenders with mental disorders, the most common pattern remains a mixture of pharmacological, psychological and social interventions.

Though to date relatively under-researched, psychological methods have been shown to be valuable in the treatment of delusions. In Chapter 5 we saw that certain positive symptoms of psychosis, such as paranoid threat/control-override symptoms, have been associated with violent acts. Several studies have shown that psychological interventions such as cognitive therapies can be effective in reducing the intensity and frequency of delusional beliefs. There are reports of successful outcomes from both single case studies and the application of the methods in groups (Fowler *et al.* 1995; Chadwick *et al.* 1996).

Community management

In general, however, by comparison with the work that has been done in criminal justice settings, for offenders with mental disorders there is much less outcome research to draw upon. It is difficult, therefore, to give anything other than preliminary indications of what might contribute to 'success' with this population. To address the question of criminal recidivism, one implication of the work that has been done is that the most likely-to-succeed interventions will be broadly similar to those applied with other offender groups.

Currently, the most favoured approach to the provision of community services for those clients thought to be at risk of antisocial behaviour is *assertive case management* or *assertive outreach*. Evidence concerning its usefulness has come from follow-up studies of hospital in-patients discharged into the community, and made subject to supervision varying in levels of intensity (e.g. Bloom *et al.* 1988; Tellefsen *et al.* 1992; Wiederanders *et al.* 1997). However, the findings so obtained are often very difficult to interpret, as studies are carried out in different jurisdictions (American states) where the rules regarding whether someone is coping well, or needs to be returned to hospital, may be applied differently. Nevertheless, the general conclusion drawn some time ago was that 'the keys to reducing the risk of violence by persons with mental disorder in the community are aggressive case management and a comprehensive array of support services' (Dvoskin and Steadman 1994: 684).

The support services provided should have two features. First, they need to be well coordinated; second, each element in the package needs to be of high quality in itself. There are several well-documented studies of projects in which considerable extra resources were invested in services with the principal aim of improving integration between them (Lehman *et al.* 1994; Morrissey *et al.* 1994; Bickman 1996). This did not, however, necessarily lead to better outcomes for service users. Reviewing these innovations, Morrissey (1999) held that enhanced case management and allied service improvements were 'a necessary but not sufficient condition for positive outcome effects for clients' (p. 462).

In the absence of clear and interpretable research findings that can inform the design of interventions in this field, Heilbrun and Peters (2000) have forwarded a set of principles for effective community-based forensic services. These combine guidelines for sound ethical practice with such recommendations as can be extracted from the limited evidence base. They include:

- an emphasis on the importance of communications between agencies;
- an explicit balance between individual rights, the need for treatment, and public safety;
- an awareness of the range of treatment needs of clients;
- the use of demonstration models in assessing risk of harm and treatability;
- clarification of legal requirements such as confidentiality and duty to protect;
- application of sound risk management procedures;
- the practice of principles for promoting healthcare adherence.

Personality disorders
Until recently, there was a widely held assumption that people classified as having personality disorders are resistant to change and may even be 'untreatable'. This was thought to apply particularly to the cluster of indicators used to diagnose or classify recidivist offenders as 'psychopathic'. Some recent studies have begun to shift the balance of expectations about what can be achieved with this group.

Serin (1995) questioned the validity of the idea of 'treatment resistance'. Long-term follow-up of 'psychopathic offenders' showed that, with the passage of time, decreasing proportions of people who are diagnosed in this way retain features of the disorder. This has been amplified in a review by Sanislow and McGlashan (1998) of 44 studies of the 'natural course' of personality disorders. Rather than finding a fixed, immutable pattern as virtually everyone expected, this review showed a pattern of fluctuation over time.

Other researchers have collated available evidence concerning the possibility of effective treatment with this group (Perry *et al.* 1999; Bateman and Fonagy 2000). Most studies focused on borderline or avoidant personality disorder where the average treatment effect sizes are much higher than anticipated. However, with reference to antisocial personality disorder, which is the diagnostic category closest to psychopathy, very few controlled evaluations have been done.

Nevertheless, there are tentative suggestions from these initial reviews that some behavioural, cognitive-behavioural and therapeutic-community programmes may be successful in reducing antisocial behaviour among individuals classed as personality disordered. While to date positive results are few, this is an absence of evidence rather than a firm finding that nothing works. Lösel (1998) accordingly recommended that services for this group could be based on a similar set of principles to those guiding offender services in general. Similarly, Blackburn (2000b) reviewed several studies suggesting that those designated as psychopathic are capable of forming therapeutic alliances, and are amenable to a number of psychosocial interventions; such that short-term improvements in mental health status have been obtained.

Salekin (2002) has reported a meta-analysis of 42 outcome studies. Only eight included control groups and many were single cases, so any conclusions must remain tentative at present. A few, however, could be regarded as more robust: for example, five studies of cognitive-behavioural therapy incorporated a cumulative sample of 246 individuals. There were high effect sizes for several therapeutic approaches, including cognitive-behaviour therapy, personal construct therapy and other approaches that '. . . addressed patients' thoughts about themselves, others and society. Thus, they tended to directly treat some psychopathic traits' (Salekin 2002: 93). Salekin also observed that there was a strong association between effect size and time in treatment: interventions lasting less than six months were less likely to produce benefits than longer ones. Where attendance was maintained for more than a year, a considerably higher fraction of the samples benefited. In opposition, therefore, to what has been called 'therapeutic nihilism' (Reid and Gacono 2000), evidence suggests that gains can be made with populations of offenders generally considered at highest risk, and whose problems of antisocial conduct have hitherto been regarded as intractable.

Further reading

Two recent volumes that provide details of the interventions described in this chapter, and much other background material, are: Lawrence W. Sherman, David P. Farrington, Brandon C. Welsh and Doris L. Mackenzie (eds., 2002) *Evidence-Based Crime Prevention* (London: Routledge); and James McGuire (ed., 2002) *Offender Rehabilitation and Treatment: Effective Programmes and Policies to Reduce Re-Offending* (Chichester: Wiley). Another valuable source is Clive Hollin's (2001) *Handbook of Offender Assessment and Treatment* (Chichester: Wiley), which has recently (2004) been issued in a briefer form containing key chapters as *The Essential Handbook of Offender Assessment and Treatment* (Chichester, Wiley).

Details of research concerning young people involved in persistent, serious offending can be found in Rolf Loeber and David P. Farrington (eds., 1998) *Serious & Violent Juvenile Offenders: Risk Factors and Successful Interventions* (Thousand Oaks, CA: Sage Publications). Also useful are Clive R. Hollin (ed., 1996) *Working with Offenders: Psychological Approaches in Offender Rehabilitation* (Chichester: Wiley); and James McGuire (ed., 1995) *What Works: Reducing Re-offending. Guidelines from Research and Practice* (Chichester: Wiley). For a discussion of the penal context related to these findings, see Ian Crow (2001) *The Treatment and Rehabilitation of Offenders* (London: Sage Publications).

For an outline of an integrative approach to offenders with drug problems, see David W. Springer, C. Aaron McNeece and Elizabeth Mayfield Arnold (2002) *Substance Abuse Treatment for Criminal Offenders: An Evidence-based Guide for Practitioners* (Washington, DC: American Psychological Association). On work with sexual offenders, see William L. Marshall, Dana Anderson and Yolanda Fernandez (1999) *Cognitive Behavioural Treatment of Sexual Offenders* (Chichester: Wiley). Approaches to work with offenders who have mental disorders are addressed in Sheilagh Hodgins and Rüdiger Müller-Isberner (eds., 2000) *Violence, Crime and Mentally Disordered Offenders: Concepts and Methods for Effective Treatment and Prevention* (Chichester: Wiley). For a volume focused on long-term developmental prevention, see David P. Farrington and Jeremy W. Coid (eds., 2003) *Early Prevention of Adult Antisocial Behaviour* (Cambridge: Cambridge University Press).

Crime and punishment: a psychological view

The evidence surveyed in the previous chapter, to the effect that psychologically based interventions have been shown to be effective in reducing criminal recidivism, probably forms the single most important reason for the current resurgence of interest in psychology in criminal justice. In that chapter, we also saw that the most frequently used strategy when responding to offenders, so widespread and firmly established that it could be called the standard or mainstream approach to criminal conduct, is the use of punishment. However, the outcomes of its use are far from satisfactory. There are few instances in which it has been shown to 'work' in the sense of serving to ensure that those who have committed criminal offences do not do so again. Almost certainly, professionals working in various criminal justice settings may be able to cite anecdotal instances where that occurred. But they tend to be the exceptions; and for the most part punishment of offenders singly fails to achieve its publicly appointed objectives. The bulk of the findings available indicate either that its effects are virtually non-existent, or that in some instances it actually makes matters worse. Put another way, it is on balance unproductive, and it can often be counter-productive.

In the present chapter, we will examine this issue in more detail. To do so the chapter is divided into four sections. First, it is helpful to make some conceptual distinctions, as there are different rationales underpinning punishment, and confusing them with one another can make it difficult to judge both arguments and evidence. Second, we will survey and scrutinize a range of findings that call into question the value of punishment as an effective way to achieve the goals that the law proclaims for it, and citizens notionally expect of it. Third, the assumption that punishment ought to work appears to be deeply embedded in many people's thinking; it is almost a part of the taken-for-granted fabric of social life. It is important then to propose an explanation of why people's expectations of it are tantamount to an illusion. This will draw on relevant findings from psychological research. Finally, given the confounding state of affairs in which one of society's chief weapons in the 'war on crime' abjectly misses its intended target, we will briefly discuss why, despite the evidence, it goes on being applied.

Our habit of thinking that punishment is the answer to crime is so deeply ingrained that, whenever bad news concerning crime hits the streets (and most news concerning crime tends to be bad), there are near-ubiquitous demands for even more of it. For example, in the wake of the publication of the annual Criminal Statistics for 2002 showing an increase in crime rates (Home Office 2003), there were once again calls for greater use of severe sanctions against offenders. The phrases used are familiar and well-worn: 'crack down', 'get tough', 'show less understanding', 'teach the culprits a lesson', 'turn up the heat'. Debates concerning 'law and order' seem to exist on a single dimension along which opinions are expressed. The language typically casts the issue in terms of a polarity between 'hard' and 'soft' in our basic disposition towards crime and criminals.

The 'hard' end of the scale is purportedly grounded in a more realistic picture of what people are like. Those who commit crimes are bad; they are unlikely to change unless compelled to do so. They need to be dealt with more strictly, and the only way to do it is to make the costs of crime higher, or its consequences as unpleasant as possible. At the 'soft' end, there is perhaps a belief that people who commit crimes are no different from anyone else; they have the capacity to live decent lives and to reform themselves, but they have grown up in adverse surroundings, and need to have better opportunities given to them. Such liberalism is discredited when it is discovered that some offenders reportedly 'get away with it' by being dealt with in ways that are thought too lenient. Evidence that even prison sentences do not deter is interpreted by many as proving that prisons are too much like 'holiday camps' and punishments should be more severe. Worse still, some offenders seem to be virtually rewarded for their crimes, for example when staff of residential centres take them on outdoor pursuits trips, in one infamous instance overseas. Within this debate, while the precise phraseology changes slightly over time, the underlying arguments remain the same.

Key concepts in sentencing and punishment

The pivotal agent in the dispensation of justice is the criminal court, and the main means of doing so at its disposal is the sentence it is able to impose. Sentencing is a complex process with several interlinked aims (Walker and Padfield 1996). This is the field of penology, and one with which traditionally, psychology has had little connection. There are several reasons for punishing offenders (Hudson 1996) but they are generally condensed into three principal justifications for its use: *retribution*, *incapacitation* and *deterrence*.

Retribution

The concept of retribution is also a complex one, and different approaches to it emphasize different elements. The fundamental principle at stake is that when an individual offends against society (by breaking its laws), this causes harm to society, giving us an automatic right, even a duty, to inflict pain on the offender as a result. The basis of this comes from within the philosophical tradition of *deontology*, a theoretical framework that achieved its fullest development in the thought of the eighteenth-century German philosopher Immanuel Kant (1724–1804). Within this, morality is codified in a set of prescripts, which, in turn, are derived from higher-order abstract rules that are viewed as virtually axiomatic. This is not concerned with outcomes at an individual level, but with the principled administration of justice. One facet of it is the idea of censure, in which society through the agency of the court utters a statement of disapproval, and acts on it through its treatment of the offender. This is contained in the popular notion of 'just deserts'. It takes its crudest form in the *lex talionis*, the law of retaliation, where the punishment corresponds to the crime ('an eye for an eye'). A subtler and more analytic version is subsumed in the concept of *proportionality* (von Hirsch and Ashworth 1998). This approach is not primarily concerned with instrumental effects or outcomes; the cycle of crime and societal retribution is, as it were, complete in itself.

Incapacitation

Incapacitation refers to the possibility of crime control by removing from offenders the ability to commit crimes. This entails punishing them by imposing restrictions on their freedom to act. The most obvious means of doing this is incarceration in prisons or other secure residential settings (from children's homes to high security hospitals). Thereby, offenders are removed from society and from situations in which they have opportunities to steal cars, break into houses or commit assaults. Liberty can be restricted to varying degrees within community penalties, too, for example by prohibiting individuals from attendance at football matches, or placing them under home curfews monitored by electronic tags. These measures almost certainly prevent crimes those individuals would have committed in the short term. And undoubtedly, there are sound justifications for the restraint or incapacitation of persons who are inflicting serious or repeated harm upon others (or, in some instances, themselves). However, the extent of incapacitation effects is limited. One aspect often overlooked is that many crimes are 'displaced' into prison where, for example, substance abuse and assaults are by no means uncommon.

With regard to the crime-preventive effects of incapacitation, criminologists have constructed elaborate models for its evaluation. Doing so entails, for example, projecting from data on the numbers of dwellings broken into by the average burglar in a year, and estimating the number of crimes then prevented by sentencing larger numbers of house burglars to imprisonment. While the logic of this appears straightforward, it turns out to be a proportionately very expensive method of reducing crime. For example, applying such a model to England and Wales, Tarling (1993) concluded that even if the prison population were to be increased by 25%, the net effect on the rate of crime would be a reduction of just 1%.

Deterrence

A third declared intention that underpins the sentencing process, and our main focus here, is that it should alter criminal behaviour by attempting to manage its consequences. This is the core of what is entitled the *utilitarian* or *consequentialist* rationale for punishment as a response to crime (Walker 1991). It is founded on the idea that legal sanctions will have an impact on those made subject to them. Punishment is thought to be one route towards rehabilitation of the offender. This set of expectations is sometimes referred to as deterrence theory.

Deterrence effects can be sub-divided into different kinds of intended outcomes. Gibbs (1986) defined and clarified some of the terms used in this area, noting first the conventional distinction between *specific* and *general* deterrence. The former refers to the influence of punishment on the individual made subject to it: if you are punished for committing a crime, you will be less likely to do it again. The latter refers to the wider impact this is assumed to have on others and in the community as a whole: if you are punished for committing a crime, many other people will be less likely to commit one, because we don't want the same thing happening to us. Stafford and Warr (1993) argued that the distinction between specific and general deterrence is difficult to sustain in other than broad and abstract terms. In everyday reality for most actual and potential offenders, there is likely to be a complex interplay between individual and general deterrence effects. The convicted prisoner is aware of both the sentence imposed upon him or her, alongside a wider knowledge that these are the penalties likely to be incurred by anyone else who commits these crimes. Conceptually, however, in analysing deterrence effects, it can be useful to keep these anticipated outcomes separate in one's mind.

A second and less familiar type of distinction outlined by Gibbs (1986) is between *absolute* and and *restrictive* detterence. The former refers to a situation in which an individual contemplates a crime but does not commit it for fear of being punished. Note that this refers to more than just the fact that no crime has been committed: for deterrence to occur, individuals must have considered the crime but not proceeded with it. The latter refers to the possibility that highly active offenders reduce their frequency or severity of offending to lower the likelihood of being caught. Gibbs gives the example of a driver exceeding the speed limit, but only by a certain amount so as to keep the risk of detection to a minimum. Wright and Decker (1994) carried out an ethnographic study of highly active house burglars. They found that their respondents were not susceptible to deterrence to the extent of simply not committing their crimes. But while inside premises they sometimes left without taking too much, sacrificing higher rewards in order to reduce their time at risk of discovery. They were wary of the possibility of 'getting greedy' in the course of a burglary and being tempted to stay longer than they otherwise would. Something similar may happen with drink-driving offences, where many drivers are over the legal alcohol limit but perhaps only marginally so. It may help to explain why those committing armed robberies in building society offices select one target per location then move elsewhere; or some patterns of sexual offending, where despite strong urges to offend perpetrators confine themselves to situations in which they can best control access to their victims.

Gibbs (1986) also set out in detail a theory of the hypothesized linkages in deterrence theory between 'objective' features of sentences on the one hand, and 'subjective' or 'perceptual' features on the other, together with their hypothesized causal relationships to rates of crime. Objective properties are those that might be measured by a government statistician or a researcher in criminology, showing for example rates of detection or arrest for different types of crime, or the numbers of offenders successfully prosecuted who are then sent to prison. Subjective or perceptual properties are those which are visible to an individual offender, who may be unaware of statistics of police detection rates but well aware of friends who have escaped arrest for specific misdemeanours. The real operative factors in decision-making by would-be offenders are likely to be the latter rather than the former.

The characteristics of deterrence measures include their certainty, celerity, severity and scope. *Certainty* refers to the likelihood of legal punishment as a result of committing a crime; *celerity* to the amount of time that lapses between an offence being committed and an official sanction being imposed; *severity* to the magnitude of a punishment or the estimated amount of pain or discomfort a convicted offender would endure; while *scope* refers to the relationship between types of crimes defined in statute books and types of punishments imposed by the courts. In each case, these features may be objective, certainty for example being the proportion of crimes of a specific type that result in formal punishment; severity being measured as the amount of a fine or length of a prison sentence. Alternatively, they may be perceptual, reflecting individual offenders' estimates of the chances of being caught or of just how bad it would be for them if they were.

Evidence for deterrence effects

Returning to our central theme, in general terms it is a traditional expectation of sentencing practices that they should deter individuals from committing crimes. Outside the realm of penology and legal philosophy, this is also an expectation of the citizenry-at-large. Much has been written about whether the public believe that the courts are too lenient or too punitive, and it is widely thought that the news media play a pivotal role in shaping perceptions of this, for example by giving more publicity to sentences that are thought too lenient than those that seem unduly harsh. These influences notwithstanding, more soberly conducted opinion surveys do not show the public to be as punitive or as vengeful as is often alleged (Cullen *et al.* 1988); on the contrary, they are often firmly in favour of rehabilitation (Moon *et al.* 2000). It is nevertheless commonly assumed that there is a widespread, fundamental belief that crime and punishment belong together; that the latter brings home to the individual what he or she has done and thereby engenders appropriate change. If that expectation is indeed widespread, how well-founded is it?

There are seven types of evidence that are potentially relevant to the question of whether deterrence measures in criminal justice have an impact on recidivism. In what follows we will examine each of them in turn. They are:

- the effects of sentencing, as judged from criminal statistics;
- relationships between imprisonment and crime rates;
- effects of enhanced punishments;

- meta-analytic reviews of outcome studies;
- controlled trials of deterrence measures;
- self-report surveys;
- research on the death penalty.

The impact of sentencing

A first source of doubt regarding the impact of punishment arises from official statistics of offender re-convictions. In the United Kingdom, the effectiveness of sentencing has traditionally been assessed by employing large-scale criminological data on the sequelae of different court 'disposals'. During the 1990s, this exercise achieved a higher level of sophistication by applying the tools of statistical prediction. It is now fairly well established in criminology that rates of criminal recidivism among groups of offenders can be predicted with a reasonable degree of accuracy on the basis of a combination of certain key variables. They include gender, age at first offence, current age, number of previous convictions, number of previous incarcerations (including any youth custody sentences) and type of current offence. This process of prediction is limited to aggregate data and cannot be extrapolated for use at the individual level. In the United Kingdom, the Home Office, through its Research Development and Statistics Directorate (RDS), developed an instrument of this kind, the Offender Group Reconviction Scale (OGRS). The original version of this scale (Copas 1995; Copas et al. 1996) was employed for the prediction of discretionary conditional release and also to enable comparisons to be made between different types of court sentences. A second, refined version (OGRS-2) has since been developed, which allows prediction over a wider age range and for specific offence types (violent and sexual offences), though only in very broad categorical terms (Copas and Marshall 1998; Taylor 1999).

The advent of this measure thus allowed comparisons to be made between custodial and community penalties, respectively. One long-standing problem is that simple comparisons between raw rates of re-conviction following different types of court disposals are not valid or meaningful, due to prior differences in risk levels between groups. For example, if people sent to prison are regularly found to be poorer risks for re-conviction, it is hardly surprising if larger numbers of them are later re-convicted than those subject to other disposals. Thus 'any attempt to compare the effectiveness of sentences through the simple comparison of reconviction rates is likely to produce very misleading results' (Lloyd *et al.* 1994: 43). These difficulties were resolved by Lloyd and his associates (1994), who reported on a carefully controlled comparison of the four main types of sentence used by the criminal courts for more serious offences. In England and Wales, when this study was done, these were imprisonment, community service orders, probation orders and probation with additional requirements. The *actual* rates of re-conviction over two years following release from prison or discharge from community penalties were compared with the *predicted* rates: those which would be expected on the basis of offenders' previous criminal histories.

Lloyd and his colleagues found some interesting differences between the groups given different types of sentence. But the real import of their data lies in the side-by-side comparison of predicted with actual rates within each sentence type. In no case was this difference larger than 3%. 'When account was taken of background variables and pseudo-reconvictions, most of the differences between the disposal groups disappeared' (Lloyd *et al.* 1994: 43). In other words, the rate at which individuals re-offended was very close to the rate at which they were probably going to re-offend, regardless of the type of sentence imposed upon them. The sentence of the court had no clear differential impact on the outcome. It could be argued that it is a virtual irrelevance. Walker and Padfield (1996) expressed similar dismay at the result: 'the differences between expected and actual percentages are disappointingly small' (p. 93).

When similar analyses are done across successive years, fairly consistent patterns emerge. Figure 7.1 shows one such set of officially published data, based on large samples. This powerfully bears out the trend originally found by Lloyd and his colleagues. Summarizing these trends, Kershaw (1999) concluded that 'After taking into account all relevant factors, there is no discernible difference between the effect of immediate custody and

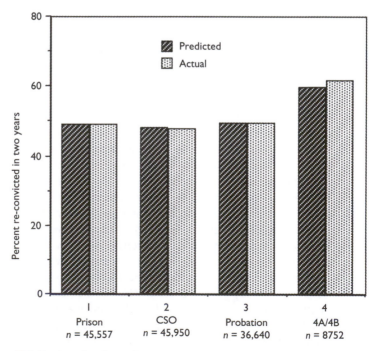

Figure 7.1 Predicted and actual re-conviction rates for four types of sentence

community penalties on reconviction rates' (p. 1). We might reasonably have expected that some suppressant effect of the more punitive sanction, imprisonment, would emerge from these figures, especially given almost unanimous acceptance of a necessary and desirable link between 'crime and punishment'. On the contrary, the findings imply that the sentencing system has a virtually negligible impact on criminal behaviour, certainly as far as the perspective of utilitarian justice is concerned.

Imprisonment and crime rates

At any one time, only a fraction of those committing crimes in society is apprehended and punished. Yet the public visibility of this process is held to act as a general deterrent for the remainder of the population, including those likely to offend. If general deterrence operates to an extent that justifies its central position in society, there should be some association between the activity of the criminal justice system and the total amount of crime.

The broadest, though possibly weakest, kind of evidence pertaining to this comes from studies of the relationship between the numbers of persons incarcerated in a society and its general rate of recorded crime. For example, where opportunities have been available to monitor recorded levels of crime across periods when rates of incarceration were steadily changing, no clear relationship materializes, even allowing for possible time-lags (Zimring and Hawkins 1994, 1995). This emerges particularly in studies of, and projections based upon, the increased use of incarceration in parts of the United States (Greenwood et al. 1996). Reviewing the evidence bearing on this point up to 1997, Nagin (1998) described the conceptual and other difficulties posed in researching this question, but could find no study that can be taken seriously as demonstrating a deterrence effect of imprisonment on general rates of crime.

Furthermore, recent research has failed to establish any relationship, in a direction that would be predicted by deterrence theory, between lengths of prison sentences and rates of recidivism. Gendreau et al. (1999a) have systematically reviewed this area in a report for the Solicitor General of Canada. The research group reviewed 23 studies yielding 222 comparisons of groups of offenders (total sample size, 68,248) who spent longer (an average of 30 months) versus shorter (an average of 17 months) periods in prison. The groups were similar on a series of five risk factors. Contrary to what would be predicted by deterrence theory, offenders who served longer sentences had slight increases in recidivism of between 2 and 3%; there was a small positive correlation between sentence length and subsequent rates of re-conviction. Incidentally, even Robert Martinson (1974), in his widely cited and highly influential paper which gave 'very little reason to hope that we have in fact found a sure way of reducing recidivism through rehabilitation' (p. 49), also concluded that there was no evidence of an association between recidivism and sentence length.

The foregoing review integrated information from many sources and was conducted on a mammoth scale. But smaller-scale research, for example on the comparative impact of fines and short jail sentences on rates of drinking and driving, have not unequivocally shown that the deterrence effect of the latter is necessarily any more powerful than that of the former (Evans *et al.* 1991; Martin *et al.* 1993). Another frequently heard claim regarding deterrence is that it is more likely to work with 'white-collar' crimes, committed by mainly middle- or upper-class offenders. Weisburd and Chayet (1995) followed the criminal careers of 742 offenders convicted of such crimes. The sample, which was divided into those who received and those who did not receive prison sentences, was followed up for a total of more than ten years. There was no observable effect that could be attributed to specific deterrence.

Enhanced punishments

During the 1970s, the proclaimed failure of education, training or psychotherapy to have their intended impact on criminal recidivism has been associated with a shift towards a more punitive stance in a number of legislatures. Particularly in the United States, from that decade onwards there was a progressive move towards harsher punishments and 'turning up the heat' on offenders (Byrne *et al.* 1992; Shichor and Sechrest 1996). At an institutional level, such sentences included the use of boot camps and shock incarceration. In the community, intensive supervision, electronic surveillance, random drug testing, curfews and various permutations of each were tried and tested.

Primary studies and evaluations of 'enhanced' and intermediate punishment therefore flourished during the 1980s and 1990s as the use of these types of sanction became more widespread. This created opportunities for controlled trials, in which more severe punishments were compared with standard punishments or 'business as usual' within the criminal justice system. Participants in the stricter forms of treatment were sometimes allocated randomly, on other occasions selected on a voluntary basis. Analysis of outcomes in such studies is made difficult by the fact that although the harshness of punishment was intensified, in many cases additional elements of education, counselling and other types of rehabilitative activity were also introduced.

Petersilia and Turner (1993) reported an evaluation of intensive supervision in probation and parole conducted in 14 American states. A sample of nearly 2,000 individuals across numerous sites was allocated randomly to experimental and control groups. Follow-up evaluation found no impact of the more intensive and restrictive supervision, which in some agencies included close surveillance, electronic monitoring, random drug testing and other innovations, on recidivism. The only positive result along these lines to emerge was an association between clients' participation in drugs and alcohol counselling and subsequent reductions in re-offending rates of the order of 10–20%. However, the possibility that this was due to a selection effect could not be eliminated (Petersilia and Turner 1993). Nevertheless, Petersilia (1998) was led to conclude that 'The empirical evidence regarding intermediate sanctions is decisive: Without a rehabilitation component, reductions in recidivism are elusive' (p. 6). Examining this and other evaluations of intermediate punishment, Gendreau et al. (1993) concluded that none of the hoped-for goals of reduced prison numbers, reduced costs or reduced recidivism were delivered by these programmes. A more recent evaluation of the effectiveness of electronic monitoring in Canada (Bonta et al. 2000), taking account of participants' risk levels, also drew negative conclusions. Bonta and his colleagues judged that the effectiveness of electronic monitoring 'as a true alternative to incarceration and reducing recidivism has yet to be demonstrated . . . If one is interested in reducing recidivism, then offender treatment, rather than sanctions, is the most promising approach' (Bonta et al. 2000: 71, 72).

For institutionally based sanctions, a similar large-scale evaluation was undertaken of the impact of shock incarceration or 'boot camps' for the US National Institute of Justice (MacKenzie and Souryal 1994; MacKenzie et al. 1995). Here, boot camp inmates were compared with other prisoners, prison parolees or probationers at a number of sites in eight states. Again, however, the results were not supportive of deterrence theory. The impact on recidivism was concluded to be 'at best, negligible . . . based on the totality of the evidence, boot camp programs did not reduce offender recidivism' (MacKenzie and Souryal 1994: 28, 41). This overall finding is very close to that obtained from evaluation of detention centres designed to deliver a 'short, sharp shock' in the United Kingdom in the early 1980s. Evaluation of this initiative concluded that 'the introduction of the pilot project regimes had no discernible effect on the rate at which trainees were reconvicted. A number of ways in which effects on reconviction might have been masked were considered and discounted' (Thornton et al. 1984: 243).

In a further test of deterrence effects, MacKenzie et al. (2001) have recently reported a review of 29 evaluative studies of correctional boot camps. The authors found that there was 'an almost equal odds of recidivating between the boot camps and comparison groups' (p. 130). On the basis of their review, they therefore concluded that, 'in our overall meta-analysis of recidivism, we found no differences between the boot camp and comparison samples . . . the results of this systematic review and meta-analysis will be disappointing for many people . . . boot camps by themselves have little to offer as far as moving offenders away from criminal activities' is concerned (pp. 137, 139).

In both institutional and community settings, then, while the innovations being researched here were ones designed to impose stiffer penalties on offenders, no useful effect of this escalation in toughness was found. Where positive outcomes were observed, they were usually associated with an investment of time and effort in rehabilitative activities.

Meta-analytic reviews

The findings from large-scale reviews of 'offender treatment' were surveyed in Chapter 6. Some of the meta-analytic reviews described there included studies of criminal sanctions. We noted that the estimated 'grand mean' across all reviews, of the order of an approximately 10% reduction in recidivism levels, was probably diminished to some extent by the incorporation of studies that reported predominantly zero or negative effects. The average effect size was, in other words, dragged down by these particular results.

Reviews that have examined criminal sanctions separately within a wide range of approaches to intervention have typically found deterrence-based programmes to have zero or negative effect sizes (Andrews *et al.* 1990b; Lipsey 1992, 1995; Pearson *et al.* 1997). One meta-analysis specifically designed to dissect the relevant literature on community-based intermediate punishments yielded negative conclusions regarding the impact of the initially much-lauded enhanced punishments. In their reviews of 135 outcome studies of surveillance, 'smart sentencing' and other measures of this type, Gendreau *et al.* (1993, 2001) found a mean effect size just below zero.

Deterrence on (controlled) trial

The studies just discussed involved evaluation of changes in sentencing practices in criminal justice services where many other factors that were operating could not be easily or satisfactorily controlled. A possibly more robust approach is to examine deterrence effects when these have been directly manipulated, though published reviews of this field are hard to find. Sherman (1988) has reviewed studies in which the effect of deterrence practices has been evaluated using randomized designs. The use of randomization in this context clearly raises ethical issues. The focus here is upon those circumstances where it has been feasible to evaluate the use of criminal sanctioning because offenders were randomly allocated to experimental and control conditions.

Of 21 studies included in Sherman's review, 14 found no differences in recidivism between experimental and control samples. In five studies, increased severity of penalties resulted in increased recidivism. Only two studies showed any impact of punitive sanctions. In one, this effect was observed only in some sub-samples and not across the experimental group as a whole. (There were also indications that a proportion of the experimental group had been treated more roughly by the police.) The remaining report, by Sherman *et al.* (1984), focused on the effect of arrest and brief incarceration on perpetrators of domestic violence in Minneapolis. However, subsequent extension and replications of this study at other sites obtained mixed results, so much so that the question of whether arrest should be mandatory for spousal abuse has been re-opened by other authors. For example, in another study responding to 1,200 cases of domestic violence in Milwaukee, criminal justice intervention in some cases precipitated further harm. Short-term arrest had an initial deterrence effect, but had a criminogenic effect in the following 12 months; full arrest with many more hours detention made no difference either way (Sherman *et al.* 1991). On that basis, alongside other factors, it has been argued that the nature of legal decisions made should be tailored to the circumstances and demands of each individual case (Schmidt and Sherman 1993).

The most comprehensive attempt to catalogue the potential impact of punitive sanctions as specific deterrents was undertaken by Weisburd *et al.* (1990), who compiled a 'Registry' of randomized experiments. The Registry provides details of a series of 68 studies published between 1951 and 1984 involving random allocation to different levels of criminal justice sanction. The definition of the word 'sanction' was very broad, and encompassed both heightened levels of strictness in terms of prison, probation or parole, as well as other experiments in which rehabilitative activities were included in traditional sanctioning procedures. Of the 68 studies available, 44 reported no differences between experimental and control samples. Only two showed apparently better outcomes for interventions that could be construed as more punitive. In neither case did the authors report statistical significance and the conclusions they drew were based solely on apparent trends in the data.

In the remaining 22 experiments, rates of recidivism, parole violation or other similar outcomes favoured experimental over control groups. However, in all the latter studies, the increased 'sanction' consisted of provision of individual counselling, participation in group treatments such as social skills training, or other forms of intervention that entailed sanctioning only in the respect that participation was non-voluntary. Though defined as sanctions for the purpose of the Registry, and involving some coercion in terms of limits on an offender's freedom, these interventions contained few if any elements that would ordinarily be considered directly punitive. In another context, that of work with substance-abusing offenders, coercion into treatment has been shown to have effects equivalent to voluntary participation, and the provision of services within such a framework may not be intrinsically punishing (Farabee *et al.* 1998).

Another type of research though in a similar vein has more direct bearing on the question of general than of specific deterrence. Sherman (1990) reviewed a series of 18 studies of the impact of police 'crackdowns' on rates of crime. Crackdowns were defined as combinations of three tactical elements: increased police presence, greater use of sanctions and threats of increased sanction certainty, conveyed through the media. That is, the police announced to the public that they would be working more intensively on certain types of crime, that people were more likely to be arrested and would be more severely dealt with by the courts. In six of the studies, crackdowns were short-term (a period of less than six months), and most of these experiments focused on illegal parking, drink-driving and other 'distinctly middle-class' vehicle-related offences (Sherman 1990: 36). In five studies in this group, residual effects of deterrence were observed; in other words, the effect continued after police 'back-off' or lifting of the crackdown. The remaining experiments were longer-term, and focused on offences such as drug sales and trafficking. However, only two of the 12 studies in this category obtained residual effects. In another two studies, there was disturbing evidence that other kinds of crimes had increased (for example, rates of homicide associated with illegal drug markets).

Self-report surveys

This category of evidence could be regarded as relatively weaker than some of the others discussed here, since it involves reliance on the verbal reports of people already convicted of crimes, some of whom may be dishonest, and indeed have convictions for offences involving dishonesty. However, there is no reason to believe that participants have anything to gain or lose according to how they respond to questioners in research of this kind. Some investigators have focused on the reactions of individuals arrested and then punished for crimes, inviting them to comment on the extent to which their experience of the process might be likely to deter them from future offending. Other researchers have focused more closely on patterns in individuals' thinking in the period immediately before committing offences. Some of this work has been based on interviews with offenders during which they have been asked to describe their offending behaviour in some detail. The types of offences committed by those taking part in these research studies varied considerably in seriousness, from shop theft and vehicle-taking to drug-trafficking and armed robbery. We will return to these studies a little later in the chapter.

In a series of surveys, Klemke (1982) and his colleagues collected self-report information on shoplifting by teenagers. Young people were interviewed at two points several months apart. Researchers found little evidence of deterrence in preventing repeated acts of shoplifting by this age group. While only a small proportion of those arrested was apprehended a second time, a far higher proportion admitted to further acts of theft. Thus the experience of arrest appeared to have had little impact on their behaviour. Conversely, although we cannot rule out the possibility that another proportion was deterred, other factors such as increasing age and maturation could also have explained their desistance.

The impact of arrest has also been investigated in some of the longitudinal studies outlined earlier in Chapter 5. In the Denver Youth Survey, Huizinga *et al.* (2003) collected data on the relationship between ongoing involvement in offending and experience of being arrested by the police. First, they found that the majority of offenders whatever their level of seriousness were not arrested at all. Second, for those who were, their delinquent behaviour did 'not appear to be well described by their arrests' (p. 80). That is, the more serious offenders were rarely apprehended for their gravest offences: they were more likely to be detained for a fairly minor offence. Third, the majority of cases showed either no change in behaviour or an actual worsening of behaviour following arrest; and 'in only 8% of the cases was the serious offending rate of the arrested juvenile less than the matched control ... being arrested is not a very strong deterrent against future delinquent behavior' (p. 81).

The death penalty

Research on the most extreme of sanctions, capital punishment or 'judicial execution', self-evidently has no bearing on the question of specific deterrence, but may provide evidence on the effectiveness of this extreme measure as a general deterrent. The presumption that it is a deterrent is certainly invoked as a rationale for imposing it. Among the 71 countries that still retained its use up to the year 2001, 'the most common political justification is the belief that it has a unique general deterrent capacity to save further innocent lives or reduce significantly other capital offences' (Hood 2002: 209). Of course, the issue of the death penalty is a highly emotive one and attitudes towards it are primarily influenced by a range of ethical and political beliefs, rather than by evidence bearing on its outcomes. But as this evidence has nevertheless been collected and is relevant to the present discussion, it is included in this survey.

Such research as is available has failed to find that the availability of the death penalty as a sentencing option has any clear suppressant effect on rates of the most serious crimes, such as homicide, including the murder of police or prison officers. Some researchers (most notably Ehrlich 1975) claimed to have found deterrence effects in the United States for the period 1935–1969, to the extent of calculating a ratio of executions to numbers of lives saved (in Ehrlich's case, seven or eight homicides averted for each additional person executed). But other researchers who have analysed the same data or attempted to replicate the analyses with other data sets have ultimately dismissed such claims.

In a global survey conducted on behalf of the United Nations, Hood (2002) compared different countries (or their composite member states) allotted to discrete categories according to their pattern of usage of capital punishment over a 40-year period. Some countries or states were *retentionist* – they had retained the use of the sentence throughout that period. Others were *abolitionist* – they either had not used it throughout the same period, or had at some point halted its use. Others, most notably all states of the USA, had a period when execution was not used (1967–1976; as a result of a moratorium and subsequent rulings by the Supreme Court), but following which its use was reinstated (except in 13 jurisdictions which do not have capital punishment on their statute books).

Analysis of the data for rates of serious crimes such as homicide under these different jurisdictions yielded no evidence that capital punishment was associated with reductions in their frequency. The assumed effects of capital punishment in suppressing rates of homicide or violent crime have proved similarly elusive even when side-by-side comparisons are made between roughly equivalent localities differing only in their usage of it (Cheatwood 1993). They also fail to appear in other circumstances predicted by general deterrence theory, for example where effects might be amplified through the publicity given to executions (Stack 1993). Even in the state of Texas, 'by far the most active death penalty state' (Sorensen *et al.* 1999: 483), analysis of crime statistics for the period 1984–1997 has found no relationship between the execution rate and the murder rate.

One other kind of evidence might seem only tangentially relevant to the points at issue here but is nevertheless worth considering. Does the potential threat of sudden death at the hands of a fellow citizen dissuade individuals from committing crimes? McDowall *et al.* (1991) tested the widely held view that possession of lethal weapons acts as a general deterrent to crime. Such an argument is often forwarded in defence of widespread gun ownership in the United States. McDowall *et al.* (1991) analysed five sets of crime data covering periods before and after significant changes in levels of gun ownership. In two of these cases, following an apparent upsurge in serious crimes (rape and robbery), police forces offered training to citizens in the use of firearms, and levels of ownership increased. In one instance in the town of Kennesaw, Georgia, a law was passed making it a legal requirement for every household to maintain a firearm. In two other cases, new laws were passed in local communities prohibiting the sale or ownership of handguns. Extended time-series analysis of rates of the target offences showed no impact (either upwards or downwards) of these changes. This was despite widely publicized claims that guns made a difference; based, as McDowall and his colleagues showed, on misleading analyses of data over short and unrepresentative periods of time.

The failure of punishment

We have probed among several sources for evidence of the deterrence effects supposedly associated with the administration of official punishment. Those effects seem to be absent or so weak as to be invisible, though the evidence is perhaps not conclusive enough to say they simply don't exist. But given the centrality and assumed importance of the crime–punishment connection, are we not entitled to expect a pattern rather stronger than we have found? The most appropriate overall conclusion from this search appears to be that punishment just does not work. Such an assertion may be thought to require firmer support. In most people's minds, the aphorism of 'crime and punishment' is so firmly embedded that one seems to follow the other as a near-necessity. Two kinds of psychological evidence can be adduced that help to elucidate the failure to realize suppressant effects from punitive sanctions in the criminal justice system.

The lack of evidence concerning their effectiveness can be understood on a behavioural and a cognitive level.

Strategies and methods of behaviour change

Punishment can be effective as a means of changing behaviour, and it is people's everyday appreciation of this – supposed clear-cut 'common sense' – that perhaps leads them to expect that a similar outcome will be obtained in the larger setting of the criminal justice system. The evidence surveyed above suggests the latter is not what happens. This apparent contradiction can be resolved when we look at other research showing that punishment only works when certain conditions are met in its application. Behavioural psychologists have traditionally drawn a distinction between two broad strategies for altering patterns of behaviour, with particular reference to the reduction of some type of activity agreed to be socially undesirable – in this case, criminal recidivism (Goldiamond 1974).

Eliminative strategies are based on the expectation that problem behaviour can be suppressed or even eradicated by linking it to negative consequences for the individual. In behaviour modification, examples of such procedures include punishment and aversive conditioning. In criminal justice, this consists instead of deterrence-based sentences or punitive sanctions. As we have seen, they include financial penalties and restriction of liberty to varying degrees, including the use of custody, surveillance, shock incarceration or the imposition of demanding physical regimes.

Constructional strategies, by contrast, are based on the proposal that a reduction of socially undesirable behaviour can be achieved more efficiently, and more ethically, through the building of new 'repertoires' of action. Rather than making the immediate consequences of an act unpleasant, in a constructional system effort is directed towards increasing the frequency of alternative behaviours through which goals can be achieved. If the new behaviours are designed to be incompatible with the problem behaviour, they can even wholly replace it. This can be done through a variety of methods, such as behavioural skills training, attitude change, education, employment and other forms of intervention.

Punishment and other eliminative strategies have consistently been shown to be a much weaker method of behaviour change than constructional techniques involving positive reinforcement and variations upon it. The provision of rewards for increasing certain types of behaviour, or developing skilled responses, proves to be a much more dependable method of behaviour change than aversive conditioning or other measures designed primarily to reduce the rate of a behaviour.

Behavioural analysis of punishment

In behavioural research, there is a large number of studies with a direct bearing on the issue. In the mid-1990s, Gendreau (1996b) estimated that cumulatively, the pertinent research literature amounted to more than 25,000 source references. Its findings, obtained primarily but by no means exclusively from laboratory studies, establish fairly firmly a number of features of punishment. The conditions necessary to make it 'work' or achieve its optimum effects have been reviewed by a number of authors (Axelrod and Apsche 1983; Sundel and Sundel 1993), as have aspects of the ethical implications of using it (Matson and Kazdin 1981).

The first is that for punishment to achieve maximum effectiveness it should first be inevitable or unavoidable; escape should be impossible, or the chances of it very remote. Second, it should be administered immediately following the 'target' behaviour, or at least with maximum possible speed or celerity. Third, for best effects it should be applied at a high level of severity. Fourth, even when these conditions are satisfactorily met, punishment may still fail to be effective when the individual being punished cannot resort to alternative behaviours for pursuing a desired goal.

It is extremely difficult, if not actually impossible, to fulfil these requirements sufficiently well in the complex real-world environment of the criminal justice system, or in the lifestyles of those who regularly come into contact with it as offenders. First, only a surprisingly small fraction of criminal behaviours results in punishment, if the latter is taken to mean significant loss of liberty. The objective chances of being arrested, convicted and then punished for a crime are, from the standpoint of the well-informed offender, reassuringly low. With reference to the United Kingdom, Home Office figures have suggested that on average only 2% of all offences committed (taking official statistics and victim surveys into account) result in a conviction. Following conviction, only one in seven indictable offences leads to a custodial sentence (Home Office 1993). This yields an approximate probability of being sent to prison for a crime of one in 300. That means, with no need whatsoever to resort to a calculator, the other 299 offences go virtually unpunished. Similar figures can be cited for the United States: based on the National Crime Survey, Felson (1994) estimated that only ten burglaries per 1,000 result in a custodial sentence, with the corresponding figure for larceny even lower at three per 1,000. Using the terminology borrowed earlier from Gibbs (1986), the certainty factor is a long way from being operative.

Second, when punitive sanctions are administered, this usually occurs after a gap of weeks or months following the occurrence of the offence. During that period, many other behaviours occur, from among which the individual's offence behaviour cannot be extracted and linked to punitive consequences (Blackman 1996). You may know that being locked up today is a consequence of the burglary you committed six months ago, but it is now rather late for this punitive consequence to set up a conditioned reaction in your nervous system. To reduce this period to any meaningful degree would require a massive expansion of police, court and penal services. So much so that, for the government treasury, there would be no money left over for anything else.

Third, court sentences are graded on a loose scale of severity known colloquially as the 'tariff'. Yet this bears only a fairly lax and uncertain relationship to the seriousness of crimes (Fitzmaurice and Pease 1986). The vagaries of sentencing decisions have been much lamented within penology, and for many offenders it is not until sentence is finally pronounced that they know for sure what their fate will be. But despite calls from some segments of society for heavier sentences, including the restoration of corporal punishments and the death penalty, many citizens have reservations about the use of exclusively severe sanctions. For example, the implementation of 'three strikes' policies in the United States has been surrounded by considerable controversy.

The use of draconian methods may well have a dramatic impact. It has been reported that 'the most effective drug control policy of modern times' was that practised by the Taleban militia during the latter part of their reign over Afghanistan in 2000–2001. The use of harsh punishments against poppy farmers, which included blackening their faces, parading them in the streets, imprisonment and the threat of 'eradication', reduced the global supply of heroin by 65% (BBC News World Edition 2004). Even in the context of widespread abhorrence of heroin use, it is doubtful whether many people would see such extreme measures as justified.

Finally, given the goal-directed nature of much crime and the limited personal resources and life circumstances of many persistent offenders, it is unlikely that many alternative courses of action are readily available to them; though certainly efforts can be made to increase the range of such options. In all these respects, official punishment departs markedly from the required parameters, in behaviourist parlance, of an effective 'aversive conditioner'.

Some time ago Moffitt (1983) posed the question of whether findings from laboratory research can be extrapolated to the more complex, uncontrolled circumstances of criminal justice services. Examining evidence pertaining to the principal dimensions of this (temporal proximity, intensity of the aversive stimulus, availability of reward, availability of alternate responses), Moffitt concluded that while significant gaps remained in the existing research, 'awareness of the principles of punishment may be of use to the deterrence theoretician' (p. 154). Some might hope that such an awareness could allow application of deterrence-based on learning theory principles. 'Achieving such optimal conditions in real-world correctional settings, however, is problematic' (Cullen *et al.* 2002: 282). The cumulative evidence merely attests to the difficulty of applying punishment in correctional settings in ways that would approximate to those needed for it to accomplish its stated objectives.

Cognitive factors

One of the gaps identified by Moffitt (1983) in respect of punishment effectiveness was 'the role of human cognitive and verbal abilities in attenuating delay of punishment' (p. 154). Evidence from other sources suggests that in this respect, too, there are major obstacles to ensuring that deterrence can be applied effectively through the criminal justice system. Perhaps reflecting the actual nature of the circumstances in which they operate, for most individuals contemplating an offence the perceived or subjective chances of being punished are probably very low. Research on perceptual characteristics of sentencing policies supports the validity of the triad of conditions identified by Gibbs (1986) – certainty, severity and celerity – as key elements in deterrence (Paternoster 1987; Howe and Loftus 1996). On the other hand, most research suggests that deterrence plays only a fairly weak part in suppressing potentially criminal behaviour (Paternoster *et al.* 1983) as compared with positive attachments to social norms and institutions. Using data from a sample of 298 inner-city youths in the age range 13–17, Foglia (1997) found that there was no relationship between self-reported delinquency and perceived risk of arrest. However, involvement in delinquency was related to 'internalized norms' assimilated through contact with peers, and experiences of parental discipline.

To make these generalizations more concrete, let us draw an everyday parallel. Most people are presumably aware in general terms of the possibility of being arrested and eventually punished should they break the law. Why does this not have the effect of stopping some individuals from committing crimes? Imagine that each morning you commute to work in your car. You appreciate, at some level of consciousness, the possibility that you could be involved in a collision. You may even know that in an average year in most European countries, several thousand people die in road traffic accidents, and many more are seriously injured. However, you drive off because you don't think it will happen to you. If the thought does enter your mind, other ideas will counter it, reflecting your confidence that you are a careful driver, you do not take risks, you have a car with good safety features (and besides, you need to get to work). The divergence between a kind of 'blanket' versus a 'here-and-now' awareness, between long-term and short-term risks or satisfactions, arises in many types of situation. It occurs when we attempt to lose weight, to quit smoking or drinking, to comply with an exercise regime, to revise for an exam . . . or write a book.

Now transpose this to a situation where someone is poised to commit a crime. He or she is perfectly aware, in what we might call loose or distant terms, of the possibility of being caught: arrested, charged, convicted, punished, even imprisoned. For crimes of any notoriety, there might be stories in the local newspaper, perhaps the added humiliation of being photographed by the press, or filmed by a TV news team going into court. In metaphorical terms, you could say this is at the back of everyone's collective mind. But for it to have a decisive influence on behaviour, it would need – continuing the metaphor – to come more to the forefront.

Studies of several different types of offence indicate that the prospect of arrest is not in the foreground of people's thinking in the moments before embarking on a criminal act. This clearly applies in the case of offences that result from strong feelings of anger or aggression leading to acts of violence; and also where offending is associated with addictive substance abuse. In these instances, people are not in control of themselves and they are not looking very far into the future. They are dominated by 'here-and-now' thinking. Findings from a number of studies based on in-depth interviews, or *in vivo* observational work, suggest that prior to committing an offence, most individuals are preoccupied with the implementation of the act, rather than deliberating upon the consequences should they be caught.

There is comparatively little research on this issue, but what is available suggests that in the period immediately preceding a criminal act, such regulatory mechanisms as might activate a self-deterrent process are not engaged or are deliberately 'switched off'. Studies of property offences of varying levels of seriousness indicate that the prospect of arrest is not salient during these crucial moments. They include the project by Carroll and Weaver (1986) described in Chapter 4, in which high-frequency shoplifters walked around Chicago stores, thinking aloud and recording their thoughts on tape via a lapel microphone. Their cognitions were exclusively focused on the immediate situation, with no evidence of ongoing concern over the possibility of arrest. By contrast, the thoughts of a group of aspiring ('novice') shoplifters were pervaded by apprehensive images of arrest, shame and other negative repercussions. Light *et al.* (1993) interviewed young people involved in vehicle-taking on a deprived Bristol housing estate. Their accounts of their offences and motivations contained little indication that the prospect of being caught was a manifest feature of their thinking. Turning to other types of offence, when Bennett and Wright (1984) invited professional burglars to describe the factors that influenced their decision-making and selection of suitable targets, again no obvious thoughts of deterrence consequences were uppermost. While minimizing risk was one factor in their decisions, their cognitive processing had gone beyond a stage where the possibility of punishment carried any meaningful force.

This parallels the findings of Wright and Decker (1994) with house burglars in the city of St Louis, Missouri. Most of their interviewees 'consciously refused to dwell on the possibility of getting caught', a process which effectively 'robbed the threatened sanctions of their deterrence value' (p. 137). All were aware of this potential outcome, though they perceived the objective chances of it as slim. Some denied that such thoughts were active at the time of committing an offence. Most, however, engaged in a kind of self-discipline to dismiss such ideas from their minds. For a few, there was even a belief that thinking about getting caught made it more likely: a superstition they called 'burning bread on yourself' (p. 130). One efficient way to banish all these doubts was simply to focus on the task and the success that awaited at the end. Similarly in their interviews with a series of 88 prisoners convicted of armed robbery, Morrison and O'Donnell (1994) found their thinking pre-occupied with planning and executing the offence, despite the real danger, having launched on this particular path, of being confronted with armed police. Comparable findings were obtained by Corbett and Simon (1992) in their study of attitudes towards a variety of road traffic offences (speeding, running red lights, drink-driving). Whether their self-disclosed offence frequency was high or low, all offenders were more or less equally eager to avoid getting caught. But high-rate offenders 'dwelled upon their beliefs about the relatively low risk of apprehension to facilitate their decisions to break the law' (p. 543).

These results are complemented by others from a study by Zamble and Quinsey (1997) of the processes involved in recidivism. The researchers interviewed and obtained detailed information from a series of 311 male repeat offenders returning to prison following a further re-conviction. Offences were typically preceded by personal crises, difficulties in coping and poor self-management. These men's problems had accumulated to intolerable levels, yet they rarely applied a positive problem-oriented approach. For some an offence was a by-product of stressful events, for others a bungled attempt to escape their ongoing problems. Again there was little evidence that the potential legal consequences of criminal activity played any significant part in determining the paths they took. The overall and compelling message from all of these findings is that, hovering on the brink of a criminal act, would-be law-breakers are not for the most part in what Walker (1991: 15) called 'deterrable states of mind'. Rather, they are in what Wright and Decker (1994, borrowing a phrase from Lofland) called a state of 'psychosocial encapsulation': a 'qualitatively different state of mind' inside which 'the potentially negative consequences of their actions become attenuated' (p. 133).

Carroll and Weaver (1986) discussed their own findings and others in the context of a model of *bounded rationality* in which individuals apply reasoning processes, but within a narrow and circumscribed frame of reference which maps onto only one segment of the situation in which they are acting. Similarly, research on aggression typically shows that for affective or angry aggression, the type likely to manifest itself in most fights, individuals are influenced by very short-term motivations and lose sight of longer-term consequences (Berkowitz 1993). That increased severity of penalties does not have the deterrence effect of instilling fear is additionally demonstrated by research on drug-trafficking (Dorn *et al.* 1992). As law-enforcement strategies have become progressively more intensive and punishments more severe, offenders have simply redoubled their efforts and increased the flexibility of their methods.

Finally, it is likely that for punishment to have an influence on individuals it must also appear comprehensible to them. Criminological researchers have shown that many individuals can account for their illegal actions in terms that make them acceptable. This entails employing elaborate cognitive mechanisms such as the techniques of neutralization that we encountered in Chapter 2. These function to isolate individuals from the consequences of their actions, to help them avoid responsibility, and to perceive the experience of punishment as unfair (Sykes and Matza 1957; Vold *et al.* 1998).

As mentioned earlier, it may be that many people's expectations that punishment will serve its purpose are based on inferring from 'common sense knowledge' that suffering pain as a result of our actions will stop us from doing something. That may be derived partly from the experience of growing up and being chastised by parents; source of the ancient adage 'spare the rod and spoil the child'. Ironically, however, punishment does not appear especially effective on that level either. Research suggests that the main elements of parenting that contribute most to whether children are well or badly behaved are expressions of warmth and support, parents' levels of interest through monitoring what children are doing, and their use of inductive reasoning when exercising discipline and explaining rules. In the absence of warmth, or at lower levels of it, the use of corporal punishment is associated with an increased risk of delinquency among young people. This was shown, for example, in a cross-cultural study of American and Taiwanese families by Simons et al. (2000), using as a measure the proportion of disciplinary encounters that involved physical punishment. While the patterns found were slightly different between the two cultural settings, overall 'our analyses provided little evidence that corporal punishment serves to deter adolescent conduct problems' (p. 74).

Deterrence effects

It appears to be widely accepted that the existence of punitive sanctions in society contributes to the maintenance of order through the suppression of criminal activity among the population. It is equally plausible, of course, that the continuation of law-abiding behaviour by most citizens most of the time is a function of other factors such as positive reinforcement or reward for socially approved behaviour, and informal social controls exercised within proximate social groups. Conversely, for those who have become marginalized as a result of previous involvement in crime, punitive sanctions may have become diluted in their effects.

These dimensions of deterrence may be illustrated by comparing the outcomes of studies reporting success and failure among deterrence-based interventions. In some circumstances, certain kinds of sanctions can be shown to work. This applies, for example, to the use of random drug-testing in conditions in which there is a great deal at stake for those found using drugs. Borack (1998) has described the impact of such procedures in the US Navy. This study employed baseline estimates of frequency of drug use obtained from general population studies. In the Navy, a positive drug test results in dismissal. Under conditions in which a randomly selected 20% of the personnel were subjected to urinalysis per 30-day period, a suppressant effect of 56.5% was obtained. When the variable of uncertainty is manipulated in circumstances where potential offenders may risk significant loss, similar findings emerge. Extensive studies in Australia concerning the suppressant effect of random breath-testing on rates of vehicle accidents have also yielded evidence firmly supportive of its efficacy

(Henstridge *et al.* 1997). In a follow-up of 700 men arrested for domestic violence, Thistlethwaite *et al.* (1998) found that even if imprisoned, only those with a high 'stake in conformity' were less likely to re-offend. 'Conformity' for this purpose was measured by a complex scale taking into account aspects of employment, education, residence and marital status.

By contrast, little effect of deterrence was observed in a study by Baron and Kennedy (1998) of the sentencing of homeless street youths. As these authors noted, 'perceptions of sanctions differ depending upon one's position in the social structure' (p. 30). These very different studies illustrate the polarities of deterrence effects. While the naval recruits described by Borack had much to lose by testing positive for drugs, the reverse was true for the homeless, impoverished youths studied by Baron and Kennedy.

Perceptual deterrence appears to have some fairly enduring characteristics. In a study using data from the US National Youth Survey, Massoglia and Macmillan (2002) found evidence of considerable steadiness in the perceived certainty and severity of sanctions across a three-year period between late adolescence and early adulthood. Massoglia and MacMillan called this 'legal subjectivity' and concluded that it is 'reasonably reliable over time and highly stable' and is 'developed in the early part of the life course through childhood socialisation and experience and then likely remains part of one's psychological toolkit for the remainder of the life course' (p. 335).

The totality of evidence cannot then support the claim that deterrence is never effective, or that no-one has ever been prevented from further offending by criminal sanctions. 'Glimmers of a deterrence effect pop up once in a while' (Cullen *et al.* 2002: 283). In all likelihood there is a proportion of any sample of offenders who will be deterred by official punishments. Similarly, as Gibbs (1986) has asserted, it may be that deterrence works widely in its restrictive form (defined earlier), in which some offenders hold back from unmitigated indulgence in crime, so as to reduce possible exposure to arrest. The extent of any such effect is probably unmeasurable. The question posed is whether specific deterrence effects are of sufficient reliability or generalizability to form the basis for a systematic policy, let alone one that is accorded the cardinal place in society's overall response to criminal behaviour.

Considering ways in which deterrence effects might be manipulated, the available evidence points to certainty as the most promising instrumental variable. Complete certainty is of course impossible to ensure. Even increased probability of arrest is difficult to attain, but comparatively small increases in the perceived risk of arrest may be sufficient to deter. This direction may present the likeliest route for increasing the efficacy of deterrence. Von Hirsch *et al.* (1999) have reviewed evidence that changes in the perceived uncertainty of punishment can have marginal deterrence effects. When studies have been conducted on the relationship between probability of conviction and rates of certain crimes (robbery, assault, burglary and vehicle theft), most have found a negative correlation. By contrast, evidence of achieving effects by varying the severity of punishment remains exceedingly weak, making it all the more ironic that this is so commonly advocated as the solution to the 'law-and-order problem'.

Other evidence showing some initial deterrence effects of sanctions has been reviewed by Nagin (1998). The most suitable interpretation of these findings is that they are due to manipulation of the perceptual certainty variable. For example, the passing of the British Road Safety Act in 1967 and the introduction of the 'breathalyser' test had an immediate impact on rates of fatal road accidents at night (Von Hirsch 1976). The effect was, however, temporary and, as in the other studies reviewed by Sherman (1990), was followed by a phenomenon he called *deterrence decay*. The introduction of similar legislation in Norway and Sweden had no parallel effect, though as we saw above the Australian experiments with random breath-testing proved more positive. One suggestion for building on the results obtained is to maintain ambiguity and uncertainty by the constant creation of novelty (if that is not a contradiction in terms). This would place an onus on the police and other justice agencies to be ceaselessly inventive and innovative in finding new ruses through which to convince the public that the probability of arrest was higher than it objectively is. But even this might only work with certain types of offences or offenders. Such deterrence effects as have been found have been harder to reproduce with more serious types of crime (Sherman 1990) and are less likely to be obtained with more experienced offenders (Nagin 1998). Paradoxically, the results of some studies suggest that 'the criminally uninitiated had unrealistically high expectations of sanction risks and . . . experience with offending caused them to lower their unrealistically high expectations' (Nagin 1998: 13). In other words, when deterrence works it appears most likely to do so with the people who need it least, and least likely with the people who need it most!

To boost certainty on any meaningful scale, however, would entail an injection of resources that few societies if any could afford. Take the example given by Felson (1994) of the policing of Los Angeles County, California, which then had a population of nearly nine million (the greater LA conurbation has a population of 16 million). Based on the area of the city, the number of properties to be protected and the availability of police on foot patrol, Felson calculated that the average house, shop, restaurant or office in LA is under visible police protection for an average of 29 seconds per day. This throws into perspective the idea that crime will be reduced if police numbers can be expanded. Usually, calls for the latter are proportionately quite modest; so let us imagine that the number of 'Bobbies on the beat' is suddenly *doubled*. That would mean each property in LA could now be offered not quite one minute of police coverage each day. 'Doubling the number of police in a U.S. metropolis is like doubling a drop in the bucket' (Felson 2002: 5). Felson regarded the possibility of protecting property through increased policing as a fairly grotesque illusion, which he dubbed the 'Cops-and-courts fallacy'.

In the previous chapter, we saw that a commentary published by Martinson (1974) has been widely considered to have played a seminal part in casting doubt on the value of rehabilitation, and of ushering in an era of greater punitiveness. Martinson's conclusion was that treatment added nothing to what he called 'the networks of criminal justice' (p. 254). The only conclusion that can seriously be sustained by all the available data is surely just the opposite. Legal frameworks and networks are essentially ineffective for their proclaimed purposes with regard to convicted offenders. Perhaps it is only by the addition of services that entail active, constructive interventions that criminal justice personnel will be likely to achieve the avowed aims of the entire process.

Ineffective – but indispensable?

In summary, the evidence reviewed here cumulatively suggests that punishing offenders simply fails to achieve what is informally assumed, and officially pronounced, to be one of its central goals. On the surface, this might at first be thought to be a purely sociological question. Here are several sets of data – on rates of conviction or imprisonment, rates of crime, and the like – which are aggregate social statistics, and which can be studied closely to test ideas about whether one might have a causal effect upon the other. I hope that this chapter has clarified why, to make sense of any such connection, or as it transpires the absence of one, psychological variables need to be taken into account.

That a supposedly intelligent society continues to employ a method that so singly fails to accomplish its goals, causes other kinds of pain, and incidentally entails considerable monetary cost, could be seen as irrational. To put it bluntly, when we say it will deter offenders from crime, we are simply kidding ourselves. But from a sociological standpoint it may well be that punishment serves other symbolic functions for society, related to group cohesion, shared morality or civil governance. From that perspective, it is viewed as imperative to avoid falling into what Garland (1990) called 'the trap of thinking of it solely in crime-control terms' (p. 20).

Nevertheless, some philosophers have argued that whether or not punishment can be justified is at least partly an empirical question (Farrell 1985). Crime-control and the creation of a 'safer society' is one of the stated roles of government, and a keenly debated theme in the manifestos of most political parties. Punishment is usually perceived as one of the key implements in delivering it. Hence, the incongruity of its continued use alongside evidence that it fails to serve that purpose merits systematic inquiry. It is difficult to imagine that in other fields of policy, such as health, education or employment, so ineffective a procedure could be so avidly pursued in the face of so much evidence of its futility. The argument that punishment is somehow an intrinsic feature of human symbolic relations, and therefore cannot be changed, is similarly unimpressive. Because something always has been so in society is no guide to whether it should continue to be so. Were that the case, the power of monarchs, the subjugation of women, the right to enslave the conquered, would all have remained unchallenged.

The philosopher Ted Honderich (1976) argued some years ago that punishment could be justified if it were, among other things, 'economically preventive of offences' (p. 176). We would have moral grounds for continuing to use it if it secured 'the reduction of distress at an economical rate' (p. 181). Based on all the findings reviewed earlier, punishment does not reduce and may well worsen the problem which it is designed to cure. The following conclusion reached by Gibbs (1986) appears as accurate now as when first written: 'The bulk of findings indicate that offenders are not deterred when punished. More precisely, numerous researchers have reported either that recidivism is greater for offenders who have been punished the most severely or that there is no significant relation between punishment severity and recidivism' (p. 122). Summarizing evidence from controlled trials of sanctions outlined earlier, Sherman (1988) endorsed the same viewpoint: 'The prevailing wisdom that punishment deters the future crimes of those punished is contradicted by the majority of the experimental evidence . . . the most frequent finding from randomized experiments is that sanctions make no difference' (p. 86). Note that the latter two statements were both written some time ago, and before the publication of considerably larger volumes of evidence reinforcing the same essential point, and subsumed in the meta-analytic reviews. More recently, considering the relationship between punishment and motivation to change, Hollin (2002c) has acknowledged that punishment can be shown to serve the purposes of retribution and incapacitation. However, viewing it as a deterrent, he concludes that 'examination of the evidence with regard to *general* deterrence suggested that there is very little consistent support for the proposition that punishing offenders inhibits the antisocial behaviour of other members of society . . . Moving from general to *specific* deterrence, it is also doubtful whether punishment motivates long-term behaviour change at the individual level' (p. 246).

Further reading

Key concepts in penology are discussed by Nigel Walker (1991) *Why Punish? Theories of Punishment Re-assessed* (Oxford: Oxford University Press) and Barbara A. Hudson (1996) *Understanding Justice: An Introduction to Ideas, Perspectives and Controversies in Modern Penal Theory* (Buckingham: Open University Press). For a mammoth volume devoted to these and related issues, see Michael Tonry (ed., 1998) *The Handbook of Crime and Punishment* (Oxford: Oxford University Press). Further discussion of the ineffectiveness of punitive sanctions can be found in Donald A. Andrews and James Bonta (2003) *The Psychology of Criminal Conduct* (3rd edn. Cincinnati, OH: Anderson).

Applications and values

This book carries the sub-title *Perspectives on theory and action* and this concluding chapter has three objectives. The first is to survey some of the kinds of action to which the application of psychology can contribute in addressing problems of crime and the administration of justice. The second is to consider some critical issues, notably ethical ones, in working with offenders on an individual basis. The third is to discuss psychology's status in the broader context of the politics of criminal justice and the sociology of knowledge.

Psychology and the criminal justice process

In a large and steadily expanding field, any book must be selective in its focus. The present one has considered certain core questions in a psychological approach to crime. There are many other topics that could be covered in companion volumes. Let us therefore first embark on a brief survey of some adjoining branches of the field. As psychology can potentially contribute to every stage of the criminal justice process, that chain of events provides a framework for organizing this account.

Police investigation

If individuals differ in ways we can understand and even predict, such patterns may also be reflected in variations in their *modus operandi* when committing offences, and in the kinds of traces they leave behind following a criminal act. That is the key assumption underpinning an influential development in crime investigation called *offender profiling*. It in turn is now part of a specialized field of research known as *investigative psychology* (Canter and Alison 2000).

The first well-known case of profiling, the capture of George Metesky, the 'mad bomber' of New York City in the 1950s, was the work of psychiatrist Dr James Brussel. As subsequently used by the Behavioral Science Unit of the Federal Bureau of Investigation, profiling involved detailed analysis of the scenes of serious crimes to extract information that revealed characteristics of the perpetrator. Hence the basic premise is that 'the crime scene reflects the personality of the offender' (Holmes and Holmes 2002: 41). For example, one distinction that emerged among serial murderers is between *disorganized asocial* and *organized non-social* offenders. The former is typically a 'nonathletic, introverted white male' (Holmes and Holmes 2002: 72), who is likely to be anxious, socially inadequate, of below average intelligence, working in an unskilled job, with a very disorganized lifestyle and poor personal hygiene. The latter by contrast is socially adequate and skilled, sexually competent, highly intelligent, living with a partner, with a well-controlled lifestyle and a high level of spatial and occupational mobility. Both types may be solitary people; but for the former, it is because of their strangeness; for the latter, it is because no-one else is good enough for them. They also differ in their post-offence behaviour and in how they respond when interviewed by the police. If individual qualities can be reliably inferred from the traces left behind at a crime scene, such information will be valuable in enabling police to channel the direction of an inquiry or narrow their range of suspects.

Given the types of the offences usually involved, this is a field in which specific cases have attracted sensationalist press coverage, influencing public perceptions of what the work involves and giving rise to a number of myths. Profiling also raises grave ethical questions, particularly from one notorious instance in which a profile was used in what practically amounted to an attempt at entrapment of the suspect (Ainsworth 2001).

While initially profiling was used mainly for serious violent crimes, more sophisticated versions are now being researched that show spatial and psychological characteristics of property offenders (Canter and Alison 2001). There are several approaches to the task (Ainsworth 2001). Some place greatest reliance on the analysis of the crime scene, and on evidence from victims where they have survived attacks. Others focus on the environmental range and hypothesized routines of likely offenders and entail detailed statistical analysis to detect any regularities in offences. Still others are closer to a process of clinical diagnosis and involve using case information to estimate the offender's motives.

The question of whether psychological profiling 'works' has remained controversial. If this is taken to mean that the information produced is so precise that it enables detectives to track a serial attacker to his front door, the chances of such an outcome are remote. A survey conducted within the Metropolitan Police suggested that the process did not add a great deal that should not already be there in good detective work, and profiles proved helpful in only 16% of cases (Copson 1995). However, many investigating officers describe psychological profiles as useful in guiding their inquiries and clarifying the options worth pursuing (Ainsworth 2001).

Separately, other psychological research has exposed some of the sources of error in cases of mistaken identification and wrongful conviction, the numbers of which are alarmingly high. This has included work on the usage of face-fits or photo-spreads, 'wanted' posters, and identification parades or line-ups (Wrightsman *et al.* 2002; Wells and Olson 2003).

Gathering evidence: the testimony of witnesses

The second phase on which psychology has applications occurs after someone is arrested. Police officers investigating a case interview and record the statements of suspects, victims and witnesses. For evidence to be admissible in a court of law, it should be gathered according to specified rules. If it is to allow a jury to make an impartial decision, it should be reliable and accurate. But given the confusing circumstances of many offences and the fraught processes that ensue, numerous factors affect the outcome of crime investigations.

Witness testimony is often the most powerful type of evidence given in court. Regrettably it is far from infallible. Observing events, and storing, retrieving and communicating information about them, are all imperfect cognitive processes. Hence psychology has copious applications in this area, through studies of attention, perception, memory, motivation and social interaction. The degree of witness confidence does not necessarily correspond to the accuracy of testimony; the quality of the evidence to a court is influenced by many variables. They include the time interval since the incident occurred; aspects of the crime scene, such as the level of lighting; the emotion induced by the event; *weapon focus*, which may cause a witness to pay less attention to other details; and differences between the witness, defendant and victim in gender, age or ethnicity (Bartol and Bartol 1994; Wells and Olson 2003). Taking account of the factors that lead to forgetting, or that produce errors, there is evidence that the recall of witnesses can be improved using certain techniques such as the *cognitive interview* (Memon 1998).

In addition, it has been shown that some witnesses are *suggestible* or *acquiescent* when interviewed by the police, and may make what in due course transpire to be misleading statements. This can happen to the extent that some individuals will confess to crimes they did not commit. Some false confessions may be given under the pressure of interrogation, while others are actuated by internal states such as emotional needs (Gudjonsson 2002). Colloquially, some forms of this are known as 'faking bad'. Psychological evidence concerning this has proved vitally important in a large number of cases.

Special care needs to be taken when victims or witnesses of a crime are emotionally or socially vulnerable. This may apply when interviewing children or adults with learning or communication difficulties, and psychologists have helped prepare and evaluate recommendations for good practice, including frameworks for how to conduct such interviews (Bull 1995, 1998), or testing the use of courtroom video-links (Davies and Noon 1991). This is allied with other developments for evaluating the status of children's testimony in allegations of sexual abuse, employing methods such as *statement validity assessment* (Vrij and Akehurst 1998).

Finally, and not surprisingly, given what is at stake when charged with a serious crime, people in that predicament are not always honest: they may tell lies to protect themselves or others. Colloquially this is known as 'faking good'. Is it possible to gauge when someone is doing this? Many people think they can. Unfortunately research in social psychology shows that the cues that most of us believe are indicators of lying are not, whereas other features that we usually discount are better for this purpose (Zuckerman and Driver 1985). There is now a significant volume of psychological research on the detection of deception (Canter and Alison 1999; De Paulo *et al.* 2003).

The sentence of the court

Society's response to someone convicted of a crime is determined by those passing sentence (judges, magistrates, sheriffs) who interpret and act upon the statutes of the criminal law. The main factors steering the imposition of any given sentence are the relevant legislation, previous judicial decisions, tariffs or sentencing guidelines, aggravating or mitigating features, and a range of informal influences (Walker and Padfield 1996; Ashworth 2000). But given the accumulating evidence that some approaches to working with offenders can reduce criminal recidivism, there has been a growing interest in the inclusion of such methods as an element in prison and community sentences. Many of the directions this has taken are informed by psychological research of the kinds reviewed in Chapter 6.

In 1996, the provision of programmes designed to reduce recidivism was made a *key performance indicator* of the Prison Service in England and Wales. In 1998, the British government announced a major policy initiative, the Crime Reduction Programme, under which resources were made available for a series of innovations in criminal justice services. This departure drew on the findings of the meta-analytic reviews of tertiary prevention, and Home Office research studies summarized portions of that research (Vennard *et al.* 1997; Nuttall *et al.* 1998).

Aspects of the work focused on the design and systematic delivery of structured programmes. Before these can be accepted as suitable for use, they have to be scrutinized and validated by an independent expert group appointed within the Home Office, the Correctional Services Accreditation Panel. The Panel has devised and published a set of accreditation criteria that inform the selection of appropriate interventions (Joint Prison/Probation Services Accreditation Panel 2002). For a programme to be approved under this procedure, it must be accompanied by a set of documents describing the theory and research on which it is based; alongside manuals specifying how it should be delivered, and how staff should be trained and supervised.

Programmes accredited in this way have been widely disseminated through prison and probation services, and similar quality-control mechanisms have been established in several countries. In the Probation Service, a set of rehabilitative programmes given the title 'Pathfinders' was introduced from 2000 onwards. Some are included within Community Punishment projects (Rex *et al.* 2004); others address the resettlement needs of short-term prisoners (Lewis *et al.* 2003); while still others entail the delivery of structured offending behaviour programmes (Hollin *et al.* 2002). Among the third group, some approaches are *generic* and include scope for working on multiple types of offence, as the focus is on dynamic risk factors that may contribute to different criminal acts. Other approaches are *offence-specific* and are designed for individuals with a pattern dominated by one type of offence. There are specialized programmes focused on alcohol-impaired driving, substance abuse, general violence, domestic violence and sexual offending.

The magnitude of this change in policy and practice is unprecedented. Some observers have criticized the pace and scale of the innovation (Ellis and Winstone 2002). Others have expressed fears that the focus, mainly deploying cognitive-behavioural interventions, was too limited and neglected social factors in crime (Rex 2001). Outcome evaluations from the prison-based programmes have so far yielded mixed results. At the time of writing, outcome evaluations from the probation programmes were about to appear.

As Ogloff and Davis (2004) have commented, there is a great deal at stake in such large-scale, government-sponsored investment in rehabilitative activities. If the outcomes of the enterprise prove to be disappointing, pressure could mount for a return to more punitive approaches. Such a turn of events would be derisory, given that evidence for the effectiveness of those approaches is to all intents and purposes non-existent (as we saw in Chapter 7).

Implementation: organizational and social contexts

The advent of criminal justice programming on the scale just described has raised other important issues, and identified omissions, in the outcome research. Many researchers now acknowledge that the process of *implementation* was badly neglected when drawing lessons from the literature reviews (Gendreau *et al.* 1999b). Fortunately, this issue has begun to receive more of the attention it requires (Harris and Smith 1996; Bernfeld *et al.* 2001).

Bernfeld *et al.* (1990) argued that programme implementation was only likely to be successful if attention was paid to issues grouped under four headings: *clients, programmes, organizations* and *society*. It may be that in recent policy developments in some countries, there have been disproportionate amounts of attention given to the second, at the expense of the other three ingredients. The most effective agencies, therefore, will locate rehabilitative efforts within wider organizational arrangements, paying attention to local variations in context, and adapting services accordingly.

Andrews (2001), too, has proposed that successfully embarking on evidence-based initiatives necessitates attention to more than the outcome studies alone. Other elements should also be in place. First, agencies should begin by developing and making available a service plan, or set of policies and guidelines regarding application of new knowledge. Second, steps should be taken to ensure that managers genuinely understand background principles, and possess the ability to coordinate processes of quality control or accreditation. Third, there should be a concerted focus on staff skills and extensive portfolio of training, including competence in developing relationships and motivating others, as well as in delivering programme sessions. Finally, it is vital to foster multi-level ownership and to avoid simply imposing decisions 'top-down'. This includes identifying and clarifying areas in which staff may exercise personal discretion within the agreed policy frameworks.

Costs and benefits of interventions

An impressive addendum to the outcomes research, and one with potentially considerable policy significance, is a set of findings to the effect that intervention programmes with offenders can be relatively cost-effective. Some years ago, Prentky and Burgess (1990) reported an econometric study of the Massachusetts Treatment Center (MTC), a specialist facility for the treatment of men who had committed serious sexual offences. The background to this was a sardonic recognition that if the state treasury was reluctant to invest in treatment facilities on purely humane grounds, its views might change if such interventions yielded monetary savings.

This type of research involves calculating and comparing two sets of costs. One consists of *victim-related expenses*, which include a range of expenditures such as repairing damage to a car or home, hospitalization costs in cases of injury, supportive counselling, compensation and associated legal costs. The other is *offender-related expenses*, which include the costs of police work, prosecution and court hearings, imprisonment or community supervision. When the two sets of figures are placed side by side in a balance sheet, it is possible to compute the ratio of one to the other and test whether there is any return on the investment made in a particular course of action.

The MTC study showed that for each individual allocated to it, not only was there a reduced risk of further victimization (on average 15%) but a net saving of US$68,000 to Massachusetts taxpayers. A similar study in Australia used an average treatment impact of 8% (based on prior evaluations). This showed that for every 100 sexual offenders treated there were net benefits to the treasury of between AU$258,000 and AU$1.85 million (Donato and Shanahan 1999).

There are now several reviews pertaining to this question. One analysis of seven studies of tertiary intervention found benefit–cost ratios ranging from 1.13 : 1 to 7.14 : 1 (Welsh and Farrington 2000, 2001). Another wider-ranging review has adduced evidence of significant cost-efficiency in evidence-based criminal justice programmes, as compared with negative economic returns for punitive sanctions (S. L. Brown 2001). Using a different approach, McDougall *et al.* (2003) attempted to compare the relative costs and benefits of different types of sentences, but the small number of studies they found and some major differences between them prohibited the drawing of any clear conclusions. In the largest review to date, Aos *et al.* (2001) reported on a series of comparisons between different interventions in their benefit–cost ratios. They identified numerous interventions that achieved a 'win–win' outcome; that is, they lowered crime *and* reduced costs. Monetary savings could be made even when reductions in crime were relatively small. While the savings from many programmes were moderate, several approaches emerged very positively, including *multi-systemic therapy, multidimensional treatment foster care, functional family therapy* and *aggression replacement training*. For example, the benefit-to-cost ratio for aggression replacement training was US$45.91 for every dollar spent.

Integrating psychology and law: therapeutic jurisprudence

Either directly or symbolically, the law affects and regulates many other sectors of life (to the extent that it has been called 'imperialist': Hudson

1996). Legal decisions, concerning guilt or innocence, type of sentence, detention or discharge from security, have profound and far-reaching repercussions for those subject to them. We may not be accustomed to thinking of it in this way, but the operation of law is essentially a process of social influence, though until recently very little attention was paid to that aspect of it. However, a new approach to this has emerged within law itself, advocating a more careful scrutiny of the meaning of events for everyone affected.

Therapeutic jurisprudence (Wexler and Winick 1991, 1996; Stolle *et al.* 2000) is a specific approach to thinking about the law in which the central focus of interest is the impact of legal processes and decisions. It is defined simply as 'the study of the role of law as a therapeutic agent' (Wexler and Winick 1996: xvii) and is based in part on a convergence between the law and behavioural sciences (Carson 2000). Its key principles originated from studies of the operation of mental health law, hence these effects are expressed in terms of whether they are *therapeutic* or *anti-therapeutic* for various parties involved. If a decision or process is therapeutic, that means it helps a person to recover or improve; if it is anti-therapeutic, it produces negative or adverse reactions.

Since their inception, these ideas have been successively applied to analysis of other legal specialisms. Wexler (1996) examined some aspects of criminal court activities and decisions. The traditional model of a courtroom depicts the central decision-maker as a 'dispassionate, disinterested magistrate'. Some writers on criminal courts, for example, see sentencing as in certain respects being an 'expressive ritual'. It entails 'denunciatory justification', the effect of which is to 'signify disapproval in a particularly dramatic way' (Walker and Padfield 1996: 117). In therapeutic jurisprudence, 'What is at issue . . . is the extent to which the law itself causes or contributes to psychological dysfunction' (Wexler 1991: 19). For example, one area of application may be in relation to persons who have committed sexual offences. With particular reference to factors such as cognitive distortions, we might ask whether the law impacts therapeutically or anti-therapeutically on them, and whether it could operate in such a way as to promote processes of cognitive change. Another issue may be whether principles of treatment adherence that operate in healthcare settings could be invoked in the interactions between courts and individuals being considered for conditional release or placement on probation. This requires fostering a closer dialogue between court personnel and offenders.

Wexler (1998) has also explored the potential import of findings concerning psychologically based interventions with offenders. If courts of law were acquainted with and able to act on the evidence concerning outcomes of that work, they might be able to facilitate it directly through a number of adjustments in procedure. First, training could be provided for sentencers to familiarize them with the relevant research literature. Putting the research into practice would entail making the defendant central rather than peripheral in proceedings, and courts would engage more actively with the process of motivating change. This could be accomplished through individuals' participation in the preparation of supervision or parole plans; the involvement of significant others where appropriate; and setting conditions or providing support through which agreed plans were to be implemented. Courts might additionally make use of some of the principles and methods that have played a prominent part in effective programmes, such as problem-solving training and relapse prevention (Wexler 1998).

Scholars in the field of therapeutic jurisprudence have pointed to a number of developments in court procedures and practice that open up routes through which legal decision-making could become more therapeutic both in its process and its effects. They include, for example, the development of specialized courts that address the complexities of domestic violence; and other departures such as drug courts, teen courts, mental health courts and problem-solving courts. There are evaluations of the impact of some of these procedures on both client participation and recidivism, with very encouraging results (Minor *et al.* 1999; Peters and Murrin 2000; Springer *et al.* 2002). McGuire (2003) has discussed ways in which concepts derived from psychological therapy or behaviour change are potentially applicable in legal settings.

Professional organizations

The development of psychology since its appearance as an independent discipline has been such that the numbers of people studying, researching and practising it has shown an almost exponential growth. Like other groups of workers, psychologists have progressively formed themselves into associations that represent their interests, set standards, regulate entry and perform other functions that sociologists describe as characteristics of a *profession* (Johnson 1972; Torstendahl and Burrage 1990). Such bodies also serve the purpose of communicating with external groups including the public, other professions and government.

Professional psychology associations have been established in many countries. The *American Psychological Association* (APA), founded in 1892, is the oldest and the largest, with more than 120,000 members. The *British Psychological Society* (BPS), founded in 1901, is the oldest in Europe, though the *Colegio Oficial de Psicologos* of Spain is numerically larger. Every European country has a national association, and several, such as the *Berufsverband Deutscher Psychologen* (BDP) of Germany, have sub-divisions dedicated to psychology and law (*Section Recht-psychologie*). Within the BPS the corresponding group is the *Division of Forensic Psychology*; in the APA it is the *American Psychology-Law Society* (APLS). Beyond national boundaries, there are also international networks that perform various liaison roles. The *European Federation of Psychologists' Associations* (EFPA) coordinates issues of common interest for its 31 member associations; there are similar networks in other continents. In addition, there are specialist international organizations such as the *European Association of Psychology and Law* (EAPL) and the *Australia and New Zealand Association of Psychiatry, Psychology and Law* (ANZAPPL).

Psychology and crime: the social context

Rates of crime, its seriousness, and the frequency of different types of it, all vary considerably from one country to another (Newman *et al.* 2001; Barclay and Tavares 2002). That could of course be a reflection of varying definitions and recording methods rather than underlying differences. But large-scale studies suggest that in England and Wales in recent years, there have been in the region of 12–17 million crimes per annum. Those figures come from successive sweeps of the British Crime Survey (Kershaw *et al.* 2001). The subjectively experienced fear of crime also shows sizeable variations (Mayhew and White 1997), but they are only circuitously related to the patterns of crime recorded in official statistics.

Whatever the exact details, the upshot is that directly or indirectly, crime touches the lives of nearly everyone. Given that context, it is rarely out of the media spotlight. Research shows that crime events take the largest single share of stories in every news medium (Carrabine *et al.* 2002). Furthermore, the proportion of news devoted to crime has been rising over the last 50 years (Reiner 2002). The level of saturation is such that almost everyone has an opinion, and a theory, and some evidence to back them up. Yet discussion of law-and-order inexorably reveals what could be described as an attitudinal minefield. Individuals' perspectives are more likely to be shaped by their prior attitudes and beliefs on a range of social issues than by systematic evidence concerning crime itself.

Can an approach that claims to be scientific really be applicable to what most people think of as moral or political questions? In the prevalent imagery, science aims towards detachment and objectivity. Surely that prohibits an appreciation of subjective experiences, meanings, ideals, values and other elemental qualities of the human condition. On the contrary: psychology is very much concerned with those spheres. Moreover, a scientific outlook can be perfectly compatible with exploring them, and with a system of values.

If psychology is to inform social action or public policy, it needs to take account of ethical and political dimensions. Nevertheless, there is a view that its methodological aspirations and close connection with biological sciences render it unsuitable for addressing social problems. If it does have a stance, its focus on individual differences leads some writers to perceive it as affiliated, intrinsically, to the conservative end of the political spectrum.

Individual and community

Let us examine these issues first at the individual level. Working with persons who have broken the law raises a number of complex ethical questions. There is an inherent tension between providing services to meet individual needs while also attempting to serve collective or community interests.

Recalling the terminology used by Garland (2002), many of the activities described earlier might make it sound as if psychology has switched its historic allegiances. While traditionally it looked like part of the Lombrosian project in criminology, perhaps it has now been assimilated into the governmental project. Psychologists help the police with their inquiries, assist courts of law in evaluating evidence, assess risk levels of offenders, and develop methods of managing them inside the penal system. Their basic agenda is to help explain crime and find means of controlling it. In Garland's (2002) view, such a 'science of causes' is a 'deeply flawed' undertaking (p. 8). And all of it is done in the service of the state!

But before the idea takes off that this is one-sidedly part of a totalitarian agenda, note that much of it can also help individual citizens. It may safeguard them from being wrongfully convicted; reduce severity of punishments if they are; and protect potential victims from genuine risks of exploitation or assault (reducing recidivism *means* reducing victimization). Outside criminal justice, psychology has many further uses in health, education and the workplace.

Furthermore, it is possible simultaneously to meet the needs of both society *and* of the individual who has broken the law. The behaviour of those who frequently offend is evidently troublesome for the community. But much research suggests that often, members of that group are themselves very troubled people. Helping such individuals re-orient their lives can be of immense value both to them as well as to others if it effectively reduces offending.

For the 1,527 young people followed in the Denver Youth Survey, there was a strong association between numbers of self-reported problems and seriousness of offending. 'Amongst those facing only one problem, 7% are serious offenders, but among those facing four problems, 85% are serious offenders' (Huizinga *et al.* 2003: 62). This pattern emerged for both males and females. The experience of personal difficulties across several areas of life is unfortunately sometimes accompanied by a lack of skills for addressing those problems and solving them in an effective way. For example, Wesner (1996) found poorer problem-solving skills among offenders than in a non-offending comparison sample.

Whitton and McGuire (submitted) gave a series of questionnaires designed to assess aspects of problems and styles of coping to young people under the supervision of youth offender teams in the Manchester conurbation, and to a matched sample of non-offenders in a secondary school. Young offenders reported a significantly higher frequency of serious problems in their lives, and this was correlated with their numbers of previous convictions. However, in depicting the ways they coped, they showed higher rates of using fairly futile, unproductive methods, and lower rates of more active, problem-focused coping.

In a study we have encountered before, Zamble and Quinsey (1997) interviewed highly repetitive adult offenders, with an average of 25 previous convictions, concerning factors that appeared to contribute to new offences. The crimes for which they were re-arrested were often preceded by difficulties in coping and by poor self-management, characterized by an absence of a positive problem-oriented approach. For example, individuals ignored problems they were experiencing, so allowing them to accumulate to intolerable levels, then adopted drastic solutions. In other research on how adult prisoners cope with problems, Zamble and Porporino (1988) found that more poorly adjusted prison inmates had more limited problem-solving skills. Morrison-Dyke (1996) found that having limited skills for solving problems was associated with homelessness among offenders with mental disorder. Exploring the factors that were associated with giving up offending in an adult community sample, Farrall (2002: 212) observed that 'as the total number of "problem" social circumstances facing the probationer increased, so desistance became less likely'.

Many structured interventions are expressly designed to impart skills in solving personal problems (McGuire 2002c) but focus in addition on difficulties posed by the situations in which participants live. Programme materials often emphasize the importance of finding solutions that are most likely to work given certain constraints; depending on circumstances that may generate courses of action that involve changing external situations. Participants in this form of exercise are not extracted or dislodged from their environments (as is sometimes alleged). Training enables them to locate the sources of their difficulties, which does not automatically imply that problems reside solely within themselves.

Ethical dilemmas: risk assessment, prediction and change

The ethical tension alluded to above becomes particularly sharp in relation to assessment and prediction of risk, and different writers have taken conflicting stances on whether such a task can be performed ethically (Grisso and Appelbaum 1992; McGuire 1997b; Zinger and Forth 1998). Whether that is feasible depends on the predictive accuracy of the methods used. Some authors have designated a level of accuracy that should be reached before predictions can be ethically acceptable. Whatever that standard might be, it is important only to use the outputs from such assessments in conjunction with various other sources of information, and to inform decisions rather than dictate them. Writing reports and making recommendations are not value-free processes. The principal objective of a psychological report is to change the beliefs and influence the actions of the person who will be reading it (Ownby 1997). It is incumbent upon psychologists to pay attention to ethical dimensions arising in such work.

Other dilemmas arise when contemplating the process of change. This has several interconnected aspects. The paramount question is whether participation in 'change-related activities' should be entirely voluntary, or can somehow be required by criminal justice staff. Even if we believe that someone would change if compelled to do so, is it ethical to enforce compliance? From one perspective, the right to decide whether to participate resides solely with individuals themselves. From another, society can over-rule the offender and is entitled to impose change. Having disregarded the rights of others, it is argued, he or she has forfeited the right to be left alone.

We would expect that for people to make meaningful changes, for example of the immensity required when learning to control substance use, it is a prerequisite that they should participate in services on a purely voluntary basis. That is certainly the optimal arrangement. But some findings show that there are also circumstances in which a compulsory framework can be conducive to change. Farabee *et al.* (1998) reported a review of 11 evaluation studies of treatment programmes for drug-abusing offenders. The programmes varied in the extent of legal pressure applied, but in all of them participation was coerced to some extent. Of the 11 studies, 'five found a positive relationship between criminal justice referral and treatment outcomes, four reported no difference, and two studies reported a negative relationship' (p. 5). The authors challenged the orthodox view that the existence of external pressure implies that individuals lack any internal motivation to change. On the contrary, change often results from a complex interplay of internal and external factors. The authors concluded that the findings supported 'the use of the criminal justice system as an effective source of treatment referral, as well as a means for enhancing retention and compliance' (p. 7). The importance of the latter was underpinned in further work by Fiorentino *et al.* (1999).

But change might not need to be coerced; it can be induced. With reference to high-frequency behaviours such as occur in substance abuse, it is possible to influence people towards change by a refined form of counselling known as *motivational interviewing* (Miller and Rollnick 2002). This involves the use of a number of interactive strategies on the part of counsellors. They include, for example, encouraging clients to make statements that attribute to themselves the capacity to change, and drawing to their attention discrepancies between the things they say and the things they do. While this is not blatantly coercive, it nevertheless raises ethical difficulties. Subtly influencing someone in this way is done without their full, informed consent and is open to the charge of being manipulative (Miller 1994).

Blackburn (2002) has discussed whether there are circumstances in which coercion could be ethically justifiable. This is based on a recognition that psychologists and other professionals working with offenders in criminal justice services are in a dual role, 'simultaneously helper and agent of social control' (p. 143), a conflict that can cause considerable strain. Evidence that coercion achieves desirable ends does not in itself excuse its use. But given certain types of offence or risks of harm, 'total rejection of compulsion does not seem a viable option' (p. 149).

Professional codes of ethics

The need to address complexities such as these has led the national psychological associations of most countries to develop and publish professional codes of ethics. Such codes are usually based on the *deontological* approach to moral reasoning: the doctrine (as we saw in Chapter 7, emanating from the work of Kant) that actions have immanent properties of rightness or wrongness independently of their consequences, and that fundamental moral values can be deduced from first principles. It is contrasted with a *utilitarian* approach in which the morality of actions is decided by their consequences or net outcomes (Bersoff 2003).

Although the precise contents of ethics codes vary, most enunciate several basic precepts:

- *Beneficence*: the acceptance of a responsibility or obligation to do good.
- *Non-maleficence*: the acceptance of a responsibility to avoid doing harm.
- *Autonomy*: observing individuals' freedom of thought and action, and their right to self-determination.
- *Justice*: basing actions on justice and fairness between individuals.
- *Integrity*: trustworthiness and faithfulness to commitments; acting within one's competence.

The American Psychological Association first published its code of ethics in 1953. It has since undergone several revisions (Canter *et al.* 1994). In 1995, the constituent members of the European Federation of Psychologists' Associations formulated a joint *meta-code* of ethics (published on the EFPA website, 2004). Codes are binding upon members of the respective regulatory bodies, and violations of them may lead to disciplinary action. However, they cannot possibly cover all the concrete situations in which an ethical problem might surface. Some psychologists have developed problem-solving and decision-making sequences to apply in circumstances like these (Pryzwansky and Wendt 1999), an approach known as *practical ethics*.

Augmenting models: risk factors and good lives

Many current developments in criminal justice programmes are derivatives of the *risk–needs* model propounded by Andrews and Bonta (2003). Some critics contend that dissecting persons in this way represents them solely as a package of risks, a 'dissolution of the subject into a cluster of factors' (Hudson 1996: 155), so denigrating their individuality and completeness.

While that misconstrues the approach in important ways, recently a few researchers have proposed major revisions to risk–needs analysis. Some revive a long-standing assumption that in helping people to change, it may be necessary to alter the 'whole person'.

Based on such a critique, Ward and Stewart (2003) have forwarded an alternative to the risk factors model, which they contend provides a sounder basis for integrating what have been called criminogenic needs within a wider analysis of motivation and change. They argue that what Andrews and Bonta term *needs* are not ones that offenders themselves would recognize. Rather, they reflect factors that other members of society would wish to change if (as Andrews and Bonta claim, and the evidence confirms) doing so will lead to lowered rates of recidivism.

Ward and Stewart (2003) propose instead that we can enrich and strengthen our understanding of need by locating it within a general model of human motivation. Within this they outline certain basic motives and 'primary human goods'. These include, for example, health, self-directedness, freedom from turmoil, and relatedness to or intimacy with others. This leads to a framework for providing offender services that Ward and Stewart call the *good lives* model, in which the objective is promotion of general psychological well-being. Bonta and Andrews (2003) have retorted that risk–needs assessment encompasses a very broad range of areas, and offenders should have access to high-quality services to meet all their needs. The question is whether it is the appointed role of criminal justice services to address ones not demonstrably linked to offending. Arguably, criminal justice personnel have no clear mandate to probe factors in an individual's life other than his or her criminal acts, and to attempt more than that is invasive. Davison and Stuart (1975) distinguish *minimal goals*, the reduction of problematic behaviour, from *optimal goals*, the enhancement of other aspects of individual functioning. The relative weight given to each may have to be negotiated afresh in every case.

Desistance: the whole person

One of the most consistent findings in criminology, the *age–crime curve*, shows lucidly that as age increases from approximately 20 onwards, there is a substantial decline in the portion of the population committing crimes. Until recently, comparatively little was known about this process (Laub and Sampson 2001). However, several researchers have explored the reasons individuals give when they have successfully reduced their involvement in crime. One important discovery is that this is far more like a journey than a sudden event. As with the pathway into offending, it involves changes of speed and reversals of direction, as individuals' priorities and lifestyles unevenly evolve.

Jamieson *et al.* (1999) found that many of the young people they interviewed talked straightforwardly about growing up, maturing, and making other transitions in terms of jobs, education, partners, breaking away from offending peers, taking on responsibilities and 'settling down'. Maruna (2001) reported a series of in-depth interviews explicitly focused on desistance processes, and found that (like anyone else) offenders need to make sense of their lives, and in doing so they construct life stories or *personal narratives* developed around specific themes. These *generative scripts* helped them to forge evolving identities within which, metaphorically speaking, they gradually become different people, or new versions of themselves, capable of acting in different ways. In a study of the impact of probation supervision, Farrall (2002) found that the process of desistance bore relatively little relation to the efforts of supervising officers, and was much more a function of life events and circumstances. Externally, progress in desistance was associated with getting jobs, meeting partners and other key events. Others who were stuck in a pattern of offending attributed this to a 'lack of change' in their lives, meaning unsatisfactory circumstances with regard to jobs and relationships.

These studies have in common an emphasis on what might be called the 'whole person' approach. While to some extent it challenges the more analytical risk factors model, the two can be complementary, as Maruna's (2001) work amply illustrates.

Psychology, science and politics

The preceding sections have surveyed applications of psychology to crime, illustrating ways in which findings can be useful to criminal justice services and to individuals, and the intricacies that arise in attempting to choose between or to balance these sometimes competing demands. Even if all these issues were somehow resolved, there are larger questions to address concerning the role of psychology in the study of crime. In the final section of the book, I would like to consider the extent to which psychology provides a perspective for political action on crime and justice, and the status of psychological knowledge alongside other approaches in social science.

From some standpoints, the very act of talking about individual offenders as if they posed a problem is an ideological stance. We saw in Chapter 1 that psychology's focus on individual diversity and how to understand it is sometimes taken to imply that social environments, structural inequalities, power relations and other contextual influences are unimportant. But on a different conceptual plane, the very idea itself of locating causes or effects within persons appears suspect. The model presented in this book does not invoke concepts of madness or disease. Nevertheless, from some standpoints, any reference to individual difference conjures up just those ideas. They are shifting apparitions of a ghost that haunts the on/off alliance between criminology and psychology: the ghost of pathology.

At various points in this book we have discussed the existence of *problems*, meaning states of distress within individuals, or discord between them; and analysed processes that could have better or worse outcomes. According so some commentators, this carries the implication that some aspect of the situation has been pathologized. Siegal (quoted by Hollin 2002a) comments that while psychological theories may be useful for understanding the behaviour of deeply damaged or destructive people, they are of no use for explaining crime in general. Since crime is widespread, that would imply that more or less everyone is disturbed. Similarly, the use of a psychological approach is thought to lead ineluctably to the notion of the 'criminal mind', caused by warped socialization and adjustment.

The *Sage Dictionary of Criminology* (McLaughlin and Muncie 2001) defines *pathology* in terms that make almost any attempt to comprehend the uneven patterns of harm in society, and their possible links to other individual or social processes, a form of biomedical discourse. The latter is almost self-evidently pernicious. 'The psy-sciences employ the nexus of power/knowledge to produce – and offer to control – pathology, as they have done with madness, crime and sexual dissidence' (pp. 202, 203). These criticisms are closely tied to the idea that any form of thinking in this vein feeds into a process of *censure*. This is a partially unconscious process by which psy-scientists deem certain practices in society as normative, and make disapproving judgements of others that diverge from them. It carries the implication that attempting to explain why one person harmed another creates a condition in which 'the interests of the state have been inserted into most dimensions of private morality' (p. 266).

This keen sense of repugnance also arises regarding biology. To cite Rutter *et al.* (1998: 156), some criminologists 'dismiss biological findings on the grounds that, because crime is socially and legally defined, it could not have its roots in biology . . . any considerations of possible biological influences necessarily "medicalizes" crime, misleadingly transforming a social phenomenon into a disease'. Perhaps this aversive attitude originates from British criminology's initial phase of consolidation in the late nineteenth and early twentieth centuries. During that era, what might collectively be called the mental sciences were represented more or less exclusively by psychiatry (Garland 2002).

Polemics of criminal justice

Nevertheless, it may be no surprise that as part-producers of the aforementioned power/knowledge, psychologists are not best known for challenging criminal justice policy-makers or mounting robust protests against ideologies of control. Critical voices are more frequently heard from other sources. Taking the advent of intermediate, community-based punishments as an example, Petersilia (1990) researched the fears and misgivings aroused among those on the receiving end. Von Hirsch (1990) drew attention to ethical dimensions of decisions to use these sanctions. Worrall (1997) analysed the historical and political context of these departures in England and Wales. Similarly, the front line in arguments for *abolitionism* (minimizing the use of imprisonment, advocating prisoners' rights, eliminating custody for juveniles, and other goals; see Hudson 1996) tends to be occupied by professionals other than psychologists.

In the wake of meteoric rises in prison populations in the United States, Haney (1999; Haney and Zimbardo 1998) castigated his fellow psychologists for having failed to raise vocal objections to the trend. Ironically, Andrews and Bonta (2003) have noted that the steady swing towards more punitive measures in several countries from the 1970s onwards was not the doing of the political right, which consistently supported punishment before then. Responsibility lies with the ideological left, which was absorbed in cultural analysis and deviance theory and abandoned rehabilitation both as an ideal and as on ongoing project.

Psychologists may not have had the highest profile in opposing abuses or inequities in justice administration, but they have certainly not remained silent on crucial issues. James (1995) discussed at length the repercussions of British government policies in the early 1980s for deprived families, and the long-term impact on youth offending. Allen *et al.* (1998) have researched and exposed the impact of jurors' attitudes to the death penalty on the likelihood that a defendant will be convicted. Steinberg and Scott (2003) have confronted the use of the death penalty for young people in the United States. Haney (2003) has marshalled evidence and arguments concerning the uses of solitary confinement in American 'supermax' prisons, and the implications for mental health. On a broader front, Joseph (2003) has disputed the alleged evidence concerning the role of genes in mental disorder and criminal conduct.

Perhaps psychologists hesitate to volunteer opinions on criminal justice issues because our training makes us 'slaves to data' (in a manner reminiscent of Lombroso, though that is not an embracement of positivism!). Advancing any argument, there is a constant wish to back it up – the more profusely the better. My conclusions regarding punishment given in Chapter 7 of this book are based on an appeal to empirical evidence about effects. That may look utterly utilitarian, a point amplified by Boone (2004) in a scrutiny of the 'what works' literature. But it is motivated by an ethical value-base of the kind outlined above. There is a gratifying concordance between the research findings and basic beliefs.

Psychology and the sociology of science

This book has been written within what philosophers of science call a *critical realist* paradigm (Searle 1995; Klee 1997; Norris 1997), not dissimilar to the text by Andrews and Bonta (2003), which adopts a *rational empiricist* stance. This involves certain epistemological assumptions. Some of the events, processes or other phenomena we seek to understand possess a reality that is independent of human minds. Others are socially constructed through human development, interaction and the use of language. It is possible to gain systematic knowledge of both, and using a scientific approach to psychology, this is permissible by a variety of means, adopting the outlook of methodological pluralism as described in Chapter 1. The form of inquiry chosen is tailored to the question asked. There is a long-standing distinction in psychology that may help to make sense of this. Approaches to investigation, and their conclusions, may be:

- *Nomothetic*: this refers to knowledge about what is recurrent across situations; states of affairs that are replicated across time and place, allowing us to make generalized statements. In a side-by-side comparison, Hedges (1987) found that the level of consistency and cumulativeness of such research findings in psychology was commensurate with that found in an archetypal 'hard' science (particle physics).
- *Idiographic*: this refers to knowledge of experiences or patterns that are found only within a single person, cultural group, language, religion, legal system or other entity in a given place at a given time. The focus is on understanding the diversity, complexity and uniqueness of individual lives, personal situations, belief structures or other aspects of experience within their local contexts, through self-reports, subjective accounts and life histories.

These words come originally from the German philosopher William Windelband (1848–1915). In his writing, he characterized the former as 'what always is', and the latter as 'what once was' (Lamiell 1995).

Hence some psychologists embark on controlled experiments, measure quantifiable variables and try to make inferences about cause and effect. (This can be done with single cases as well as large samples.) Others pursue qualitative, social-constructionist studies of previously marginalized aspects of human experience. Separate research projects address discrete though intersecting questions. Each provides a different kind of understanding; they are not in competition, each tells us something new. The assembled result is accumulated knowledge and theoretical understanding.

To critics of the scientific paradigm, however, those are illusory gains. There are several current antagonisms within social sciences, between positivist and constructionist, essentialist and idealist, modernist and post-modernist approaches. Some contemporary cultural theorists will call the above formulation 'modernist', a label that may render this book, *ipso facto*, out of date in their eyes. Cultural theorists assert that the Enlightenment idea of applying 'science' to 'social problems', yielding projects such as 'offender rehabilitation', is ideologically driven (Hudson 1996). Its adherents might not be malevolent, but they are probably naïve, and do not appreciate how their unwitting participation in the power/knowledge complex constitutes an endorsement of it, thereby sustaining it.

Going beyond this, some contemporary thinkers assert that all discourses or 'texts' are equally valid. Science has no more claim upon our attention than any other sphere of activity. It is just that historically and culturally, it became a privileged or dominant discourse. This critique has been extended to include physical science, as shown in the Strong Programme in the sociology of knowledge (Klee 1997). Sometimes science is equated with its own worst excesses. That is, the exploitative, technocratic manifestations of science are taken to signify all of it (Norris 1997). The same intellectual currents also run through psychology (which like other disciplines has a 'critical' strand).

The predicament such extreme relativism leaves us with, however, is that if we accept it, then *Principia Mathematica, The Origin of Species*, the *Oxford Handbook of Criminology*, the *Bible*, the *Koran, Mein Kampf*, and a leaflet distributed by some neo-fascist cell, are all equivalent documents. As indicated above, there are many potential sources of understanding. But we need a standard by which claims regarding human beings can be evaluated, in relation to which ideas can be anchored. Our best hope of obtaining it is through the kind of reflective reasoning and systematic empirical testing of ideas that characterize scientific inquiry.

Further reading

There is a useful and relatively concise overview of different approaches to offender profiling by Peter Ainsworth (2001) *Offender Profiling and Crime Analysis* (Cullompton: Willan Publishing). For source texts on issues of witness testimony, see Amina Memon, Aldert Vrij and Ray Bull (2003) *Psychology and Law: Truthfulness, Accuracy and Credibility* (2nd edn. Chichester: Wiley); Gisli H. Gudjonsson (2002) *The Psychology of Interrogations and Confessions: A Handbook* (Chichester: Wiley). Broader accounts of forensic and legal psychology are given by Gisli H. Gudjonsson and Lionel Hayward (1998) *Forensic Psychology: Practitioner's Guide* (London: Routledge); by Ronald Roesch, Stephen D. Hart and James R. P. Ogloff (eds., 1999) *Psychology and Law: The State of the Discipline* (New York: Kluwer Academic/Plenum Publishers); and Lawrence S. Wrightsman, Edie Greene, Michael T. Nietzel and William H. Fortune (2002) *Psychology and the Legal System* (5th edn. Belmont, CA: Wadsworth).

For an invaluable series of discussions on aspects of implementing programmes in criminal justice services, see Gary A. Bernfeld, Alan Leschied and David P. Farrington (eds., 2001) *Offender Rehabilitation in Practice: Implementing and Evaluating Effective Programs* (Chichester: Wiley); and for a similarly useful review of issues surrounding the question of offender motivation, see Mary McMurran (ed., 2002) *Motivating Offenders to Change: A Guide to Enhancing Engagement in Therapy* (Chichester: Wiley).

Glossary

Affect General term for feeling or emotion, an internal state and personal experience associated with specific ideas or events.

Aggression The intentional infliction of physical or psychological harm; usually divided into an *angry, hostile* or *expressive* form and an *instrumental* or *incentive-motivated* form.

Aggressiveness Recurrent readiness to act in an aggressive manner in a range of different situations.

Alternative thinking The cognitive capacity or skill of generating a variety of ideas that may be useful for solving an everyday practical or interpersonal problem.

Attribution Hypothesized cognitive process in which individuals represent to themselves assumed explanations for (or conclusions concerning) motives for action, or cause-effect relationships in the behaviour of others and of themselves.

Anger control training An intervention that combines relaxation with the learning of new self-instructions, applied in provocative situations to reduce levels of angry feelings or behaviour; sometimes called anger management training.

Assertive case management, assertive outreach A pattern of services in work with offenders with mental disorders thought to pose a risk to themselves or others; involving a high level of contact and support and frequent monitoring, usually requiring collaboration between agencies.

Automatic process, automaticity Cognitive activity, usually outside awareness, for management of information in large quantities, and coordination of highly routinized, habitual responses essential for the performance of frequently repeated tasks.

Automatic thoughts Rapid, almost instantaneous cognitive events or patterns, usually outside awareness, with an important role in the patterning of current behaviour.

Behaviour modification An approach to altering patterns of behaviour based on learning theory, notably on the operant conditioning model of B.F. Skinner and his associates.

Behaviour therapy A psychotherapeutic approach to behavioural and emotional problems employing methods derived from learning theory, based on the Classical conditioning model.

Behaviourism One of the major 'schools' of psychological thought throughout the twentieth century, which asserted that a scientific approach to psychology required focusing exclusively on externally observable events. In later versions, this was altered to include inferences about cognitive and other hypothesized internal processes.

Binomial effect size display In an intervention/outcome study or collection of studies, a 2×2 table showing the respective proportions of success/failure or improvement/no improvement in experimental and control conditions, respectively.

Birth cohort study A type of research in which a sample (cohort), usually of children or adolescents, is followed prospectively over time and data are collected on the subject-matter of interest to facilitate understanding of the temporal and causal patterning of developmental change; a type of *longitudinal study*.

Cognition, cognitive process Psychological processes entailing the gathering, storage and use of information about the external or internal environment, enabling an organism or individual to adapt accordingly. It is usually taken to include attention, perception, memory, reasoning, problem-solving, creativity and language use.

Cognitive-behavioural A form of psychological therapy that emerged from an integration of behavioural and social learning theory with the study of cognitive processes. There are several varieties of this approach, each founded on a variant balance or relatively different emphasis on behavioural or cognitive change.

Cognitive distortion Patterns or contents of thinking at odds with expectations or reactions of others with regard to norms for behaviour, particularly in personal relationships. The term is most frequently employed with specific reference to self-serving thoughts or beliefs of offenders that allow or encourage sexual activity between adults and children.

Cognitive therapy A form of psychological therapy based on the view that the origin of many kinds of distress lie in the way individuals think about themselves and the world, or in their belief systems regarding them. Therapy is designed to help individuals self-assess and, if necessary, alter their recurrent thoughts and beliefs.

Conditioning A mechanism of learning that occurs in the central nervous system through which new stimuli can elicit responses previously elicited through reflex action. Initially thought to occur through temporal association only, it was subsequently shown to be strengthened by repetition and reinforcement.

Constructional strategies In behaviour modification, an approach to change that emphasizes the development and establishment of new 'repertoires' of behaviour that can replace previous dysfunctional or damaging patterns, and avoids the use of aversive techniques.

Constructivism An approach within psychology that places particular emphasis on individuals' unique perspectives and capacities for making sense of themselves and their surroundings, and on the meanings they attach to or derive from experiences and events.

Control theory A collection of theories in criminology with the basic premise that individuals will pursue their own self-interest unless constrained either by external social forces (sociological control theory) or internal restraints (psychological control theory).

Controlled process Cognitive activity that entails reflective review of plans or actions in conscious awareness; includes activities such as self-observation, problem-solving, self-regulation and decision-making.

Criminogenic need An alternative term used to describe *dynamic risk factors*, specifying features of individuals that are associated with the risk of involvement in crime but which change over time. They are susceptible to change by direct effort and where that is achieved risks of criminal activity are reduced.

Criminological psychology A specialized division of applied psychology focusing on the links between psychology and the study of crime.

Desistance Among persons who have been involved in offending for some time, a gradual reduction in the frequency or seriousness of, or eventual cessation of, criminal activity.

Deterrence In penology, the doctrine that the costs of committing crimes will have a suppressant effect on the frequency or severity of criminal activity. *General deterrence* refers to the effect of visible punishments on the population as a whole. *Specific deterrence* refers to the impact on the subsequent behaviour of individuals convicted and sentenced. *Restrictive deterrence* refers to an effect in which individuals who do offend limit the seriousness of crimes to avoid more severe penalties.

Differential psychology A major branch of psychology concerned with all aspects of difference between individuals, including variations in ability, aptitude, personality, attitudes, or self-image, and the causes and consequences of this variability.

Dynamic risk factor An aspect of an individual's functioning that is associated with his or her risk of involvement in crime but which fluctuates over time and is also susceptible to change by direct effort. This includes variables such as numbers of criminal associates, antisocial attitudes, impulsiveness, limited social or problem-solving skills, anger or other mood states, and involvement in substance abuse.

Effect size In a research study, an outcome measure indicating the scale or degree of either (a) the relationship between two variables, or (b) the impact of an intervention. In meta-analysis, statistics of this kind are combined across several studies to produce a *mean effect size*.

Emotion The experience and manifestation of feeling, an internal state or subjective experience associated with specific ideas or events; entailing physiological, personal/experiential and expressive/behavioural components.

Empathy In psychology, the capacity to experience and resonate with the emotional state of another person, with important consequences for attitudes and behaviour. Used more widely, it can also refer to the ability to project oneself into an 'object of contemplation' such as a work of art.

Forensic psychology Application of psychology to study the provision of and process of using evidence in courts of law or other legal settings; including the study of witness testimony, credibility, methods of gathering evidence, use of photo-fits, line-ups and other procedures involving cognitive and psychosocial processes. More recently the term has been extended to include the work of psychologists in prison, probation and related settings.

Idiographic An approach to knowledge in psychology as an attempt to understand experiences or patterns that are found only within a single person, cultural group, language, system of beliefs or other phenomena in a given place at a given time.

Impulsiveness, impulsivity The tendency to act immediately, or quickly, without deliberation or consideration of the impact or consequences of one's actions.

Interactionism An integrative model in which behaviour is understood as a net product of personal and situational factors operating in conjunction.

Interpersonal skills training A set of methods for helping individuals to improve their abilities in interaction with others in social encounters: a widely used component of intervention programmes designed to reduce recidivism; also known as social skills training.

Investigative psychology The use of psychology to assist criminal investigation by the police, in particular the study of psychological factors influencing patterns of crime by repeat offenders.

Legal psychology The application of psychology to the process of law, focused on psychological factors in legal decisions, including the admissibility of evidence, fitness to stand trial, decision-making by juries and sentencers, and related issues.

Longitudinal study A research design in which a cohort of individuals is followed over an extended period of time and data collected concerning life events and patterns, and social, psychological or other variables of interest.

Means–end thinking A cognitive skill involved in formulating realistic connections or sequences of action between a problem and a proposed solution to it.

Meta-analysis A method of integrating the quantitative findings from a number of primary studies, using statistical analysis to detect trends among the results obtained.

Motivational interviewing A stategic counselling approach, involving a range of interactive techniques designed to influence an individual's state of readiness and capacity to change entrenched or repetitive patterns of behaviour, such as dependent substance abuse.

Multi-modal programme Type of intervention programme with a number of targets of change, each associated with a separate risk factor, including appropriate methods for addressing each.

Neutralization A term used in both criminology and psychology to describe a cognitive event or process in which individuals make statements (to themselves or others) that will negate unpleasant feelings or other reactions they might have to their own behaviour.

Nomothetic An approach to the accumulation of knowledge in psychology as a task centred mainly on discovering patterns that are recurrent across situations, or states of affairs that are replicated across time and place, so allowing the formulation of generalized statements.

Observational learning In social learning theory, acquisition of new patterns of behaviour without the direct experience of reinforcement or punishment, through the observation of actions of others and of the consequences that result.

Odds ratio The odds of a successful outcome (such as reduction in recidivism) for a given group is defined by the probability that that event will occur, relative to the probability that it will not. The odds ratio is then a statistical expression of the relationship between the two odds – that is, those for experimental and control samples, respectively.

Offending behaviour A generic term for actions or sequences of action codified as unlawful in the statutes of a given society.

Personality Usually conceptualized as a relatively stable, slowly evolving and complex configuration of features including cognitions, affects and behaviours that gives coherence to an individual's life. It marks the uniqueness of individuals, while allowing them to be known and understood within a shared framework of their culture. Note that there is no universally accepted definition, but most formulations contain the foregoing items as common elements.

Personality disorder There is currently no consensus regarding how this can be defined. However, it is generally taken to refer to an enduring configuration of character or personality that repeatedly induces distress or causes harm to self or others, without symptoms of and not explicable in terms of other forms of mental disorder.

Perspective-taking The cognitive capacity for imagining or considering the nature of a situation from a standpoint of another person or persons, and taking account of this in action.

Positivism A word with a range of meanings, most commonly taken to refer a philosophy of science with a focus on the description of facts or factual relations that can be confirmed or disconfirmed by empirical test, and a sceptical attitude towards the value of theorizing about phenomena that are not directly observable. In its most radical version, *logical positivism* asserts that the only meaningful statements are ones that can be anchored in observations about external states of affairs. In a looser sense, it is another word for *empiricism* and the idea that knowledge is derived through the senses.

Problem-solving training A set of methods for enabling individuals to improve their skills in addressing and managing everyday problems in living, aspects of which may contribute to risks of involvement in crime.

Programme A specially designed series of methods and exercises to provide opportunities for learning and change: most familiar in the form of structured, 'manualized' intervention programmes used in criminal justice services for the reduction of offending behaviour.

Programme integrity The extent to which a structured programme adheres to the model on the basis of which it was designed, in terms of the methods of intervention used and the quality and style of delivery of its sessions.

Protective factor Variables that counter the influence of risk factors and enhance the resilience of those exposed to them; associated with a decreased likelihood of personally or socially undesirable outcomes.

Punishment In behavioural psychology, an aversive or unpleasant consequence of a behavioural response that reduces the probability of its recurrence. In criminal justice, a set of procedures for conveying society's disapproval of a criminal act and applying sanctions that will induce change in the offender.

Realism, scientific A philosophy of science that takes for granted the existence of an external, mind-independent reality that is potentially knowable by human minds through systematic inquiry.

Recidivism Usually taken to refer to repeated involvement in crime or offending behaviour. However, this can be defined in specific ways, with reference to self-reported crime, arrests or police contacts, appearances in court, convictions, or in the case of persons with mental disorders, re-admission to hospital.

Reciprocal determinism In social learning theory, the proposal that there is a two-way, bi-directional process of influence between individual and environmental variables.

Reductionism In philosophy of science, the assumption that events or phenomena at a given level of description can be accounted for by the study of other events or phenomena at a simpler level.

Reinforcement In behavioural approaches, a process in which environmental events whose occurrence is contingent on behavioural responses alter the frequency of those responses.

Relapse prevention A term derived from research and practice in people with alcohol or other substance abuse problems. It entails a set of self-management and allied methods for enabling individuals who have participated in treatment or training to avoid repetition of the problem behaviour.

Resilience A pattern in which individuals exposed to high levels of risk factors for occurrence of a problem nevertheless do not do so; usually associated with the presence and operation of protective factors.

Responsivity A design feature that contributes to effectiveness of intervention programmes with offenders. *General responsivity* refers to an overall approach in which activities have clear objectives and structure, and entail active engagement of participants in processes focused on behavioural or attitudinal change. *Specific responsivity* requires taking into account factors that reflect diversity among participants in terms of age, gender, ethnicity, language, ability level or learning style.

Risk factor An individual or environmental variable that has been shown through empirical research to be associated with greater likelihood of involvement in criminal activity (or other type of problem).

Risk–needs assessment A combined approach to working with offenders, the first stage of which is collecting information concerning the probability of future offending and the factors likely to influence it.

Schema A hypothesized set of relatively enduring relationships between ideas and beliefs, usually outside awareness, that influence individuals' patterns of thinking, feeling and action across many situations.

Self-control In criminology, a theory that holds that variations in the likelihood of offending are influenced mainly by individual differences in a psychological construct reflecting the extent to which people can restrain the tendency to act on impulse. In cognitive social learning theory, the finding that individuals can self-consciously acquire mastery over habitual, automatic modes of thinking or responding that are dysfunctional for themselves or others.

Self-efficacy Individuals' general expectations or beliefs concerning their capabilities to take action, achieve goals, solve problems or in other ways act as effective agents in their own lives.

Self-instruction A statement or series of statements individuals can use to alter previously established patterns of thinking, feeling or reacting.

Self-regulation An acquired or learned capacity in developing children, usually involving the use of automatic processes and language, in which individual patterns of thoughts, feelings and behaviour become less dependent on the immediate environment.

Situationism The assumption that environmental determinants are of paramount importance in influencing a person's actions or reactions.

Social constructionism In philosophy of science and in psychology, an approach that asserts that experience of the social world, and thereby understanding of the self, results from a process of interaction and exchange involving the use of language and other symbols. Such a process and its products are viewed as more important than the 'objective' features of the situation.

Social learning theory A generalized account of human learning based on behavioural principles, but proposing that a large proportion of learning occurs through indirect experience or observational processes in the interpersonal environment.

Socialization The totality of experiences of a developing child as he or she interacts with and responds to the behaviour and communications of parents or other caregivers, within a wider familial, social and cultural context, and acquires patterns of acting, feeling and thinking that are acceptable in that context.

Standardized mean difference In meta-analysis, a type of statistic that expresses the extent of change in the experimental group relative to that of the comparison group.

Temperament A collection of patterns or propensities to feel or act in certain ways, evident from shortly after birth onwards, and exhibiting relatively stable differences between individuals. Usually considered to have psychophysiological features, this interacts with socialization to influence the early development of individuality.

Theory integration A process with criminology, psychology and other social sciences, as an alternative to competitive elimination, in which theoretical concepts from different sources are combined in appropriate ways to construct and test models with greater validity or breadth of reference.

Therapeutic jurisprudence An approach within law by which legal processes and decisions are studied in terms of their potential therapeutic or anti-therapeutic effects on the individuals involved; representing a combination of ideas from law and behavioural sciences.

Trait A description of how people typically behave that also helps to account for individual differences between them; sometimes used on a purely descriptive level, at other times to denote hypothesized underlying causal patterns that account for relative stability across situations or over time.

Under-determination of theory A principle in the philosophy of science, referring to circumstances in which the available data are compatible with two or more theoretical accounts, with insufficient information to choose between them.

References

Aarts, H. and Dijksterhuis, A. (2000) Habits as knowledge structures: automaticity in goal-directed behavior. *Journal of Personality and Social Psychology*, 78, 53–63.

Agnew, R. (1994) The techniques of neutralization and violence. *Criminology*, 34, 555–80.

Agnew, R. and White, H. R. (1992) An empirical test of General Strain Theory. *Criminology*, 30, 475–500.

Ainsworth, P. (2001) *Offender Profiling and Crime Analysis*. Cullompton: Willan Publishing.

Akers, R. L., Krohn, M. D., Lanza-Kaduce, L. and Radosevich, M. (1979) A social learning theory of deviant behavior. *American Sociological Review*, 44, 635–55.

Akhtar, N. and Bradley, E. J. (1991) Social information processing deficits of aggressive children: present findings and implications for social skills training. *Clinical Psychology Review*, 11, 621–44.

Alexander, M. A. (1999) Sexual offender treatment efficacy revisited. *Sexual Abuse: Journal of Research and Treatment*, 11, 101–16.

Allen, M., Mabry, E. and McKelton, D.-M. (1998) Impact of juror attitudes about the death penalty on juror evaluations of guilt and punishment: a meta-analysis. *Law and Human Behavior*, 22, 715–31.

American Psychiatric Association (2000) *Diagnostic and Statistical Manual of Mental Disorders*, 4th edn. Text Revision. Washington, DC: American Psychiatric Association.

Anderson, C. A. and Bushman, B. J. (2002) Human aggression. *Annual Review of Psychology*, 53, 27–51.

Andrews, D. A. (1989) Recidivism is predictable and can be influenced: using risk assessments to reduce recidivism. *Forum on Corrections Research*, 1, 11–18.

Andrews, D. A. (1995) The psychology of criminal conduct and effective treatment. In J. McGuire (ed.) *What Works: Reducing Re-offending. Guidelines from Research and Practice*. Chichester: Wiley.

Andrews, D. A. (2001) Principles of effective correctional programs. In L. L.

Motiuk and R. C. Serin (eds.) *Compendium 2000 on Effective Correctional Programming*. Ottawa: Correctional Service Canada.

Andrews, D. A. and Bonta, J. (1995) *LSI-R: The Level of Service Inventory – Revised*. Toronto: Multi-Health Systems.

Andrews, D. A. and Bonta, J. (2003) *The Psychology of Criminal Conduct*, 3rd edn. Cincinnati, OH: Anderson Publishing Co.

Andrews, D. A., Bonta, J. and Hoge, R. D. (1990a) Classification for effective rehabilitation: rediscovering psychology. *Criminal Justice and Behavior*, 17, 19–52.

Andrews, D. A., Zinger, I., Hoge, R. D. *et al.* (1990b) Does correctional treatment work? A clinically relevant and psychologically informed meta-analysis. *Criminology*, 28, 369–404.

Antonowicz, D. and Ross, R. R. (1994) Essential components of successful rehabilitation programs for offenders. *International Journal of Offender Therapy and Comparative Criminology*, 38, 97–104.

Aos, S., Phipps, P., Barnoski, R. and Lieb, R. (2001) *The Comparative Costs and Benefits of Programs to Reduce Crime*. Olympia, WA: Washington State Institute for Public Policy.

Aromaeki, A. S., Haebich, K. and Lindman, R. E. (2002) Age as a modifier of sexually aggressive attitudes in men. *Scandinavian Journal of Psychology*, 43, 419–23.

Aronson, E. and Mettee, D. R. (1968) Dishonest behavior as a function of differential levels of induced self-esteem. *Journal of Personality and Social Psychology*, 9, 121–7.

Ashworth, A. (2000) *Sentencing and Criminal Justice*, 3rd edn. London: Butterworths.

Aust, A. (1987) Gaining control of compulsive shop theft. *National Association of Probation Officers' Journal*, December, pp. 145–6.

Aust, R., Sharp, C. and Goulden, C. (2002) *Prevalence of Drug Use: Key Findings from the 2001/2002 British Crime Survey*. Findings 182. London: Home Office Research, Development and Statistics.

Axelrod, S. and Apsche, J. (eds.) (1983) *The Effects of Punishment on Human Behavior*. New York: Academic Press.

Bakker, L., Hudson, S. M. and Ward, T. (2000) Reducing recidivism in driving while disqualified: a treatment evaluation. *Criminal Justice and Behavior*, 27, 531–60.

Bakker, L., Ward, T., Cryer, M. and Hudson, S. M. (1997) Out of the rut: a cognitive-behavioral treatment program for driving-while-disqualified offenders. *Behaviour Change*, 14, 29–38.

Baldwin, J., Bottoms, A. E. and Walker, M. A. (1976) *The Urban Criminal: A Study in Sheffield*. London: Tavistock Publications.

Bandura, A. (1977) *Social Learning Theory*. New York: Prentice-Hall.

Bandura, A. (1997) *Self-Efficacy: The Exercise of Control*. New York: W. H. Freeman & Co.

Bandura, A. (2001) Social cognitive theory: an agentic perspective. *Annual Review of Psychology*, 52, 1–26.

Barak, G. (ed.) (1998) *Integrative Criminology*. Aldershot: Ashgate.

Barclay, G. C. and Tavares, C. (2002) *International Comparisons of Criminal Justice Statistics 2000*. London: Home Office Research, Development and Statistics Directorate.

Bargh, J. A. (1997) The automaticity of everyday life. In R. S. Wyer (ed.) *The Automaticity of Everyday Life: Advances in Social Cognition*, Vol. 10. Mahwah, NJ: Erlbaum.

Bargh, J. A. and Chartrand, T. L. (1999) The unbearable automaticity of being. *American Psychologist*, 54, 462–79.

Bargh, J. A. and Ferguson, M. J. (2000) Beyond behaviorism: on the automaticity of higher mental processes. *Psychological Bulletin*, 126, 925–45.

Barker, C., Pistrang, N. and Elliott, R. (2002) *Research Methods in Clinical Psychology: An Introduction for Students and Practitioners*. Chichester: Wiley.

Barker, L. M. (1994) *Learning and Behavior: A Psychobiological Perspective*. New York: Macmillan.

Baron, L., Straus, M. A. and Jaffee, D. (1988) Legitimate violence, violent attitudes, and rape: a test of the Cultural Spillover Theory. In R. A. Prentky and V. L. Quinsey (eds.) Human Sexual Aggression: Current Perspectives. *Annals of the New York Academy of Sciences*, 528, 79–110.

Baron, S. W. and Kennedy, L. W. (1998) Deterrence and homeless male street youths. *Canadian Journal of Criminology*, 40, 27–60.

Bartol, C. R. and Bartol, A. M. (1994) *Psychology and Law*, 2nd edn. Pacific Grove, CA: Brooks/Cole.

Bateman, A. W. and Fonagy, P. (2000) Effectiveness of psychotherapeutic treatment of personality disorder. *British Journal of Psychiatry*, 177, 1138–43.

BBC News World Edition (2004) Taleban drugs control 'effective' (available online: http://news.bbc.co. uk/2/hi/south_asia/3408353.stm).

Becker, J. V. (1998) What we know about the characteristics and treatment of adolescents who have committed sexual offenses. *Child Maltreatment*, 3, 317–29.

Becker, J. V. and Kaplan, M. S. (1988) The assessment of adolescent sexual offenders. *Advances in Behavioral Assessment of Children and Families*, 4, 97–118.

Beech, A. R., Erikson, M., Friendship, C. and Ditchfield, J. (2001) *A Six-Year Follow-up of Men Going Through Probation-Based Sex Offender Treatment Programmes*. Research Findings 144. London: Home Office Research, Development and Statistics Directorate.

Beech, A. R. and Mann, R. (2002) Recent developments in the assessment and treatment of sexual offenders. In J. McGuire (ed.) *Offender Rehabilitation and Treatment: Effective Programmes and Policies to Reduce Re-Offending*. Chichester: Wiley.

Bell, S. T., Kuriloff, P. J., Lottes, I. and Nathanson, J. (1992) Rape callousness in college freshmen: an empirical investigation of the sociocultural model of aggression towards women. *Journal of College Student Development*, 33, 454–61.

Bem, D. J. and Allen, A. (1974) On predicting some of the people some of the time: the search for cross-situational consistencies in behavior. *Psychological Review*, 81, 506–20.

Bennett, T. and Wright, R. (1984) *Burglars on Burglary: Prevention and the Offender*. Aldershot: Gower.

Benton, T. and Craib, I. (2001) *Philosophy of Social Science: The Philosophical Foundations of Social Thought*. Basingstoke: Palgrave.

Berkowitz, L. (1993) *Aggression: Its Causes, Consequences, and Control*. New York: McGraw-Hill.

Bernard, T. J. (1990) Twenty years of testing theories: what have we learned and why? *Journal of Research in Crime and Delinquency*, 27, 325–47.

Bernard, T. J. and Snipes, J. B. (1996) Theoretical integration in criminology. *Crime and Justice: A Review of Research*, 20, 301–48.

Bernfeld, G. A. (2001) The struggle for treatment integrity in a 'dis-integrated' service delivery system. In G. A. Bernfeld, D. P. Farrington and A. W. Leschied (eds.) *Offender Rehabilitation in Practice: Implementing and Evaluating Effective Programs*. Chichester: Wiley.

Bernfeld, G. A., Blase, K. A. and Fixsen, D. L. (1990) Towards a unified perspective on human service delivery systems: application of the teaching-family model. In R. J. McMahon and R. DeV. Peters (eds.) *Behavioral Disorders of Adolescence*. New York: Plenum Press.

Bernfeld, G. A., Farrington, D. P. and Leschied, A. W. (eds.) (2001) *Offender Rehabilitation in Practice: Implementing and Evaluating Effective Programs*. Chichester: Wiley.

Bersoff, D. N. (ed.) (2003) *Ethical Conflicts in Psychology*, 2nd edn. Washington, DC: American Psychological Association.

Bickman, L. (1996) A continuum of care: more is not always better. *American Psychologist*, 51, 689–701.

Blackburn, R. (1992) Criminal behaviour, personality disorder, and mental illness: the origins of confusion. *Criminal Behaviour and Mental Health*, 2, 66–77.

Blackburn, R. (1993) *The Psychology of Criminal Conduct*. Chichester: Wiley.

Blackburn, R. (1996) What *is* forensic psychology? *Legal and Criminological Psychology*, 1, 3–16.

Blackburn, R. (2000a) Risk assessment and prediction. In J. McGuire, T. Mason and A. O'Kane (eds.) *Behaviour, Crime and Legal Processes: A Guidebook for Practitioners*. Chichester: Wiley.

Blackburn, R. (2000b) Treatment or incapacitation? Implications of research on personality disorders for the management of dangerous offenders. *Legal and Criminological Psychology*, 5, 1–21.

Blackburn, R. (2002) Ethical issues in motivating offenders to change. In M. McMurran (ed.) *Motivating Offenders to Change: A Guide to Enhancing Engagement in Therapy*. Chichester: Wiley.

Blackman, D. E. (1996) Punishment: an experimental and theoretical analysis. In J. McGuire and B. Rowson (eds.) *Does Punishment Work?* London: Institute for the Study and Treatment of Delinquency.

Blaske, D. M., Borduin, C. M., Henggeler, S. W. and Mann, B. J. (1989) Individual, family and peer characteristics of adolescent sex offenders and assaultive offenders. *Developmental Psychology*, 25, 846–55.

Bloom, J. D., Bradford, J. M. and Kofoed, L. (1988) An overview of psychiatric treatment approaches to three offender groups. *Hospital and Community Psychiatry*, 39, 151–8.

Bonta, J. (1996) Risk–needs assessment and treatment. In A. T. Harland (ed.) *Chooosing Correctional Options that Work: Defining the Demand and Evaluating the Supply*. Thousand Oaks, CA: Sage Publications.

Bonta, J. and Andrews, D. A. (2003) A commentary on Ward and Stewart's model of human needs. *Psychology, Crime and Law*, 9, 215–18.

Bonta, J., Law, M. and Hanson, K. (1998) The prediction of criminal and violent recidivism amongst mentally disordered offenders: a meta-analysis. *Psychological Bulletin*, 123, 123–42.

Bonta, J., Wallace-Capretta, S. and Rooney, J. (2000) Can electronic monitoring make a difference? An evaluation of three Canadian programs. *Crime and Delinquency*, 46, 61–75.

Boone, M. (2004) Does What Works lead to less repression? The justification of punishment according to What Works. Paper delivered to the *Societies of Criminology, First Key Issues Conference*, Paris.

Borack, J. I. (1998) An estimate of the impact of drug testing on the deterrence of drug use. *Military Psychology*, 10, 17–25.

Borduin, C. M., Mann, B. J., Cone, L. T. and Hengeller, S. W. (1995) Multi-systemic treatment of serious juvenile offenders: long-term prevention of criminality and violence. *Journal of Consulting and Clinical Psychology*, 63, 569–78.

Bottoms, A. and McWilliams, W. (1979) A non-treatment paradigm for probation practice. *British Journal of Social Work*, 9, 159–202.

Bowers, K. S. (1973) Situationism in psychology: an analysis and a critique. *Psychological Review*, 80, 307–36.

Breggin, P. R. (1991) *Toxic Psychiatry: Drugs and Electroconvulsive Therapy. The Truth and the Better Alternatives*. London: HarperCollins.

Brennan, P. A., Mednick, S. A. and Volavka, J. (1995) Biomedical factors in crime. In J. Q. Wilson and J. Petersilia (eds.) *Crime*. San Francisco, CA: CIS Press.

Brezina, T. (2002) Assessing the rationality of criminal and delinquent behavior: a focus on actual utility. In A. R. Piquero and S. G. Tibbetts (eds.) *Rational Choice and Criminal Behavior: Recent Research and Future Challenges*. New York: Routledge.

Brody, S. (1976) *The Effectiveness of Sentencing*. Home Office Research Study 35. London: HMSO.

Brown, I. (1997) A theoretical model of the behavioural addictions – applied to offending. In J. Hodge, M. McMurran and C. R. Hollin (eds.) *Addicted to Crime?* Chichester: Wiley.

Brown, J. (2001) The effectiveness of treatment. In N. Heather, T. J. Peters and T. Stockwell (eds.) *International Handbook of Alcohol Dependence and Problems*. Chichester: Wiley.

Brown, S. L. (2001) Cost-effective correctional treatment. In L. L. Motiuk and R. C. Serin (eds.) *Compendium 2000 on Effective Correctional Programming*. Ottawa: Correctional Service Canada.

Brownfield, D. and Thompson, K. (1991) Attachment to peers and delinquent behaviour. *Canadian Journal of Criminology*, 33, 45–60.

Buchanan, A. (1998) Criminal conviction after discharge from special (high security) hospital: incidence in the first 10 years. *British Journal of Psychiatry*, 172, 472–6.

Buehler, R. E., Patterson, G. R. and Furniss, J. M. (1966) The reinforcement of behavior in institutional settings. *Behavior Research and Therapy*, 4, 157–67.

Buikhuisen, W. and Mednick, S. A. (eds.) (1988) *Explaining Criminal Behaviour*. Leiden: E. J. Brill.

Bull, R. (1995) Interviewing people with communicative disabilities. In R. Bull and D. Carson (eds.) *Handbook of Psychology in Legal Contexts*. Chichester: Wiley.

Bull, R. (1998) Obtaining information from child witnesses. In A. Memon, A. Vrij and R. Bull (eds.) *Psychology and Law: Truthfulness, Accuracy and Credibility*. London: McGraw-Hill.

Bull, R. and Carson, D. (eds.) (1995) *Handbook of Psychology in Legal Contexts*. Chichester: Wiley.

Burke, B. L., Arkowitz, H. and Dunn, C. (2002) The efficacy of motivational interviewing and its adaptations: what we know so far. In W. R. Miller and S. Rollnick (eds.) *Motivational Interviewing: Preparing People for Change*, 2nd edn. New York: Guilford Press.

Bush, J. (1995) Teaching self-risk-management to violent offenders. In J. McGuire (ed.) *What Works: Reducing Reoffending. Guidelines from Research and Practice*. Chichester: Wiley.

Byrne, J. M., Lurigio, A. J. and Petersilia, J. (eds.) (1992) *Smart Sentencing: The Emergence of Intermediate Sanctions*. Newbury Park, CA: Sage Publications.

Cann, J., Falshaw, L., Nugent, F. and Friendship, C. (2003) *Understanding What Works: Accredited Cognitive Skills Programmes for Adult Men and Young Offenders*. Findings 226. London: Home Office Research, Development and Statistics Directorate.

Canter, D. and Alison, L. (eds.) (1999) *Interviewing and Deception*. Aldershot: Ashgate.

Canter, D. and Alison, L. (eds.) (2000) *Profiling Property Crimes*. Aldershot: Ashgate.

Canter, M. B., Bennett, B. E., Jones, S. E. and Nagy, T. F. (1994) *Ethics for Psychologists: A Commentary on the APA Ethics Code*. Washington, DC: American Psychological Association.

Capaldi, D. and Patterson, G. R. (1987) An approach to the problem of recruitment and retention rates for longitudinal research. *Behavioral Assessment*, 9, 169–77.

Caprara, G. V. (1986) Indicators of aggression: the Dissipation-Rumination Scale. *Personality and Individual Differences*, 7, 763–9.

Carrabine, E., Cox, P., Lee, M. and South, N. (2002) *Crime in Modern Britain*. Oxford: Oxford University Press.

Carroll, J. and Weaver, F. (1986) Shoplifters' perceptions of crime opportunities: a process-tracing study. In D. B. Cornish and R. V. Clarke (eds.) *The Reasoning Criminal: Rational Choice Perspectives on Offending*. New York: Springer-Verlag.

Carson, D. (2000) The legal context: obstacle or opportunity? In J. McGuire, T. Mason and A. O'Kane (eds.) *Behaviour, Crime and Legal Processes: A Guidebook for Practitioners*. Chichester: Wiley.

Casey, L. R. and Shulman, J. L. (1979) Police-probation shoplifting reduction program in San José, California: a synergetic approach. *Crime Prevention Review*, 6, 1–9.

Caspi, A., Elder, G. H. and Herberner, E. S. (1990) Childhood personality and the prediction of life course patterns. In L. Robins and M. Rutter (eds.) *Straight and Devious Pathways from Childhood to Adulthood*. Cambridge: Cambridge University Press.

Caspi, A., Henry, B., McGee, R. O., Moffitt, T. E. and Silva, P. A. (1995) Temperamental origins of child and adolescent behavior problems: from age three to age fifteen. *Child Development*, 66, 55–68.

Caspi, A., Moffitt, T. E., Silva, P. A. *et al.* (1994) Are some people crime-prone? Replications of the personality–crime relationship across countries, genders, races and methods. *Criminology*, 32, 163–96.

Caspi, A. and Silva, P. A. (1995) Temperamental qualities at age 3 predict personality traits in young adulthood: longitudinal evidence from a birth cohort. *Child Development*, 66, 486–98.

Catalano, R. F. and Hawkins, J. D. (1996) The social development model: a theory of antisocial behavior. In J. D. Hawkins (ed.) *Delinquency and Crime: Current Theories*. Cambridge: Cambridge University Press.

Cervone, D. and Shoda, Y. (1999) Social-cognitive theories and the coherence of personality. In D. Cervone and Y. Shoda (eds.) *The Coherence of Personality: Social-Cognitive Bases of Consistency, Variability, and Organization*. New York: Guilford Press.

Chadwick, P., Birchwood, M. and Trower, P. (1996) *Cognitive Therapy for Delusions, Voices and Paranoia*. Chichester: Wiley.

Chalmers, A. F. (1999) *What Is This Thing Called Science? An Assessment of the Nature and Status of Science and Its Methods*, 3rd edn. Buckingham: Open University Press.

Chamberlain, P. (2003) *Treating Chronic Juvenile Offenders: Advances Made Through the Oregon Multidimensional Treatment Foster Care Model*. Washington, DC: American Psychological Association.

Chamberlain, P. and Reid, J. B. (1998) Comparison of two community alternatives to incarceration for chronic juvenile offenders. *Journal of Consulting and Clinical Psychology*, 66, 624–33.

Chandler, M. J. (1973) Egocentrism and anti-social behavior: the assessment and training of social perspective-taking skills. *Developmental Psychology*, 9, 326–32.

Cheatwood, D. (1993) Capital punishment and the deterrence of violent crime in comparable counties. *Criminal Justice Review*, 18, 165–81.

Chesney-Lind, M. and Pasko, L. (2004) *The Female Offender: Girls, Women and Crime*, 2nd edn. Thousand Oaks, CA: Sage Publications.

Chess, S. and Thomas, A. (1990) Continuities and discontinuities in temperament. In L. Robins and M. Rutter (eds.) *Straight and Devious Pathways from Childhood to Adulthood*. Cambridge: Cambridge University Press.

Churchland, P. M. (1995) *The Engine of Reason, The Seat of the Soul: A Philosophical Journey into the Brain*. Cambridge, MA: MIT Press.

Clark, L. A., Watson, D. and Reynolds, S. (1995) Diagnosis and classification of psychopathology: challenges to the current system and future directions. *Annual Review of Psychology*, 46, 121–53.

Clarke, R. V. and Felson, M. (1993) Introduction: criminology, routine activity, and rational choice. In R. V. Clarke and M. Felson (eds.) *Routine Activity and Rational Choice*. Advances in Criminological Theory, Vol. 5. New Brunswick, NJ: Transaction Publishers.

Cleland, C. M., Pearson, F. S., Lipton, D. S. and Yee, D. (1997) Does age make a difference? A meta-analytic approach to reductions in criminal offending for juveniles and adults. Paper delivered to the *Annual Meeting of the American Society of Criminology*, San Diego, CA.

Cohen, J. (1988) *Statistical Power Analysis for the Behavioral Sciences*. Hillsdale, NJ: Erlbaum.

Cohen, L. E. and Felson, M. (1979) Social change and crime rate trends: a routine activity approach. *American Sociological Review*, 44, 588–608.

Cohen, L. E. and Machalek, R. (1988) A general theory of expropriative crime: an evolutionary ecological approach. *American Journal of Sociology*, 94, 465–501.

Coie, J. D., Lochman, J. E., Terry, R. and Hyman, C. (1992) Predicting early adolescent disorder from childhood aggression and peer rejection. *Journal of Consulting and Clinical Psychology*, 60, 783–92.

Coleman, C. and Moynihan, J. (1996) *Understanding Crime Data: Haunted by the Dark Figure*. Buckingham: Open University Press.

Collins, K. and Bell, R. (1997) Personality and aggression: the Dissipation-Rumination Scale. *Personality and Individual Differences*, 22, 751–5.

Collins, R. L. and Bradizza, C. M. (2001) Social and cognitive learning processes. In N. Heather, T. J. Peters and T. Stockwell (eds.) *International Handbook of Alcohol Dependence and Problems*. Chichester: Wiley.

Conger, R. D., Ge, X., Elder, G. H., Lorenz, F. O. and Simons, R. L. (1994) Economic stress, coercive family process, and developmental problems of adolescents. *Child Development*, 65, 541–61.

Conger, R. D., Patterson, G. R. and Ge, X. (1995) It takes two to replicate: a mediational model for the impact of parents' stress on adolescent adjustment. *Child Development*, 66, 80–97.

Conklin, J. E. (1992) *Criminology*. 4th edition. New York: Macmillan Publishing Company.

Cook, C. and Gurling, H. (2001) Genetic predisposition to alcohol dependence and problems. In N. Heather, T. J. Peters and T. Stockwell (eds.) *International Handbook of Alcohol Dependence and Problems*. Chichester: Wiley.

Copas, J. (1995) On using crime statistics for prediction. In M. A. Walker (ed.) *Interpreting Crime Statistics*. Oxford: Clarendon Press.

Copas, J. and Marshall, P. (1998) The offender group reconviction scale: a statistical reconviction score for use by probation officers. *Applied Statistics*, 47, 159–71.

Copas, J., Marshall, P. and Tarling, R. (1996) *Predicting Reoffending for Discretionary Conditional Release*. Home Office Research Study 150. London: Home Office Research and Statistics Directorate.

Copson, G. (1995) *Coals to Newcastle? Part 1: A Study of Offender Profiling*. Police Research Group, Special Interest Paper 7. London: Home Office.

Corbett, C. and Simon, F. (1992) Decisions to break or adhere to the rules of the road, viewed from the rational choice perspective. *British Journal of Criminology*, 32, 537–49.

Cottle, C. C., Lee, R. J. and Heilbrun, K. (2001) The prediction of criminal recidivism in juveniles: a meta-analysis. *Criminal Justice and Behavior*, 28, 367–94.

Crick, N. R. and Dodge, K. A. (1994) A review and reformulation of social information-processing mechanisms in children's social adjustment. *Psychological Bulletin*, 115, 74–101.

Cronbach, L. J. (1975) Beyond the two disciplines of scientific psychology. *American Psychologist*, 30, 116–27.

Crow, I. (2001) *The Treatment and Rehabilitation of Offenders*. London: Sage Publications.

Cullen, F. T., Cullen, J. B. and Wozniak, J. F. (1988) Is rehabilitation dead? The myth of the punitive public. *Journal of Criminal Justice*, 16, 313–17.

Cullen, F. T., Pratt, T. C., Miceli, S. L. and Moon, M. M. (2002) Dangerous liaison? Rational choice theory as the basis for correctional intervention. In A. R. Piquero and S. G. Tibbetts (eds.) *Rational Choice and Criminal Behavior: Recent Research and Future Challenges*. New York: Routledge.

Daly, K. and Chesney-Lind, M. (1988) Feminism and criminology. *Justice Quarterly*, 5, 497–538.

Davies, G. and Noon, E. (1991) *An Evaluation of the Live Link for Child Witnesses.* London: Home Office.

Davies, H. (1993) *Evaluation of Motor Offender Projects.* Birmingham: West Midlands Probation Service.

Davies, J. B. (1992) *The Myth of Addiction: An Application of the Psychological Theory of Attribution to Illicit Drug Use.* Reading: Harwood Academic Publishers.

Davison, G. C. and Stuart, R. B. (1975) Behavior therapy and civil liberties. *American Psychologist*, 30, 755–63.

Dean, K. E. and Malamuth, N. M. (1997) Characteristics of men who aggress sexually and of men who imagine aggressing: risk and moderating variables. *Journal of Personality and Social Psychology*, 72, 449–55.

De Coverley Veale, D. M. W. (1987) Exercise dependence. *British Journal of Addiction*, 82, 735–40.

Del Vecchio, T. and O'Leary, K. D. (2004) Effectiveness of anger treatments for specific anger problems: A meta-analytic review. *Clinical Psychology Review*, 24, 15–34.

Dembo, R., Ramírez-Garnica, G., Rollie, M. W. and Schmeidler, J. (2000) Impact of a family empowerment intervention on youth recidivism. *Journal of Offender Rehabilitation*, 30, 59–98.

De Paulo, B. M., Lindsay, J. J., Malone, B. E. *et al.* (2003) Cues to deception. *Psychological Bulletin*, 129, 74–118.

DiGuiseppe, R. and Tafrate, R. C. (2003) Anger treatment for adults: a meta-analytic review. *Clinical Psychology: Science and Practice*, 10, 70–84.

Dobash, R. E. and Dobash, R. P. (2000) Evaluating criminal justice interventions for domestic violence. *Crime and Delinquency*, 46, 252–70.

Dobash, R. P., Dobash, R. E., Cavanagh, K. and Lewis, R. (1996) *Re-education Programmes for Violent Men – An Evaluation.* Research Findings 46. London: Home Office Research and Statistics Directorate.

Dodge, K. A. and Pettit, G. S. (2003) A biopsychosocial model of the development of chronic conduct problems in adolescence. *Developmental Psychology*, 39, 349–71.

Dodge, K. A., Pettit, G. S. and Bates, J. E. (1994) Socialisation mediators of the relation between socioeconomic status and child conduct problems. *Child Development*, 65, 649–65.

Dodge, K. A. and Schwartz, D. (1997) Social information processing mechanisms in aggressive behavior. In D. M. Stoff, J. Breiling and J. D. Maser (eds.) *Handbook of Antisocial Behavior.* New York: Wiley.

Donato, R. and Shanahan, M. (1999) *The Economics of Implementing Intensive In-prison Sex-offender Treatment Programs.* Trends and Issues in Crime and Justice 134. Canberra, ACT: Australian Institute of Criminology.

Dorn, N., Murji, K. and South, N. (1992) *Traffickers: Drug Markets and Law Enforcement.* London: Routledge.

Dowden, C. and Andrews, D. A. (1999a) What works in young offender treatment: a meta-analysis. *Forum on Corrections Research*, 11, 21–4.

Dowden, C. and Andrews, D. A. (1999b) What works for female offenders: a meta-analytic review. *Crime and Delinquency*, 45, 438–52.

Dowden, C. and Andrews, D. A. (2000) Effective correctional treatment and violent reoffending: a meta-analysis. *Canadian Journal of Criminology*, 449–67.

Dowden, C., Blanchette, K. and Serin, R. C. (1999) *Anger Management Programming for Federal Male Inmates: An Effective Intervention.* Research Report R-82. Ottawa, ON: Correctional Service of Canada.

Dunawayk, R. G., Cullen, F. T., Burton, V. S. and Evans, T. D. (2000) The myth of social class and crime revisited: an examination of class and adult criminality. *Criminology*, 38, 589–632.

Dvoskin, J. A. and Steadman, H. J. (1994) Using intensive case management to reduce violence by mentally ill persons in the community. *Hospital and Community Psychiatry*, 45, 679–84.

East, K. and Campbell, S. (2000) *Aspects of Crime: Young Offenders 1999.* London: Home Office Research, Development and Statistics Directorate (available online: http://www.Justice.statsapollo@homeoffice.gsi.gov.uk).

Eastman, N. (2000) Psycho-legal studies as an interface discipline. In J. McGuire, T. Mason and A. O'Kane (eds.) *Behaviour, Crime and Legal Processes: A Guidebook for Practitioners.* Chichester: Wiley.

Eck, J. E. (2002) Preventing crime at places. In L. W. Sherman, D. P. Farrington, B. C. Welsh and D. L. MacKenzie (eds.) *Evidence-Based Crime Prevention.* London: Routledge.

Edmondson, C. B. and Conger, J. C. (1996) A review of treatment efficacy for individuals with anger problems: conceptual, assessment, and methodological issues. *Clinical Psychology Review*, 16, 251–75.

Edwards, D. and Roundtree, G. (1982) Assessment of short-term treatment groups with adjudicated first offender shoplifters. *Journal of Offender Counseling, Services and Rehabilitation*, 6, 89–102.

Ehrlich, I. (1975) The deterrent effect of capital punishment: a question of life and death. *American Economic Review*, 65, 397–417.

Elliott, D. S., Ageton, S. S. and Cantor, R. J. (1979) An integrated theoretical perspective on delinquent behavior. *Journal of Research in Crime and Delinquency*, 16, 3–27.

Elliott, D. S., Wilson, W. J., Huizinga, D. *et al.* (1996) The effects of neighborhood disadvantage on adolescent development. *Journal of Research on Crime and Delinquency*, 33, 389–426.

Ellis, T. and Winstone, J. (2002) The policy impact of a survey of programme evaluations in England and Wales. In J. McGuire (ed.) *Offender Rehabilitation and Treatment: Effective Programmes and Policies to Reduce Re-Offending.* Chichester: Wiley.

Ellsworth, P. C., Carlsmith, J. M. and Henson, A. (1972) The stare as a stimulus to flight in human subjects: a series of field experiments. *Journal of Personality and Social Psychology*, 21, 302–11.

Epstein, S. and O'Brien, E. J. (1985) The person–situation debate in historical and current perspective. *Psychological Bulletin*, 98, 513–37.

Esbensen, F.-A., Winfree, L. T., He, N. and Taylor, T. J. (2001) Youth gangs and definitional issues: when is a gang a gang, and why does it matter? *Crime and Delinquency*, 47, 105–30.

European Federation of Psychologists' Associations (2004) *Ethics* (available online: http://www.efpa.be/Home/newpagina.htm).

Evans, W. N., Neville, D. and Graham, J. D. (1991) General deterrence of drunk driving: evaluation of recent American policies. *Risk Analysis*, 11, 279–89.

Eysenck, H. J. (1977) *Crime and Personality*, 3rd edn. London: Routledge and Kegan Paul.

Falshaw, L., Friendship, C., Travers, R. and Nugent, F. (2003) *Searching for 'What Works': An Evaluation of Cognitive Skills Programmes*. Findings 206. London: Home Office Research, Development and Statistics Directorate.

Farabee, D., Prendergast, M. and Anglin, M. D. (1998) The effectiveness of coerced treatment for drug-abusing offenders. *Federal Probation*, 62, 3–10.

Farber, I. E. (1963) The things people say to themselves. *American Psychologist*, 18, 185–97.

Farrall, S. (2002) *Rethinking What Works with Offenders: Probation, Social Context and Desistance from Crime*. Cullompton: Willan Publishing.

Farrell, D. M. (1985) The justification of general deterrence. *Philosophical Review*, XCIV, 367–94.

Farrington, D. P. (1993) Have any individual, family or neighbourhood influences on offending been demonstrated conclusively? In D. P. Farrington, R. J. Sampson and P. H. Wikström (eds.) *Integrating Individual and Ecological Aspects of Crime*. Stockholm: National Council for Crime Prevention.

Farrington, D. P. (1994) Childhood, adolescent and adult features of violent males. In L. R. Huesmann (ed.) *Aggressive Behavior: Current Perspectives*. New York: Plenum Press.

Farrington, D. P. (1995) The development of offending and antisocial behaviour from childhood: key findings from the Cambridge Study in Delinquent Development. *Journal of Child Psychology and Psychiatry*, 36, 929–64.

Farrington, D. P. (1996) The explanation and prevention of youthful offending. In J. D. Hawkins (ed.) *Delinquency and Crime: Current Theories*. Cambridge: Cambridge University Press.

Farrington, D. P. (2002) Developmental criminology and risk-focused prevention. In M. Maguire, R. Morgan and R. Reiner (eds.) *The Oxford Handbook of Criminology*, 3rd edn. Oxford: Oxford University Press.

Farrington, D. P. (2003) Key results from the first forty years of the Cambridge Study in Delinquent Development. In T. P. Thornberry and M. D. Krohn (eds.) *Taking Stock of Delinquency: An Overview of Findings from Contemporary Longitudinal Studies*. New York: Kluver Academic/Plenum Publishers.

Farrington, D. P. and Coid, J. W. (eds.) (2003) *Early Prevention of Adult Antisocial Behaviour*. Cambridge: Cambridge University Press.

Farrington, D. P., Jolliffe, D., Loeber, R., Stouthamer-Loeber, M. and Kalb, L. M. (2001) The concentration of offenders in families, and family criminality in the prediction of boys' delinquency. *Journal of Adolescence*, 24, 579–96.

Farrington, D. P. and Welsh, B. C. (2002) Developmental prevention programmes: effectiveness and benefit–cost analysis. In J. McGuire (ed.) *Offender Rehabilitation and Treatment: Effective Programmes and Policies to Reduce Re-Offending*. Chichester: Wiley.

Farrington, D. P. and Welsh, B. C. (2003) Family-based prevention of offending: a meta-analysis. *Australian and New Zealand Journal of Criminology*, 36, 127–51.

Farrington, D. P. and West, D. (1993) Criminal, penal and life histories of chronic offenders: risk and protective factors and early identification. *Criminal Behaviour and Mental Health*, 3, 492–523.

Fazel, S. and Danesh, J. (2002) Serious mental disorder in 23,000 prisoners: A systematic review of 62 surveys. *Lancet*, 359, 545–50.

Feindler, E. L. and Ecton, R. B. (1986) *Adolescent Anger Control: Cognitive-Behavioral Techniques*. New York: Pergamon Press.

Felson, M. (1994) *Crime and Everyday Life: Insight and Implications for Society*. Thousand Oaks, CA: Pine Forge Press.

Felson, M. (2002) *Crime and Everyday Life*, 3rd edn. Thousand Oaks, CA: Sage Publications.

Fergusson, D. M., Horwood, L. J. and Nagin, D. S. (2000) Offending trajectories in a New Zealand birth cohort. *Criminology*, 38, 525–52.

Field, S. (1990) *Trends in Crime and their Interpretation: A Study of Recorded Crime in Post-War England and Wales*. Home Office Research Study 119. London: HMSO.

Field, S. (1999) *Trends in Crime Revisited*. Home Office Research Study 195. London: Home Office Research, Development and Statistics Directorate.

Fiorentino, R., Nakashima, J. and Anglin, M. D. (1999) Client engagement in drug treatment. *Journal of Substance Abuse Treatment*, 17, 199–206.

Fitzmaurice, C. and Pease, K. (1986) *The Psychology of Judicial Sentencing*. Manchester: Manchester University Press.

Foglia, W. D. (1997) Perceptual difference and the mediating effect of internalized norms among inner-city teenagers. *Journal of Research in Crime and Delinquency*, 34, 414–42.

Foglia, W. D. (2000) Adding an explicit focus on cognition to criminological theory. In D. H. Fishbein (ed.) *The Science, Treatment, and Prevention of Antisocial Behaviors: Application to the Criminal Justice System*. Kingston, NJ: Civic Research Institute.

Ford, M. E. and Linney, J. A. (1995) Comparative analysis of juvenile sex offenders, violent nonsexual offenders, and status offenders. *Journal of Interpersonal Violence*, 10, 56–70.

Fowler, D., Garety, P. and Kuipers, E. (1995) *Cognitive Behaviour Therapy for Psychosis*. Chichester: Wiley.

Friendship, C., Blud, L., Erikson, M. and Travers, R. (2002) *An Evaluation of Cognitive-Behavioural Treatment for Prisoners*. Findings 161. London: Home Office Research, Development and Statistics Directorate.

Friendship, C., Mann, R. and Beech, A. (2003) *The Prison-Based Sex Offender Treatment Programme: An Evaluation*. Findings 205. London: Home Office Research, Development and Statistics Directorate.

Fry, P. S. (1975) Affect and resistance to temptation. *Developmental Psychology*, 11, 466–72.

Funder, D. C. (2001) Personality. *Annual Review of Psychology*, 52, 197–221.

Furnham, A. F. (1988) *Lay Theories: Everyday Understanding of Problems in the Social Sciences*. Oxford: Pergamon Press.

Gaes, G. G. (1998) Correctional treatment. In M. Tonry (ed.) *The Handbook of Crime and Punishment*. Oxford: Oxford University Press.

Gallagher, C. A., Wilson, D. B., Hirschfield, P., Coggeshall, M. B. and MacKenzie, D. L. (1999) A quantitative review of the effects of sexual offender treatment on sexual reoffending. *Corrections Management Quarterly*, 3, 19–29.

Garland, D. (1990) *Punishment and Modern Society: A Study in Social Theory*. Oxford: Clarendon Press.

Garland, D. (2002) Of crimes and criminals: the development of criminology in Britain. In M. Maguire, R. Morgan and R. Reiner (eds.) *The Oxford Handbook of Criminology*, 3rd edn. Oxford: Oxford University Press.

Garrett, C. G. (1985) Effects of residential treatment on adjudicated delinquents: a meta-analysis. *Journal of Research in Crime and Delinquency*, 22, 287–308.

Gauthier, J. and Pellegrin, D. (1982) Management of compulsive shoplifting through covert sensitisation. *Journal of Behavior Therapy and Experimental Psychiatry*, 13, 73–5.

Gendreau, P. (1996a) Offender rehabilitation: what we know and what needs to be done. *Criminal Justice and Behavior*, 23, 144–61.

Gendreau, P. (1996b) The principles of effective intervention with offenders. In A. T. Harland (ed.) *Choosing Correctional Options that Work: Defining the Demand and Evaluating the Supply*. Thousand Oaks, CA: Sage Publications.

Gendreau, P. and Andrews, D. A. (1990) Tertiary prevention: what the meta-analyses of the offender treatment literature tell us about 'what works'. *Canadian Journal of Criminology*, 32, 173–84.

Gendreau, P. and Goggin, C. (1996) Principles of effective correctional programming. *Forum on Corrections Research*, 8, 38–41.

Gendreau, P., Goggin, C. and Cullen, F. T. (1999a) *The Effects of Prison Sentences on Recidivism*. Report to the Corrections Research and Development and Aboriginal Policy Branch. Ottawa: Solicitor General of Canada.

Gendreau, P., Goggin, C., Cullen, F. T. and Paparozzi, M. (2001) The effects of community sanctions and incarceration on recidivism. In L. L. Motiuk and R. C. Serin (eds.) *Compendium 2000 on Effective Correctional Programming*. Ottawa: Correctional Service Canada.

Gendreau, P., Goggin, C., Cullen, F. T. and Paparozzi, M. (2002a) The common-sense revolution and correctional policy. In J. McGuire (ed.) *Offender Rehabilitation and Treatment: Effective Programmes and Policies to Reduce Re-Offending*. Chichester: Wiley.

Gendreau, P., Goggin, C. and Smith, P. (1999b) The forgotten issue in effective correctional treatment: program implementation. *International Journal of Offender Therapy and Comparative Criminology*, 43, 180–7.

Gendreau, P., Goggin, C. and Smith, P. (2002b) Is the PCL-R really the 'unparalleled' measure of offender risk? A lesson in knowledge cumulation. *Criminal Justice and Behavior*, 29, 397–426.

Gendreau, P., Little, T. and Goggin, C. (1996) A meta-analysis of predictors of adult recidivism: what works! *Criminology*, 34, 575–607.

Gendreau, P., Paparozzi, M., Little, T. and Goddard, M. (1993) Does 'punishing smarter' work? An assessment of the new generation of alternative sanctions in probation. *Forum on Corrections Research*, 5, 31–4.

Gendreau, P. and Ross, R. R. (1980) Effective correctional treatment: bibliotherapy for cynics. In R. R. Ross and P. Gendreau (eds.) *Effective Correctional Treatment*. Toronto: Butterworths.

Gensheimer, L. K., Mayer, J. P., Gottschalk, R. and Davidson, W. S. (1986) Diverting youth from the juvenile justice system: a meta-analysis of intervention efficacy. In S. A. Apter and A. P. Goldstein (eds.) *Youth Violence: Programs and Prospects*. Elmsford, NJ: Pergamon Press.

Gibbs, J. P. (1986) Deterrence theory and research. In G. B. Melton (ed.) *The Law as a Behavioral Instrument: Nebraska Symposium on Motivation 1985*. Lincoln, NB: University of Nebraska Press.

Glass, G. V. (1976) Primary, secondary and meta-analysis of research. *Educational Researcher*, 5, 3–8.

Glass, G. V., McGaw, B. and Smith, M. L. (1981) *Meta-analysis in Social Research*. Newbury Park, CA: Sage Publications.

Glatt, M. M. and Cook, C. C. H. (1987) Pathological spending as a form of psychological dependence. *British Journal of Addiction*, 82, 1257–8.

Glick, L. (1995) *Criminology*. Boston, MA: Allyn and Bacon.

Glover, J. H. (1985) A case of kleptomania treated by covert sensitisation. *British Journal of Clinical Psychology*, 24, 213–14.

Gold, M. (1987) Social ecology. In H. C. Quay (ed.) *Handbook of Juvenile Delinquency*. New York: Wiley.

Goldiamond, I. (1974) Toward a constructional approach to social problems: ethical and constitutional issues raised by applied behavior analysis. *Behaviorism*, 2, 1–84.

Goldstein, A. P. (1996) *The Psychology of Vandalism*. New York: Plenum Press.

Goldstein, A. P. (2002) Low-level aggression: definition, escalation, intervention. In J. McGuire (ed.) *Offender Rehabilitation and Treatment: Effective Programmes and Policies to Reduce Re-Offending*. Chichester: Wiley.

Goldstein, A. P. and Glick, B. (2001) Aggression replacement training: application and evaluation management. In G. A. Bernfeld, D. P. Farrington and A. W. Leschied (eds.) *Offender Rehabilitation in Practice: Implementing and Evaluating Effective Programs*. Chichester: Wiley.

Goldstein, A. P., Glick, B., Carthan, W. and Blancero, D. A. (1994) *The Prosocial Gang: Implementing Aggression Replacement Training*. Thousand Oaks, CA: Sage Publications.

Goode, E. (1997) *Deviant Behavior*, 5th edn. Upper Saddle River, NJ: Prentice-Hall.

Gordon, D. A. (2002) Intervening with families of troubled youth: functional family therapy and parenting wisely. In J. McGuire (ed.) *Offender Rehabilitation and Treatment: Effective Programmes and Policies to Reduce Re-Offending*. Chichester: Wiley.

Gordon, D.A., Graves, K. and Arbuthnot, J. (1995) The effect of functional family therapy for delinquents on adult criminal behavior. *Criminal Justice and Behavior*, 22, 60–73.

Gossop, M., Marsden, J., Stewart, D. and Kidd, T. (2003) The National Treatment Outcome Research Study (NTORS): 4–5 year follow-up results. *Addiction*, 98, 291–303.

Gottfredson, D. C., Wilson, D. B. and Najaka, S. S. (2002) School-based crime prevention. In L. W. Sherman, D. P. Farrington, B. C. Welsh and D. L. Mackenzie (eds.) *Evidence-Based Crime Prevention*. London: Routledge.

Gottfredson, M. R. and Hirschi, T. (1990) *A General Theory of Crime*. Stanford, CA: Stanford University Press.

Gottfredson, M. R. and Hirschi, T. (1993) A control theory interpretation of psychological research on aggression. In R. B. Felson and J. T. Tedeschi (eds.) *Aggression and Violence: Social Interactionist Perspectives*. Washington, DC: American Psychological Association.

Gottschalk, R., Davidson, W. S., Gensheimer, L. K. and Mayer, J. P. (1987a) Community-based interventions. In H. C. Quay (ed.) *Handbook of Juvenile Delinquency*. New York: Wiley.

Gottschalk, R., Davidson, W. S., Mayer, J. and Gensheimer, L. K. (1987b) Behavioral approaches with juvenile offenders: a meta-analysis of long-term treatment efficacy. In E. K. Morris and C. J. Braukmann (eds.) *Behavioural Approaches to Crime and Delinquency*. New York: Plenum Press.

Gould, S. J. (1981) *The Mismeasure of Man*. Harmondsworth: Penguin Books.

Graf, R. G. (1971) Induced self-esteem as a determinant of behavior. *Journal of Social Psychology*, 85, 213–17.

Graham, K. and West, P. (2001) Alcohol and crime: examining the link. In N. Heather, T. J. Peters and T. Stockwell (eds.) *International Handbook of Alcohol Dependence and Problems*. Chichester: Wiley.

Greenwood, P., Rydell, C. P., Abrahamse, A. F. *et al.* (1996) Estimated costs and benefits of California's new mandatory-sentencing law. In D. Shichor and D. K. Sechrest (eds.) *Three Strikes and You're Out: Vengeance as Public Policy*. Thousand Oaks, CA: Sage Publications.

Grisso, T. and Appelbaum, P. S. (1992) Is it unethical to offer predictions of future violence? *Law and Human Behavior*, 16, 621–33.

Grubin, D. (1998) *Sex Offending Against Children: Understanding the Risk*. Police Research Series Paper 99. London: Home Office Policing and Reducing Crime Unit.

Gudjonsson, G. H. (2002) *The Psychology of Interrogations and Confessions: A Handbook*. Chichester: Wiley.

Gudjonsson, G. H. and Hayward, L. (1998) *Forensic Psychology: Practitioner's Guide*. London: Routledge.

Guerra, N. G., Tolan, P. H. and Hammond, W. R. (1994) Prevention and treatment of adolescent violence. In L. D. Eron, J. H. Gentry and P. Schlegel (eds.) *Reason to Hope: A Psychosocial Perspective on Violence and Youth*. Washington, DC: American Psychological Association.

Guidry, L. S. (1975) Use of a covert punishment contingency in compulsive stealing. *Journal of Behavior Therapy and Experimental Psychiatry*, 6, 169.

Gulbenkian Foundation (1995) *Children and Violence*. London: Calouste Gulbenkian Foundation.

Guttenplan, S. (1994) *A Companion to the Philosophy of Mind*. Oxford: Blackwell.

Guttridge, P., Gabrielli, W. F., Mednick, S. A. and Van Dusen, K. T. (1983) Criminal violence in a birth cohort. In K. T. Van Dusen and S. A. Mednick (eds.) *Prospective Studies of Crime and Delinquency*. Hingham, MA: Kluwer Nijhoff.

Hadi, A. (2000) Prevalence and correlates of the risk of marital sexual violence in Bangladesh. *Journal of Interpersonal Violence*, 15, 787–805.

Hagell, A. and Newburn, T. (1994) *Persistent Young Offenders*. London: Policy Studies Institute.

Halfpenny, P. (1982) *Positivism and Sociology: Explaining Social Life*. London: Allen & Unwin.

Hall, G. C. N. (1995) Sexual offender recidivism revisited: a meta-analysis of recent treatment studies. *Journal of Consulting and Clinical Psychology*, 63, 802–9.

Hall, J. A., Herzberger, S. D. and Skowronski, K. J. (1998) Outcome expectancies and outcome values as predictors of children's aggression. *Aggressive Behavior*, 24, 439–54.

Hämäläinen, M. and Pulkkinen, L. (1995) Aggressive and non-prosocial behaviour as precursors of criminality. *Studies on Crime and Crime Prevention*, 4, 6–20.

Haney, C. (1999) Ideology and crime control. *American Psychologist*, 54, 786–8.

Haney, C. (2003) Mental health issues in long-term solitary and 'supermax' confinement. *Crime and Delinquency*, 49, 124–56.

Haney, C. and Zimbardo, P. (1998) The past and future of U.S. prison policy: twenty-five years after the Stanford Prison Experiment. *American Psychologist*, 53, 709–27.

Hanson, R. K., Gordon, A., Harris, A. J. R. *et al.* (2002) First report of the Collaborative Outcome Data Project on the effectiveness of psychological treatment for sex offenders. *Sexual Abuse: A Journal of Research and Treatment*, 14, 169–94.

Hare, R. D. (1996) Psychopathy: a clinical construct whose time has come. *Criminal Justice and Behavior*, 23, 25–54.

Harland, A. T. (ed.) (1996) *Choosing Correctional Options that Work: Defining the Demand and Evaluating the Supply*. Thousand Oaks, CA: Sage Publications.

Harris, P. and Smith, S. (1996) Developing community corrections: an implementation perspective. In A. T. Harland (ed.) *Choosing Correctional Options that Work: Defining the Demand and Evaluating the Supply*. Thousand Oaks, CA: Sage Publications.

Harway, M. and O'Neil, J. M. (eds.) (1999) *What Causes Men's Violence Against Women?* Thousand Oaks, CA: Sage Publications.

Hawkins, J. D., Smith, B. H., Kill, K. J. *et al.* (2003) Understanding and preventing crime and violence: findings from the Seattle Social Development Project. In T. P. Thornberry and M. D. Krohn (eds.) *Taking Stock of Delinquency: An Overview of Findings from Contemporary Longitudinal Studies*. New York: Kluver Academic/Plenum Publishers.

Hedges, L. V. (1987) How hard is hard science, how soft is soft science? The empirical cumulativeness of research. *American Psychologist*, 42, 443–55.

Heidensohn, F. (2002) Gender and crime. In M. Maguire, R. Morgan and R. Reiner (eds.) *The Oxford Handbook of Criminology*, 3rd edn. Oxford: Oxford University Press.

Heilbrun, K. and Peters, L. (2000) The efficacy of community treatment programmes in preventing crime and violence. In S. Hodgins and R. Muller-Isberner (eds.) *Violence, Crime and Mentally Disordered Offenders: Concepts and Methods for Effective Treatment and Prevention*. The Hague: Kluwer Academic Publishers.

Henderson, J. Q. (1981) A behavioural approach to stealing: a proposal for treatment based on ten cases. *Journal of Behavior Therapy and Experimental Psychiatry*, 12, 231–6.

Henggeler, S. W., Schoenwald, S. K., Borduin, C. M., Rowland, M. D. and Cunningham, P. B. (1998) *Multisystemic Treatment of Antisocial Behavior in Children and Adolescents*. New York: Guilford Press.

Henning, K. R. and Frueh, B. C. (1996) Cognitive-behavioral treatment of incarcerated offenders: an evaluation of the Vermont Department of Corrections' Cognitive Self-Change Program. *Criminal Justice and Behavior*, 23, 523–42.

Henry, S. and Milovanovic, D. (1991) Constitutive criminology: the maturation of critical theory. *Criminology*, 29, 293–315.

Henstridge, J., Homel, R. and Mackay, P. (1997) *The Long-term Effects of Random Breath Testing in Four Australian States: A Time Series Analysis*. Canberra, ACT: Federal Office of Road Safety.

Hill, K. G., Howell, J. C., Hawkins, J. D. and Battin-Pearson, S. R. (1999) Childhood risk factors for adolescent gang membership: results from the Seattle Social Development Project. *Journal of Research in Crime and Delinquency*, 36, 300–22.

Hirschi, T. (1979) Separate and unequal is better. *Journal of Research in Crime and Delinquency*, 16, 34–8.

Hodgins, S. and Côté, G. (1990) The prevalence of mental disorders among penitentiary inmates. *Canada's Mental Health*, 38, 1–5.

Hodgins, S. and Müller-Isberner, R. (eds.) (2000) *Violence, Crime and Mentally Disordered Offenders: Concepts and Methods for Effective Treatment and Prevention*. Chichester: Wiley.

Hoge, R. D. (2002) Standardized instruments for assessing risk and need in youthful offenders. *Criminal Justice and Behavior*, 29, 380–96.

Hoge, R. D. and Andrews, D. A. (1996) *Assessing the Youthful Offender: Issues and Techniques*. New York: Plenum Press.

Hollenhorst, P. S. (1998) What do we know about anger management programs in corrections? *Federal Probation*, 62, 52–64.

Hollin, C. R. (1989) *Psychology and Crime: An Introduction to Criminological Psychology*. London: Routledge.

Hollin, C. R. (1990) *Cognitive-Behavioral Interventions with Young Offenders*. New York: Pergamon.

Hollin, C. R. (1995) The meaning and implications of program integrity. In J. McGuire (ed.) *What Works: Reducing Reoffending. Guidelines from Research and Practice*. Chichester: Wiley.

Hollin, C. R. (1999) Treatment programmes for offenders: meta-analysis, 'what works', and beyond. *International Journal of Law and Psychiatry*, 22, 361–71.

Hollin, C. R. (ed.) (2001a) *Handbook of Offender Assessment and Treatment*. Chichester: Wiley.

Hollin, C. R. (2001b) To treat or not to treat? An historical perspective. In C. R. Hollin (ed.) *Handbook of Offender Assessment and Treatment*. Chichester: Wiley.

Hollin, C. R. (2002a) Criminological psychology. In M. Maguire, R. Morgan and R. Reiner (eds.) *The Oxford Handbook of Criminology*, 3rd edn. Oxford: Oxford University Press.

Hollin, C. R. (2002b) Risk–needs assessment and allocation to offender programmes. In J. McGuire (ed.) *Offender Rehabilitation and Treatment: Effective Programmes and Policies to Reduce Re-Offending*. Chichester: Wiley.

Hollin, C. R. (2002c) Does punishment motivate offenders to change? In M. McMurran (ed.) *Motivating Offenders to Change: A Guide to Enhancing Engagement in Therapy*. Chichester: Wiley.

Hollin, C. R., McGuire, J., Palmer, E. *et al.* (2002) *Introducing Pathfinder Programmes to the Probation Service*. Home Office Research Study 247. London: Home Office.

Holmes, R. M. and Holmes, S. T. (2002) *Profiling Violent Crimes: An Investigative Tool*, 3rd edn. Thousand Oaks, CA: Sage Publications.

Home Affairs Committee (1993) *Juvenile Offenders: Memoranda of Evidence*. London: HMSO.

Home Office (1993) *Digest 2: Information on the Criminal Justice System in England and Wales*. London: Home Office Research and Statistics Department.

Home Office (2003) *Criminal Statistics for England and Wales 2002*. London: Home Office.

Honderich, T. (1976) *Punishment: The Supposed Justifications*. Harmondsworth: Penguin Books.

Honderich. T. (2002) *How Free Are You? The Determinism Problem*, 2nd edn. Oxford: Oxford University Press.

Hood, R. (2002) *The Death Penalty: A Worldwide Perspective*, 3rd edn. Oxford: Oxford University Press.

Howe, E. S. and Loftus, T. C. (1996) Integration of certainty, severity and celerity information in judged deterrence value: further evidence and methodological equivalence. *Journal of Applied Social Psychology*, 26, 226–42.

Howells, K. and Day, A. (2003) Readiness for anger management. *Clinical Psychology Review*, 23, 319–37.

Howells, K., Day, A., Bubner, S., Jauncey, S., Williamson, P., Parker, A. and Heseltine, K. (2002) *Anger management and violence prevention: Improving effectiveness*. Trends and Issues No.207. Canberra: Australian Institute of Criminology.

Howells, K., Watt, B., Hall, G. and Baldwin, S. (1997) Developing programmes for violent offenders. *Legal and Criminological Psychology*, 2, 117–28.

Hubbard, D. J. and Pratt, T. C. (2002) A meta-analysis of the predictors of delinquency among girls. *Journal of Offender Rehabilitation*, 34, 1–13.

Hudson, B. A. (1996) *Understanding Justice: An Introduction to Ideas, Perspectives and Controversies in Modern Penal Theory*. Buckingham: Open University Press.

Hudson, S. M. and Ward, T. (2001) Adolescent sexual offenders: assessment and treatment. In C. R. Hollin (ed.) *Handbook of Offender Assessment and Treatment*. Chichester: Wiley.

Huesmann, R. L., Moise-Titus, J., Podolski, C. L. and Eron, L. P. (2003) Longitudinal relations between children's exposure to TV violence and their aggressiveness and violent behaviour in young adulthood: 1977–1992. *Developmental Psychology*, 39, 201–21.

Huizinga, D., Weiher, A. W., Espiritu, E. and Esbensen, F. (2003) Delinquency and crime: some highlights from the Denver Youth Survey. In T. P. Thornberry and M. D. Krohn (eds.) *Taking Stock of Delinquency: An Overview of Findings from Contemporary Longitudinal Studies*. New York: Kluver Academic/Plenum Publishers.

Izzo, R. L. and Ross, R. R. (1990) Meta-analysis of rehabilitation programmes for juvenile delinquents. *Criminal Justice and Behavior*, 17, 134–42.

Jakob, R. (1992) On the development of psychologically oriented legal thinking in German speaking countries. In F. Lösel, D. Bender and T. Bliesener (eds.) *Psychology and Law: International Perspectives*. Berlin: Walter De Gruyter.

James, O. (1995) *Juvenile Violence in a Winner–Loser Culture: Socio-Economic and Familial Origins of the Rise in Violence Against the Person*. London: Free Association Books.

Jamieson, J., McIvor, G. and Murray, C. (1999) *Understanding Offending Among Young People*. Edinburgh: The Stationery Office.

Janson, C. G. (1983) Delinquency among metropolitan boys: a progress report. In K. T. Van Dusen and S. A. Mednick (eds.) *Prospective Studies of Crime and Delinquency*. Hingham, MA: Kluwer Nijhoff.

Jarvis, G. and Parker, H. (1989) Young heroin users and crime: how do the 'new users' finance their habits? *British Journal of Criminology*, 29, 175–85.

Johnson, T. J. (1972) *Professions and Power*. London: Macmillan.

Joint Prison/Probation Services Accreditation Panel (2002) *Performance Standards Manual for the Delivery of Accredited Individual Programmes*. London: National Probation Service.

Jolliffe, D. and Farrington, D. P. (2003) Empathy and offending: A systematic review and meta-analysis. *Aggression and Violent Behaviour*, 9, 441–476.

Joseph, J. (2003) *The Gene Illusion: Genetic Research in Psychiatry and Psychology under the Microscope*. Ross-on-Wye: PCCS Books.

Juby, H. and Farrington, D. P. (2001) Disentangling the link between disrupted families and delinquency. *British Journal of Criminology*, 41, 22–40.

Kandel, E. R., Schwartz, J. H. and Jessell, T. M. (eds.) (2000) *Principles of Neural Science*, 4th edn. New York: McGraw-Hill.

Kapardis, A. (1997) *Psychology and Law: A Critical Introduction*. Cambridge: Cambridge University Press.

Kaplan, H. B. (2003) Testing an integrative theory of deviant behavior: theory-syntonic findings from a long-term multi-generation study. In T. P. Thornberry and M. D. Krohn (eds.) *Taking Stock of Delinquency: An Overview of Findings from Contemporary Longitudinal Studies*. New York: Kluver Academic/Plenum Publishers.

Kassinove, H. and Tafrate, R. C. (2002) *Anger Management: The Complete Treatment Guidebook for Practitioners*. Atascedero, CA: Impact Publishers.

Kendall, P. C. (1993) Cognitive-behavioral therapies with youth: guiding theory, current status, and emerging developments. *Journal of Consulting and Clinical Psychology*, 61, 235–47.

Kershaw, C. (1999) *Reconviction of Offenders Sentenced or Released from Prison in 1994*. Research Findings 90. London: Home Office Research, Development and Statistics Directorate.

Kershaw, C., Chivite-Matthews, N., Thomas, C. and Aust, R. (2001) *The 2001 British Crime Survey: First Results, England and Wales*. London: Home Office Research, Development and Statistics Directorate.

Kilpatrick, R. (1987) Joyriding: an addictive behaviour? In J. Hodge, M. McMurran and C. R. Hollin (eds.) *Addicted to Crime?* Chichester: Wiley.

Klee, R. (1997) *Introduction to the Philosophy of Science: Cutting Nature at its Seams*. New York: Oxford University Press.

Klein, N. C., Alexander, J. F. and Parsons, B. V. (1977) Impact of family systems intervention on recidivism and sibling delinquency: A model or primary prevention and program evaluation. *Journal of Consulting and Clinical Psychology*, 45, 469–474.

Klemke, L. W. (1982) Reassessment of Cameron's apprehension-termination of shoplifting finding. *California Sociologist*, 5, 88–95.

Kolman, A. S. and Wasserman, C. (1991) Theft groups for women: a cry for help. *Federal Probation*, 55, 48–54.

Kolvin, L., Miller, F. J. W., Fleeting, M. and Kolvin, P. A. (1988) Social and parenting factors affecting criminal-offence rates: findings from the Newcastle Thousand Family Study (1947–1980). *British Journal of Psychiatry*, 152, 80–90.

Krug, E. G., Dahlberg, L. L., Mercy, J. A., Zwi, A. B. and Lozano, R. (eds.) (2002) *World Report on Violence and Health*. Geneva: World Health Organization.

Kutchins, H. A. and Kirk, S. A. (1997) *Making Us Crazy: DSM: The Psychiatric Bible and the Creation of Mental Disorders*. Glencoe, IL: The Free Press.

Lamb, H. R. and Weinberger, L. E. (1998) Persons with severe mental illness in jails and prisons: a review. *Psychiatric Services*, 49, 483–92.

Lamiell, J. T. (1995) Rethinking the role of quantitative methods in psychology. In J. A. Smith, R. Harré and L. Van Langenhove (eds.) *Rethinking Methods in Psychology*. London: Sage Publications.

Lanis, K. and Covell, K. (1995) Images of women in advertisements: effects on attitudes related to sexual aggression. *Sex Roles*, 32, 639–49.

Laub, J. H. and Sampson, R. J. (1993) Turning points in the life course: why change matters to the study of crime. *Criminology*, 31, 301–25.

Laub, J. H. and Sampson, R. J. (2001) Understanding desistance from crime. *Crime and Justice: A Review of Research*, 28, 1–70.

Leahy, T. H. (1997) *A History of Psychology: Main Currents in Psychological Thought*, 4th edn. Upper Saddle River, NJ: Prentice-Hall.

Leavitt, G. (1999) Criminological theory as an art form: implications for criminal justice policy. *Crime and Delinquency*, 45, 389–99.

LeBlanc, M. (1993) Prevention of adolescent delinquency: an integrative multi-layered control theory based perspective. In D. P. Farrington, R. J. Sampson and P. H. Wikström (eds.) *Integrating Individual and Ecological Aspects of Crime*. Stockholm: National Council for Crime Prevention.

LeBlanc, M. and Girard, S. (1997) The generality of deviance: replication over two decades with a Canadian sample of adjudicated boys. *Canadian Journal of Criminology*, 39, 171–83.

Leeman, L. W., Gibbs, J. C. and Fuller, D. (1993) Evaluation of a multi-component group treatment program for juvenile delinquents. *Aggressive Behavior*, 19, 281–92.

Lehman, A., Postrado, L., Roth, D., McNary, S. and Goldman, H. (1994) An evaluation of the continuity of care, case management, and client outcomes in the Robert Wood Johnson program on chronic mental illness. *The Milbank Quarterly*, 72, 105–22.

Leslie, J. C. (2002) *Essential Behaviour Analysis*. London: Arnold.

Levi, M. and Maguire, M. (2002) Violent crime. In M. Maguire, R. Morgan and R. Reiner (eds.) *The Oxford Handbook of Criminology*, 3rd edn. Oxford: Oxford University Press.

Lewis, S., Maguire, M., Raynor, P., Vanstone, M. and Vennard, J. (2003) *The Resettlement of Short-term Prisoners: An Evaluation of Seven Pathfinder Programmes*. Findings 200. London: Home Office Research, Development and Statistics Directorate.

Light, R., Nee, C. and Ingham, H. (1993) *Car Theft: The Offender's Perspective*. Home Office Research Study 130. London: HMSO.

Lilly, J. R., Cullen, F. T. and Ball, R.A. (2002) *Criminological Theory: Context and Consequences*, 3rd edn. Thousand Oaks, CA: Sage Publications.

Link, B., Andrews, D. and Cullen, F. (1992) The violent and illegal behavior of mental patients reconsidered. *American Sociological Review*, 57, 275–92.

Link, B. and Stueve, A. (1994) Psychotic symptoms and the violent/illegal behavior of mental patients compared to community controls. In J. Monahan and H. J. Steadman (eds.) *Violence and Mental Disorder: Developments in Risk Assessment*. Chicago, IL: University of Chicago Press.

Lipsey, M. W. (1992) Juvenile delinquency treatment: a meta-analytic inquiry into the variability of effects. In T. Cook, D. Cooper, H. Corday *et al.* (eds.) *Meta-Analysis for Explanation: A Casebook*. New York: Russell Sage Foundation.

Lipsey, M. W. (1995) What do we learn from 400 studies on the effectiveness of treatment with juvenile delinquents? In J. McGuire (ed.) *What Works: Reducing Re-offending. Guidelines from Research and Practice*. Chichester: Wiley.

Lipsey, M. W., Chapman, G. L. and Landenberger, N. A. (2001) Cognitive-behavioral programs for offenders. *Annals of the American Academy of Political and Social Science*, 578, 144–57.

Lipsey, M. W. and Derzon, J. H. (1998) Predictors of violent or serious delinquency in adolescence and early adulthood: a synthesis of longitudinal research. In R. Loeber and D. P. Farrington (eds.) *Serious & Violent Juvenile Offenders: Risk Factors and Successful Interventions*. Thousand Oaks, CA: Sage Publications.

Lipsey, M. W. and Wilson, D. B. (1993) The efficacy of psychological, educational, and behavioral treatment: confirmation from meta-analysis. *American Psychologist*, 48, 1181–209.

Lipsey, M. W. and Wilson, D. B. (1998) Effective intervention for serious juvenile offenders: a synthesis of research. In R. Loeber and D. P. Farrington (eds.) *Serious & Violent Juvenile Offenders: Risk Factors and Successful Interventions*. Thousand Oaks, CA: Sage Publications.

Lipsey, M. W. and Wilson, D. B. (2001) *Practical Meta-Analysis*. Thousand Oaks, CA: Sage Publications.

Lipton, D. S., Martinson, R. and Wilks, J. (1975) *The Effectiveness of Correctional Treatment: A Survey of Treatment Evaluation Studies*. New York: Praeger.

Lipton, D. S., Pearson, F. S., Cleland, C. M. and Yee, D. (1997) Synthesizing correctional treatment outcomes: preliminary CDATE findings. Paper delivered to the *5th Annual National Institute of Justice Conference on Research and Evaluation in Criminal Justice*, Washington, DC, July.

Lipton, D. S., Pearson, F. S., Cleland, C. M. and Yee, D. (2002a) The effects of therapeutic communities and milieu therapy on recidivism. In J. McGuire (ed.) *Offender Rehabilitation and Treatment: Effective Programmes and Policies to Reduce Re-Offending*. Chichester: Wiley.

Lipton, D. S., Pearson, F. S., Cleland, C. M. and Yee, D. (2002b) The effectiveness of cognitive-behavioural treatment methods on recidivism. In J. McGuire (ed.) *Offender Rehabilitation and Treatment: Effective Programmes and Policies to Reduce Re-Offending*. Chichester: Wiley.

Lishman, W. A. (1997) *Organic Psychiatry: The Psychological Consequences of Cerebral Disorder*, 3rd edn. Oxford: Blackwell.

Lloyd, C., Mair, G. and Hough, M. (1994) *Explaining Reconviction Rates: A Critical Analysis*. Home Office Research Study 136. London: HMSO.

Loeber, R. (1990) Development and risk factors of juvenile antisocial behavior and delinquency. *Clinical Psychology Review*, 10, 1–41.

Loeber, R. and Farrington, D. P. (1997) Strategies and yields of longitudinal studies on antisocial behavior. In D. M. Stoff, J. Breiling and J. D. Maser (eds.) *Handbook of Antisocial Behavior*. New York: Wiley.

Loeber, R., Farrington, D. P., Stouthamer-Loeber, M. *et al.* (2003) The development of male offending: key findings from fourteen years of the Pittsburgh Youth Study. In T. P. Thornberry and M. D. Krohn (eds.) *Taking Stock of Delinquency: An Overview of Findings from Contemporary Longitudinal Studies*. New York: Kluver Academic/Plenum Publishers.

Loeber, R., Farrington, D. P. and Waschbusch, D. A. (1998) Serious and violent juvenile offenders. In R. Loeber and D. P. Farrington (eds.) *Serious & Violent Juvenile Offenders: Risk Factors and Successful Interventions*. Thousand Oaks, CA: Sage Publications.

Loeber, R. and LeBlanc, M. (1990) Toward a developmental criminology. *Crime and Justice: A Review of Research*, 12, 375–473.

Loeber, R. and Stouthamer-Loeber, M. (1987) Prediction. In H. C. Quay (ed.) *Handbook of Juvenile Delinquency*. New York: Wiley.

Logan, C. H. and Gaes, G. G. (1993) Meta-analysis and the rehabilitation of punishment. *Justice Quarterly*, 10, 245–63.

Lösel, F. (1995) The efficacy of correctional treatment: a review and synthesis of meta-evaluations. In J. McGuire (ed.) *What Works: Reducing Re-offending. Guidelines from Research and Practice*. Chichester: Wiley.

Lösel, F. (1998) Treatment and management of psychopaths. In D. Cooke, A. E. Forth and R. A. Hare (eds.) *Psychopathy: Theory, Research and Implications for Society*. Amsterdam: Kluwer Academic Publishers.

Lösel, F. (2001) Evaluating the effectiveness of correctional programs: bridging the gap between research and practice. In G. A. Bernfeld, D. P. Farrington and A. W. Leschied (eds.) *Offender Rehabilitation in Practice: Implementing and Evaluating Effective Programs*. Chichester: Wiley.

Lösel, F. and Bender, D. (2003) Protective factors and resilience. In D. P. Farrington and J. W. Coid (eds.) *Early Prevention of Adult Antisocial Behaviour*. Cambridge: Cambridge University Press.

Lösel, F. and Bliesener, T. (1994) Some high-risk adolescents do not develop conduct problems: a study of protective factors. *International Study of Behavioral Development*, 17, 753–77.

Lösel, F. and Koferl, P. (1989) Evaluation research on correctional treatment in West Germany: a meta-analysis. In H. Wegener, F. Lösel and J. Haisch (eds.) *Criminal Behavior and the Justice System: Psychological Perspectives*. New York: Springer-Verlag.

MacDevitt, J. W. and Kedzierzawski, G. D. (1990) A structured group format for first offense shoplifters. *International Journal of Offender Therapy and Comparative Criminology*, 34, 155–64.

MacKenzie, D. L. (1997) Criminal justice and crime prevention. In L. W. Sherman, D. Gottfredson, D. L. Mackenzie et al., *Preventing Crime: What Works, What Doesn't, What's Promising*. Washington, DC: Office of Justice Programs.

MacKenzie, D. L. (2002) Reducing the criminal activities of known offenders and delinquents: crime prevention in the courts and corrections. In L. W. Sherman, D. P. Farrington, B. C. Welsh and D. L. MacKenzie (eds.) *Evidence-Based Crime Prevention*. London: Routledge.

MacKenzie, D. L., Brame, R., McDowall, D. and Souryal, C. (1995) Boot camp prisons and recidivism in eight states. *Criminology*, 33, 327–57.

MacKenzie, D. L. and Souryal, C. (1994) *Multisite Evaluation of Shock Incarceration*. Washington, DC: National Institute of Justice.

MacKenzie, D. L., Wilson, D. B. and Kider, S. B. (2001) Effects of correctional boot camps on offending. *Annals of the American Academy of Political and Social Science*, 578, 126–43.

Maguire, M. (2002) Crime statistics: the 'data explosion' and its implications. In M. Maguire, R. Morgan and R. Reiner (eds.) *The Oxford Handbook of Criminology*, 3rd edn. Oxford: Oxford University Press.

Mahoney, M. J. (1974) *Cognition and Behavior Modification*. Cambridge, MA: Ballinger.

Marshall, W. L. (2001) Adult sexual offenders against women. In C. R. Hollin (ed.) *Handbook of Offender Assessment and Treatment*. Chichester: Wiley.

Marshall, W. L., Anderson, D. and Fernandez, Y. (1999) *Cognitive Behavioural Treatment of Sexual Offenders*. Chichester: Wiley.

Marshall, W. L. and McGuire, J. (2003) Effect sizes in the treatment of sexual offenders. *International Journal of Offender Therapy and Comparative Criminology*, 47, 653–63.

Martens, P. L. (1993) An ecological model of socialisation in explaining offending.

In D. P. Farrington, R. J. Sampson and P. H. Wikström (eds.) *Integrating Individual and Ecological Aspects of Crime*. Stockholm: National Council for Crime Prevention.

Martin, S. E., Annan, S. and Forst, B. (1993) The special deterrent effects of a jail sanction on first-time drunk drivers: a quasi experimental study. *Accident Analysis and Prevention*, 25, 561–8.

Martinson, R. (1974) What works? Questions and answers about prison reform. *The Public Interest*, 10, 22–54.

Martinson, R. (1979) New findings, new views: a note of caution regarding sentencing reform. *Hofstra Law Review*, 7, 243–58.

Maruna, S. (2001) *Making Good: How Ex-convicts Reform and Rebuild Their Lives*. Washington, DC: American Psychological Association.

Marzagao, L. R. (1972) Systematic desensitization treatment of kleptomania. *Journal of Behavior Therapy and Experimental Psychiatry*, 3, 327–8.

Massoglia, M. and Macmillan, R. (2002) Deterrence, rational choice, and criminal offending: a consideration of legal subjectivity. In A. R. Piquero and S. G. Tibbetts (eds.) *Rational Choice and Criminal Behavior: Recent Research and Future Challenges*. New York: Routledge.

Matson, J. L. and Kazdin, A. E. (1981) Punishment in behavior modification: pragmatic, ethical and legal issues. *Clinical Psychology Review*, 1, 197–210.

Matsueda, R. L. and Anderson, K. (1998) The dynamics of delinquent peers and delinquent behavior. *Criminology*, 36, 269–308.

Mattia, J. I. and Zimmerman, M. (2001) Epidemiology. In W. J. Livesley (ed.) *Handbook of Personality Disorders: Theory, Research and Treatment*. New York: Guilford Press.

May, C. (1999) *Explaining Reconviction Following a Community Sentence: The Role of Social Factors*. Home Office Research Study 192. London: Home Office.

May, T., Warburton, H., Turnball, P. J. and Hough, M. (2002) *Times They Are A-Changing: Policing of Cannabis*. York: Joseph Rowntree Foundation.

Mayer, J. P., Gensheimer, L. K., Davidson, W. S. and Gottschalk, R. (1986) Social learning treatment within juvenile justice: a meta-analysis of impact in the natural environment. In S. A. Apter and A. P. Goldstein (eds.) *Youth Violence: Programs and Prospects*. Elmsford, NJ: Pergamon Press.

Mayhew, P. and White, P. (1997) *The 1996 International Crime Victimisation Survey*. Research Findings 57. London: Home Office Research and Statistics Directorate.

McAdams, D. P. (2001) *The Person: An Integrated Introduction to Personality Psychology*, 3rd edn. Fort Worth, TX: Harcourt Brace.

McDougall, C., Cohen, M. A., Swaray, R. and Perry, A. (2003) The costs and benefits of sentencing: a systematic review. *Annals of the American Academy of Political and Social Science*, 587, 160–77.

McDowall, D., Lizotte, A. J. and Wiersma, B. (1991) General deterrence through civilian gun ownership: an examination of the quasi-experimental evidence. *Criminology*, 29, 541–59.

McGillivray, M. (1993) *Putting the Brakes on Car Crime: A Local Study of Auto-related Crime among Young People*. London and Cardiff: The Children's Society and Mid Glamorgan Social Services Department.

McGue, M., Bacon, S. and Lykken, D. T. (1993) Personality stability and change in early adulthood: a behavioral genetic analysis. *Developmental Psychology*, 29, 96–109.

McGuire, J. (ed.) (1995a) *What Works: Reducing Re-offending. Guidelines from Research and Practice*. Chichester: Wiley.

McGuire, J. (1995b) Reasoning and rehabilitation programs in the UK. In R. R. Ross and B. Ross (eds.) *Thinking Straight: The Reasoning and Rehabilitation Program for Delinquincy Prevention and Offender Rehabilitation*. Ottawa: Air Training & Publications.

McGuire, J. (1997a) 'Irrational' shoplifting and models of addiction. In J. Hodge, M. McMurran and C. R. Hollin (eds.) *Addicted to Crime?* Chichester: Wiley.

McGuire, J. (1997b) Ethical dilemmas in forensic clinical psychology. *Legal and Criminological Psychology*, 2, 177–92.

McGuire, J. (2000a) Explanations of criminal behaviour. In J. McGuire, T. Mason and A. O'Kane (eds.) *Behaviour, Crime and Legal Processes: A Guidebook for Practitioners*. Chichester: Wiley.

McGuire, J. (2000b) *Cognitive-Behavioural Approaches: An Introduction to Theory and Research*. London: Home Office.

McGuire, J. (2001a) Property offences. In C. R. Hollin (ed.) *Handbook of Offender Assessment and Treatment*. Chichester: Wiley.

McGuire, J. (2001b) Treatment approaches for offenders with mental disorder. In L. L. Motiuk and R. C. Serin (eds.) *Compendium 2000 on Effective Correctional Programming*. Ottawa: Correctional Service Canada.

McGuire, J. (2001c) Defining correctional programs. In L. L. Motiuk and R. C. Serin (eds.) *Compendium 2000 on Effective Correctional Programming*. Ottawa: Correctional Service Canada.

McGuire, J. (2002a) Criminal sanctions versus psychologically-based interventions with offenders: a comparative empirical analysis. *Psychology, Crime and Law*, 8, 183–208.

McGuire, J. (ed.) (2002b) *Offender Rehabilitation and Treatment: Effective Practice and Policies to Reduce Re-offending*. Chichester: Wiley.

McGuire, J. (2002c) What is problem-solving? Theory, research, and applications. *Criminal Behaviour and Mental Health*, 11, 210–35.

McGuire, J. (2003) Maintaining change: converging legal and psychological initiatives in a therapeutic jurisprudence framework. *Western Criminology Review*, 4, 18–32 (available online: http://wcr.sonoma.edu/v4n2/mcguire. html).

McGuire, J., Priestley, P. and Gates, E. (submitted) Evaluation of a probation-based programme for learning control of aggression. Manuscript submitted for publication.

McLaughlin, E. and Muncie, J. (eds.) (2001) *The Sage Dictionary of Criminology*. London: Sage Publications.

McMurran, M. (2001) Offenders with personality disorders. In C. R. Hollin (ed.) *Handbook of Offender Assessment and Treatment*. Chichester: Wiley.

McMurran, M. (2002) Alcohol, aggression, and violence. In J. McGuire (ed.) *Offender Rehabilitation and Treatment: Effective Programmes and Policies to Reduce Re-Offending*. Chichester: Wiley.

McNiel, D. E. (1994) Hallucinations and violence. In J. Monahan and H. J. Steadman (eds.) *Violence and Mental Disorder: Developments in Risk Assessment*. Chicago, IL: University of Chicago Press.

Mechanic, D. (1999) Mental health and mental illness: definitions and perspectives. In A. V. Horwitz and T. L. Scheid (eds.) *A Handbook for the Study of Mental Health: Social Contexts, Theories and Systems*. Cambridge: Cambridge University Press.

Meichenbaum, D. (1977) *Cognitive-Behavior Modification: An Integrative Approach*. New York: Plenum Press.

Meichenbaum, D. (1995) Cognitive-behavioral therapy in historical perspective. In B. Bongar and L. E. Buetler (eds.) *Comprehensive Textbook of Psychotherapy*. New York: Oxford University Press.

Meichenbaum, D. and Gilmore, J. B. (1984) The nature of unconscious processes: a cognitive-behavioral perspective. In K. S. Bowers and D. Meichenbaum (eds.) *The Unconscious Reconsidered*. New York: Wiley.

Melton, G., Petrila, J., Poythress, N. and Slobogin, C. (1998) *Psychological Evaluations for the Courts: A Handbook for Lawyers and Mental Health Practitioners*, 2nd edn. New York: Guilford Press.

Memon, A. (2003) Telling it all: the cognitive interview. In A. Memon, A. Vrij and R. Bull (eds.) *Psychology and Law: Truthfulness, Accuracy and Credibility* (2nd edn). London: McGraw-Hill.

Memon, A., Vrij, A. and Bull, R. (eds.) (1998) *Psychology and Law: Truthfulness, Accuracy and Credibility*. London: McGraw-Hill.

Messner, S. F., Krohn, M. D. and Lisak, A. E. (eds.) (1989) *Theoretical Integration in the Study of Deviance and Crime*. Albany, NY: State University of New York Press.

Miller, W. R. (1994) Motivational interviewing III: On the ethics of motivational intervention. *Behavioural and Cognitive Psychotherapy*, 22, 111–23.

Miller, W. R. and Rollnick, S. (eds.) (2002) *Motivational Interviewing: Preparing People for Change*, 2nd edn. New York: Guilford Press.

Minor, K. I., Wells, J. B., Soderstrom, I. R., Bingham, R. and Williamson, D. (1999) Sentence completion and recidivism among juveniles referred to teen courts. *Crime and Delinquency*, 45, 467–80.

Mirrlees-Black, C. and Allen, J. (1998) *Concern About Crime: Findings from the 1998 British Crime Survey*. Research Findings 83. London: Home Office Research, Development and Statistics Directorate.

Mischel, W. (1968) *Personality and Assessment*. New York: Wiley.

Mischel, W. (1999) *Introduction to Personality*, 6th edn. Forth Worth, TX: Harcourt Brace.

Mischel, W. (2004) Toward an integrative science of the person. *Annual Review of Psychology*, 55, 1–22.

Mischel, W. and Shoda, Y. (1998) Reconciling processing dynamics and personality dispositions. *Annual Review of Psychology*, 49, 229–58.

Moffitt, T. E. (1983) The learning theory model of punishment: implications for delinquency deterrence. *Criminal Justice and Behavior*, 10, 131–58.

Moffitt, T. E. (1993) Adolescence-limited and life-course-persistent anti-social behavior: a developmental taxonomy. *Psychological Review*, 100, 674–701.

Moffitt, T. E., Caspi, A., Rutter, M. and Silva, P. A. (2001) *Sex Differences in Antisocial Behaviour: Conduct Disorder, Delinquency and Violence in the Dunedin Longitudinal Study*. Cambridge: Cambridge University Press.

Monahan, J. (1997) Clinical and actuarial predictions of violence. In D. Faigman, D. Kaye, M. Saks and J. Sanders (eds.) *West's Companion to Scientific Evidence*. St.Paul, MN: West Publishing Company.

Monahan, J. and Steadman, H. J. (eds.) (1994) *Violence and Mental Disorder: Developments in Risk Assessment*. Chicago, IL: Chicago University Press.

Monahan, J., Steadman, H. J., Silver, E. *et al.* (2001) *Rethinking Risk Assessment: The MacArthur Study of Mental Disorder and Violence*. New York: Oxford University Press.

Moon, M. M., Sundt, J. L., Cullen, F. T. and Wright, J. P. (2000) Is child saving dead? Public support for juvenile rehabilitation. *Crime and Delinquency*, 46, 38–60.

Morison, R. S. (1960) 'Gradualness, gradualness, gradualness'. *American Psychologist*, 15, 187–97.

Morrison, S. and O'Donnell, I. (1994) *Armed Robbery: A Study in London*. Oxford: Centre for Criminological Research.

Morrison-Dyke, D. F. (1996) Interpersonal cognitive problem-solving skills and severity of criminal behavior among homeless mentally disordered criminal offenders. *Dissertation Abstracts International*, 56(8-B): 4589.

Morrissey, J. P. (1999) Integrating service delivery systems for persons with a severe mental illness. In A. V. Horwitz and T. L. Scheid (eds.) *A Handbook for the Study of Mental Health: Social Contexts, Theories and Systems*. Cambridge: Cambridge University Press.

Morrissey, J. P., Calloway, M., Bartko, W. T. *et al.* (1994) Local mental health authorities and service system change: evidence from the Robert Wood Johnson program on chronic mental illness. *Milbank Quarterly*, 72, 49–80.

Motiuk, L. and Porporino, F. J. (1991) *The Nature and Severity of Mental Health Problems Among Federal Inmates in Canadian Penitentiaries*. Research Report R4. Ottawa: Correctional Service Canada.

Motiuk, L. L. and Serin, R. C. (eds.) (2001) *Compendium 2000 on Effective Correctional Programming*. Ottawa: Correctional Service Canada.

Muncie, J. (2001) The construction and deconstruction of crime. In J. Muncie and E. McLaughlin (eds.) *The Problem of Crime*, 2nd edn. London: Sage Publications in association with the Open University.

Nagin, D. S. (1998) Criminal deterrence research at the outset of the twenty-first century. *Crime and Justice: A Review of Research*, 23, 51–91.

Nettler, G. (1984) *Explaining Crime*, 3rd edn. New York: McGraw-Hill.

Newman, G. (1976) *Comparative Deviance: Perception and Law in Six Cultures*. New York: Elsevier.

Newman, G. (1977) Social institutions and the control of deviance: a cross-national opinion survey. *European Journal of Social Psychology*, 7, 39–59.

Newman, G., Bouloukos, A. C. and Cohen, D. (eds.) (2001) *World Factbook of Criminal Justice Systems*. Washington, DC: Department of Justice (available online: http://www.ojp.usdoj.gov/bjs/pub/ascii/wfbcjhon.txt).

Nietzel, M. T. (1979) *Crime and its Modification: A Social Learning Perspective*. New York: Pergamon Press.

Norris, C. (1997) *Against Relativism: Philosophy of Science, Deconstruction and Critical Theory*. Oxford: Blackwell.

Novaco, R. W. (1975) *Anger Control: Development and Evaluation of an Experimental Treatment*. Lexington, KT: D. C. Heath.

Novaco, R. W. (1997) Remediating anger and aggression with violent offenders. *Legal and Criminological Psychology*, 2, 77–88.

Nuttall, C., Goldblatt, P. and Lewis, C. (1998) *Reducing Offending: An Assessment of Research Evidence on Ways of Dealing with Offending Behaviour*. Home Office Research Study 187. London: Home Office.

Ogloff, J. R. P. and Davis, M. R. (2004) Advances in offender assessment and rehabilitation: contributions of the risk–needs–responsivity approach. *Psychology, Crime and Law*, 10, 229–242.

Olweus, D. (1979) Stability of aggressive reaction patterns in males: a review. *Psychological Bulletin*, 86, 852–75.

Olweus, D. (1988) Environmental and biological factors in the development of aggressive behaviour. In W. Buikhuisen and S. A. Mednick (eds.) *Explaining Criminal Behaviour*. Leiden: E. J. Brill.

O'Neil, J. M. and Harway, M. (1999) Revised multivariate model explaining men's risk factors for violence against women: theoretical propositions, new hypotheses, and proactive recommendations. In M. Harway and J. M. O'Neil (eds.) *What Causes Men's Violence Against Women?* Thousand Oaks, CA: Sage Publications.

Orobrio de Castro, B., Veerman, J. W., Koops, W., Bosch, J. D. and Monshouwer, H. (2002) Hostile attribution of intent and aggressive behaviour: A meta-analysis. *Child Development*, 73, 916–934.

O'Toole, M. E. (2001) *The School Shooter: A Threat Assessment Perspective*. Washington, DC: Federal Bureau of Investigation.

Ouellette, J. A. and Wood, W. (1998) Habit and intention in everyday life: the multiple processes by which past behavior predicts future behavior. *Psychological Bulletin*, 124, 54–74.

Ownby, R. L. (1997) *Psychological Reports: A Guide to Report Writing in Professional Psychology*, 3rd edn. New York: Wiley.

Palmer, T. (1975) Martinson re-visited. *Journal of Research in Crime and Delinquency*, 12, 133–52.

Palmer, T. (1992) *The Re-Emergence of Correctional Intervention*. Newbury Park, CA: Sage Publications.

Paternoster, R. (1987) The deterrent effect of the perceived certainty and severity of punishment: a review of evidence and issues. *Justice Quarterly*, 4, 173–217.

Paternoster, R., Saltzman, L. E., Waldo, G. P. and Chiricos, T. G. (1983) Perceived risk and social control: do sanctions really deter? *Law and Society Review*, 17, 457–79.

Patterson, G. R. (1982) *Coercive Family Process*. Eugene, OR: Castalia Publishing Company.

Patterson, G. R. and Yoerger, K. (1993) Developmental models for delinquent behavior. In S. Hodgins (ed.) *Mental Disorder and Crime*. Newbury Park, CA: Sage Publications.

Pearson, F. S. and Lipton, D. S. (1999) A meta-analytic review of the effectiveness of corrections-based treatments for drug abuse. *The Prison Journal*, 79, 384–410.

Pearson, F. S., Lipton, D. S. and Cleland, C. M. (1997) Rehabilitative programs in adult corrections: CDATE meta-analyses. Paper delivered to the *Annual Meeting of the American Society of Criminology*, San Diego, CA.

Pease, K. (2002) Crime reduction. In M. Maguire, R. Morgan and R. Reiner (eds.) *The Oxford Handbook of Criminology*, 3rd edn. Oxford: Oxford University Press.

Peay, J. (2002) Mentally disordered offenders, mental health, and crime. In M. Maguire, R. Morgan and R. Reiner (eds.) *The Oxford Handbook of Criminology*, 3rd edn. Oxford: Oxford University Press.

Peck, C. P. (1986) Risk-taking behavior and compulsive gambling. *American Psychologist*, 41, 461–5.

Perry, J. C., Banon, E. and Ianni, F. (1999) Effectiveness of psychotherapy for personality disorders. *American Journal of Psychiatry*, 1156, 1312–21.

Peters, R. H. and Murrin, M. R. (2000) Effectiveness of treatment-based drug courts in reducing criminal recidivism. *Criminal Justice and Behavior*, 27, 72–96.

Petersilia, J. (1990) When probation becomes more dreaded than prison. *Federal Probation*, 54, 23–7.

Petersilia, J. (1998) A decade of experimenting with intermediate sanctions: what have we learned? *Federal Probation*, 62, 3–9.

Petersilia, J. and Turner, S. (1993) Intensive probation and parole. *Crime and Justice: A Review of Research*, 17, 281–335.

Petrosino, A. (2000) Crime, drugs and alcohol. In *Evidence from Systematic Reviews of Research Relevant to Implementing the Wider Public Health Agenda*. York: University of York, NHS Centre for Reviews and Dissemination (available online: http://www.york.ac.uk/inst/crd/wph.htm).

Petrosino, A., Turpin-Petrosino, C. and Finckenauer, J. O. (2000) Well-meaning programs can have harmful effects! Lessons from experiments of programs such as Scared Straight. *Crime and Delinquency*, 46, 354–79.

Phillipson, M. (1971) *Sociological Aspects of Crime and Delinquency*. London: Routledge & Kegan Paul.

Pilgrim, D. and Rogers, A. (1993) *A Sociology of Mental Health and Illness*. Buckingham: Open University Press.

Platt, J. J., Perry, G. and Metzger, D. (1980) The evaluation of a heroin addiction treatment program within a correctional environment. In R. R. Ross and P. Gendreau (eds.) *Effective Correctional Treatment*. Toronto: Butterworths.

Plattner, M. F. (1976) The rehabilitation of punishment. *The Public Interest*, 44, 104–14.

Polaschek, D. L. L. and Reynolds, N. (2001) Assessment and treatment: violent offenders. In C. R. Hollin (ed.) *Handbook of Offender Assessment and Treatment*. Chichester: Wiley.

Polizzi, D. M., MacKenzie, D. L., and Hickman, L. J. (1999) What works in adult sex offender treatment? A review of prison- and non-prison-based treatment programs. *International Journal of Offender Therapy and Comparative Criminology*, 43, 357–74.

Pratt, T. C. and Cullen, F. T. (2000) The empirical status of Gottfredson and Hirschi's general theory of crime: a meta-analysis. *Criminology*, 38, 931–64.

Prentky, R. A. (1995) A rationale for the treatment of sex offenders: *pro bono publico*. In J. McGuire (ed.) *What Works: Reducing Re-offending. Guidelines from Research and Practice*. Chichester: Wiley.

Prentky, R. A. and Burgess, A. W. (1990) Rehabilitation of child molesters: a cost–benefit analysis. *American Journal of Orthopsychiatry*, 60, 108–17.

Pryzwansky, W. B. and Wendt, R. N. (1999) *Professional and Ethical Issues in Psychology: Foundations of Practice*. New York: W. W. Norton.

Raine, A. (1997) Antisocial behavior and psychophysiology: a biosocial perspective and a prefrontal dysfunction hypothesis. In D. M. Stoff, J. Breiling and J. D. Maser (eds.) *Handbook of Antisocial Behavior*. New York: Wiley.

Raynor, P. and Vanstone, M. (1996) Reasoning and rehabilitation in Britain: the results of the straight thinking on probation (STOP) programme. *International Journal of Offender Therapy and Comparative Criminology*, 40, 272–84.

Reckless, W. C. (1967) *The Crime Problem*, 4th edn. New York: Appleton-Century-Crofts.

Reckless, W. C., Dinitz, S. and Murray, E. (1956) Self-concept as an insulator against delinquency. *American Sociological Review*, 21, 744–6.

Redondo, S., Garrido, V. and Sánchez-Meca, J. (1997) What works in correctional rehabilitation in Europe: a meta-analytical review. In S. Redondo, V. Garrido, J. Pérez and R. Barberet (eds.) *Advances in Psychology and Law: International Contributions*. Berlin: Walter de Gruyter.

Redondo, S., Sánchez-Meca, J. and Garrido, V. (1999) The influence of treatment programmes on the recidivism of juvenile and adult offenders: a European meta-analytic review. *Psychology, Crime and Law*, 5, 251–78.

Redondo, S., Sánchez-Meca, J. and Garrido, V. (2002) Crime treatment in Europe: a review of outcome studies. In J. McGuire (ed.) *Offender Rehabilitation and Treatment: Effective Programmes and Policies to Reduce Re-Offending*. Chichester: Wiley.

Reed, A. and Seago, P. (1999) *Criminal Law*. London: Sweet & Maxwell.

Reid, J. B. and Patterson, G. R. (1977) The modification of aggression and stealing behaviour of boys in the home setting. In E. Ribes-Inesta and A. Bandura (eds.) *Analysis of Delinquency and Aggression*. Hillsdale, NJ: Erlbaum.

Reid, J. B., Patterson, G. R. and Snyder, J. (2002) *Antisocial Behavior in Children and Adolescents: A Developmental Analysis and Model for Intervention*. Washington, DC: American Psychological Association.

Reid, W. H. and Gacono, C. (2000) Treatment of antisocial personality, psychopathy and other characterologic antisocial syndromes. *Behavioral Sciences and the Law*, 18, 647–62.

Reiner, R. (2002) Media made criminality: the representation of crime in the mass media. In M. Maguire, R. Morgan and R. Reiner (eds.) *The Oxford Handbook of Criminology*, 3rd edn. Oxford: Oxford University Press.

Reith, M. (1998) *Community Care Tragedies*. Birmingham: Venture Press.

Rex, S. (2001) Beyond cognitive-behaviouralism? Reflections on the effectiveness literature. In A. Bottoms, L. Gelsthorpe and S. Rex (eds.) *Community Penalties: Change and Challenges*. Cullompton: Willan Publishing.

Rex, S., Gelsthorpe, L., Roberts, C. and Jordan, P. (2004) *What's Promising in Community Service: Implementation of Seven Pathfinder Projects*. Findings 231. London: Home Office Research, Development and Statistics Directorate.

Roberts, A. R. and Camasso, M. J. (1991) The effect of juvenile offender treatment programs on recidivism: a meta-analysis of 46 studies. *Notre Dame Journal of Law, Ethics and Public Policy*, 5, 421–41.

Robins, L. N. (1974) *Deviant Children Grown Up: A Sociological and Psychiatric Study of Psychiatric Morbidity*. Huntington, NY: Robert E. Krieger Publishing Company.

Robinson, D. (1995) *The Impact of Cognitive Skills Training on Post-Release Recidivism among Canadian Federal Offenders*. Ottawa: Correctional Service Canada.

Robinson, D. and Porporino, F. J. (2001) Programming in cognitive skills: the reasoning and rehabilitation programme. In C. R. Hollin (ed.) *Handbook of Offender Assessment and Treatment*. Chichester: Wiley.

Rock, P. (2002) Sociological theories of crime. In M. Maguire, R. Morgan and R. Reiner (eds.) *The Oxford Handbook of Criminology*, 3rd edn. Oxford: Oxford University Press.

Roesch, R., Hart, S. D. and Ogloff, J. R. P. (eds.) (1999) *Psychology and Law: The State of the Discipline*. New York: Kluwer Academic/Plenum Publishers.

Rosenthal, R. (1994) Parametric measures of effect size. In H. Cooper and L. V. Hedges (eds.) *Handbook of Research Synthesis*. New York: Russell Sage Foundation.

Rosenthal, R. and Rubin, D. B. (1982) A simple, general purpose display of magnitude of experimental effect. *Journal of Educational Psychology*, 74, 166–9.

Roshier, B. (1989) *Controlling Crime: The Classical Perspective in Criminology*. Milton Keynes: Open University Press.

Ross, R. R., Antonowicz, D. H. and Dhaliwal, G. K. (1995) *Going Straight: Effective Delinquency Prevention and Offender Rehabilitation*. Ottawa: Air Training and Publications.

Ross, R. R. and Fabiano, E. A. (1985) *Time to Think: A Cognitive Model of Delinquency Treatment and Offender Rehabilitation*. Ottawa: Institute of Social Sciences and Arts.

Ross, R. R., Fabiano, E. A. and Ewles, C. D. (1988) Reasoning and rehabilitation. *International Journal of Offender Therapy and Comparative Criminology*, 20, 165–73.

Rothbart, M. K., Derryberry, D. and Posner, M. I. (1994) A psycho-biological approach to the development of temperament. In J. E. Bates and T. D. Wachs (eds.) *Temperament: Individual Differences at the Interface of Biology and Behavior*. Washington, DC: American Psychological Association.

Royse, D. and Buck, S. A. (1991) Evaluation of a diversion program for first-offence shoplifters. *Journal of Offender Rehabilitation*, 17, 147–58.

Russell, M. N. (1995) *Confronting Abusive Beliefs: Group Treatment for Abusive Men*. Thousand Oaks, CA: Sage Publications.

Russell, M. N. (2002) Changing beliefs of spouse abusers. In J. McGuire (ed.) *Offender Rehabilitation and Treatment: Effective Programmes and Policies to Reduce Re-Offending*. Chichester: Wiley.

Rutter, M. (1981) Epidemiological-longitudinal strategies and causal research in child psychiatry. *Journal of the American Academy of Child Psychiatry*, 20, 513–44.

Rutter, M. (1989) Pathways from childhood to adult life. *Journal of Child Psychology and Psychiatry*, 30, 23–51.

Rutter, M., Giller, H. and Hagell, A. (1998) *Antisocial Behavior by Young People*. Cambridge: Cambridge University Press.

Salekin, R. T. (2002) Psychopathy and therapeutic pessimism: clinical lore or clinical reality? *Clinical Psychology Review*, 22, 79–112.

Sanday, P. R. (1981) *Female Power and Male Dominance: On the Origins of Sexual Inequality*. Cambridge: Cambridge University Press.

Sanday, P. R. (2003) Rape-free versus rape-prone: how culture makes a difference. In C. B. Travis (ed.) *Evolution, Gender, and Rape*. Cambridge, MA: MIT Press.

Sanislow, C. A. and McGlashan, T. H. (1998) Treatment outcomes of personality disorders. *Canadian Journal of Psychiatry*, 43, 237–50.

Schmidt, J. D. and Sherman, L. W. (1993) Does arrest deter domestic violence? *American Behavioral Scientist*, 36, 601–9.

Schwartz, M. D. and Friedrichs, D. O. (1994) Postmodern thought and crimino-logical discontent: new metaphors for understanding violence. *Criminology*, 32, 221–46.

Schweinhart, L. J., Barnes, H. V. and Weikart, D. P. (1993) *Significant Benefits: The High/Scope Perry Preschool Project*. Ypsilanti, MI: High/Scope Press.

Scully, D. (1990) *Understanding Sexual Crime: A Study of Convicted Rapists*. New York: Routledge.

Searle, J. R. (1995) *The Construction of Social Reality*. London: Penguin Books.

Serin, R. C. (1995) Treatment responsivity in criminal psychopaths. *Forum on Corrections Research*, 7, 23–6.

Serin, R. C. and Preston, D. L. (2000) Programming for violent offenders. *Forum on Corrections Research*, 12, 45–8.

Sherman, L. W. (1988) Randomized experiments in criminal sanctions. In H. S. Bloom, D. S. Cordray and R. J. Light (eds.) *Lessons from Selected Program and Policy Areas*. New Directions for Program Evaluation 37. San Francisco, CA: Jossey-Bass.

Sherman, L. W. (1990) Police crackdowns: initial and residual deterrence. *Crime and Justice: A Review of Research*, 12, 1–48.

Sherman, L. W., Berk, R. A. and 42 officers of the Minneapolis Police Department (1984) The specific deterrent effects of arrest for domestic assault. *American Sociological Review*, 49, 261–72.

Sherman, L. W., Farrington, D. P., Welsh, B. C. and MacKenzie, D. L. (eds.) (2002) *Evidence-Based Crime Prevention*. London: Routledge.

Sherman, L. W., Gottfredson, D., McKenzie, D. *et al.* (1997) *Preventing Crime: What Works, What Doesn't, What's Promising*. Washington, DC: Office of Justice Programs.

Sherman, L. W., Schmidt, J. D., Rogan, D. P. *et al.* (1991) From initial deterrence to long-term escalation: short custody arrest for poverty ghetto domestic violence. *Criminology*, 29, 821–50.

Shichor, D. and Sechrest, D. K. (eds.) (1996) *Three Strikes and You're Out: Vengeance as Public Policy*. Thousand Oaks, CA: Sage Publications.

Shields, I. W. and Jordan, S. A. (1995) Young sex offenders: a comparison with a control group of non-sex offenders. *Forum on Corrections Research*, 7, 17–19.

Shoda, Y., Mischel, W. and Wright, J. C. (1994) Intra-individual stability in the organisation and patterning of behavior: incorporating psychological situations into the idiographic analysis of personality. *Journal of Personality and Social Psychology*, 65, 1023–35.

Simmons, J. and colleagues (2002) *Crime in England and Wales 2001/2002*. London: Home Office Research, Development and Statistics Directorate.

Simon, L. M. J. (1998) Does criminal offender treatment work? *Applied and Preventive Psychology*, 7, 137–59.

Simons, R. L., Wu, C-I., Lin, K-H., Gordon, L. and Conger, R. D. (2000) A cross-cultural examination of the link between corporal punishment and adolescent antisocial behavior. *Criminology*, 38, 47–79.

Simourd, D. J. and Olver, M. E. (2002) The future of criminal attitudes research and practice. *Criminal Justice and Behavior*, 29, 427–46.

Simourd, L. and Andrews, D. A. (1994) Correlates of delinquency: a look at gender differences. *Forum on Corrections Research*, 6, 26–31.

Singleton, N., Meltzer, H., Gatward, R., Coid, J. and Deasy, D. (1998) *Psychiatric Morbidity among Prisoners: Summary Report*. London: Office for National Statistics.

Snyder, H. N. (1998) Appendix: serious, violent, and chronic juvenile offenders – an assessment of the extent of and trends in officially recognised serious criminal behavior in a delinquent population. In R. Loeber and D. P. Farrington (eds.) *Serious & Violent Juvenile Offenders: Risk Factors and Successful Interventions*. Thousand Oaks, CA: Sage Publications.

Snyder, J. J. and Patterson, G. R. (1987) Family interaction and delinquent behavior. In H. C. Quay (ed.) *Handbook of Juvenile Delinquency*. New York: Wiley.

Solomon, G. S. and Ray, J. B. (1984) Irrational beliefs of shoplifters. *Journal of Clinical Psychology*, 40, 1075–7.

Sommerhoff, G. (2000) *Understanding Consciousness: Its Function and Brain Processes*. London: Sage Publications.

Sorensen, J., Wrinkle, R., Brewer, V. and Marquart, J. (1999) Capital punishment and deterrence: examining the effect of executions on rates of murder in Texas. *Crime and Delinquency*, 45, 481–93.

Spivack, G. and Cianci, N. (1987) High-risk early behavior pattern and later delinquency. In J. D. Burchard and S. N. Burchard (eds.) *Prevention of Delinquent Behavior*. Newbury Park, CA: Sage Publications.

Spivack, G., Platt, J. J. and Shure, M. B. (1976) *The Problem-Solving Approach to Adjustment*. San Francisco, CA: Jossey-Bass.

Springer, D. W., McNeece, C. A. and Arnold, E. M. (2002) *Substance Abuse Treatment for Criminal Offenders: An Evidence-based Guide for Practitioners*. Washington, DC: American Psychological Association.

Stack, S. (1993) Execution publicity and homicide in Georgia. *American Journal of Criminal Justice*, 18, 25–39.

Stafford, M. C. and Warr, M. (1993) A reconceptualisation of general and specific deterrence. *Journal of Research on Crime and Delinquency*, 30, 123–35.

Staub, E. (1989) *The Roots of Evil: The Origins of Genocide and other Group Violence*. New York: Plenum Press.

Steadman, H. J., Fabisiak, S., Dvoskin, J. and Holohean, E. J. (1989) A survey of mental disability among state prison inmates. *Hospital and Community Psychiatry*, 38, 1086–90.

Steadman, H. J., Mulvey, E. P., Monahan, J. *et al.* (1998) Violence by people discharged from acute psychiatric inpatient facilities and by others in the same neighborhoods. *Archives of General Psychiatry*, 55, 393–401.

Steinberg, L. and Scott, E. S. (2003) Less guilty by reason of adolescence: developmental immaturity, diminished responsibility, and the juvenile death penalty. *American Psychologist*, 58, 1009–18.

Stolle, D. P., Wexler, D. B. and Winick, B. J. (eds.) (2000) *Practicing Therapeutic Jurisprudence: Law as a Helping Profession*. Durham, NC: Carolina Academic Press.

Stumphauzer, J. S. (1976) Elimination of stealing by self-reinforcement and alternative behaviour and family contracting. *Journal of Behavior Therapy and Experimental Psychiatry*, 7, 265–8.

Sukhodolsky, D. G., Kassinove, H. and Gorman, B. S. (2004) Congnitive-behavioral therapy for anger in children and adolescents: A meta-analysis. *Aggression and Violent Behaviour*, 9, 247–69.

Sugg, D. (1998) *Motor Projects in England and Wales: An Evaluation*. Research Findings 81. London: Home Office Research Development and Statistics Directorate.

Sundel, S. S. and Sundel, M. (1993) *Behavior Modification in Human Services: A Systematic Introduction to Concepts and Applications*. Newbury Park, CA: Sage Publications.

Surgeon General (2001) *Youth Violence: A Report of the Surgeon General*. Washington, DC: US Department of Health and Human Services (available online: http://www.surgeongeneral.gov/library/youthviolence/youvioreport. htm).

Swanson, J. W. (1994) Mental disorder, substance abuse, and community violence: an epidemiological approach. In J. Monahan and H. J. Steadman (eds.) *Violence and Mental Disorder: Developments in Risk Assessment*. Chicago, IL: University of Chicago Press.

Swanson, J. W., Estroff, S., Swartz, M. *et al.* (1997) Violence and severe mental disorder in the clinical and community populations: the effects of psychotic symptoms, comorbidity and lack of treatment. *Psychiatry*, 60, 1–22.

Swanson, J. W., Holzer, C. E., Ganju, V. K. and Jono, R. T. (1990) Violence and psychiatric disorder in the community: evidence from the Epidemiological Catchment Area surveys. *Hospital and Community Psychiatry*, 41, 761–70.

Sykes, G. and Matza, D. (1957) Techniques of neutralization: a theory of delinquency. *American Sociological Review*, 22, 664–73.

Szasz, T. S. (1961) *The Myth of Mental Illness: Foundations of a Theory of Personal Conduct*. New York: Harper & Row.

Tafrate, R. C. (1995) Evaluation of treatment strategies for adult anger disorders. In H. Kassinove (ed.) *Anger Disorders: Definition, Diagnosis and Treatment*. Washington, DC: Taylor & Francis.

Tarling, R. (1993) *Analysing Crime: Data, Models and Interpretations*. London: Home Office.

Taylor, I., Walton, P. and Young, J. (1973) *The New Criminology*. London: Routledge & Kegan Paul.

Taylor, P. J. and Gunn, J. (1999) Homicides by people with mental illness: myth and reality. *British Journal of Psychiatry*, 174, 9–14.

Taylor, R. (1999) *Predicting Reconvictions for Sexual and Violent Offences Using the Revised Offender Group Reconviction Scale*. Research Findings 104. London: Home Office Research, Development and Statistics Directorate.

Tellefsen, C., Cohen, M. I., Silver, S. B. and Dougherty, C. (1992) Predicting success on conditional release for insanity acquittees: regionalized versus nonregionalized hospital patients. *Bulletin of the American Academy of Psychiatry and Law*, 20, 87–100.

Teplin, L. A. (1990) The prevalence of severe mental disorder among male urban jail detainees: comparison with the Epidemiological Catchment Area program. *American Journal of Public Health*, 80, 663–9.

Teplin, L. A., Abram, K. M. and McClelland, G. M. (1996) Prevalence of psychiatric disorders among incarcerated women. *Archives of General Psychiatry*, 53, 505–12.

Thistlethwaite, A., Wooldredge, J. and Gibbs, D. (1998) Severity of dispositions and domestic violence recidivism. *Crime and Delinquency*, 44, 388–98.

Thornberry, T. P. (1987) Toward an interactional theory of delinquency. *Criminology*, 25, 863–91.

Thornberry, T. P. (1996) Empirical support for interactional theory: a review of the literature. In J. D. Hawkins (ed.) *Delinquency and Crime: Current Theories*. Cambridge: Cambridge University Press.

Thornberry, T. P. and Krohn, M. D. (2003) The development of panel studies of delinquency. In T. P. Thornberry and M. D. Krohn (eds.) *Taking Stock of Delinquency: An Overview of Findings from Contemporary Longitudinal Studies*. New York: Kluwer Academic/Plenum Publishers.

Thornberry, T. P., Lizotte, A. J., Krohn, M. D., Smith, C. A. and Porter, P. (2003) Causes and consequences of delinquency: findings from the Rochester Youth Development Study. In T. P. Thornberry and M. D. Krohn (eds.) *Taking Stock of Delinquency: An Overview of Findings from Contemporary Longitudinal Studies*. New York: Kluwer Academic/Plenum Publishers.

Thornton, D., Curran, L., Grayson, D. and Holloway, V. (1984) *Tougher Regimes in Detention Centres: Report of an Evaluation by the Young Offender Psychology Unit*. London: HMSO.

Thornton, T. N., Craft, C. A., Dahlberg, L. L., Lynch, B. S. and Baer, K. (2000) *Best Practices of Youth Violence Prevention: A Sourcebook for Community Action*. Atlanta, GA: National Center for Injury Prevention and Control.

Todorov, A. and Bargh, J. A. (2002) Automatic sources of aggression. *Aggression and Violent Behavior*, 7, 53–68.

Torstendahl, R. and Burrage, M. (eds.) (1990) *The Formation of Professions: Knowledge, State and Strategy*. London: Sage Publications.

Tracy, P. E., Wolfgang, M. E. and Figlio, R. M. (1985) *Delinquency in Two Birth Cohorts: Executive Summary*. Washington, DC: US Department of Justice.

Trasler, G. (1993) Conscience, opportunity, rational choice, and crime. In R. V. Clarke and M. Felson (eds.) *Routine Activity and Rational Choice*. Advances in Criminological Theory, Vol. 5. New Brunswick, NJ: Transaction Publishers.

Traverso, G. B. and Manna, P. (1992) Law and psychology in Italy. In F. Lösel, D. Bender and T. Bliesener (eds.) *Psychology and Law: International Perspectives*. Berlin: Walter De Gruyter.

Tremblay, R. E., Vitaro, F., Nagin, D. S., Pagani, L. and Séguin, J. R. (2003) The Montreal Longitudinal and Experimental Study: rediscovering the power of descriptions. In T. P. Thornberry and M. D. Krohn (eds.) *Taking Stock of Delinquency: An Overview of Findings from Contemporary Longitudinal Studies*. New York: Kluwer Academic/Plenum Publishers.

United Nations Office on Drugs and Crime (2003) *Global Illicit Drugs Trends 2003*. Geneva: UNODC (available online: http://www.unodc.org/unodc/global_illicit_ drug_trends.html).

Vazsonyi, A. T., Pickering, L. E., Belliston, L. M., Hessing, D. and Junger, M. (2002) Routine activities and deviant behaviors: American, Dutch, Hungarian and Swiss youth. *Journal of Quantitative Criminology*, 18, 397–422.

Vazsonyi, A. T., Pickering, L. E., Junger, M. and Hessing, D. (2001) An empirical test of a general theory of crime: a four-nation comparative study of self-control and the prediction of deviance. *Journal of Research in Crime and Delinquency*, 38, 91–131.

Vennard, J., Sugg, D. and Hedderman, C. (1997) *Changing Offenders' Attitudes and Behaviour: What Works?* Home Office Research Study 171. London: HMSO.

Vila, B. (1994) A general paradigm for understanding criminal behaviour: extending evolutionary ecological theory. *Criminology*, 32, 311–59.

Vizard, E., Monck, E. and Misch, P. (1995) Child and adolescent sex abuse perpetrators: a review of the research literature. *Journal of Child Psychology and Psychiatry*, 36, 731–59.

Vold, G. B., Bernard, T. J. and Snipes, J. B. (1998) *Theoretical Criminology*, 4th edn. New York: Oxford University Press.

Von Hirsch, A. (1976) *Doing Justice: The Choice of Punishments. Report of the Committee for the Study of Incarceration*. New York: Hill & Wang.

Von Hirsch, A. (1990) The ethics of community-based sanctions. *Crime and Delinquency*, 36, 162–73.

Von Hirsch, A. and Ashworth, A. (eds.) (1998) *Principled Sentencing: Readings on Theory and Policy*, 2nd edn. Oxford: Hart Publishing.

Von Hirsch, A., Bottoms, A. E., Burney, E. and Wikström, P. O. (1999) *Criminal Deterrence and Sentencing Severity: An Analysis of Recent Research*. Oxford: Hart Publishing.

Vrij, A. and Akehurst, L. (1998) Verbal communication and credibility: statement validity. In A. Memon, A. Vrij and R. Bull (eds.) *Psychology and Law: Truthfulness, Accuracy and Credibility*. London: McGraw-Hill.

Walker, M. A. (ed.) (1995) *Interpreting Crime Statistics*. Oxford: Clarendon Press.

Walker, N. (1991) *Why Punish? Theories of Punishment Reassessed*. Oxford: Oxford University Press.

Walker, N. and Padfield, N. (1996) *Sentencing: Theory, Law and Practice*. London: Butterworths.

Walklate, S. (1997) *Understanding Criminology: Current Theoretical Debates*. Buckingham: Open University Press.

Walters, G. D. (1992) A meta-analysis of the crime–gene relationship. *Criminology*, 30, 595–613.

Walters, G. D. (1998) *Changing Lives of Crime and Drugs: Intervening with Substance-Abusing Offenders*. Chichester: Wiley.

Ward, T., Hudson, S. M. and Keenan, T. R. (2001) The assessment and treatment of sexual offenders against children. In C. R. Hollin (ed.) *Handbook of Offender Assessment and Treatment*. Chichester: Wiley.

Ward, T. and Stewart, C. (2003) Criminogenic needs and human needs: a theoretical model. *Psychology, Crime and Law*, 9, 125–43.

Warr, M. and Stafford, M. (1991) The influence of delinquent peers: what they think or what they do? *Criminology*, 29, 851–66.

Webster, C. D., Douglas, K. S., Eaves, D. and Hart, S. D. (1997) *HCR-20: Assessing Risk for Violence. Version 2*. Burnaby, BC: Mental Health, Law and Policy Institute, Simon Fraser University.

Wegner, D. M. (2002) *The Illusion of Conscious Will*. Cambridge, MA: MIT Press.

Weiner, I. B. and Hess, A. K. (eds.) (2000) *Handbook of Forensic Psychology*, 2nd edn. New York: Wiley.

Weisburd, D. and Chayet, E. (1995) Specific deterrence in a sample of offenders convicted of white-collar crimes. *Criminology*, 33, 587–607.

Weisburd, D., Sherman, L. and Petrosino, A. J. (1990) *Registry of Randomized Criminal Justice Experiments in Sanctions*. Unpublished report, Rutgers University, University of Maryland and Crime Control Institute.

Wells, G. L. and Olson, E. A. (2003) Eyewitness testimony. *Annual Review of Psychology*, 54, 277–95.

Wells-Parker, E., Bangert-Drowns, R., McMillen, R. and Williams, M. (1995) Final results from a meta-analysis of remedial interventions with drink/drive offenders. *Addiction*, 9, 907–26.

Welsh, B. C. and Farrington, D. P. (2000) Correctional intervention programs and cost benefit analysis. *Criminal Justice and Behavior*, 27, 115–33.

Welsh, B. C. and Farrington, D. P. (2001) Evaluating the economic efficiency of correctional intervention programs. In G. A. Bernfeld, D. P. Farrington and A. W. Leschied (eds.) *Offender Rehabilitation in Practice: Implementing and Evaluating Effective Programs*. Chichester: Wiley.

Werner, E. E. (1987) Vulnerability and resiliency in children at risk for delinquency: a longitudinal study from birth to adulthood. In J. D. Burchard and S. N. Burchard (eds.) *Prevention of Delinquent Behavior*. Newbury Park, CA: Sage Publications.

Wesner, D. W. (1996) Cognitive factors mediating the social problem-solving ability of adolescent offenders. *Dissertation Abstracts International*, 57(1-B): 0768.

Wexler, D. B. (1991) An introduction to therapeutic jurisprudence. In D. B. Wexler and B. J. Winick (eds.) *Essays in Therapeutic Jurisprudence*. Durham, NC: Academic Press.

Wexler, D. B. (1996) Therapeutic jurisprudence and the criminal courts. In D. B. Wexler and B. J. Winick (eds.) *Law in a Therapeutic Key: Developments in Therapeutic Jurisprudence*. Durham, NC: Carolina Academic Press.

Wexler, D. B. (1998) How the law can use *What Works*: a therapeutic jurisprudence look at recent research on rehabilitation. *Behavioral Sciences and the Law*, 15, 368–9.

Wexler, D. B. and Winick, B. J. (1991) *Essays in Therapeutic Jurisprudence*. Durham, NC: Carolina Academic Press.

Wexler, D. B. and Winick, B. J. (eds.) (1996) *Law in a Therapeutic Key: Developments in Therapeutic Jurisprudence*. Durham, NC: Carolina Academic Press.

Whitehead, J. T. and Lab, S. P. (1989) A meta-analysis of juvenile correctional treatment. *Journal of Research in Crime and Delinquency*, 26, 276–95.

Whitton, A. and McGuire, J. (submitted) Problems and coping skills in adolescent offenders. Manuscript submitted for publication.

Widom, C. S. (1989) The intergenerational transmission of violence. In N. A. Weiner and M. E. Wolfgang (eds.) *Pathways to Criminal Violence*. Newbury Park, CA: Sage Publications.

Widom, C. S. and Maxfield, M. G. (2001) *An Update on the Cycle of Violence*. Washington, DC: National Institute of Justice (available online: http://www.ojp.usdoj.gov/nij).

Wiederanders, M., Bromley, D. L. and Choate, P. A. (1997) Forensic conditional release programs and outcomes in three states. *International Journal of Law and Psychiatry*, 20, 249–57.

Wikström, P. (ed.) (1990) *Crime and Measures Against Crime in the City*. Stockholm: National Council for Crime Prevention.

Wikström, P. and Loeber, R. (2000) Do disadvantaged neighborhoods cause well-adjusted children to become adolescents? A study of male juvenile serious offending, individual risk and protective factors, and neighborhood context. *Criminology*, 38, 1109–42.

Wilkinson, J. (1997) The impact of Ilderton motor project on motor vehicle crime and offending. *British Journal of Criminology*, 37, 568–81.

Williams, N. (1995) Cognitive skills groupwork. *Issues in Criminological and Legal Psychology*, 23, 22–30.

Wilson, D. B. (2001) Meta-analytic methods for criminology. *Annals of the American Academy of Political and Social Science*, 578, 71–89.

Wilson, D. B., Gallagher, C. A. and MacKenzie, D. L. (2000) A meta-analysis of corrections-based education, vocation and work programs for adult offenders. *Journal of Research in Crime and Delinquency*, 37, 568–81.

Wilson, D. B., Gottfredson, D. C. and Najaka, S. S. (2001) School-based prevention of problem behaviors: a meta-analysis. *Journal of Quantitative Criminology*, 17, 247–72.

Wilson, J. Q. and Herrnstein, R. J. (1985) *Crime and Human Nature*. New York: Simon & Schuster.

Wilson, S. J. and Lipsey, M. W. (2000) Wilderness challenge programs for delinquent youth: a meta-analysis of outcome evaluations. *Evaluation and Program Planning*, 23, 1–12.

Wilson, S. J., Lipsey, M. W. and Soydan, H. (2003) Are mainstream programs for juvenile delinquency less effective with minority youth than majority youth? A meta-analysis of outcomes research. *Research on Social Work Practice*, 13, 3–26.

Woolfenden, S. R., Williams, K. and Peat, J. K. (2002) Family and parenting interventions for conduct disorder and delinquency: a meta-analysis of randomised controlled trials. *Archives of Disease in Childhood*, 86, 251–6.

World Health Organization (1992) *The International Classification of Mental and Behavioural Disorders (ICD-10)*. 10th edn. Geneva: WHO.

Worling, J. R. and Långström, N. (2003) Assessment of criminal recidivism risk with adolescents who have offended sexually: a review. *Trauma, Violence and Abuse*, 4, 341–62.

Worrall, A. (1997) *Punishment in the Community: The Future of Criminal Justice*. Harlow: Addison Wesley Longman.

Wright, B. R. E., Caspi, A., Moffitt, T. E., Miech, R. A. and Silva, P. A. (1999) Reconsidering the relationship between SES and delinquency: causation but not correlation. *Criminology*, 37, 175–94.

Wright, B. R. E., Caspi, A., Moffitt, T. E. and Silva, P. A. (2001) The effects of social ties on crime vary by criminal propensity: a life-course model of interdependence. *Criminology*, 39, 321–51.

Wright, R. T. and Decker, S. H. (1994) *Burglars on the Job: Streetlife and Residential Break-ins*. Boston, MA: Northeastern University Press.

Wrightsman, L. S., Greene, E., Nietzel, M. T. and Fortune, W. H. (2002) *Psychology and the Legal System*, 5th edn. Belmont, CA: Wadsworth.

Yoshikawa, H. (1994) Prevention as cumulative protection: effects of early family support and education on chronic delinquency and its risks. *Psychological Bulletin*, 115, 28–54.

Zamble, E. and Porporino, F. J. (1988) *Coping, Behavior, and Adaptation in Prison Inmates*. New York: Springer.

Zamble, E. and Quinsey, V. (1997) *The Criminal Recidivism Process*. Cambridge: Cambridge University Press.

Zimring, F. E. and Hawkins, G. (1994) The growth of imprisonment in California. *British Journal of Criminology*, 34 (special issue), 83–96.

Zimring, F. E. and Hawkins, G. (1995) *Incapacitation: Penal Confinement and the Restraint of Crime*. New York: Oxford University Press.

Zinger, I. and Forth, A. E. (1998) Psychopathy and Canadian criminal proceedings: the potential for human rights abuses. *Canadian Journal of Criminology*, 40, 237–76.

Zuckerman, M. and Driver, R. E. (1985) Telling lies: verbal and non-verbal correlates of deception. In A. W. Siegman and S. Feldstein (eds.) *Multichannel Integration of Nonverbal Behaviors*. Hillsdale, NJ: Erlbaum.

Zumkley, H. (1994) The stability of aggressive behavior: a meta-analysis. *German Journal of Psychology*, 18, 273–81.

Subject index

Name index

Focus on PRONUNCIATION 1

THIRD EDITION

Linda Lane

American Language Program
Columbia University

Focus on Pronunciation 1, Third Edition

Pearson Education, 10 Bank Street, White Plains NY 10606

Staff credits: The people who made up the *Focus on Pronunciation 1, Third Edition* team, representing editorial, production, design, and manufacturing, are Dave Dickey, Nancy Flaggman, Ann France, Shelley Gazes, Maria Pia Marrella, Lise Minovitz, Liza Pleva, and Lynn Sobotta.

Cover image: Shutterstock.com
Text composition: ElectraGraphics, Inc.
Text font: 10/12 New Aster
Illustrations: Gary Torrisi and Jill Wood

Library of Congress Cataloging-in-Publication Data

Lane, Linda (Linda L.)
  Focus on pronunciation : [v.] 1 / Linda Lane. — 3rd ed.
      p. cm.
  ISBN 0-13-231493-2 (v. 1) — ISBN 0-13-231494-0 (v. 2) — ISBN 0-13-231500-9 (v. 3) 1. English language—Pronunciation—Problems, exercises, etc. 2. English language—Textbooks for foreign speakers.   I. Title.
  PE1137.L22 2012
  428.3'4—dc23

                                                              2011047246

ISBN 10: 0-13-231493-2
ISBN 13: 978-0-13-231493-0

Printed in the United States of America

2 3 4 5 6 7 8 9 10—V011—17 16 15 14 13

CONTENTS

INTRODUCTION

Focus on Pronunciation 1 is a comprehensive course that helps beginning students speak English more clearly, confidently, and accurately. The course covers important topics from all aspects of pronunciation—sounds, stress, rhythm, and intonation.

The vowel and consonant sounds presented are those that occur frequently in English and that students recognize as new or difficult. Stress, rhythm, or intonation topics focus on pronunciation features that are important for clear English communication and that students can easily notice.

Each unit ends with Communication Practice about a theme (for example, shopping and volunteering). As such, the activities and practice provide students with opportunities to improve their pronunciation and communication skills in context.

ORGANIZATION OF *FOCUS ON PRONUNCIATION 1*

Focus on Pronunciation 1 is divided into three parts: Vowels; Consonants; and Stress, Rhythm, and Intonation. Each unit deals with specific pronunciation points and has the following organization:

STEP 1   PRESENTATION

This section introduces, explains, and provides information about the pronunciation point. It may show how sounds are made or present other useful information. This is often achieved through the use of diagrams or illustrations. Pronunciation explanations are student friendly and easy to understand.

STEP 2   FOCUSED PRACTICE

This section consists of controlled classroom activities that allow students to develop skill and proficiency with the pronunciation point.

STEP 3   COMMUNICATION PRACTICE

This section provides communicative practice activities that focus on a theme. The activities are more open-ended and they ensure student involvement through the use of games and interactive tasks. When students are engaged in the communicative activities, they should be encouraged to keep in mind these global features of clear speaking:

- Speak slowly.
- Speak loudly enough.
- Pay attention to the ends of words.
- Use your voice to speak expressively.

NEW!   NATURAL ENGLISH

New to this edition, the Natural English box in each unit highlights ways to speak English more naturally. In some cases, the Natural English box reviews or "pulls in" another important aspect of pronunciation that is not the focus of the current unit. Students might, for example, be reminded to group words together in a consonant or vowel unit in order to make their English more understandable to others. Additionally, the Natural English box may highlight the pronunciation of useful expressions (such as the use of *me too* for agreement).

This section consists of recorded homework activities. Accuracy Practice reviews key controlled exercises within the unit and serves as a warm-up for Fluency Practice, a freer speaking task that deals with the content of the unit. Students who have access to a computer can record their voices and review their pronunciation. The teacher can also listen to these recordings and provide feedback. Directions for how to make and send electronic files are at the back of the Student Book.

AUDIO PROGRAM

The **Classroom Audio CDs** have the recordings for all the pronunciation and listening exercises in the Student Book.

The **Student Audio CD-ROM** in the back of the book has all the recordings needed to complete the Accuracy Practice exercises in MP3 format.

KEY TO ICONS

🎧 —material recorded as part of the Classroom Audio CDs

🎧 —material recorded as part of the Student Audio CD-ROM in the Student Book

🎤 —material for students to record and give to the teacher

PLANNING A SYLLABUS

The units in *Focus on Pronunciation 1* can be used in any order. Teachers can "skip around"—for example, teaching the overview unit for Vowels, then a specific vowel unit, then the overview for Stress, Rhythm, and Intonation, then a specific unit dealing with rhythm, and so on. Teachers who adopt this approach could also cover all the overview units at the beginning of the course and then skip around within the sections. The units can also be taught in order, first covering vowels, then consonants, and so on.

GENERAL REFERENCES

Most students have difficulty with English vowels and with stress, rhythm, and intonation, regardless of their native language background. With the exception of a few consonants (for example, the first sound in *think*), consonant difficulty depends more on the native language. The following references provide information on pronunciation problems related to native language:

Avery, Peter and S. Ehrlich. *Teaching American English Pronunciation*. Oxford: Oxford University Press, 1992.

Lane, Linda. *Tips for Teaching Pronunciation*. Pearson Longman, 2010.

Swan, M. and Smith, B. *Learner English, 2nd Ed.* Cambridge, UK: Cambridge University Press, 2001.

The following research influenced the content and approach of this book:

Avery, Peter and S. Ehrlich. *Teaching American English Pronunciation*. Oxford: Oxford University Press, 1992.

Celce-Murcia, Marianne, D. M. Brinton and J. M. Goodwin. *Teaching Pronunciation: A Reference for Teachers of English to Speakers of Other Languages*. Cambridge: Cambridge University Press, 1996.

Lane, Linda. *Tips for Teaching Pronunciation*. Pearson Longman, 2010.

Linda Lane is a senior faculty member in the American Language Program of Columbia University. In addition to the *Focus on Pronunciation* series, she is also the author of *Tips for Teaching Pronunciation,* Pearson, 2010. She served as director of the Columbia University Humanities Media Center for 10 years and coordinated Columbia's TESOL Certificate Program for another 10 years, teaching classes in Applied Phonetics and Pronunciation Teaching and Introduction to Second Language Acquisition. She received her EdD in Applied Linguistics from Teachers College, Columbia University, her MA in Linguistics from Yale University, and her BS in Mathematics from the University of Washington, Seattle.

ACKNOWLEDGMENTS

I am indebted to a number of people whose support, patience, and good humor made this book possible. I am grateful for the help and suggestions of my editors at Pearson: Lise Minovitz, Lynn Sobotta, and Shelley Gazes.

I would like to thank the reviewers who offered suggestions that shaped the new edition: Ashkhen Strack, Tunxis Community College, Farmington, CT; Victor Matthews, Assumption College, Lampang, Thailand; Judy Gilbert, Columbia University, New York, NY; Joanna Ghosh, University of Pennsylvania, Philadelphia, PA.

In addition, I would like to thank those reviewers whose insights shaped the previous edition: Dr. John Milbury-Steen, Temple University, Philadelphia, PA; Michele McMenamin, Rutgers University, Piscataway, NJ; Gwendolyn Kane, Rutgers University, Piscataway, NJ; William Crawford, Georgetown University, Washington, D.C.; Linda Wells, University of Washington, Seattle, WA; Tara Narcross, Columbus State Community College, Columbus, OH; Robert Baldwin, UCLA, Los Angeles, CA; Mary Di Stefano Diaz, Broward Community College, Davie, FL; Barbara Smith-Palinkas, University of South Florida, Tampa, FL; Susan Jamieson, Bellevue Community College, Bellevue, WA; Andrea Toth, City College of San Francisco, San Francisco, CA; Fernando Barboza, ICPNA, Lima, Peru; Adrianne P. Ochoa, Georgia State University, Atlanta, GA; Greg Jewell, Drexel University, Philadelphia, PA; Cindy Chang, University of Washington, Seattle, WA; Emily Rosales, Université du Québec à Montréal/École de Langues, Montréal, QC, Canada.

My colleagues at the American Language Program at Columbia University have always been an inspiration and source of generous support.

For the encouragement and patience of my family, Mile, Martha, Sonia, and Luke, and of my dear friend Mary Jerome, whom I miss every day, I am also deeply grateful.

Finally, I want to thank my students—for teaching me how they learn pronunciation, for wanting to improve their pronunciation, and for showing me how to help them.

–Linda Lane

VOWELS

Vowel Overview

STEP 1 PRESENTATION

There are 14 vowel sounds in English.

1. tr<u>ee</u> /iy/
2. f<u>i</u>sh /ɪ/
3. m<u>ai</u>l /ey/
4. b<u>e</u>d /ɛ/
5. h<u>a</u>t /æ/
6. c<u>u</u>p /ə/
7. b<u>o</u>x /ɑ/

8. f<u>oo</u>d /uw/
9. b<u>oo</u>k /ʊ/
10. r<u>oa</u>d /ow/
11. j<u>aw</u>[1] /ɔ/
12. h<u>ou</u>se /aw/
13. <u>eye</u> /ay/
14. b<u>oy</u> /oy/

There are six vowel letters.[2]

1. A, a /ey/
2. E, e /iy/
3. I, i /ay/ (sounds like *eye*)

4. O, o /ow/
5. U, u /yuw/ (sounds like *you*)
6. Y, y /way/ (sounds like *why*)

STEP 2 FOCUSED PRACTICE

EXERCISE 1: Four Vowels End in a /y/ Sound

A | *Listen to the words.*

1. /ay/	2. /oy/	3. /ey/	4. /iy/
a. <u>eye</u>	a. b<u>oy</u>	a. pl<u>ay</u>	a. t<u>ea</u>
b. tr<u>y</u>	b. j<u>oy</u>	b. s<u>ay</u>	b. s<u>ee</u>

---

[1] *Many Americans say* jaw *with the vowel in* stop; [2] *The letter* y *is sometimes a vowel sound.*

B | *Listen and repeat the words.*

1. coin
2. day
3. fly
4. why
5. table
6. tree
7. bee
8. please
9. oil
10. toys
11. my
12. face

C | *Write each word from Part B in the correct column.*

/ay/ **eye**	/oy/ **boy**	/ey/ **play**	/iy/ **tea**
_____	_coin_	_____	_____
_____	_____	_____	_____
_____	_____	_____	_____

EXERCISE 2: Join Words Together

Listen and repeat the sentences. Use /y/ to join the vowel sound to the next word.

1. The boy is sick.
2. Please say it again.
3. Today is Saturday.
4. Why are you laughing?
5. Try it.
6. Let's seeʸ a movie.

EXERCISE 3: Three Vowels End in a /w/ Sound

A | *Listen to the words.*

1. /aw/
   a. cow
   b. town

2. /ow/
   a. go
   b. show

3. /uw/
   a. shoe
   b. do

B | *Listen and repeat the words.*

1. towel
2. know
3. how
4. pool
5. brown
6. student
7. two
8. boat
9. toes

C | *Write each word from Part B in the correct column.*

/aw/ **cow**	/ow/ **go**	/uw/ **shoe**
towel	_____	_____
_____	_____	_____
_____	_____	_____

EXERCISE 4: Join Words Together

Listen and repeat the sentences. Use /w/ to join the vowel sound to the next word.

1. Do^w it now.
2. It's too^w easy.
3. Go^w out.
4. Show it to me.
5. How is your friend?
6. Now I'm ready.

EXERCISE 5: Listen for Differences

A | *Listen and repeat the words.*

1. a. wait
   b. wet

2. a. seat
   b. sit

3. a. Luke
   b. look

4. a. head
   b. had

5. a. leave
   b. live

6. a. hat
   b. hot

7. a. cup
   b. cop

8. a. will
   b. well

9. a. lock
   b. luck

B | *Listen again. Which word do you hear? Circle **a** or **b**.*

C | *GROUPS: Say a word from Part A. Pronounce the vowel carefully. Your classmates will say **a** or **b**.*

EXERCISE 6: Differences in Meaning

A | *Listen to the questions and answers.*

Questions	Answers
1. a. How do you spell *seat*?	S-E-A-T.
b. How do you spell *sit*?	S-I-T.
2. a. How do you spell *had*?	H-A-D.
b. How do you spell *head*?	H-E-A-D.
3. a. How do you spell *leave*?	L-E-A-V-E.
b. How do you spell *live*?	L-I-V-E.
4. a. How do you spell *cup*?	C-U-P.
b. How do you spell *cop*?	C-O-P.

Natural English

The line above each question shows the intonation. Intonation is the rise or fall of your voice, or the music of your voice. Intonation usually falls at the end of information questions.

A: How do you spell *Steven*?

B: S-T-E-V-E-N.

A: Where are you from?

B: Spain.

B | *PAIRS: Ask a question from Part A. Follow the intonation lines. Pronounce the underlined word carefully. Your partner will spell the word.*

CURRENCY

EXERCISE 7: Currencies and Countries

People use money to buy things. The money people use in a certain country is called *currency*. Different countries have different currencies. In the United States, the currency is the dollar.

A | *Listen to the currencies. Match each currency in column A with the word in column B that has the same vowel sound.*

	A	B
United States	**1.** d<u>o</u>llar	**a.** w<u>e</u>t /ɛ/
_____	**2.** p<u>e</u>so	**b.** st<u>o</u>p /ɑ/
_____	**3.** r<u>u</u>ble	**c.** sh<u>oe</u> /uw/
_____	**4.** y<u>e</u>n	**d.** g<u>o</u> /ow/
_____	**5.** kr<u>o</u>na	**e.** pl<u>ay</u> /ey/

B | *PAIRS: Match the countries and their currencies. Write the name of each country on the correct line in Part A. Then check your answers on page 6.*

Japan	Mexico	Russia	Sweden	~~United States~~

EXERCISE 8: Your Turn

GROUPS: Use the sentences to talk about the currency used in your country.

I'm from _____. In _____, we use the _____.
      (country name)   **(country name)**   **(currency name)**

"_____" is spelled _____.
  (currency name)   **(letters)**

🎧🎤 **Accuracy Practice** *Listen again to Exercise 5A on page 4. Then record the words.*

🎤 **Fluency Practice** *Use the information from Exercise 7 on page 5 to talk about currencies. Complete the sentences and record them.*

EXAMPLE: The currency in the United States is the ___*dollar*___.
(currency name)

"___*Dollar*___" is spelled ___D-O-L-L-A-R___.
(currency name)   (letters)

1. The currency in Japan is the _____. "_____" is

   spelled _____.

2. The currency in Mexico is the _____. "_____" is

   spelled _____.

3. The currency in Russia is the _____. "_____" is

   spelled _____.

4. The currency in Sweden is the _____. "_____" is

   spelled _____.

5. I'm from _____. In _____ we use the

   _____. "_____" is spelled _____.

Exercise 7B: 1. United States, 2. Mexico, 3. Russia, 4. Japan, 5. Sweden

/iy/ eat and /ɪ/ it

The pictures show you how to say the sounds /iy/ and /ɪ/.

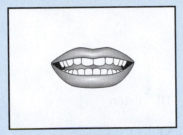

eat /iy/

Spread your lips.
End the vowel with /y/.

it /ɪ/

Relax your lips.
Lower your tongue a little.

Spellings for /iy/	Spellings for /ɪ/
Common feet, need, see believe, piece east, read police, ski	**Common** sit, dish, minute
Other receive people key	**Other** build business, busy give, live

EXERCISE 1: Words with /iy/

A | *Listen and repeat the words.*

1. see
2. tree
3. green
4. teeth
5. people
6. police
7. leave
8. receive
9. machine
10. sheep
11. please
12. teacher

B | *Choose four words from Part A. Write them in the left column.*

Your Words   **Your Partner's Words**

1. _____   1. _____

2. _____   2. _____

3. _____   3. _____

4. _____   4. _____

C | *PAIRS: Listen to your partner's words. Write them in the right column.*

EXERCISE 2: Words with /ɪ/

A | *Listen and repeat the words.*

1. v<u>i</u>sit   4. qu<u>i</u>ck   7. th<u>i</u>s   10. l<u>i</u>sten

2. m<u>i</u>lk   5. f<u>i</u>sh   8. b<u>i</u>g   11. s<u>i</u>t

3. m<u>i</u>nute   6. sw<u>i</u>m   9. s<u>i</u>ster   12. s<u>i</u>ck

B | *Choose four words. Write them in the left column.*

Your Words   **Your Partner's Words**

1. _____   1. _____

2. _____   2. _____

3. _____   3. _____

4. _____   4. _____

C | *PAIRS: Listen to your partner's words. Write them in the right column.*

EXERCISE 3: Listen for Differences: /iy/ vs. /ɪ/

A | *Listen and repeat the words.*

1. **a.** m<u>ea</u>t   4. **a.** s<u>ea</u>t   7. **a.** h<u>ee</u>l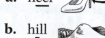

   b. m<u>i</u>tt   **b.** s<u>i</u>t   **b.** h<u>i</u>ll

2. **a.** sh<u>ee</u>p   5. **a.** <u>ea</u>t   8. **a.** r<u>ea</u>ch

   b. sh<u>i</u>p   **b.** <u>i</u>t   **b.** r<u>i</u>ch

3. **a.** h<u>ea</u>t   6. **a.** gr<u>ee</u>n   9. **a.** l<u>ea</u>ve

   b. h<u>i</u>t   **b.** gr<u>i</u>n   **b.** l<u>i</u>ve

8   UNIT 2

C | *GROUPS: Say a word from Part A. Pronounce the vowel carefully. Your classmates will say **a** or **b**.*

EXERCISE 4: Differences in Meaning

A | *Listen and repeat the sentences.*

1. **a.** That's a high <u>hill</u>.   **b.** That's a high <u>heel</u>.

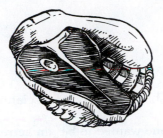

2. **a.** The <u>meat</u> is on the <u>mitt</u>.   **b.** The <u>mitt</u> is on the <u>meat</u>.

3. **a.** The <u>ship</u> is on the <u>sheep</u>.   **b.** The <u>sheep</u> is on the <u>ship</u>.

B | *Listen again. Which sentence do you hear? Circle **a** or **b**.*

C | *PAIRS: Say a sentence from Part A. Your partner will point to the correct sentence, **a** or **b**.*

/iy/ <u>ea</u>t and /ɪ/ <u>i</u>t   **9**

JOBS

EXERCISE 5: Famous People and Their Jobs

A | *Listen and repeat the sentences. Use /y/ to join words.*

____*a.*____ **1.** She wanted to be^y a tennis player.

_____ **2.** She wanted to be^y a singer.

_____ **3.** He wanted to be^y a soccer star.

_____ **4.** She wanted to be^y a scientist.

_____ **5.** She wanted to be^y an actress.

_____ **6.** He wanted to be^y a leader.

B | *Write the letter of each famous person's name next to the correct sentence in Part A.*

a. ~~Maria Sharapova~~	**c.** Lady Gaga	**e.** Barack Obama
b. David Beckham	**d.** Marie Curie	**f.** Natalie Portman

C | *GROUPS: What did each famous person want to do? Make sentences.*

EXERCISE 6: Do You Have a Job?

Listen and repeat the conversations.

1. A: Do you have a job?*

   B: Yes.

   A: What do you do?

   B: I'm an office manager.

   A: Do you like your job?

   B: Yes. The people at work are very nice.

> ***Natural English**
>
> In questions, *do you* is often pronounced "d'you."
>
> D'you have a job?
>
> What d'you do?
>
> D'you like your job?

2. A: Do you have a job?

   B: Not a paying job—I'm a student.

   A: What kind of job would you like?

   B: I'd like to be a singer.

   A: Why?

   B: I love to sing, and I want to be famous.

EXERCISE 7: Your Turn

A | *PAIRS: Ask and answer the questions in the chart.*

Do you have a job now?	Your Name _____	Your Partner's Name _____
1. If yes:		
a. What do you do?		
b. Do you like your job? Why or why not?		
2. If no:		
a. What kind of job would you like?		
b. Why?		

B | *Tell the class about your partner. Follow the example.*

   EXAMPLE: My partner's name is Keiko. She doesn't have a job right now.

                  She'd like to be a dentist.

STEP 4 EXTENDED PRACTICE

Accuracy Practice *Listen again to Exercise 5A on page 10. Then record the sentences.*

Fluency Practice *Talk about a job you have or want. Make complete sentences using your answers from the chart in Exercise 7A. Then record your sentences.*

/æ/ b**a**d and /ɛ/ b**e**d

STEP 1 PRESENTATION

The pictures show you how to say the sounds /æ/ and /ɛ/.

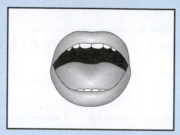

ba**d** /æ/

Open your mouth.
Spread your lips.
Push your tongue down
    and to the front.

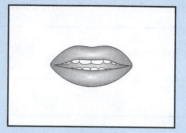

be**d** /ɛ/

Your mouth is almost closed.
Spread your lips.

Spellings for /æ/	Spellings for /ɛ/
Common b**a**d, h**a**t, c**a**b	**Common** b**e**d, g**e**t, n**e**ver
Other l**au**gh	**Other** br**ea**kfast, w**ea**ther ag**ai**n, s**ai**d fr**ie**nd **a**ny, m**a**ny

STEP 2 FOCUSED PRACTICE

EXERCISE 1: Words with /æ/

A | *Listen and repeat the words.*

1. b**a**d
2. h**a**ve
3. **a**nswer
4. **a**sk
5. h**a**nd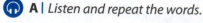
6. h**a**t
7. f**a**mily
8. st**a**nd
9. f**a**t
10. d**a**nce
11. h**a**ppy
12. bl**a**ck

B | *Choose four words from Part A. Write them in the left column.*

Your Words   **Your Partner's Words**

1. _____   1. _____

2. _____   2. _____

3. _____   3. _____

4. _____   4. _____

C | *PAIRS: Listen to your partner's words. Write them in the right column.*

EXERCISE 2: Words with /ɛ/

A | *Listen and repeat the words.*

1. b<u>e</u>d	4. b<u>e</u>lt	7. fri<u>e</u>nd	10. br<u>ea</u>kfast
2. s<u>ai</u>d	5. h<u>ea</u>vy	8. y<u>e</u>llow	11. l<u>e</u>g
3. w<u>e</u>st	6. m<u>e</u>n	9. d<u>ea</u>d	12. y<u>e</u>sterday

B | *Choose four words. Write them in the left column.*

Your Words   **Your Partner's Words**

1. _____   1. _____

2. _____   2. _____

3. _____   3. _____

4. _____   4. _____

C | *PAIRS: Listen to your partner's words. Write them in the right column.*

EXERCISE 3: Listen for Differences: /æ/ vs. /ɛ/

A | *Listen and repeat the words.*

1. a. Br<u>a</u>d	4. a. l<u>au</u>ghed	7. a. b<u>a</u>d
b. br<u>ea</u>d	b. l<u>e</u>ft	b. b<u>e</u>d
2. a. h<u>a</u>d	5. a. m<u>a</u>n	8. a. D<u>a</u>d
b. h<u>ea</u>d	b. m<u>e</u>n	b. d<u>ea</u>d
3. a. s<u>a</u>d	6. a. <u>A</u>nnie	9. a. th<u>a</u>n
b. s<u>ai</u>d	b. <u>a</u>ny	b. th<u>e</u>n

B | *Listen again. Which word from Part A do you hear? Circle* **a** *or* **b**.

C | *GROUPS: Say a word from Part A. Pronounce the vowel carefully. Your classmates will say* **a** *or* **b**.

EXERCISE 4: Bingo

A | *Listen and repeat the words on the Bingo card.*

1. left	5. bread	9. laughed	13. Dad
2. said	6. dead	10. Brad	14. bad
3. had	7. head	11. sad	15. men
4. man	8. any	12. Annie	16. bed

B | *Now play Bingo. Use the card in Part A. Put an "X" over the words you hear. When you have four Xs in a row, say "Bingo!"*

EXAMPLE:

EXERCISE 5: Differences in Meaning

A | *Listen to the sentences and answers.*

Sentences	**Answers**
1. **a.** Do you like <u>bread</u>?	Yes, with butter.
b. Do you like <u>Brad</u>?	Yes, he's very nice.
2. **a.** Spell *head*.	H-E-A-D.
b. Spell *had*.	H-A-D.
3. **a.** He took my <u>pan</u>.	Now you can't cook.
b. He took my <u>pen</u>.	Now you can't write.
4. **a.** My father just <u>left</u>.	When is he coming back?
b. My father just <u>laughed</u>.	Did you say something funny?

B | *PAIRS: Say a sentence. Pronounce the underlined word carefully. Your partner will choose the correct answer and say it aloud.*

BREAKFAST

EXERCISE 6: Breakfast Foods

A | *Listen to the items on the breakfast menu.*

Breakfast Menu

Main Dishes

Cereal with milk	$2.00
Fried eggs	$4.00
Scrambled eggs	$4.00
Pancakes with syrup	$5.00
Waffles with berries	$6.00

Beverages

Apple juice	$1.50
Orange juice	$1.50
Coffee	$1.50
Hot chocolate	$2.00
Milk	$1.50
Tea	$1.50

Side Dishes

Bagel with cream cheese	$2.00
Bacon	$3.00
Ham	$3.00
Hash-brown potatoes	$2.00
Muffin (corn, bran)	$1.50

Healthy Choices

Fruit bowl	$4.00
Yogurt, plain	$2.00
Yogurt with fruit	$3.00

/æ/ b<u>a</u>d and /ɛ/ b<u>e</u>d   **15**

B | *Look at the words with underlined letters in Part A. Write each word in the correct column.*

/æ/	/ɛ/
scrambled	_____
_____	_____
_____	_____
_____	_____
_____	_____
	_____

EXERCISE 7: Conversations

Natural English
Use *me too* to show that you feel the same.
A: I'm hungry!
B: Me too.
Use *me neither* to agree with a negative sentence.
A: I'm not hungry.
B: Me neither. I just ate.
Use *not me* to show that you don't feel the same.
A: I want a big breakfast.
B: Not me.

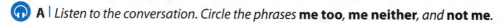

A | *Listen to the conversation. Circle the phrases* **me too**, **me neither**, *and* **not me**.

DAN: Do you want to go out for breakfast?

GREG: Yeah. I'm hungry!

DAN: Me too. When I get up, I'm starving! I want pancakes.

GREG: Not me! I don't like pancakes.

DAN: Really? What do you want to eat—eggs?

GREG: No, I don't like eggs.

DAN: Me neither.

B | *PAIRS: Practice the conversation. Take turns.*

EXERCISE 8: Your Turn

PAIRS: Talk about your breakfast habits. You can use the language from Exercises 6A and 7A on pages 15 and 16 or answer the questions.

1. What do people usually eat for breakfast in your country?

2. What do you have for breakfast?

3. Do you always eat breakfast?

4. Do you ever skip (miss) breakfast? Why?

STEP 4 EXTENDED PRACTICE

Accuracy Practice *Listen again to Exercises 1A, 2A, and 3A on pages 12 and 13. Then record the words.*

Fluency Practice *Record your answers to the questions in Exercise 8.*

UNIT 4 /ɑ/ cop and /ə/ cup

STEP 1 PRESENTATION

The pictures show you how to say the sounds /ɑ/ and /ə/.

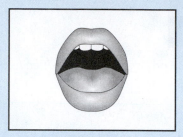

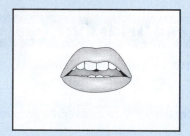

cop /ɑ/

Open your mouth.

cup /ə/

Your mouth is almost closed.

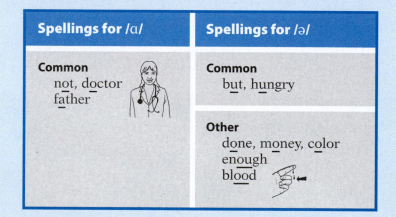

Spellings for /ɑ/	Spellings for /ə/
Common not, doctor father	**Common** but, hungry
	Other done, money, color enough blood

STEP 2 FOCUSED PRACTICE

EXERCISE 1: Words with /ɑ/

A | *Listen and repeat the words.*

1. top
2. watch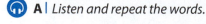
3. clock

4. job
5. cop
6. father

7. bottle
8. hot
9. problem

10. want
11. shop
12. soccer

B | *Choose four words from Part A. Write them in the left column.*

Your Words   **Your Partner's Words**

1. _____   1. _____

2. _____   2. _____

3. _____   3. _____

4. _____   4. _____

C | *PAIRS: Listen to your partner's words. Write them in the right column.*

EXERCISE 2: Words with /ə/

A | *Listen and repeat the words.*

1. cup

2. money

3. bus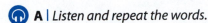

4. brother

5. young

6. country

7. one

8. sun

9. mother

10. month

11. color

12. love

B | *Choose four words. Write them in the left column.*

Your Words   **Your Partner's Words**

1. _____   1. _____

2. _____   2. _____

3. _____   3. _____

4. _____   4. _____

C | *PAIRS: Listen to your partner's words. Write them in the right column.*

EXERCISE 3: Listen for Differences: /ɑ/ vs. /ə/

A | *Listen and repeat the words.*

1. **a.** shot   **b.** shut

2. **a.** boss[1] 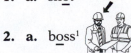   **b.** bus

3. **a.** collar[2] 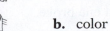   **b.** color

4. **a.** dock 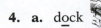   **b.** duck

5. **a.** cot   **b.** cut

[1–2] *Some people pronounce* boss *and* collar *with /ɔ/, a vowel similar to /ɑ/.*

B | *Listen again. Which word from Part A do you hear? Circle* **a** *or* **b.**

C | *GROUPS: Say a word from Part A. Pronounce the vowel carefully. Your classmates will say* **a** *or* **b.**

EXERCISE 4: Sentences with /ɑ/ and /ə/

A | *Listen and repeat the sentences.*

1. Chickens go "cl<u>u</u>ck-cl<u>u</u>ck" and cl<u>o</u>cks go "tick-t<u>o</u>ck."

2. What c<u>o</u>lor is your c<u>o</u>llar?
3. My b<u>o</u>ss takes the b<u>u</u>s.
4. The c<u>o</u>t is not c<u>o</u>mfortable.
5. How m<u>u</u>ch m<u>o</u>ney is en<u>ou</u>gh?
6. The d<u>u</u>cks are swimming near the d<u>o</u>cks.

B | *Look at the words with the underlined letters. Write each word in the correct column.*

/ɑ/		/ə/
clocks	_____	_____
_____	_____	_____
_____	_____	_____
_____	_____	_____
_____		
_____		

EXERCISE 5: Differences in Meaning

A | *Listen to the sentences and answers.*

Sentences	**Answers**
1. **a.** How do you spell *once*?	O-N-C-E.
b. How do you spell *wants*?	W-A-N-T-S.
2. **a.** Let's go swimming near the <u>duck</u>.	No. We'll scare it.
b. Let's go swimming near the <u>dock</u>.	No. Boats stop there.
3. **a.** That's a new <u>cop</u>.	He looks very young.
b. That's a new <u>cup</u>.	Yes. The old one broke.
4. **a.** Is that your <u>boss</u>?	Yes. She's very nice.
b. Is that your <u>bus</u>?	Yes. I'll see you later.

B | *PAIRS: Say a sentence. Pronounce the underlined word carefully. Your partner will choose the correct answer and say it aloud.*

SHOPPING

EXERCISE 6: One-Stop Shopping

A | *Listen to the sentences.*

1. Do you like to sh<u>o</u>p?

2. Do you like one-st<u>o</u>p shopping?

3. *One-stop shopping* means you can buy j<u>u</u>st about everything in one store.

4. BigMart is an example. It's c<u>a</u>lled[1] a superstore.

5. You can buy food, toys, clothes, and electr<u>o</u>nics there.*

6. You can even get a hairc<u>u</u>t at BigMart!

7. Shoppers go to BigMart because they w<u>a</u>nt to save m<u>o</u>ney.

8. B<u>u</u>t others say BigMart is bad for sm<u>a</u>ll[2] businesses.

9. They also say BigMart d<u>oe</u>sn't pay its workers en<u>ou</u>gh money.

---

*Natural English

Pronounce *clothes* like the verb in <u>Close</u> *the door* (do not pronounce the letters *th*). Remember: *Clothes* is always plural.

They sell clothes ("close") there.

B | *PAIRS: Practice the sentences. Pronounce the underlined vowels carefully.*

[1–2] *Some people pronounce* called *and* small *with* /ɔ/.

EXERCISE 7: Your Turn

A | *Read each sentence in the list. Follow the directions.*

Check (✔) the sentence that describes you.

_____ I like to shop.

_____ I like to shop sometimes.

_____ I don't like shopping at all.

Check (✔) the items you like to buy.

_____ clothes

_____ electronics

_____ food

Check (✔) the places you like to shop.

_____ online

_____ small stores

_____ superstores

What's important to you when you shop in stores? Write *1* (very important) or *2* (not very important) in each blank.

_____ good quality

_____ good service

_____ low prices

_____ one-stop shopping

_____ the size of the store

_____ The store should be close to my home.

B | *PAIRS: Compare your answers. How are your answers the same? How are they different?*

STEP 4   EXTENDED PRACTICE

Accuracy Practice   *Listen again to Exercises 1A and 2A on pages 18 and 19. Then record the words.*

Fluency Practice   *Record your answers from Exercise 7.*

UNIT 5 — Review of /ə/, /æ/, and /ɑ/

STEP 1   PRESENTATION

The pictures show you how to say the sounds /ə/, /æ/, and /ɑ/.

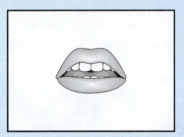

r<u>u</u>n /ə/

Your mouth is almost closed.

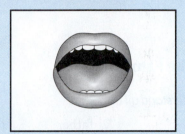

r<u>a</u>n /æ/

Open your mouth.
Spread your lips.

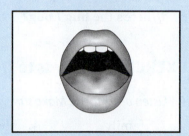

c<u>o</u>p /ɑ/

Open your mouth.
Don't spread your lips.

> **Spellings for /ə/, /æ/, and /ɑ/**
>
> See Units 3 and 4.

STEP 2   FOCUSED PRACTICE

EXERCISE 1: Words with /ə/, /æ/, and /ɑ/

A | *Listen and repeat the words.*

	/ə/		/æ/		/ɑ/
1.	a. c<u>u</u>p	b. c<u>a</u>p		c. c<u>o</u>p	
2.	a. d<u>o</u>ne	b. D<u>a</u>n		c. D<u>o</u>n	
3.	a. n<u>u</u>t	b. N<u>a</u>t		c. n<u>o</u>t	
4.	a. r<u>u</u>n	b. r<u>a</u>n		c. R<u>o</u>n	
5.	a. b<u>u</u>g	b. b<u>a</u>g		c. b<u>o</u>g[1]	

B | *Listen again. Which word do you hear? Circle **a**, **b**, or **c**.*

C | GROUPS: *Say a word from Part A. Pronounce the vowel carefully. Your classmates will say **a**, **b**, or **c**.*

[1] *Some people pronounce* bog *with /ɔ/, a vowel similar to /ɑ/.*

EXERCISE 2: Sentences with /ə/, /æ/, and /ɑ/

Listen to each sentence. Do you hear /ə/, /æ/, or /ɑ/? Circle the correct bold word. Then compare
your answers with a partner.

1. Where's the **cop / cup?**

2. **Dan / Don** is my brother.

3. Are you **Don / done?**

4. We **ran / run** together.

5. Where's the **bug / bog?**

EXERCISE 3: Words to Describe Families

A | Listen and repeat. Make sure you understand all the words.

1. family	4. husband	7. father	10. mom	13. son
2. aunt¹	5. younger	8. cousin	11. uncle	14. dad
3. daughter²	6. grandmother	9. brother	12. grandfather	15. mother

B | Write each word in the correct column. Some words belong in more than one column. Then
compare your answers with a partner.

/ə/	/æ/	/ɑ/
_____	*family*	_____
_____	_____	_____
_____	_____	_____
_____	_____	_____
_____	_____	
_____		
_____		
_____		

_____

¹⁻² *Some people pronounce* aunt *and* daughter *with* /ɔ/.

24 UNIT 5

C | *PAIRS: Complete Sam's family tree with words from Part A.*

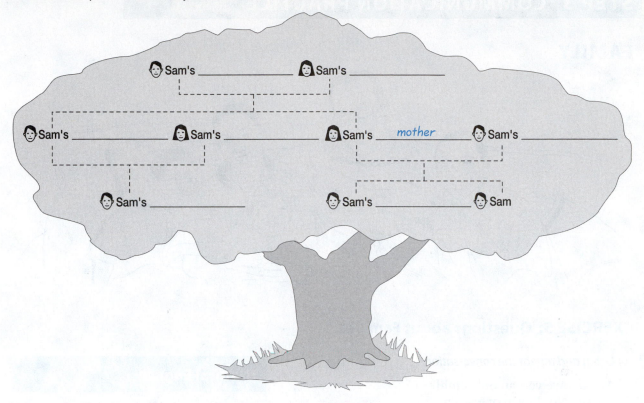

Sam's _____ Sam's _____

Sam's _____ Sam's _____ Sam's _____ *mother* Sam's _____

Sam's _____ Sam's _____ Sam

EXERCISE 4: Sentences about Families

A | *Listen. Complete the sentences with the words you hear. Then compare your answers with a partner.*

1. In some _____, only the parents and children live together.

2. In my family, my _____, _____, and

   _____ live with us.

3. My _____'s best friend is always at our house too. He's like

   one of the family.

4. Both my _____ and my sister have red hair. Red hair runs in our family.

5. Both my _____ and my _____ want me

   to be a doctor. But that's not what I want to do. I only want to write music

   and play with my band. I guess I'm the black sheep of the family.

B | *PAIRS: Practice the sentences. Take turns.*

FAMILY

EXERCISE 5: Questions about Families

A | *Listen and repeat the conversations.*

1. **A:** Are you an only child?
   B: No, I have one sister.

2. **A:** Do you have any brothers?
   B: Yes, I have two brothers.

3. **A:** Are you older or younger than your brothers? *
   B: Younger.

4. **A:** Do you have a family of your own?
   B: Yes, I do.

5. **A:** Are you married or single?
   B: Married.

6. **A:** Do you have any children?
   B: Yes, I have two sons and a daughter.

7. **A:** Do you have any grandchildren?
   B: Yes, I have a grandson.

B | *PAIRS: Practice the conversations. Take turns.*

---

*Natural English

In choice questions, your voice goes up on the first choice and down on the second.

A: Are you older or younger than your brothers?

B: Younger.

A: Are you married or single?

B: Married.

EXERCISE 6: Your Turn

A | *Answer the questions in the chart about yourself.*

	Your Name _____	**Student's Name** _____	**Student's Name** _____
Do you have any brothers or sisters?			
If so, are you the oldest child, a middle child, or the youngest child?			
Are you married or single?			
Do you have any children?			
Do you have any grandchildren?			

B | *Ask two classmates the questions. Write their answers in the chart.*

C | *Share your information with your classmates: Who has the largest family? How many of your classmates are married? How many have children? Grandchildren?*

STEP 4 EXTENDED PRACTICE

Accuracy Practice *Listen again to Exercises 1A and 3A on pages 23 and 24. Then record the words.*

Fluency Practice *Record your answers to the questions from the chart in Exercise 6A.*

Vowels + *r:* /ɑr/ c<u>ar</u>, /or/ f<u>our</u>, and /ər/ b<u>ir</u>d

STEP 1   PRESENTATION

The pictures show you how to say the sounds /r/, /ɑr/, /or/, and /ər/.

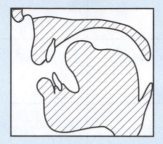

Turn the front of your tongue
up and back to make /r/.

c<u>ar</u> /ɑr/

Open your mouth. Turn your
tongue up and back.

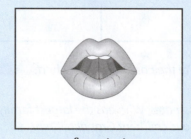

f<u>our</u> /or/

Round your lips. Turn your
tongue up and back.

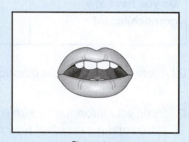

first /ər/

Your mouth is almost closed.
Turn your tongue up and back.

Spellings for /ɑr/	Spellings for /or/	Spellings for /ər/
Common c<u>ar</u>, h<u>ar</u>d	**Common** f<u>or</u>, m<u>or</u>e fl<u>oor</u>, d<u>oor</u>	**Common** h<u>er</u>, w<u>er</u>e t<u>ur</u>n, b<u>ur</u>n f<u>ir</u>st, b<u>ir</u>d
Other h<u>ear</u>t g<u>uar</u>d	**Other** f<u>our</u> w<u>ar</u>, w<u>ar</u>m	**Other** h<u>ear</u>d, <u>Ear</u>th w<u>or</u>k, w<u>or</u>d

EXERCISE 1: Words with /ɑr/

A | *Listen and repeat the words. Open your mouth. Turn your tongue up and back.*

1. hard	**4.** dark	**7.** arm
2. garden	**5.** heart	**8.** park
3. party	**6.** apartment	**9.** star

B | *Choose four words. Write them in the left column.*

Your Words   **Your Partner's Words**

1. _____   1. _____

2. _____   2. _____

3. _____   3. _____

4. _____   4. _____

C | *PAIRS: Listen to your partner's words. Write them in the right column.*

EXERCISE 2: Words with /or/

A | *Listen and repeat the words. Round your lips. Turn your tongue up and back.*

1. four	**4.** shore	**7.** north
2. more	**5.** short	**8.** war
3. floor	**6.** story	**9.** warm

B | *Choose four words. Write them in the left column.*

Your Words   **Your Partner's Words**

1. _____   1. _____

2. _____   2. _____

3. _____   3. _____

4. _____   4. _____

C | *PAIRS: Listen to your partner's words. Write them in the right column.*

EXERCISE 3: Words with /ər/

A | *Listen and repeat the words. Keep your mouth almost closed and small inside. Turn your tongue up and back.*

1. bird
2. first
3. circle ◯

4. thirsty
5. shirt
6. birthday

7. learn
8. turn
9. work

B | *Choose four words. Write them in the left column.*

Your Words

1. _____
2. _____
3. _____
4. _____

Your Partner's Words

1. _____
2. _____
3. _____
4. _____

C | *PAIRS: Listen to your partner's words. Write them in the right column.*

EXERCISE 4: Same or Different?

*Listen to the word pairs. Write **S** if the underlined sounds are the same. Write **D** if the underlined sounds are different. Then compare your answers with a partner.*

1. were, work ___S___
2. third, more _____
3. word, wore _____
4. start, hard _____
5. learn, bird _____

6. third, turn _____
7. heart, heard _____
8. war, car _____
9. circle, her _____
10. door, store _____

EXERCISE 5: Game: Vowels + *r*

Play this game in two teams—Team A and Team B.

Team A: Ask the questions on page 161 to the players on Team B.
Team B: Answer the questions with words that have /ɑr/, /or/, or /ər/ sounds. Then ask
Team A the questions on page 163. Follow the example.

EXAMPLE:

TEAM A: What number comes after 12?

TEAM B: Thirteen.

TEAM A: What's the opposite of *tall*?

TEAM B: Short.

FIRSTS

EXERCISE 6: My First Home

A | *Listen to the story.*

1. I was <u>born</u> in New Jersey on <u>March</u> 5th.

2. My father <u>worked</u> in New <u>York</u> City.

3. He grew up on a <u>farm</u>. My father didn't really like city life.

4. So we moved to the country when I was <u>four</u> years old.

5. It's the <u>first</u> home I remember.

6. We had a <u>yard</u>[1], and <u>I</u> could play outside. We could see the <u>stars</u> at night.

7. There <u>were</u> a lot of farms near our new home.

8. And there was a <u>dark</u>, empty <u>church</u>[2] next <u>door</u>.

9. I was always afraid to walk by that old church.*

---

*Natural English

Work and *walk* have different pronunciations. The vowel in *walk* is like the vowel in *father*. Also, don't say the consonant *l* in *walk*—it's silent.

Try it. Say:

  I don't want to *walk*.

  I don't want to *work*.

---

[1] yard: *the grass around a house;* [2] dark, empty church: *the church was not used by anyone*

B | *Write each underlined word from Part A in the correct column.*

/ɑr/	/ɔr/	/ər/
_____	*born*	_____
_____	_____	_____
_____	_____	_____
_____	_____	_____
_____		

C | *PAIRS: Practice the story in Part A. Take turns.*

EXERCISE 7: The First One

A | *Listen to the conversations. Complete the sentences with the words you hear. Then compare your answers with a partner.*

1. **A:** Do you remember your _____ date?

    B: Uh-huh. Rick Moore. We went to a school _____ together.

    A: That sounds exciting. How old _____ you?

    B: I was _____, but he was 15—an _____ boy!

2. **A:** Do you _____ your first teacher?

    B: Oh, yes. Her name was Mrs. Rinaldo. I'll _____ _____ her!

    A: You didn't like her?

    B: No! And she didn't like me!

3. **A:** Do you remember your first _____?

    B: I've never had one. I don't know how to drive.

4. **A:** Do you remember your first job?

    B: Of course—I still have it. I'm an _____ _____.

B | *PAIRS: Practice the conversations. Take turns.*

EXERCISE 8: Your Turn

PAIRS: Talk about some of your "firsts." Use the conversations in Exercise 7A on page 32 as models. Take notes as your partner answers your questions.

EXAMPLE:

> My partner: Matteo
>
> Matteo's first . . .
>
> date: Maria Ruiz
>
> teacher: Mr. Alonso
>
> car: Ford truck
>
> job: Food store

STEP 4 EXTENDED PRACTICE

Accuracy Practice *Listen again to Exercises 1A, 2A, and 3A on pages 29 and 30. Then record the words.*

Fluency Practice *Record your answers to the questions. Use complete sentences.*

1. When were you born?
2. Where were you born?
3. Do you remember your first home? If so, describe it.
4. Did your family ever move from your first home? If so, where did you move to?

CONSONANTS

UNIT	PRONUNCIATION FOCUS	COMMUNICATION FOCUS
7	Consonant Overview	Contact Information
8	/θ/ three and /ð/ this	Holidays
9	/p/ pen, /b/ boy, /f/ foot, /v/ very, and /w/ wet	Pets
10	/s/ sun, /z/ zoo, /ʃ/ shoe, and /ʒ/ television	Stress and Relaxation
11	/tʃ/ chair and /dʒ/ jet; /dʒ/ jet and /y/ yet	Education
12	/r/ road and /l/ love	Truth or Lies?
13	/m/ mouth, /n/ nose, and /ŋ/ sing	Time
14	Word Endings: Plurals and Present Tense	Chores and Glamorous Jobs
15	Word Endings: Past Tense	The Bus Driver
16	Consonant Groups	Nature

Consonant Overview

STEP 1 PRESENTATION

Consonant sounds are made by moving parts of the mouth close together.

Label the parts of the mouth. Use the words in the box.

| nose | lips | teeth | vocal cords | tongue |

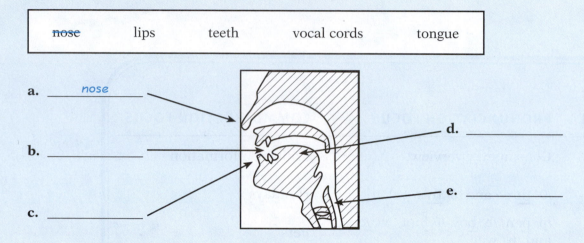

a. _____nose_____

b. _____

c. _____

d. _____

e. _____

Label the parts of the tongue. Use the words in the box.

| tip | middle | back |

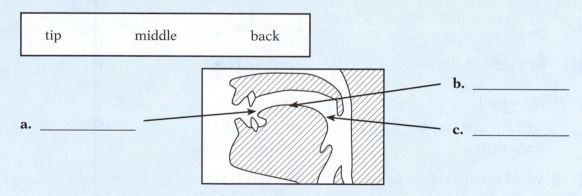

a. _____

b. _____

c. _____

EXERCISE 1: Consonants You Can See

A | *Look at the pictures. They show you how to say six consonants.*

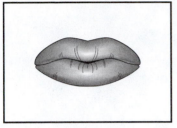

/p, b, m/

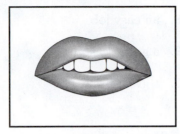

/f, v/

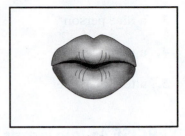

/w/

B | *Listen and repeat the words.*

1. pie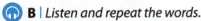
2. bike
3. mail

4. fish
5. fire
6. vest

7. west
8. wave
9. wind

C | *PAIRS: Say the words. Does your mouth look like the pictures in Part A?*

EXERCISE 2: Consonants with a Puff of Air

A | *Use a strong puff of air when you say words that begin with /p/, /t/, or /k/.*

B | *Listen and repeat the words. Say the first sound of each word with a puff of air.*

1. pay
2. park

3. time
4. tall

5. kiss
6. coat

EXERCISE 3: Voiced and Voiceless Consonants

A | */z/ is a voiced sound. The vocal cords vibrate. Try it. Say a long /z/.*
/zzzzzzzzzzzzzzzzzzzzz/

B | */s/ is a voiceless sound. The vocal cords do not vibrate. Try it. Say a long /s/.*
/ssssssssssssssssssssss/

C | *Put your fingers against your neck. Now make these sounds.*
Can you feel a difference?
/zzzzzzz/
/sssssss/

D | *Try it again. Feel the voicing go "on" and "off."*
/zzzzzzz-sssssss-zzzzzzz-sssssss/
/vvvvvvv-fffffffff-vvvvvvv-fffffffff/

🎧 **E** | *Listen and repeat the phrases and sentences.*

/s/		/z/
	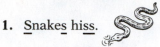	

/s/
1. Snake<u>s</u> hi<u>ss</u>.
2. a good pri<u>c</u>e
3. a ni<u>c</u>e per<u>s</u>on
4. a hard le<u>ss</u>on
5. a text me<u>ss</u>age

/z/
6. Bee<u>s</u> bu<u>zz</u>.
7. a bu<u>s</u>y day
8. an ea<u>s</u>y job
9. a good rea<u>s</u>on
10. a great pri<u>z</u>e

EXERCISE 4: Join Words Together

🎧 **A** | *Listen and repeat the phrases. Join the final consonant sound to the next vowel.*

1. come in
2. home address
3. email address
4. mailing address
5. contact information
6. online application

🎧 **B** | *Listen and repeat the phrases. Make one long consonant.*

1. phone number
2. bank card
3. bad day
4. call later
5. bus stop
6. part time

🎧 **C** | *Listen and repeat the phrases. Say the final consonant, but keep it short (ᐟ). Then say the next word clearly.*

1. apartmentᐟ building
2. zipᐟ code[1]
3. faxᐟ number
4. webᐟ site
5. smartᐟ phone
6. faceᐟ to face[2]

---

[1] zip code: *a number that you put below the address on an envelope to help the post office deliver the mail more quickly;* [2] face to face: *facing someone*

CONTACT INFORMATION

EXERCISE 5: What's Your Mailing Address?

A | *Listen to the conversation. Notice how the speakers join words together.*

MAX: Can I apply online for a part-time course this fall?

MS. ADAMS: No, we still use paper applications. And I don't have any now. Can you come back tomorrow?

MAX: Sorry, tomorrow's a bad day for me. I'm really busy.

MS. ADAMS: Well, I can mail you one. What's your address?

MAX: My mailing address is P.O. Box[1] 412, Yakima, Washington, 98908.*

MS. ADAMS: OK. I'll send you one tomorrow.

---

*Natural English

You can use the word *oh* or *zero* for the number *0*.

   90908 (nine-oh-nine-oh-eight) or 90908 (nine-zero-nine-zero-eight)

P.O. Boxes, zip codes, and phone numbers are easier to understand if you say the numbers in groups.

   P.O. Box 412 (four-twelve)

   Zip code: 98908 (nine-eight, nine-oh-eight) or 98908 (nine-eight-nine, oh-eight)

   Phone number: 509 – 555 – 6022
           (area code) phone number

B | *PAIRS: Practice the conversation in Part A. Join final consonants to vowels. Take turns.*

---

[1] P.O. Box (an abbreviation for post office box): *a box in a post office; some people get their mail sent to a post office box, not to their home address*

EXERCISE 6: Your Turn

A | *PAIRS: How do you keep in contact (communicate with) your friends and family? Check (✓) your answers. Then compare them with a partner.*

_____ I email my friends and family.

_____ I make phone calls.

_____ I send people text messages.

_____ I visit social sites on the Web.

_____ I write letters.

B | *PAIRS: Ask and answer questions about your contact information. Follow the example. Then write the answers in the chart.*

EXAMPLE:

STUDENT A: What's your _____*phone number*_____?

STUDENT B: _____*(715) 555-3018*_____

STUDENT A: Is that your cell phone or your home phone?

STUDENT B: _____*That's my cell phone.*_____

	Your Name _____	**Your Partner's Name** _____
Cell phone / Home phone number		
Email address		
Home address		
Mailing address		

STEP 4   EXTENDED PRACTICE

Accuracy Practice *Listen again to Exercises 4A, 4B and 4C on page 38. Then record the phrases.*

Fluency Practice *Record your answers to the questions.*

1. My email address is _____.

2. My (cell phone/home phone number) is _____.

3. My home address and mailing address are _____.
   (same / different)

4. My (home/mailing) address is _____.

/θ/ <u>th</u>ree and /ð/ <u>th</u>is

STEP 1 PRESENTATION

The picture shows you how to say the sounds /θ/ and /ð/.

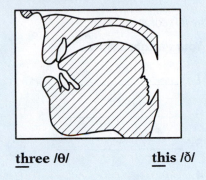

<u>th</u>ree /θ/   <u>th</u>is /ð/

Put the tip of your tongue between your teeth to make the *th* sounds /θ/ and /ð/.

/θ/ is voiceless.   /ð/ is voiced.

Notes

1. Pronounce the final *th* in *month* as /θ/. You don't need to pronounce this sound in the plural form. You can say *months* as /mənts/.
2. Pronounce the plural word *clothes* like the verb *close (the door)*. You don't need to pronounce the *th* sound.

Spellings for /θ/		Spellings for /ð/	
Common <u>th</u>ree wi<u>th</u>		**Common** <u>th</u>is mo<u>th</u>er	
Nouns ba<u>th</u> brea<u>th</u>	⟶ ⟶	**Verbs** to ba<u>th</u>e to brea<u>th</u>e	

EXERCISE 1: Words with /θ/

A | *Listen and repeat the words. Put the tip of your tongue between your teeth.*

1. think	**4.** thumb	**7.** month

1. think   **4.** thumb   **7.** month

2. thin   **5.** thousand   **8.** bath

3. throw   **6.** health   **9.** fifth

B | *Choose four words. Write them in the left column.*

Your Words   **Your Partner's Words**

1. _____   **1.** _____

2. _____   **2.** _____

3. _____   **3.** _____

4. _____   **4.** _____

C | *PAIRS: Listen to your partner's words. Write them in the right column.*

EXERCISE 2: Words with /ð/

A | *Listen and repeat the words. Put the tip of your tongue between your teeth.*

1. there   **4.** brother   **7.** clothing

2. that   **5.** weather   **8.** together

3. then   **6.** other   **9.** mother

B | *Choose four words. Write them in the left column.*

Your Words   **Your Partner's Words**

1. _____   **1.** _____

2. _____   **2.** _____

3. _____   **3.** _____

4. _____   **4.** _____

C | *PAIRS: Listen to your partner's words. Write them in the right column.*

EXERCISE 3: Game: /θ/ and /ð/

Play this game in two teams—Team A and Team B.

Team A: Ask the questions on page 161 to the players on Team B.
Team B: Answer the questions with words that have *th* sounds. Then ask Team A
the questions on page 163.

EXAMPLE:

TEAM A: What number comes after two?

TEAM B: Three.

STEP 3 COMMUNICATION PRACTICE

HOLIDAYS

EXERCISE 4: Holiday Names

A | *Listen and repeat the holiday names in column A.*

A	B
<u>_h_</u> **1.** New Year's Day	**a.** a day for workers
_____ **2.** Christmas	**b.** the birthday of the United States
_____ **3.** Halloween	**c.** a day for tricks and jokes
_____ **4.** Memorial Day	**d.** a day to give thanks
_____ **5.** Labor Day	**e.** a day of gift-giving and religious celebration
_____ **6.** New Year's Eve	**f.** the day to remember people who died in wars
_____ **7.** April Fool's Day	**g.** the last night of the year
_____ **8.** Valentine's Day	**h.** the first day of the new year
_____ **9.** Independence Day	**i.** a day to show your love
_____ **10.** Thanksgiving Day	**j.** a day to wear costumes

B | *PAIRS: Match the holidays in column A with the descriptions in column B. Then check your answers on page 45.*

EXERCISE 5: Dates

Natural English

When you give a date, stress the date more than the month.

    December 25th (December twenty-fifth)

Stress the last number of the date more than the first number.

    April 10th (April tenth)

A | *PAIRS: Do you know the dates of the holidays listed in Exercise 4A on page 43? Write the holidays next to the dates. Then check your answers on page 45.*

1. January 1st _____*New Year's Day*_____

2. October 31st _____

3. December 31st _____

4. April 1st _____

5. the last Monday of May _____

6. February 14th _____

7. December 25th _____

8. July 4th _____

9. the fourth Thursday of November _____

10. the first Monday of September _____

B | *PAIRS: Ask and answer questions about the holidays and their dates. Follow the example.*

EXAMPLE:

STUDENT A: When is Valentine's Day?

STUDENT B: It's on February 14th.

EXERCISE 6: Your Turn

PAIRS: Do you celebrate the holidays listed in Exercise 4A on page 43? Talk about the holidays and how you celebrate them. Follow the example.

EXAMPLE:

STUDENT A: Do you celebrate New Year's Eve in your country?

STUDENT B: Yes.

STUDENT A: What do you do on that day?

STUDENT B: I eat a big meal with my family. Then I go to parties with my friends. We listen to music and dance.

STEP 4 EXTENDED PRACTICE

Accuracy Practice *Listen again to Exercises 1A and 2A on page 42. Then record the words.*

Fluency Practice *Record your answers to the questions. Use complete sentences.*

1. What's your favorite holiday?
2. Why is it your favorite?
3. When is that holiday?
4. What do you do on that day?

STEP 1   PRESENTATION

The pictures show you how to say /p/, /b/, /f/, /v/, and /w/.

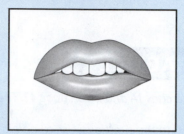

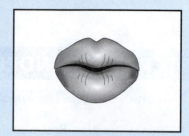

<u>p</u>en /p/, <u>b</u>oy /b/

/p/ is voiceless.
/b/ is voiced.

<u>f</u>oot /f/, <u>v</u>ery /v/

/f/ is voiceless.
/v/ is voiced.

<u>w</u>et /w/

Spellings for /p/	Spellings for /b/	Spellings for /w/
Common peo<u>p</u>le, <u>p</u>ut, kee<u>p</u>	**Common** <u>b</u>oy, <u>b</u>a<u>b</u>y	**Common** <u>w</u>et, <u>w</u>est, <u>w</u>ell <u>qu</u>estion, <u>qu</u>iet
	Other bomb, comb, (*b* is silent)	**Other** write, answer (*w* is silent)

Spellings for /f/	Spellings for /v/
Common <u>f</u>ast, li<u>f</u>e o<u>ff</u>ice	**Common** <u>v</u>ery, lo<u>v</u>e, ne<u>v</u>er
Other <u>ph</u>one, <u>ph</u>oto cou<u>gh</u>, lau<u>gh</u>	

Singular	**Plural**
a kni<u>f</u>e →	kni<u>v</u>es
a lea<u>f</u> →	lea<u>v</u>es

EXERCISE 1: Words with /p/ and /b/

🎧 **A** | *Listen and repeat the words.*

	/p/				/b/		
1.	people	4.	happy	7.	bank	10.	about
2.	picture	5.	stop	8.	book	11.	job
3.	play	6.	sleep	9.	blue	12.	robe

B | *Choose four words. Write them in the left column.*

Your Words   **Your Partner's Words**

1. _____   1. _____

2. _____   2. _____

3. _____   3. _____

4. _____   4. _____

C | *PAIRS: Listen to your partner's words. Write them in the right column.*

EXERCISE 2: Words with /f/ and /v/

🎧 **A** | *Listen and repeat the words.*

	/f/				/v/		
1.	five	4.	coffee	7.	van	10.	seven
2.	foot	5.	elephant	8.	visit	11.	love
3.	phone	6.	laugh	9.	never	12.	arrive

B | *Choose four words. Write them in the left column.*

Your Words   **Your Partner's Words**

1. _____   1. _____

2. _____   2. _____

3. _____   3. _____

4. _____   4. _____

C | *PAIRS: Listen to your partner's words. Write them in the right column.*

EXERCISE 3: Words with /w/

🎧 **A** | *Listen and repeat the words.*

1. <u>w</u>est
2. <u>w</u>ater
3. <u>w</u>inter
4. <u>w</u>eather
5. a<u>w</u>ay
6. a<u>w</u>ake
7. q<u>u</u>iet
8. lang<u>u</u>age
9. q<u>u</u>estion

B | *Choose four words. Write them in the left column.*

Your Words   **Your Partner's Words**

1. _____   1. _____

2. _____   2. _____

3. _____   3. _____

4. _____   4. _____

C | *PAIRS: Listen to your partner's words. Write them in the right column.*

EXERCISE 4: Listen for Differences: /p/, /b/, /f/, /v/, /w/

🎧 **A** | *Listen and repeat the words.*

1. **a.** co<u>p</u>y   **b.** co<u>f</u>fee

2. **a.** <u>p</u>ear   **b.** <u>f</u>air

3. **a.** <u>f</u>erret   **b.** <u>p</u>arrot

4. **a.** <u>f</u>ox   **b.** <u>b</u>ox

5. **a.** <u>v</u>ote   **b.** <u>b</u>oat

6. **a.** <u>v</u>est   **b.** <u>w</u>est

7. **a.** <u>v</u>ery   **b.** <u>b</u>erry

8. **a.** <u>V</u>   **b.** <u>w</u>e

🎧 **B** | *Listen again. Which word do you hear? Circle **a** or **b**.*

EXERCISE 5: Sounds That You Can See

A | *Write each word from Exercise 4A on page 48 under the correct picture.*

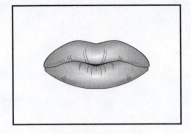   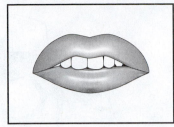   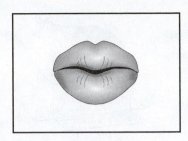

_____copy_____   _____   _____

_____   _____   _____

_____   _____

_____   _____

_____   _____

_____

_____

B | *Work with your partner. Choose one word from Part A. Face your partner. Take turns saying the word without using any sound. Use the mouth pictures above to help you. Your partner will decide which word you said by looking at the shape of your mouth. Follow your teacher's example.*

EXAMPLE:

TEACHER: *(Says the word without any sound.)* **Pear.**

STUDENT A: Did you say **fair?**

TEACHER: No, watch again. *(Says the word again without any sound.)* **Pear.**

STUDENT A: Oh! You said **pear.**

EXERCISE 6: Differences in Meaning

 **A** | *Listen and repeat the sentences.*

1. **a.** The <u>f</u>ox is on the <u>b</u>ox.   **b.** The <u>b</u>ox is on the <u>f</u>ox.

2. **a.** The <u>f</u>erret is in the cage.   **b.** The <u>p</u>arrot is in the cage.

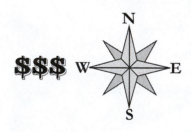

3. **a.** My money is in the <u>w</u>est.   **b.** My money is in the <u>v</u>est.

4. **a.** The co<u>p</u>y is under the co<u>ff</u>ee.   **b.** The co<u>ff</u>ee is under the co<u>p</u>y.

B | *PAIRS: Say a sentence. Your partner will point to the correct sentence, **a** or **b**.*

EXERCISE 7: Game: /p/, /b/, /f/, /v/, or /w/

Play this game in two teams—Team A and Team B.

Team A: Ask the questions on page 161 to the players on Team B.
Team B: Answer the questions with words that have /p/, /b/, /f/, /v/, or /w/ sounds.
Then ask Team A the questions on page 163.

> **EXAMPLE:**
>
> **TEAM A:** What animals fly?
>
> **TEAM B:** *Birds!*

STEP 3 COMMUNICATION PRACTICE

PETS

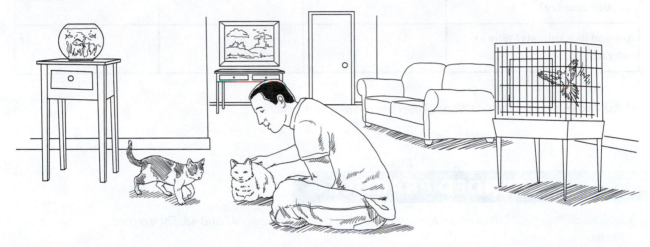

EXERCISE 8: People and Pets

A | *Listen and repeat. Make sure you understand all the words.*

1. popular	3. pigs	5. bark	7. healthy	9. bite
2. rabbits	4. snakes	6. protect	8. responsibility	10. disease

B | *PAIRS: Listen to the recording. Then answer the questions.*

1. What is the most popular pet in the United States?
2. What are some other popular pets?
3. What are some unusual pets?
4. How can pets help people?*
5. What are some problems that pets cause?

> ***Natural English**
>
> *People* is more natural and used more often than *persons*.
>
> How can pets help people?
>
> People take care of pets.

EXERCISE 9: Your Turn

A | *Answer the questions in the chart about yourself.*

	Your Name _____	Student's Name _____	Student's Name _____
Do you have a pet?			
Did you have a pet when you were a child?			
What kind of pet do/did you have?			
What kinds of pets are popular in your country?			
Do you like animals? Why or why not?			

B | *Ask two classmates the questions. Write their answers in the chart.*

STEP 4 | EXTENDED PRACTICE

Accuracy Practice *Listen again to Exercises 1A, 2A, and 3A on pages 47 and 48. Then record the words.*

Fluency Practice *Record your answers to the questions in Exercise 9.*

The pictures show you how to say the sounds /s/, /z/, /ʃ/, and /ʒ/.

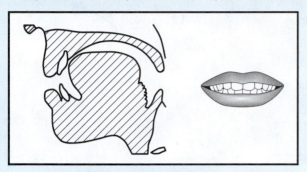

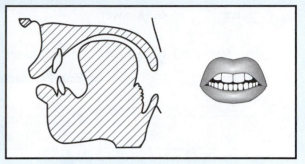

<u>s</u>un /s/, <u>z</u>ero /z/

Keep the tip of your tongue high, behind your top teeth.

/s/ is voiceless; /z/ is voiced.

<u>sh</u>oe /ʃ/, televi<u>s</u>ion /ʒ/

Pull back your tongue. Round your lips a little.

/ʃ/ is voiceless; /ʒ/ is voiced.

Spellings for /s/	Spellings for /ʃ/
Common <u>s</u>un, <u>s</u>ister, <u>s</u>top cla<u>ss</u>, ki<u>ss</u>, le<u>ss</u>on <u>c</u>ity poli<u>c</u>e, fa<u>c</u>e	**Common** <u>sh</u>oe, pu<u>sh</u>ing, wa<u>sh</u> edu<u>c</u>a<u>ti</u>on, vaca<u>ti</u>on
Other hou<u>s</u>e, hor<u>s</u>e <u>s</u>cissors e<u>x</u>plain, bo<u>x</u>, (*x* is /ks/)	**Other** spe<u>ci</u>al, musi<u>ci</u>an <u>s</u>ure, <u>s</u>ugar <u>Ch</u>icago, ma<u>ch</u>ine o<u>c</u>ean
Spellings for /z/	Spellings for /ʒ/
Common <u>z</u>oo, <u>z</u>ero ea<u>s</u>y, vi<u>s</u>it, mu<u>s</u>ic plea<u>s</u>e, becau<u>s</u>e	**Common** televi<u>s</u>ion, deci<u>s</u>ion, A<u>s</u>ia u<u>s</u>ually, plea<u>s</u>ure
Other sci<u>ss</u>ors	**Other** gara<u>g</u>e

EXERCISE 1: Words with /s/ and /z/

🎧 **A** | *Listen and repeat the words.*

/s/			/z/		
1. sorry	4. office		7. zoo		10. business
2. listen	5. police		8. zebra		11. music
3. stress¹	6. answer		9. easy		12. rose

B | *Choose four words. Write them in the left column.*

Your Words **Your Partner's Words**

1. _____ 1. _____

2. _____ 2. _____

3. _____ 3. _____

4. _____ 4. _____

C | *PAIRS: Listen to your partner's words. Write them in the right column.*

EXERCISE 2: Words with /ʃ/ and /ʒ/

🎧 **A** | *Listen and repeat the words.*

/ʃ/		/ʒ/	
1. shoe	4. wash	7. usually	10. treasure
2. machines	5. vacation	8. pleasure	11. Asia
3. ocean	6. sugar	9. decision	12. television

B | *Choose four words. Write them in the left column.*

Your Words **Your Partner's Words**

1. _____ 1. _____

2. _____ 2. _____

3. _____ 3. _____

4. _____ 4. _____

C | *PAIRS: Listen to your partner's words. Write them in the right column.*

---

¹ stress: *feelings of worry about work or other problems*

EXERCISE 3: Listen for Differences: /s/ vs. /z/

🎧 **A** | *Listen and repeat the words.*

1. **a.** ra<u>c</u>er **b.** ra<u>z</u>or

2. **a.** <u>s</u>ea **b.** <u>Z</u>

3. **a.** Ro<u>ss</u> **b.** Ro<u>z</u>

4. **a.** pla<u>c</u>e **b.** play<u>s</u>

5. **a.** <u>S</u>ue **b.** <u>z</u>oo

6. **a.** pri<u>c</u>e **b.** pri<u>z</u>e

7. **a.** pea<u>c</u>e **b.** pea<u>s</u>

8. **a.** la<u>c</u>y **b.** la<u>z</u>y

🎧 **B** | *Listen again. Which word do you hear? Circle **a** or **b**.*

C | *GROUPS: Say a word from Part A. Pronounce the consonants carefully. Your classmates will say **a** or **b**.*

EXERCISE 4: Sounds and Spellings

🎧 **A** | *Listen and repeat the words.*

1. <u>sh</u>ould
2. A<u>s</u>ia
3. mu<u>s</u>eum
4. de<u>c</u>i<u>s</u>ion
5. offi<u>c</u>e
6. bu<u>s</u>ine<u>ss</u>
7. <u>Ch</u>icago
8. ma<u>ch</u>ines
9. gara<u>g</u>e

B | *PAIRS: The underlined letters in Part A have /s/, /z/, /ʃ/, and /ʒ/ sounds. Write each word in the correct column. Words with two underlines go in more than one column.*

/s/	/z/	/ʃ/	/ʒ/
		should	

/s/ <u>s</u>un, /z/ <u>z</u>oo, /ʃ/ <u>sh</u>oe, and /ʒ/ televi<u>s</u>ion **55**

C | PAIRS: *Listen to the story. Complete the sentences with words from Part A.*

I work for a _____ in _____. We fix copy _____. But
  1.   2.   3.

sometimes I can't fix a copier. Then the people in the _____ get angry. They think I
                                                          4.

_____ be able to fix everything. There's just too much stress in my work. So I've
  5.

made a _____. I'm going to quit my job and move back to New York. Yes, there's also
          6.

a lot of stress there. But my friend says he can get me a job at the Rubin _____. It
                                                                              7.

has art from India, China, and other countries in _____. The work is relaxing[1], and
                                                      8.

that's what I need.

STEP 3   COMMUNICATION PRACTICE

STRESS AND RELAXATION

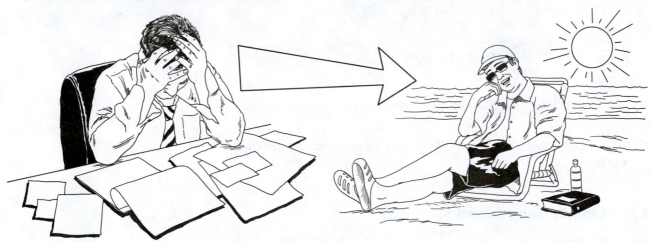

EXERCISE 5: Under Stress

A | *Listen to the conversation.*

   A: What do you do when you're stressed?

      What do you do to relax?

   B: I close my eyes and think about something nice.

   A: Like what? What do you think about?

   B: A quiet beach. I think about the warm sun on my face.

      And I think about the sound of the waves. It helps me relax.

> **Natural English**
>
> Say words in groups. Word groups tell the listener what ideas belong together. Word groups make your English clearer.
>
>   What do you do to relax?

B | *PAIRS: Practice the conversation. Use the lines to help you group words. Take turns.*

[1] relaxing: *creating calm and less worry, especially by doing something enjoyable*

56   UNIT 10

EXERCISE 6: Your Turn

A | *Listen and repeat the sentences.*

_____ 1. I watch television.

_____ 2. I go for a walk.

_____ 3. I close my eyes.

_____ 4. I think about something nice.

_____ 5. I breathe deeply, 10 times.

_____ 6. I listen to music.

_____ 7. I do a crossword puzzle.

_____ 8. I eat, but I shouldn't.

B | *Read the sentences again. Check (✓) the things you do to relax.*

C | *GROUPS: Discuss your answers to the questions.*

1. What makes you feel stressed? Work? School? Family? Traffic? Waiting in line?
2. Is it easy for you to relax when you feel stressed?
3. What do you do to relax?

STEP 4   EXTENDED PRACTICE

Accuracy Practice *Listen again to Exercises 1A and 2A on page 54. Then record the words.*

Fluency Practice *Record your answers to the questions in Exercise 6C.*

The pictures show you how to say the sounds /tʃ/, /dʒ/, and /y/.

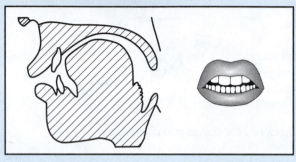

<u>ch</u>air /tʃ/   **<u>j</u>et** /dʒ/

/tʃ/ starts as a /t/ sound.   /dʒ/ starts as a /d/ sound.
/tʃ/ is voiceless.   /dʒ/ is voiced.

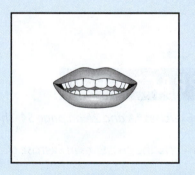

<u>y</u>et /y/

Notes

1. If you pronounce *yet* like *jet*, try this:

    Say: *iíet* (yet)—stress the second *i*

    Try it: *iíes* (yes)   *iíesterday* (yesterday)   *iíear* (year)   *iíellow* (yellow)

2. If you pronounce *much* like *mush*, try this:

    Say: A /t/ before *ch*: *mutch* (much)

    Try it: *mutch* (much)   *whitch* (which)

Spellings for /tʃ/	Spellings for /dʒ/	Spellings for /y/
Common chair, much kitchen, watch	**Common** job, June, just George, age engine, imagination bridge, judge	**Common** yes, young, yellow
Other future question	**Other** education, graduate	**Other** university, United States

STEP 2 FOCUSED PRACTICE

EXERCISE 1: Words with /tʃ/ and /dʒ/

A | *Listen and repeat the words.*

/tʃ/

1. child
2. church
3. picture
4. kitchen
5. question
6. peach

/dʒ/

7. graduate
8. job
9. jump
10. education
11. engine
12. college

B | *Choose four words. Write them in the left column.*

Your Words	Your Partner's Words
1. _____	1. _____
2. _____	2. _____
3. _____	3. _____
4. _____	4. _____

C | *PAIRS: Listen to your partner's words. Write them in the right column.*

EXERCISE 2: Words with /y/ and /dʒ/

🎧 **A |** *Listen and repeat the words.*

/y/

1. yes
2. year
3. yet
4. United States
5. young
6. university

/dʒ/

7. jail
8. June
9. jar
10. jaw
11. jet
12. jeans

B | *Choose four words. Write them in the left column.*

Your Words

1. _____
2. _____
3. _____
4. _____

Your Partner's Words

1. _____
2. _____
3. _____
4. _____

C | *PAIRS: Listen to your partner's words. Write them in the right column.*

EXERCISE 3: Listen for Differences: /y/ vs. /dʒ/, /ʃ/ vs. /tʃ/

🎧 **A |** *Listen and repeat the words.*

1. **a.** Yale   **b.** jail
2. **a.** wash   **b.** watch
3. **a.** sheep   **b.** cheap
4. **a.** ships   **b.** chips
5. **a.** share   **b.** chair
6. **a.** yes   **b.** Jess
7. **a.** catch   **b.** cash
8. **a.** mush   **b.** much

🎧 **B |** *Listen again. Which word do you hear? Circle **a** or **b**.*

C | *GROUPS: Say a word from Part A. Pronounce the consonants carefully. Your classmates will say **a** or **b**.*

EXERCISE 4: Short Conversations

A | *Listen to the conversations.*

1. **MR. JESTER:** George, did they fix my jet yet?

   GEORGE: Yes, Mr. Jester—yesterday.

2. **ALICE:** Where did you go in July?

   ELENA: You know—Juneau . . . Juneau, Alaska.

3. **MOM:** How much mush did the baby eat?

   DAD: Not much. Bring some cheese. She's a cheese lover.

4. **MOM:** You have to stay in college. You have to graduate!

   EVA: Why? Bill Gates didn't graduate! He started Microsoft, and now he's a billionaire[1].

5. **HUSBAND:** Why don't you wash the dishes, and I'll watch TV?

   WIFE: I have a much better idea. You wash, and I'll watch.

6. **LUIS:** What does the orange jelly taste like?

   ANNA: Peaches, I think. The red jelly tastes like cherries.

B | *PAIRS: Practice the conversations. Take turns.*

STEP 3 COMMUNICATION PRACTICE

EDUCATION

EXERCISE 5: Why Is College Important?

A | *Listen and repeat. Make sure you understand all the words.*

1. successful
2. producer (of a movie)
3. expensive
4. tuition
5. family income
6. debts
7. citizen
8. earn
9. Midwest

---

[1] billionaire: *someone with $1,000,000,000 (or more)*

B | *Listen to the recording. Then read the statements below. Write **T** (**True**) or **F** (**False**). Then compare your answers with a partner.*

_____ **1.** Bill Gates started his own company.

_____ **2.** Quentin Tarantino is a college graduate.*

_____ **3.** It's expensive to go to college in the United States.

_____ **4.** In 2010, there were more than 90 million students in U.S. colleges and universities.

Natural English box:

> ***Natural English**
>
> The word *graduate* has two pronunciations.
>
> When *graduate* is a noun or adjective, say /ˈɡrædʒuwət/.
>
> > He is a college graduate.
>
> When *graduate* is a verb, say /ˈɡrædʒuweyt/.
>
> > I'll get a good job after I graduate.

C | *Listen to the recording. Why is having a college education important? Check (✓) the reasons you hear. Then compare your answers with a partner.*

_____ **1.** College graduates get better jobs.

_____ **2.** College graduates are healthier.

_____ **3.** College graduates have fewer children.

_____ **4.** College graduates know more about the world.

_____ **5.** College graduates take longer vacations.

EXERCISE 6: Your Turn

GROUPS: Work with your classmates to answer the questions.

1. Is it hard to get into a college in your country?

2. Is college expensive, inexpensive,[1] or free in your country?

3. Is it easy for college graduates to find jobs in your country?

4. Do you think a college education is important? Why or why not?

STEP 4 EXTENDED PRACTICE

Accuracy Practice *Listen again to Exercises 1A and 2A on pages 59 and 60. Then record the words.*

Fluency Practice *Record your answers to the questions in Exercise 6.*

---

[1] inexpensive: *doesn't cost a lot of money*

UNIT 12 /r/ <u>r</u>oad and /l/ <u>l</u>ove

STEP 1 PRESENTATION

The pictures show you how to say the sounds /r/ and /l/.

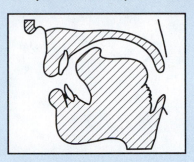

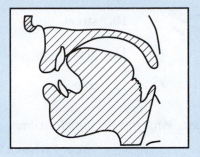

<u>r</u>oad /r/

Turn the tip of your tongue up and back. Then move the tip of your tongue down. Don't touch the top of your mouth when the tongue moves down.

<u>l</u>ove /l/

Put the tip of your tongue behind your top teeth.

Spellings for /r/	Spellings for /l/
Common <u>r</u>ed, <u>r</u>oad a<u>rr</u>ive, so<u>rr</u>y	**Common** <u>l</u>ook, <u>l</u>ove, po<u>l</u>ice he<u>ll</u>o, ye<u>ll</u>ow
Other <u>wr</u>ong <u>wr</u>ist, (*w* is silent)	

63

EXERCISE 1: Words with /r/

A | *Listen and repeat the words.*

1. right
2. rain
3. room
4. river
5. arrive
6. sorry

7. parent
8. brown
9. problem
10. street
11. green
12. tree

B | *Choose four words. Write them in the left column.*

Your Words

1. _____
2. _____
3. _____
4. _____

Your Partner's Words

1. _____
2. _____
3. _____
4. _____

C | *PAIRS: Listen to your partner's words. Write them in the right column.*

EXERCISE 2: Words with /l/

A | *Listen and repeat the words.*

1. light
2. look
3. lemon

4. late
5. television
6. family

7. color
8. ceiling
9. clock

10. slow
11. blue
12. please

B | *Choose four words from Part A. Write them in the left column.*

Your Words   **Your Partner's Words**

1. _____   1. _____

2. _____   2. _____

3. _____   3. _____

4. _____   4. _____

C | *PAIRS: Listen to your partner's words. Write them in the right column.*

EXERCISE 3: Listen for Differences: /r/ vs. /l/

A | *Listen and repeat the words.*

1. **a.** road   **b.** load
2. **a.** wrong   **b.** long
3. **a.** fry   **b.** fly
4. **a.** corrects   **b.** collects
5. **a.** arrive   **b.** alive
6. **a.** pray   **b.** play
7. **a.** pirate   **b.** pilot
8. **a.** right   **b.** light

B | *Listen again. Which word do you hear? Circle **a** or **b**.*

C | *PAIRS: Read a sentence to your partner. Choose one of the bold words to complete the sentence. Your partner will tell you which word you said.*

1. Why is this so **wrong / long?**

2. The teacher **corrects / collects** our homework every day.

3. They **pray / play** here.

4. Do you want to meet a **pirate / pilot?**

EXERCISE 4: Differences in Meaning

A | *Listen and repeat the sentences.*

1. **a.** Larry is <u>collecting</u> the papers.   **b.** Larry is <u>correcting</u> the papers.

2. **a.** The children are <u>praying</u>.   **b.** The children are <u>playing</u>.

3. **a.** Roland is a <u>pirate</u>.   **b.** Roland is a <u>pilot</u>.

   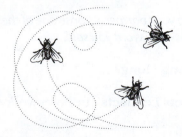

4. **a.** Those are <u>fries</u>.   **b.** Those are <u>flies</u>.

B | *Listen again. Which sentence do you hear? Circle **a** or **b**.*

C | *PAIRS: Say a sentence from Part A. Your partner will point to the correct sentence, **a** or **b**.*

TRUTH or LIES?

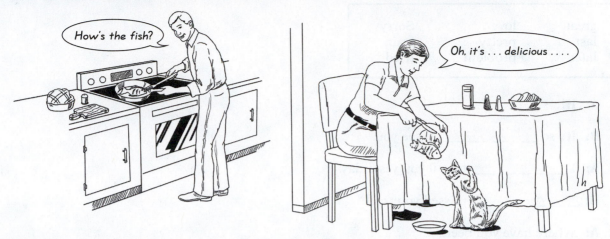

EXERCISE 5: Thirty Lies a Day

A | *Listen to the conversation. Make sure you understand all the words.*

RUTH: Do you think you're a truthful person?

LEILA: Of course! I always tell the truth!

RUTH: Well, I read an interesting article about lying.

LEILA: What did it say?

RUTH: The article said most people tell about 30 lies a day.

LEILA: Thirty? That's a lot. Well, I don't lie.

RUTH: Oh, really? Fifteen minutes ago, you told Tom you loved his new haircut.

But when he left, you told me he looked awful.

LEILA: Yes, but I didn't want to hurt his feelings.

RUTH: But you still lied. You didn't tell the truth.

LEILA: OK, maybe you're right. In fact, I remember another lie I told today.

In class, I said I left my homework at home. But the truth is, I didn't do it.

B | *PAIRS: Practice the conversation. Use the lines to help you group words together.*

EXERCISE 6: Common Lies

Listen to seven common lies. Then complete each sentence with a word from the box. Compare your answers with a partner.

great	love	Sorry
last	pretty	train
later	problem	tried

1. **A:** Hi!

   B: It's so _____ to see you.

2. **A:** I _____ to call you yesterday.

   B: _____ I missed your call.

3. **A:** Where have you been?

   B: The _____ was late.

4. **A:** I emailed you _____ week, but you didn't answer.

   B: I'm having a _____ with my email.

5. **A:** Hi, can we talk?

   B: Not right now, but I'll call you back _____.

6. **A:** Do you like my dress?

   B: It's _____.

7. **A:** I love you.

   B: I _____ you too.

EXERCISE 7: Your Turn

A | *Listen as your teacher reads the situations and conversations aloud. In each conversation, you can choose from three answers. One answer is a lie (L). One answer is the truth (T). One answer is not a lie or the truth (N). Circle **L**, **T**, or **N** next to each answer.*

1. **SITUATION:** Your friend is wearing a bright green shirt. The shirt looks awful.

   FRIEND: How does this shirt look?

   YOU: (*L / T / N*) **a.** It's great! Really nice!

   (*L / T / N*) **b.** Awful! Your face looks green!

   (*L / T / N*) **c.** Is it new?

2. **SITUATION:** You cheated on a test. You looked at a classmate's answers and wrote them down. The next day, your teacher gave you your test back.

    TEACHER: You did very well on this test.

        YOU: (*L / T / N*)   **a.** Oh, that's great!

                (*L / T / N*)   **b.** I studied really hard for this test.

                (*L / T / N*)   **c.** I cheated. I looked at my classmate's test.

3. **SITUATION:** You're late for work because you didn't want to get out of bed.

    BOSS: You're late. What happened?

        YOU: (*L / T / N*)   **a.** Sorry. I didn't feel like getting up on time.*

                (*L / T / N*)   **b.** Sorry. The train was late.

                (*L / T / N*)   **c.** Sorry. Here's the report you wanted.

---

*Natural English

Use *feel like* + verb + *-ing* to show you want to do something.
Use *don't feel like* + verb + *-ing* to show you don't want to do something.
Stress *feel* more than *like*.

  I *féel like going* out.

  I *don't féel like watching* TV.

B | *PAIRS: Compare your answers to the questions in Part A. Then practice the conversations. Read each conversation three times, each time with a different answer. Take turns.*

STEP 4   EXTENDED PRACTICE

🎧 🎤 **Accuracy Practice**   *Listen again to Exercises 1A and 2A on page 64. Then record the words.*

🎤 **Fluency Practice**   *Record a short story about a lie you told in the past.*

The pictures show you how to say the sounds /m/, /n/, and /ŋ/.

<u>m</u>outh /m/

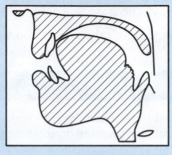

<u>n</u>ose /n/

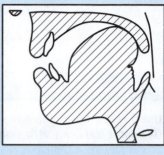

si<u>ng</u> /ŋ/

Spellings for /m/	Spellings for /n/	Spellings for /ŋ/
Common <u>m</u>ake, Ji<u>m</u> su<u>mm</u>er	**Common** <u>n</u>ow, ru<u>n</u> di<u>nn</u>er	**Common** bri<u>ng</u>, wro<u>ng</u>
Other com~~b~~, bom~~b~~ (*b* is silent)	**Other** forei~~g~~n, si~~g~~n (*g* is silent) ~~k~~now, ~~k~~nife (*k* is silent)	**Other** ba<u>n</u>k, thi<u>n</u>k

EXERCISE 1: Words with /m/ and /n/

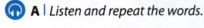 **A** | *Listen and repeat the words.*

/m/		/n/	
1. <u>m</u>eet	4. <u>M</u>om	7. <u>n</u>ight	10. ru<u>n</u>
2. co<u>m</u>e	5. <u>m</u>ovie	8. <u>kn</u>ife	11. to<u>n</u>ight
3. ho<u>m</u>e	6. re<u>m</u>e<u>m</u>ber	9. <u>n</u>i<u>n</u>e	12. agai<u>n</u>

B | *Choose four words from Part A. Write them in the left column.*

Your Words   **Your Partner's Words**

1. _____   1. _____

2. _____   2. _____

3. _____   3. _____

4. _____   4. _____

C | *PAIRS: Listen to your partner's words. Write them in the right column.*

EXERCISE 2: Words with /ŋ/ and /ŋg/

A | *Listen and repeat. Notice the difference between the /ŋ/ and /ŋg/ sounds.*

/ŋ/			/ŋg/
1. si<u>ng</u>	4. wro<u>ng</u>	7. fi<u>ng</u>er	10. si<u>ng</u>le
2. si<u>ng</u>er	5. goi<u>ng</u>	8. lo<u>ng</u>er	11. you<u>ng</u>er
3. wi<u>ng</u>	6. lo<u>ng</u>	9. stro<u>ng</u>er	12. a<u>ng</u>ry

B | *Choose four words. Write them in the left column.*

Your Words   **Your Partner's Words**

1. _____   1. _____

2. _____   2. _____

3. _____   3. _____

4. _____   4. _____

C | *PAIRS: Listen to your partner's words. Write them in the right column.*

EXERCISE 3: Join Words Together

A | *Listen and repeat the poem. Join final consonants to vowels.*

I'm leaving at night from L.A.,[1]

Arriving in Rome the next day.

I'll see some new faces.

I'll see some new places.

It's nice to be getting away.

B | *PAIRS: Practice the poem. Take turns.*

―――――――――
[1] L.A.: *an abbreviation for* Los Angeles; *pronounce the initials* /ɛléy/

TIME

EXERCISE 4: Good News

A | *Listen to the conversation.*

JOHN: Congratulations! I just heard the good news.

SIMONA: Thanks. I'm really excited.

JOHN: Have you told your family yet?

SIMONA: Just my sister. She lives in Minneapolis. It's 8:30 there, so she was just getting up when I called.

JOHN: You didn't call your mom and dad? They live in California, right?

SIMONA: Yes, they live in L.A. But it's only 6:30 there. I'll call them later. They're probably still sleeping.*

> ### *Natural English
>
> Use *probably* to mean "I think."
> Sometimes native-English speakers shorten *probably*. They say, "Probly."
>
> They're *probably* still sleeping.
>
> They're *probly* still sleeping.

B | *PAIRS: Practice the conversation. Take turns.*

C | *What do you think Simona's good news is? Share your guesses with your classmates.*

EXERCISE 5: What Time Is It?

A | *Listen and repeat. Make sure you understand all the words.*

1. area
2. west
3. Rocky Mountains
4. Midwest
5. Atlantic Ocean

B | *Listen to the recording. Then write the names of the time zones in the blanks at the top of the map. Write the times next to the cities.*

_____ _____ _____ _____

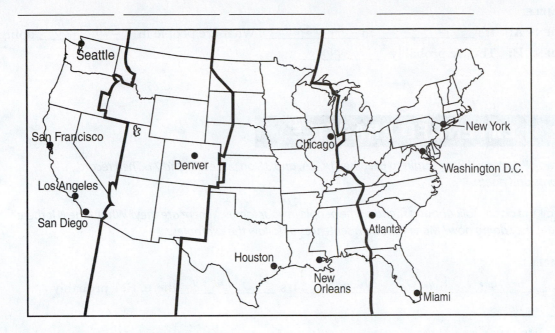

C | *PAIRS: Look at the map. Choose a time and two places. Ask and answer questions about the different time zones. Follow the example.*

EXAMPLE:

STUDENT A: It's _____ 9 A.M. _____ in _____ Denver _____. What time is it in _____ New York _____?

STUDENT B: It's _____ 11 A.M. _____.

EXERCISE 6: What in the World Are They Doing?

A | *Listen as your teacher reads the information about world times.*

4 A.M.	6 A.M.	7 A.M.	8 A.M.	12 noon	2 P.M.
• Los Angeles	• Chicago	• New York	• São Paulo, Brazil	• Madrid	• Istanbul, Turkey
• San Diego	• Mexico City			• London	

3 P.M.	5 P.M.		8 P.M.	9 P.M.	10 P.M.
• Cairo, Egypt	• New Delhi, India		• Beijing	• Tokyo	• Sydney, Australia
• Moscow				• Seoul	

B | *Listen and repeat. Make sure you understand all the verbs.*

1. exercising at the gym
2. eating breakfast
3. eating lunch
4. getting ready for work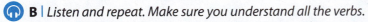
5. getting up
6. having dinner
7. sleeping
8. watching TV
9. working

C | *PAIRS: Look again at the information in Part A. Choose a time and two cities. Then use the information in Parts A and B to make a conversation. Follow the example.*

EXAMPLE:

STUDENT A: It's _____5 P.M._____ in ___New Delhi___. What are people in ___San Diego___ doing?

STUDENT B: They're probably _____sleeping_____.

STEP 4 EXTENDED PRACTICE

Accuracy Practice Listen again to Exercises 1A, 2A, and 3A on pages 70 and 71. Then record the words and poem.

Fluency Practice Talk about a friend or the people in your family. Where are they? What time is it there? What are they doing now? Make your own sentences or follow the examples.

EXAMPLES:

My ___brother___ lives in ___Chicago___. It's ___9 A.M.___ there. He's probably ___getting up___.

My ___mother and father___ live ___with me___. It's ___7 P.M.___. They're probably ___watching TV___.

UNIT 14   Word Endings: Plurals and Present Tense

STEP 1   PRESENTATION

–S endings can be pronounced as a syllable or a sound.

1. Pronounce the -s ending as a new syllable (/əz/ or /ɪz/) when the base word ends in an s-like sound (/s, z, ʃ, ʒ, tʃ, dʒ/).

    one ro<u>se</u> → two ro<u>ses</u>

2. Pronounce the -s ending as /s/ or /z/ when the base word does not end in an s-like sound.

    a. Use /s/ when the base word ends in /p, t, k, θ, f/.

    They wor<u>k</u>. → He wor<u>ks</u>.

    b. Use /z/ when the base word ends in a vowel sound or /b, d, g, ð, v, m, n, ŋ, r, l/.

    tr<u>ee</u> → two tr<u>ees</u>

Use –s endings for:

1. **Plural nouns:** two boy<u>s</u>, four book<u>s</u>
2. **Present tense (third-person singular):** She play<u>s</u> the piano.
3. **Possessives:** my mother'<u>s</u> house
4. **Contractions of *is* or *has*:** John'<u>s</u> late.

STEP 2   FOCUSED PRACTICE

EXERCISE 1: Plurals with /əz/ (or /ɪz/)

🎧 **A |** *Listen and repeat the word pairs.*

Singular	Plural	Singular	Plural
1. bus	buses	**5.** box	boxes
2. dress	dresses	**6.** rose	roses
3. dish	dishes	**7.** orange	oranges
4. language	languages	**8.** watch	watches

🎧 **B |** *Listen again to the word pairs. Tap the number of syllables in each word with your finger. Then underline each syllable.*

EXAMPLE:

   bus   bus es

75

EXERCISE 2: Plurals with /s/ and /z/

A | *Listen and repeat the word pairs.*

Singular	/s/ Plural	Singular	/z/ Plural
1. cat	cats	5. dog	dogs
2. map	maps	6. boy	boys
3. bike	bikes	7. bed	beds
4. student	students	8. pencil	pencils

B | *Choose four word pairs. Write them in the left column.*

Your Word Pairs

1. _____
2. _____
3. _____
4. _____

Your Partner's Word Pairs

1. _____
2. _____
3. _____
4. _____

C | *PAIRS: Listen to your partner's word pairs. Write them in the right column.*

EXERCISE 3: Apply the Rule

Listen to the plural words. Is the plural ending a new syllable (/əz/ or /ɪz/) or a final consonant sound (/s/ or /z/)? Write the plural words in the correct columns.

1. noses	4. horses	7. jobs	10. dishes
2. eyes	5. legs	8. towns	11. weeks
3. nights	6. ages	9. lunches	12. offices

New Syllable (/əz/ or /ɪz/)

noses _____ _____

_____ _____

_____ _____

Final Consonant Sound (/s/ or /z/)

_____ _____

_____ _____

_____ _____

EXERCISE 4: Conversation

Listen and repeat the conversation. Group words together and speak smoothly. Words with -s endings are underlined.

BILL: I just met Anna Ross. She's great! Does she have a boyfriend?

DRAGAN: Why? Are you interested?

BILL: No, not really. Well, maybe a little.

DRAGAN: I don't think she goes out much. She works a lot. She teaches dance at Steps Studio.

CHORES AND GLAMOROUS JOBS

EXERCISE 5: Chores

A | *Listen and repeat. Make sure you understand all the words.*

1. washing / does the dishes
2. groceries
3. cut the lawn
4. paying bills
5. bloggers

B | *Listen to the recording. Complete the sentences with the words you hear.*

Chores are part of life. Everybody has chores. Chores are boring jobs that you have to do.

Washing _____ is a chore. Shopping for groceries is a chore. Cutting the lawn is a
        1.

chore. Paying _____ can be a chore. Some people like doing some chores, but not
        2.

others. Listen to what two _____ had to say about their chores.
        3.

Blogger 1 wrote: I don't mind washing the car. _____ easy, and the car always
        4.

looks good. But I don't like cleaning the inside of the car. Blogger 2 wrote: I don't mind making

dinner. But, I really don't like washing dishes. So I cook, and my husband _____
        5.

the dishes.

Natural English

Use *don't mind* + verb + *-ing* to show that something doesn't bother you.

    I *don't mind washing* the car. It's easy and fun.

Native speakers may shorten *don't* in this expression.

    I *don'* mind taking out the garbage.

EXERCISE 6: Your Turn

A | *Listen as your teacher reads the list of chores in the chart. Make sure you understand all the words.*

Chore	Who does this chore in your home?	Do you like doing this chore? Write *1*, *2*, or *3*: 1: I don't mind doing this chore. 2: I don't like doing this chore. 3: I never do this chore.
wash the dishes		
cook		
do the laundry		
clean		
pay bills		
walk the dog		
take out the garbage		
wash the car		

B | *Read the questions in the chart and write your answers in the correct columns.*

C | *PAIRS: Tell your partner about your chart. Use your own words or follow the example.*

EXAMPLE: I don't like _____cleaning my room_____ at all. It's pretty messy. But I don't mind

_____cooking_____. Sometimes I cook on the weekends. My roommate

usually _____washes the dishes_____.

EXERCISE 7: Glamorous Jobs

Most people think sports stars and actors have glamorous jobs. Glamorous jobs are exciting. People with glamorous jobs are usually famous. They often make a lot of money.

A | *Listen and repeat the verb phrases. Make sure you understand all the words.*

1. **Basketball**

    a. lift weights

    b. shoot baskets

    c. guard other players

    d. pass the ball

2. Acting

    a. memorize lines

    b. read scripts

    c. wear costumes

    d. work with a director

3. President

    a. give speeches

    b. live in the White House

    c. meet with other leaders

    d. travel to other countries

B | *Use the verb phrases from Part A to answer each question. Use the present **-s** ending with each verb. How is the ending pronounced?*

    1. What does a basketball star do?

He shoots baskets.

(continued)

2. What does an actress do?

_____

_____

_____

_____

3. What does the president do?

_____

_____

_____

_____

C | *PAIRS: Take turns asking and answering the questions in Part B.*

Accuracy Practice *Listen again to Exercises 1A and 2A on pages 75 and 76. Then record the word pairs.*

Fluency Practice *Review Exercises 5B and 6A on pages 77 and 78. Then record your answers to the questions.*

1. What chores do you do?

2. Which chores do you like?

3. Which ones don't you like?

UNIT 15 Word Endings: Past Tense

STEP 1 PRESENTATION

The regular past tense -ed ending can be pronounced as a syllable or as a sound.

1. Pronounce the -ed ending as a new syllable (/əd/ or /ɪd/) when the base verb ends in /t/ or /d/.

   star**t** → It start**ed** at 7:00 P.M.

2. Pronounce the -ed ending as /t/ or /d/ when the base verb ends in other sounds.

   a. Use /t/ when the base verb ends in /p, k, θ, f, s, ʃ, tʃ/.

   wor**k** → They wor**ked**.

   b. Use /d/ when the base verb ends in a vowel sound or /b, g, ð, v, z, ʒ, dʒ, m, n, ŋ, r, l/.

   sho**w** → He sho**wed** it to me.

STEP 2 FOCUSED PRACTICE

EXERCISE 1: Past Tense Endings

A | *Listen and repeat the word pairs.*

/əd/ or /ɪd/	/t/	/d/
1. start—started	5. talk—talked	9. answer—answered
2. wait—waited	6. watch—watched	10. close—closed
3. need—needed	7. stop—stopped	11. enjoy—enjoyed
4. invite—invited	8. kiss—kissed	12. open—opened

B | *Choose four word pairs. Write them in the left column.*

Your Word Pairs	Your Partner's Word Pairs
1. _____	1. _____
2. _____	2. _____
3. _____	3. _____
4. _____	4. _____

C | *PAIRS: Listen to your partner's word pairs. Write them in the right column.*

EXERCISE 2: Apply the Rule

Is the past ending of these verbs a new syllable (/əd/ or /ɪd/) or is it a final consonant sound (/t/ or /d/)? Write the past tense form of each verb in the correct column.

1. decided
2. danced
3. visited
4. worked
5. ended
6. laughed
7. pushed
8. shouted
9. wanted
10. rained
11. painted
12. lived

New Syllable (/əd/ or /ɪd/)

decided

_____

_____

_____

_____

Final Consonant Sound (/t/ or /d/)

_____

_____

_____

_____

_____

_____

EXERCISE 3: Conversation

A | *Listen to the conversation.*

RANIA: You're late. Did you miss the bus?

MARTIN: No. I waited an hour, but it didn't come.

RANIA: How did you get here?

MARTIN: I walked. It took me an hour. You drive to school, right?

RANIA: No. I take the subway.

MARTIN: How long does it take to get here?

RANIA: Not long. Maybe 15 minutes. Is there a subway stop near you?

MARTIN: No. It's faster to take the bus—when it comes.

B | *PAIRS: Practice the conversation. Follow the intonation lines. Join words together and speak smoothly.*

C | *PAIRS: Talk about how you got to class today.*

THE BUS DRIVER

EXERCISE 4: Prepare to Listen

A | *Listen and repeat. Make sure you understand all the words.*

1. bus terminal

2. collect

3. arrest

4. passenger

5. (to) head north

6. charge someone money

7. fare

Natural English

Use the word *fare* to talk about the price of transportation. In *bus fare*, *air fare* and *cab fare*, the first word is stressed more strongly. It is also pronounced on a higher note.

　　　bús
The 　　fare is $3.00.

Áir
　　fares are higher during busy travel times.

　　　　　　cáb
How much is the 　　fare to the airport?

B | *Listen and repeat the past tense verbs.*

1. arrested

2. charged

3. collected

4. crossed

5. headed

6. looked

7. picked

8. repeated

9. returned

10. started

11. stopped

12. turned

13. walked

C | *Is the past ending of the verbs in Part B a new syllable (/əd/ or /ɪd/) or is it a final consonant sound (/t/ or /d/)? Write each verb in the correct column.*

New Syllable (/əd/ or /ɪd/)		Final Consonant Sound (/t/ or /d/)	
arrested	_____	_____	_____
_____	_____	_____	_____
_____	_____	_____	_____
		_____	_____

EXERCISE 5: The Bus Ride

A | *Listen to the story. Then write the past tense verbs you hear in the blanks. Some verbs may be used more than once.*

A 20-year-old man _____*walked*_____ into a bus terminal in New York City. He got on a bus
 1.
and sat down in the driver's seat. He _____ the bus and drove out of the terminal.
 2.
He _____ north for the George Washington Bridge. On the way, he
 3.
_____ at bus stops and _____ up passengers. He
 4. **5.**
_____ them 50 cents for the ride. He _____ the bridge into New
 6. **7.**
Jersey and _____ in Fort Lee. Then he _____ around and
 8. **9.**
_____ to New York. He _____ his trip several times and
 10. **11.**
_____ $88 in fares.
 12.

Finally, the police _____ him. They said he _____ just like a bus
 13. **14.**
driver. His passengers said he was a good driver. They were surprised he wasn't a real bus driver.

B | *PAIRS: Number the events in the order they happened within the story.*

_____ got onto a bus, <u>start</u> the engine

_____ <u>pick up</u> passengers

_____ <u>return</u> to New York City

_____ <u>decide</u> to drive to New Jersey

__*1*__ <u>walk</u> into the bus terminal

_____ <u>charge</u> 50 cents for the ride

_____ <u>arrest</u> the man

_____ <u>repeat</u> the trip several times

C | *PAIRS: Tell the story of the bus driver. Make sentences with the underlined verbs in Part B.*

EXERCISE 6: Predictions

A | *Listen to the predictions¹ about the bus driver.*

1. The man went to jail.
2. The man paid a fine.²
3. The police let the man go.
4. The man took a class and became a bus driver.

B | *GROUPS: Why do you think the man drove the bus? What do you think happened to him? Write your own prediction. Then share it with the class.*

STEP 4   EXTENDED PRACTICE

Accuracy Practice   Listen again to Exercise 1A on page 82. Then record the word pairs.

Fluency Practice   Look at the predictions in Exercise 6A. What do you think happened to the man after the police arrested him? Record your answer.

---

¹ predictions: *sentences that say something is going to happen;* ² fine: *money you pay for doing something wrong*

Consonant Groups

A consonant group is two or more consonant sounds together in a word. There are many consonant groups in English.

1. **Consonant Groups with /r/ and /l/**

   green   blue

   front   play

2. **Consonant Groups with /s/**

   snow   street

   stop   spring

3. **Consonant Groups with /w/**

   quiet   swim

   language   twelve

4. **Final Consonant Groups**

   build   month

   test   fix (/ks/)

5. **Consonant Groups Made of Grammatical Endings**

   stopped /pt/   listened /nd/

   skirts /rts/   finished /ʃt/

This is how to join words with final consonants to the next word.

1. **Final consonant + vowel:** Join the words.

   clean air

2. **Final consonant + same consonant:** Make one long consonant.

   I want to go.

3. **Final consonant + different consonant:** Keep the final consonant short. Then say the next sound clearly.

   night classes

STEP 2 FOCUSED PRACTICE

EXERCISE 1: Consonant Groups with /r/ and /l/

A | *Listen and repeat the words.*

1. <u>br</u>own
2. <u>pr</u>ice
3. <u>bl</u>ack
4. <u>cl</u>imb
5. <u>dr</u>ess
6. <u>gr</u>ass
7. <u>dr</u>ive
8. <u>thr</u>ee
9. <u>cl</u>othes
10. <u>fl</u>owers
11. <u>cr</u>y
12. <u>pr</u>oblem

B | *Choose four words. Write them in the left column.*

Your Words	Your Partner's Words
1. _____	1. _____
2. _____	2. _____
3. _____	3. _____
4. _____	4. _____

C | *PAIRS: Listen to your partner's words. Write them in the right column.*

EXERCISE 2: Consonant Groups with /s/

A | *Listen and repeat the words.*

1. <u>sk</u>y
2. <u>sk</u>ate
3. <u>st</u>ay
4. <u>sp</u>eak
5. <u>sm</u>ile
6. <u>st</u>eam
7. <u>spr</u>ing
8. <u>sm</u>ell
9. <u>st</u>op
10. <u>sn</u>ake
11. <u>sn</u>ow
12. <u>sw</u>im

B | *Choose four words. Write them in the left column.*

Your Words	Your Partner's Words
1. _____	1. _____
2. _____	2. _____
3. _____	3. _____
4. _____	4. _____

C | *PAIRS: Listen to your partner's words. Write them in the right column.*

EXERCISE 3: Consonant Groups with /w/

A | *Listen and repeat the words.*

1. question
2. quickly
3. quarter

4. quietly
5. quiz
6. Gwen

7. language
8. twins
9. between

10. twelve
11. swing
12. sweater

B | *Choose four words. Write them in the left column.*

Your Words

1. _____
2. _____
3. _____
4. _____

Your Partner's Words

1. _____
2. _____
3. _____
4. _____

C | *PAIRS: Listen to your partner's words. Write them in the right column.*

EXERCISE 4: Hearing Consonant Groups

A | *Listen and repeat the words.*

One Consonant Sound   **Consonant Group**

1. **a.** sure   **b.** shirt
2. **a.** bug   **b.** bugs
3. **a.** love   **b.** loved
4. **a.** wash   **b.** washed
5. **a.** sing   **b.** sink
6. **a.** animal   **b.** animals
7. **a.** like   **b.** liked
8. **a.** bell   **b.** belt
9. **a.** Stan   **b.** stand
10. **a.** watch   **b.** watched

B | *PAIRS: Say a word. Your partner will point to the correct word, **a** or **b**.*

NATURE

EXERCISE 5: Prepare to Listen

A | *Listen and repeat. Make sure you understand all the words.*

1. scientist
2. expert
3. wild (animals)
4. chimpanzee (chimp)
5. national park
6. protect

B | *Listen and repeat the phrases and sentences. Join final consonants to vowels.*

1. an expert
2. She's an expert.
3. in Africa
4. interested in Africa*
5. worries about
6. She worries about children.
7. as a child
8. loved animals

---

*Natural English

Many Americans shorten the word *interested*. They pronounce it as a three-syllable word.

I'm *intrested* in Africa.

When you speak, you can use the shorter pronunciation or the longer pronunciation, with four syllables.

I'm *interested* in sports.

EXERCISE 6: Jane Goodall

A | *Read along as you listen to the story. Consonant groups are underlined.*

Tanzania

1. Jane Goodall is a <u>Br</u>itish scienti<u>st</u>.
2. She's an e<u>xp</u>ert on the life of wi<u>ld</u> <u>ch</u>impa<u>nz</u>ees.
3. As a <u>ch</u>i<u>ld</u>, Goodall lov<u>ed</u> animal<u>s</u> and was interested in Africa.
4. In 1960, Goodall we<u>nt</u> to a national pa<u>rk</u> in Tanzania, Africa.
5. She <u>st</u>udied the <u>ch</u>impa<u>nz</u>ees there for 45 year<u>s</u>.
6. Goodall now wo<u>rks</u> to <u>pr</u>ote<u>ct</u> nature and wi<u>ld</u> animal<u>s</u>.
7. She worries about <u>ch</u>il<u>dr</u>en who <u>gr</u>ow up in cities, away <u>fr</u>om nature.
8. She believ<u>es</u> that city life is <u>d</u>angerous to <u>ch</u>il<u>dr</u>en's heal<u>th</u>.
9. She says young <u>ch</u>il<u>dr</u>en need <u>gr</u>ass, <u>sk</u>y, bu<u>gs</u>, and <u>fl</u>ower<u>s</u> to <u>gr</u>ow up heal<u>thy</u>.

B | *PAIRS: Answer the questions. You can use phrases and sentences from the story. Pronounce consonant groups carefully.*

1. Who is Jane Goodall?
2. What did Goodall study in Africa?
3. What does Goodall do now?
4. Why does Goodall worry about children who grow up in cities?

EXERCISE 7: Your Turn

GROUPS: Take turns asking and answering the questions.

1. Did you grow up in the city or in the country?
2. Do you like city life or country life?
3. Do you like to be outdoors in nature? Why or why not?
4. Do you like to go to parks? What do you do there?
5. Goodall says city life is dangerous to children's health. Do you agree?

STEP 4   EXTENDED PRACTICE

Accuracy Practice *Listen again to Exercises 1A, 2A, and 3A on pages 88 and 89. Then record the words.*

Fluency Practice *Record your answers to the questions in Exercise 7.*

STRESS, RHYTHM, AND INTONATION

UNIT	PRONUNCIATION FOCUS	COMMUNICATION FOCUS
17	Stress, Rhythm and Intonation Overview	Cities and Countries
18	Strong Stress and Secondary Stress in Words	Snacks
19	Weak Syllables in Words	Learning from Wild Animals
20	Stress in Compound Nouns and Numbers	Around the Neighborhood
21	Strong Words and Weak Words in Sentences	A Place to Live
22	Highlighting Information	Correcting Information
23	Common Weak Words	Abilities
24	Contractions	Dreams
25	Word Groups	Planning a Party
26	Joining Final Sounds to Beginning Sounds	Volunteering
27	Rising and Falling Intonation	Dating Customs
28	Other Uses of Intonation	Checking Information

Stress, Rhythm, and Intonation Overview

STEP 1 PRESENTATION

Stressing the correct syllable in a word helps listeners understand what you've said. Using rhythm and intonation correctly helps listeners know what words go together and what information is important.

Stress

1. Syllables

Syllables are parts of words. You can tap the syllables of a word with your finger.

car → 1 syllable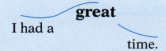

airport → 2 syllables

apartment → 3 syllables

2. Syllables and Stress

a**part**ment   **stu**dent   a**gree**

The stressed syllable is the most important syllable in a word. Listeners use the stressed syllable to identify words. Stressed syllables are long and loud. Unstressed syllables are short.

Rhythm

1. Word Groups

I'm moving to Miami Beach. It's always warm in Miami.

Word groups are phrases. Your English will be clearer if you say the words in a phrase together.

2. Important Words

I'm **sor**ry.

Important words are long and loud. Important words often have a high pitch (a musical note).

Intonation

I had a **great** time.

Intonation is the music of your voice. English has higher high notes and lower low notes than some other languages. Good intonation makes your English clearer.

STEP 2 FOCUSED PRACTICE

EXERCISE 1: Syllables

 A | *Listen to the words. Tap the syllables with your finger.*

1. parks
2. beach
3. beaches

4. popular
5. city
6. country

7. quiet
8. expensive
9. inexpensive

 B | *Listen and repeat the words. Count the syllables in each word. Write the number in the blank.*

1. church _____
2. sidewalk _____
3. hometown _____
4. university _____
5. traffic _____

6. entertainment _____
7. museum _____
8. restaurants _____
9. bridge _____
10. theater _____

EXERCISE 2: Stressed Syllables

A | *Listen and repeat. Make the stressed syllable in each word long and loud.*

1. **peo**ple
2. **o**cean
3. **tra**ffic
4. **tour**ist

5. to**mor**row
6. Sep**tem**ber
7. im**por**tant
8. de**li**cious

9. po**lice**
10. ar**rive**
11. to**day**
12. to**night**

B | *Listen to the words in the box. Place a stress mark over the stressed syllable in each word. Then write the words in the correct column.*

vacátion	enough	crowded	invite	December	noisy

First Syllable

_____

_____

Middle Syllable

vacation

_____

Last Syllable

_____

_____

EXERCISE 3: Word Groups

A | *Listen to the story.*

1. Cape Cod is a popular vacation spot on the East Coast.
2. It's in the state of Massachusetts.
3. Cape Cod looks like an arm, reaching out and up.
4. It has beautiful beaches.
5. The seafood is also great, especially the lobsters.
6. In the summer, Cape Cod is crowded.
7. There's a lot of traffic.
8. At the end of summer, the tourists go home.
9. Then the restaurants aren't crowded, and the beaches are quiet.
10. That's my favorite time in Cape Cod.

B | *PAIRS: Take turns asking and answering the questions. You can use phrases or sentences from the story. Group words together.*

1. Where is Cape Cod?
2. What is Cape Cod like in the summer?
3. When does the speaker like Cape Cod the best? Why?

EXERCISE 4: Conversation and Intonation

A | *Listen to the conversation. The lines show intonation, the music of the sentences.*

ALICIA: I don't really like Chicago. It's too big.

ENRICO: Are you from a small town?

ALICIA: Uh-huh. What about you?*

ENRICO: Me too. But I like Chicago.

ALICIA: It's noisy. There are too many people. It's crowded.

ENRICO: Yeah, but it's exciting. My hometown is really boring.

---

*Natural English

What about you? asks your partner to give you similar information.

I'm from a small town. What about you? (Are you from a small town?)

I like big cities. What about you? (Do you like big cities?)

B | *PAIRS: Practice the conversation in Part A. Take turns.*

CITIES AND COUNTRIES

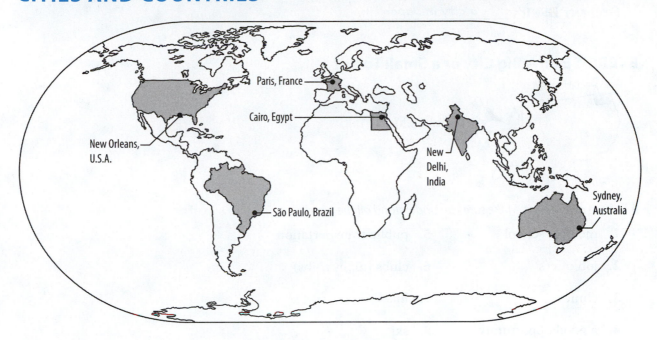

EXERCISE 5: Cities and Countries Around the World

A | *Listen to the names of cities and countries around the world. Which syllable is stressed? Put a stress mark (′) over the stressed syllable.*

1. Tókyo
2. Miami
3. Caracas
4. China
5. Chile
6. Atlanta
7. Canada
8. Korea
9. Amsterdam
10. Jamaica
11. London
12. Italy

B | *PAIRS: Look at the place names in Part A. Are they cities or countries? Write each name in the correct column. Then check your answers on page 99.*

Cities	Countries
Tokyo	

C | *PAIRS: Work with a new partner. Make a conversation about each place. Follow the example.*

EXAMPLE:

STUDENT A: What's _____ Tokyo _____?

STUDENT B: It's _____ a city in Japan _____.

EXERCISE 6: A Big City or a Small Town?

— Yakima, WA

— New York City, NY

A | *Listen and repeat. Make sure you understand all the words.*

1. medical school
2. job offers
3. clinic
4. a good opportunity
5. public transportation
6. clubs (night clubs)
7. hike
8. ski

B | *Read the sentences in the chart. Then listen to the descriptions of two cities—Yakima and New York. Which city does each sentence describe? Check (✓) the correct answer.*

	Yakima	New York
1. Fifty thousand people live here.		
2. It's expensive.		
3. There is good public transportation.		
4. Most people drive cars.		
5. Eight million people live here.		
6. There are many museums and clubs.		
7. It's less expensive.		
8. There are places to hike and ski.		

C | *GROUPS: Answer the questions.*

1. Which job should the woman take? Why?
2. Would you like to live in Yakima or New York City? Why?

Accuracy Practice *Listen again to Exercise 2A on page 95. Then record the words.*

Fluency Practice *Complete the sentences about yourself. Record your sentences.*

1. The name of my hometown is _____.
   (name of town)

2. I like these things about my hometown: _____

   _____.

3. I don't like these things about my hometown: _____

   _____.

Exercise 5B: Cities—Tokyo, Miami, Caracas, Atlanta, Amsterdam, London; **Countries**—China, Chile, Canada, Korea, Jamaica, Italy

UNIT 18 Strong Stress and Secondary Stress in Words

STEP 1 PRESENTATION

Stressing the correct syllable in a word helps listeners understand what you've said. Using rhythm and intonation correctly helps listeners know what words go together and what information is important.

Strong Stress in Words

péople   tomórrow   agáin

One syllable in each word has strong stress (′). Vowels with strong stress are l**o**ng.

1. **Strong Stress in Two-Syllable Nouns**

   páper   stúdent   déntist

   Most two-syllable nouns have strong stress on the first syllable.

2. **Strong Stress in Two-Syllable Verbs**

   ánswer   vísit   arríve   begín

   Some two-syllable verbs have strong stress on the first syllable. Many other two-syllable verbs have strong stress on the second syllable.

Strong Stress (′) and Secondary Stress (ˋ)

hómewòrk

hót dògs

Some words have strong stress (′) and secondary stress (ˋ). Strong stress is the most important stress. Say syllables with strong stress on a high pitch (musical note).

Say syllables with secondary stress on a lower pitch.

STEP 2 FOCUSED PRACTICE

EXERCISE 1: Strong Syllables

A | *Listen and repeat the words. Make the strong syllables long.*

1. d**o**ctor
2. ch**i**ldren
3. **o**pen
4. tod**ay**
5. pol**i**ce
6. ag**ai**n
7. tom**a**to
8. tom**o**rrow
9. rem**e**mber

B | *Choose four words from Part A. Write them in the left column.*

Your Words   **Your Partner's Words**

1. _____   1. _____

2. _____   2. _____

3. _____   3. _____

4. _____   4. _____

C | *PAIRS: Listen to your partner's words. Write them in the right column.*

EXERCISE 2: Hearing Strong Syllables

A | *Listen and repeat the words.*

1. próblem   4. healthy   7. arrive

2. tonight   5. salad   8. delicious

3. banana   6. potato   9. dessert

B | *Listen again. Which syllable has strong stress? Mark the strong syllable (ˈ) in each word.*

C | *PAIRS: Compare your answers. Then write each word in the correct column.*

Strong stress is on the . . .

first syllable	middle syllable	last syllable
problem	_____	_____
_____	_____	_____
_____	_____	_____

EXERCISE 3: Conversations

A | *Listen and repeat. Make sure you understand all the words.*

snacks   popcorn   delicious

B | *Listen and repeat the conversations.*

1. **ALICIA:** What kinds of snacks do you eat?
   YOUNG: I like fruit. It's not fattening.

2. **ZHANG:** Do you like popcorn?
   JINNY: Yes! It's delicious.

3. **LEE:** Do you like tacos?
   TATSUYA: I don't know. I've never tried them.

C | *PAIRS: Practice the conversations. Take turns.*

SNACKS

EXERCISE 4: Describing Food

A | *The words below describe food. Listen and repeat the words.*

1. gr**ea**sy
2. s**a**lty
3. sw**ee**t
4. del**i**cious

5. h**ea**lthy
6. unh**ea**lthy
7. h**ea**vy
8. f**a**ttening¹

9. l**i**ght
10. s**ou**r
11. sp**i**cy
12. b**i**tter²

B | *Listen to the rhyme. Complete the sentences with the words you hear.*

Lemons are _____, and sugar is _____.

Chilies are _____; they have lots of heat.³

Coffee is _____—it keeps you awake.

French fries are _____ but good with a steak.

Chips come in bags. They're a crisp, _____ treat.⁴

Natural English

The letters *ea* in *healthy, heat,* and *steak* all have different sounds.

In some words, *ea* is pronounced like the vowel in *bed*: *healthy, heavy, head, breakfast.*

In some words, *ea* is pronounced like the vowel in *see*: *heat, treat, tea.*

In some words, *ea* is pronounced like the vowel in *take*: *steak, break, great.*

---

¹ fattening: *likely to make you fat;* ² bitter: *having a strong taste, like chocolate without sugar;*
³ heat: *noun for* hot; ⁴ treat: *something good to eat*

EXERCISE 5: Snack Foods

A | Listen and repeat the words. Remember: Syllables with strong stress are long.

1. **a**pples
2. ban**a**nas
3. c**a**ndy bars
4. c**a**rrots
5. c**e**lery

6. c**oo**kies
7. Fr**e**nch fries
8. **i**ce cream
9. p**o**pcorn
10. p**ea**nuts

11. p**i**zza
12. pot**a**to chips
13. pr**e**tzels
14. r**a**isins
15. y**o**gurt

B | PAIRS: Talk about the snacks. Are they healthy or unhealthy? Some snacks may belong to both groups. Write the name of each snack on the correct line. Follow the example.

EXAMPLE:
STUDENT A: Are apples healthy?
STUDENT B: Yes, they are. They're healthy.

Healthy _apples_ _____

_____

Unhealthy _____

_____

EXERCISE 6: Your Turn

A | Write the names of some snacks you like to eat on the lines below.

_____

_____

_____

B | GROUPS: Tell your classmates about each snack. You can use your own words or those from Exercises 4A and 5A.

STEP 4 EXTENDED PRACTICE

Accuracy Practice Listen again to Exercises 1A and 4A on pages 100 and 102. Then record the words.

Fluency Practice Record a description of the snacks you like to eat.

Weak Syllables in Words

STEP 1   PRESENTATION

Learning how unstressed syllables are pronounced will help you understand English.

Weak Syllables

open   ar**rive**   **Ju**ly   **li**ons
/ə/   /ə/   /ə/   /ə/

The underlined syllables are weak syllables. They are not stressed.

Vowels in weak syllables are short. The vowels are usually pronounced /ə/ (and sometimes /ɪ/).

Final Weak Syllables

yellow   po**ta**to   **ha**ppy   **ta**xi
/ow/   /ow/   /iy/   /iy/

Final weak syllables spelled *-ow/-o* are pronounced /ow/.

Final weak syllables spelled *-y/-i* are pronounced /iy/.

STEP 2   FOCUSED PRACTICE

EXERCISE 1: Weak Syllables

A | *Listen and repeat the words. The spelling of each word shows how the weak vowel is pronounced. Make the strong syllable long and clear.*

1. ə**way**

    <u>away</u>

2. ə**gain**

    _____

3. **a**nəməl

    _____

4. d**o**ctər

    _____

5. f**a**məs

    _____

6. s**ea**sən

    _____

7. pr**o**bləm

    _____

8. tə**day**

    _____

9. **A**frəcə

    _____

B | *PAIRS: Write the correct spelling of the words in the blanks. Then practice saying the words. Use /ə/ for weak vowels.*

EXERCISE 2: Hearing Stress Patterns

A | *Listen and repeat the words. Notice the stress patterns.*

Stress Pattern	Example
1. **DÁ**da	**fá**mous
	/ə/
2. **DÁ**dada	**é**lephant
	/ə/ /ə/
3. da**DÁ**da	a**pár**tment
	/ə/ /ə/
4. da**DÁ**	Ju**lý**
	/ə/

B | *Listen to the words. Cross out the word with a different stress pattern.*

1. famous, garden, ~~today~~, chicken

2. thousand, kitchen, horses, arrive

3. tomorrow, beautiful, difficult, visitors

4. Alaska, dangerous, December, November

5. o'clock, police, again, zebra

EXERCISE 3: Conversations

A | *Listen to the conversations.*

1. **SAM:** What's a hippopotamus?
   JOSE: It's a wild animal.[1] It's big. It likes water.
   SAM: Where does it live?
   JOSE: In Africa.

2. **LYNN:** What's an eagle?
   LUPE: It's a very big bird. It's the national bird of the United States.
   LYNN: Where does it live?
   LUPE: In mountains and forests.

3. **BECCA:** What's a goat?
   TONY: It's a farm animal.[2]
   BECCA: Is it big?
   TONY: It's not too big. And it's not too small.

B | *PAIRS: Practice the conversations. Join words together.*

---

[1] wild animal: *an animal that lives in nature;* [2] farm animal: *an animal that is kept on a farm and used for food or money*

LEARNING FROM WILD ANIMALS

EXERCISE 4: Wild Animals

Natural English

Sometimes two vowel letters have two vowel sounds. Join the two vowels with a "y" sound.

One vowel sound:	Two vowel sounds:
eagle	li^{y}ons
goat	sci^{y}entists

A | *Listen and repeat the words.*

1. buffalo

2. cobras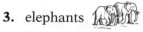

3. elephants

4. giraffes

5. gorillas

6. leopards

7. lions

8. ostriches

9. pandas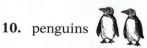

10. penguins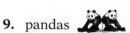

11. tigers

12. zebras

B | *PAIRS: Listen again. Mark the strong syllable (′) in each word. Follow the example.*

EXAMPLE: búffalo

EXERCISE 5: Daphne and Aisha

A | *Listen and repeat. Make sure you understand all the words.*

1. national park
2. orphaned
3. coconut oil

4. in the wild
5. female elephants
6. a broken heart

B | *CLASS: Listen to the recording. Then answer the questions.*

1. Why do orphaned baby elephants usually die?
2. Daphne found something that Aisha could eat. What was it?
3. How do baby elephants grow up in the wild?
4. Why did Daphne think Aisha "died of a broken heart"?
5. What lessons did scientists and zoos learn from Daphne and Aisha?

EXERCISE 6: The Animal Name Game

CLASS: Play this game with your classmates.

Student A: Think of an animal. You can use the animal names in Exercise 4A on page 106 or other animal names. Tell the class the first letter of the animal's name.

Class: Ask Student A questions about the animal. Try to guess the animal's name. Follow the example.

> **EXAMPLE:**
> **STUDENT A:** This animal's name starts with *c*.
> **STUDENT B:** Is it a wild animal?
> **STUDENT A:** No.
> **STUDENT C:** Is it a pet?
> **STUDENT A:** Yes.
> **STUDENT C:** Is it a cat?
> **STUDENT A:** Yes!

STEP 4 EXTENDED PRACTICE

Accuracy Practice Listen again to Exercises 1A and 3A on pages 104 and 105. Then record the words and sentences.

Fluency Practice Record descriptions of three wild animals. You can use ideas from Exercises 3A and 4A on pages 105 and 106.

Stress in Compound Nouns and Numbers

PRESENTATION

Compound nouns and some numbers have special stress patterns.

Compound Nouns (Noun + Noun)

drúgstòre   bús stòp   áirpòrt   bóokstòre

The first noun has strong stress and high pitch. The second noun has secondary stress and lower pitch.

Numbers

1. **-*teen* Numbers**

   13 thirtéen   14 fourtéen   15 fiftéen

   Pronounce the *t* of *-teen* as /t/, and stress *-teen*.

2. **Counting -*teen* Numbers**

   thirteen   **four**teen   **fif**teen

   Stress the first syllable of *-teen* numbers when you're counting.

3. **Years with -*teen* Numbers**

   1920 (n**i**neteen tw**e**nty)

   Stress the first syllable of the *-teen* number.

4. **-*ty* Numbers**

   30 th**í**rty   40 f**ó**rty   50 f**í**fty

   Stress the first syllable, and pronounce the *t* of *-ty* as a "fast" /d/. (Say /d/ fast.)

Numbers in Addresses

1. **Addresses with Two Numbers**

   22 (twenty-two) East Avenue

   Say the numbers in one group.

2. **Addresses with Three Numbers**

   535 (five thirty-five) First Street

   Say the first number. Then group the last two numbers together. Don't say *hundred*.

3. **Addresses with Four Numbers**

   5012 (fifty-twelve) Morningside Drive

   Say the numbers in two groups. Don't say *thousand*.

4. **Addresses with Zeros**

   100 (one hundred) Fifth Avenue   4000 (four thousand) First Avenue

   When zeros (0s) follow the first number, say *hundred* or *thousand*.

STEP 2   FOCUSED PRACTICE

EXERCISE 1: Compound Nouns

A | *Listen and repeat the compound nouns. Say the first word with strong stress and high pitch.*

1. sh**oe** store
2. p**o**st office
3. c**o**ffee shop
4. b**u**s stop
5. gr**o**cery store
6. p**i**zza place
7. dr**u**gstore
8. b**oo**kstore
9. s**i**dewalk

B | *Choose four compound nouns. Write them in the left column.*

Your Words	Your Partner's Words
1. _____	1. _____
2. _____	2. _____
3. _____	3. _____
4. _____	4. _____

C | *PAIRS: Listen to your partner's compound nouns. Write them in the right column.*

EXERCISE 2: Matching

A | *Listen and repeat the sentences and answers. Group words together.*

Sentences   **Answers**

___d___ 1. Where can I mail this package?   a. There's a shoe store on Main Street.

_____ 2. What do you call a long seat in   b. Yes, walk north to the next bus stop.
          a park?   The bus stops there.

_____ 3. I need some boots.   c. There's a grocery store two blocks away.

_____ 4. Where can I get a loaf of bread?   d. There's a post office on the next block.

_____ 5. I want to take a train   e. There's a bookstore on First Avenue.
          to Boston.
                                                        f. A park bench.
_____ 6. Can I take a bus to the airport?
                                                        g. The train station is downtown.
_____ 7. I want to buy a book for
          my mother.   h. Go to the drugstore.

_____ 8. I need to get some medicine.

B | *PAIRS: Make conversations by matching sentences and answers.*

EXERCISE 3: Listen for Differences: Numbers

A | *Listen and repeat the numbers.*

1. **a.** 13 (thirTEEN)   **b.** 30 (THIRty)

2. **a.** 14 (fourTEEN)   **b.** 40 (FORty)

3. **a.** 15 (fifTEEN)   **b.** 50 (FIFty)

4. **a.** 16 (sixTEEN)   **b.** 60 (SIXty)

5. **a.** 17 (sevenTEEN)   **b.** 70 (SEventy)

6. **a.** 18 (eighTEEN)   **b.** 80 (EIGHty)

7. **a.** 19 (nineTEEN)   **b.** 90 (NINEty)

B | *Listen again. Which word do you hear? Circle **a** or **b**.*

C | *GROUPS: Choose a number from Part A. Pronounce it carefully. Your classmates will say **a** or **b**.*

EXERCISE 4: Differences in Meaning

Listen. Complete the sentences with the numbers you hear.

1. **A:** When does the bus leave?

   B: It leaves at _____.

2. **A:** How old are your siblings?

   B: My brother is _____, and my sister is _____.

3. **A:** How many students are in your English class?

   B: _____.

4. **A:** How many students are in your math class?

   B: _____.

5. **A:** How many candles do we need for the birthday cake?

   B: We need _____.

6. **A:** How many people came to your party?

   B: _____.

EXERCISE 5: Conversations

A | *Listen to the conversations.*

1. **MARTA:** How much is a movie ticket?

   CLERK: $12 (twelve dollars) for adults, $7.50 (seven fifty) for children.

2. **MARTA:** How much is a gallon of milk?

   CLERK: $4.09 (four oh nine).

3. **MARTA:** How much is this couch?

   CLERK: $999.99 (nine ninety-nine ninety-nine).

4. **MARTA:** How much is this birthday card?

   CLERK: $3.95 (three ninety-five).

B | *PAIRS: Practice the conversations. Take turns.*

AROUND THE NEIGHBORHOOD

EXERCISE 6: Numbers in Addresses

> **Natural English**
>
> Stress the last number in addresses.
>
> 52 (fifty-twó) East Avenue
>
> When the number *zero (0)* comes before the last number, pronounce the zero as *oh.*
>
> 604 (six-oh-fóur) Jackson Avenue

A | *Listen and repeat the Pleasant Valley addresses.*

1. 2012 (twenty twelve) Elm Street
2. 1102 (eleven-oh-two) Elm Street
3. 1000 (one thousand) Elm Street
4. 972 (nine seventy-two) Elm Street
5. 2061 (twenty sixty-one) Pine Road
6. 1015 (ten fifteen) Linda Lane
7. 900 (nine hundred) Linda Lane
8. 114 (one fourteen) West Avenue
9. 100 (one hundred) Main Street
10. 213 (two thirteen) Main Street
11. 110 (one ten) East Avenue
12. 52 (fifty-two) East Avenue

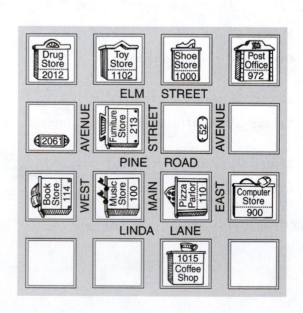

B | *PAIRS: Complete the maps of Pleasant Valley. Follow the steps.*

STUDENT A: Look at your map on page 162. Ask your partner what's at the addresses with blanks. Write the answers in the blanks.

STUDENT B: Look at your map on page 164. Find the addresses Student A asks about. Tell Student A the answers. Then ask Student A questions about the blank addresses on your map.

EXAMPLE:

STUDENT A: What's at 1102 Elm Street?   STUDENT B: _____The toy store._____

EXERCISE 7: Your Turn

A | *Living in a neighborhood with many stores and businesses is convenient.[1] Check (✓) the places in your neighborhood that are near your home. Then compare your answers with a partner.*

_____ **1.** gym   _____ **6.** park   _____ **11.** school

_____ **2.** pizzeria   _____ **7.** deli   _____ **12.** hardware store[2]

_____ **3.** bank   _____ **8.** drugstore   _____ **13.** grocery store

_____ **4.** hair salon   _____ **9.** movie theater _____ **14.** restaurant

_____ **5.** clothing store _____ **10.** shoe store   _____ **15.** cell phone store

B | *PAIRS: Answer the questions.*

1. Do you shop at businesses in your neighborhood? If so, which ones?
2. Do you think the businesses in your neighborhood are convenient?

STEP 4 EXTENDED PRACTICE

Accuracy Practice Listen again to Exercises 1A and 3A on pages 109 and 110. Then record the compound nouns and numbers.

Fluency Practice Record four addresses that you know. Use complete sentences. Follow the example.

EXAMPLE:

My grandparents' address is 42 (forty-two) Calle San Isidro.

---

[1] convenient: *makes something easier for you or saves you time;* [2] hardware store: *a place where you can buy tools you use in your home and yard*

Strong Words and Weak Words in Sentences

PRESENTATION

A word with clear meaning, like table, *is a strong word. A word with grammatical meaning, like* the, *is a weak word.*

Strong Words in Sentences

> Room for Rent
> Big, Good View, Quiet

> I have a **ROOM** for **RENT**.[1] It's **BIG**. It has a **GOOD VIEW**. It's **QUIET**.

Strong words have strong stress. They are easy to hear and have clear meanings. Strong words are usually nouns, verbs, adjectives, and adverbs.

Weak Words in Sentences

> Men's Basketball — Feb. 8 — 8:00 P.M. School Gym

> There's a **MEN'S BASKETBALL GAME** on **FEBRUARY EIGHTH** at **EIGHT** P.M. in the **SCHOOL GYM**.

Weak words are often "grammar" words, such as *the, a, it, to, in*. Weak words are not stressed, and they are harder to hear than strong words.

---

[1] rent: *the money you pay to live in a room, apartment, or house that belongs to someone else*

EXERCISE 1: Strong and Weak Words

Listen and repeat. Say the strong words clearly. Group words together.

1. for the SUMMER

   a ROOMMATE

   a ROOMMATE for the SUMMER

   I'm LOOKING

   I'm LOOKING for a ROOMMATE.

   I'm LOOKING for a ROOMMATE for the SUMMER.

2. a PLACE

   to STAY

   a PLACE to STAY

   I NEED

   to FIND

   I NEED to FIND

   I NEED to FIND a PLACE.

   I NEED to FIND a PLACE to STAY.

   I NEED to FIND a PLACE to STAY for the SUMMER.

EXERCISE 2: Hearing Weak Words

A | *People put information that they want others to see on bulletin boards. There are online bulletin boards like the one below. Read the information. It's about an apartment in New York City.*

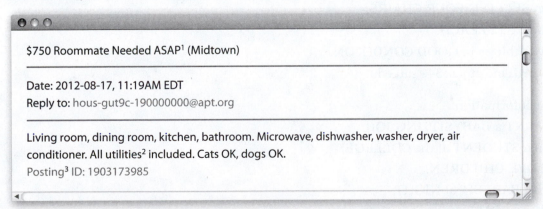

$750 Roommate Needed ASAP[1] (Midtown)

Date: 2012-08-17, 11:19AM EDT
Reply to: hous-gut9c-190000000@apt.org

Living room, dining room, kitchen, bathroom. Microwave, dishwasher, washer, dryer, air conditioner. All utilities[2] included. Cats OK, dogs OK.
Posting[3] ID: 1903173985

---

[1] ASAP: *an abbreviation for the phrase* as soon as possible; [2] utilities: *money you pay for gas, electricity, or water;*
[3] posting: *a public notice about something, pinned to a bulletin board or wall, or written on a Web site*

B| *Listen to the paragraph. Write the weak words you hear in the blanks.*

I need _____to_____ find _____ roommate _____ soon as possible.
            1.   **2.**   **3.**

_____ rent is $750 _____ month. _____ apartment _____ a
  4.   **5.**   **6.**   **7.**

living room, dining room, kitchen, _____ one bathroom. _____ a microwave,
                        8.   **9.**

a dishwasher, _____ a washer and dryer. _____ apartment _____
          10.   **11.**   **12.**

_____ air conditioner. All utilities _____ included. Cats _____ OK,
  13.   **14.**   **15.**

_____ dogs _____ OK.
  16.   **17.**

C| *What else do you want to know about the apartment in Part A? Listen and repeat the questions.*

1. Is the NEIGHBORHOOD SAFE?
2. HOW BIG is the APARTMENT?
3. Is the APARTMENT QUIET?
4. Is the BEDROOM a PRIVATE[1] ROOM?
5. HOW BIG is the ROOM?
6. Does the ROOM have any FURNITURE?
7. Is the ROOM SUNNY?

EXERCISE 3: Strong Words vs. Weak Words

José, Akiko, and Lenka want to put notices (signs) on the bulletin board at the university. That way, other students and teachers can read the information they post.[2]

A| *Listen and repeat the information. Stress only the strong words.*

1. José's information:
   a. I'm MOVING.
   b. I'm SELLING some FURNITURE.
   c. I'm SELLING a COUCH for $200.
   d. I'm SELLING a TABLE for $50.
   e. I'm SELLING FOUR CHAIRS.
   f. They're $20 EACH.
   g. Everything's in GOOD CONDITION.
   h. EMAIL me at jose34@sau.edu.

2. Akiko's information:
   a. I WANT a BABYSITTING JOB.
   b. I'm a STUDENT at the COLLEGE.
   c. I LOVE CHILDREN.
   d. I can BABYSIT at NIGHT.
   e. You can CALL me at 555–0100.

---

[1] private: *for use by one person or group, not for everyone;* [2] post: *put a public notice on a bulletin board, wall, or Web site*

3. Lenka's information:
   a. I NEED a RIDE to CHICAGO.
   b. I WANT to GO in MID-DECEMBER.
   c. I'll SHARE the DRIVING.
   d. I'll SHARE the COST of GAS.
   e. My EMAIL is jenny23@jmail.com.

B | *PAIRS: Complete the bulletin board notices for José, Akiko, and Lenka.*

1.
MOVING SALE
COUCH $200
TABLE _____
_____ , _____$20_____ EA.
_____ CONDITION
jose34@sau.edu

2.
_____ JOB WANTED
_____ STUDENT
LOVE _____
AVAILABLE at _____

CALL _____

3.
_____ NEEDED to _____
MID- _____
SHARE _____ , _____
jenny23@jmail.com

EXERCISE 4: Using Strong Words

Look at the bulletin board ads. Fill in the blanks below each ad to make complete sentences.

1.

CLASS PARTY
TONIGHT, 9:00 P.M.
MARY'S APT.
42 FIRST ST.

There will be a _____ _____ tonight at _____ P.M.

The party's at _____ _____ . Her address is 42

_____ _____ .

(continued)

2.

> ROOM for RENT
> SMALL, SUNNY
> CLOSE to BUS, $800/MO.
> NON-SMOKER ONLY
> CALL FRANCO 555-0159

I have a _____ for _____. It's _____,

_____, and _____ to the bus. The _____ is $800

a month. I only want a _____-smoker. _____ Franco at 555-0159.

3.

> ENGLISH 1101
> FINAL EXAM
> DEC. 13, 9:00–11:00 A.M.
> RM 202

The _____ _____ for English 1101 will be _____ 13th,

from _____ to _____ A.M. The exam will be in Room

_____.

4.

> SOCCER TEAM PRACTICE
> TODAY 4:30 P.M.
> WRIGHT'S FIELD

The _____ _____ will practice _____ at

_____ P.M. Practice will be at Wright's Field.

A PLACE TO LIVE

EXERCISE 5: University Residence Halls

A | *Listen and repeat. Make sure you understand all the words.*

1. residence halls

2. participate in

3. extracurricular activities

4. staff

5. cable TV

6. wireless Internet access

7. lounges

B | *Listen to the information about residence halls at an American university. How does the speaker describe the residence halls? Check (✔) the information you hear. Then compare your answers with a partner.*

_____ kitchens

_____ activities for students

_____ a dining area in every residence hall

_____ computers in every room

_____ a friendly staff

_____ TVs in every room

_____ cable TV hookups in every room

_____ free Internet access

_____ libraries

_____ exercise rooms

EXERCISE 6: Your Turn

A | *Read each question. Circle the answer that describes where you live.*

1. **Q:** Where do you live?

   A: I live in a _____.

   a. house or apartment   **b.** residence hall

2. **Q:** How quiet is your (house/apartment/residence hall)?

   A: It's usually _____.

   a. quiet   **b.** noisy

3. **Q:** Do you have your own room?

   A: I _____.

   a. have my own room   **b.** share my room

4. **Q:** How big is your room?

   A: My room is _____.

   a. big   **b.** small

5. **Q:** Do you have a good view?

   A: I _____.

   a. have a good view   **b.** don't have a good view

6. **Q:** How much sun does your room get?

   A: My room is usually _____.

   a. sunny   **b.** dark

7. **Q:** How safe is your neighborhood?

   A: It's _____.

   a. pretty safe   **b.** not very safe

B | *GROUPS: Use the questions and answers to describe where you live. Stress the strong words in each sentence.*

Accuracy Practice *Listen again to Exercises 1 and 3A on pages 115 and 116. Then record the phrases and sentences.*

Fluency Practice *Record a description of your room. You can make your own sentences or use those from Exercise 6A on page 120.*

Highlighting Information

STEP 1 PRESENTATION

Use stress and pitch (a musical note) to highlight information in a sentence.

1. The Most Important Information

I saw a **GREAT** movie.

GREAT? It was **AWFUL**!

In a sentence, one word usually has the most important information. It is often the last non-grammar word. Use your voice to "highlight" this word: Say the word with strong stress and a high pitch (a high note).

2. New Information

What's your name?

My name is **CHANG**.

Highlight new information in a sentence.

3. Correcting and Contrasting Information

We're not taking the **BUS**. We're **WALKING**.

Highlight errors and corrections.

The movie was **GOOD** but **LONG**.

Highlight information that you compare or contrast.

EXERCISE 1: Hearing the Most Important Word

A | *Listen and repeat. You will hear each sentence three times. The speaker will highlight a different word each time.*

1. I ran for two hours in the park.

   a. _____

   b. _____

   c. _____

2. My new laptop isn't very fast.

   a. _____

   b. _____

   c. _____

3. I tried to call you at home this morning.

   a. _____

   b. _____

   c. _____

B | *Listen again. Which word does the speaker highlight in each sentence? Write the highlighted word in the blank.*

EXERCISE 2: Conversation

A | *Listen to the conversation.*

STELLA: I made a dentist appointment for you on Thursday.

STANLEY: I don't need to see the doctor.

STELLA: A dentist appointment, Stanley. The dentist.

STANLEY: I can't go on Friday. I'm working.

STELLA: I said Thursday. The appointment's for Thursday.

STANLEY: I don't like Dr. Corkrum.

STELLA: We haven't seen Dr. Corkrum for years! He's retired.[1]

STANLEY: Good. Because I never liked him.

B | *Listen again and repeat. Circle the words that are highlighted.*

---

[1] retired: *stopped working, due to old age*

EXERCISE 3: What Did You Say?

PAIRS: Follow the directions.

STUDENT A: Read a numbered sentence to your partner.

STUDENT B: Ask the questions under Student A's sentence.

STUDENT A: Answer the questions. Use your voice to highlight the correct information.

> **EXAMPLE:**
>
> **STUDENT A:** I went to a beach party with my roommate last weekend.
>
> **STUDENT B:** *What kind of party did you go to?*
>
> **STUDENT A:** A BEACH party.

1. I went to a beach party with my roommate last weekend.

   a. What kind of party did you go to?

   b. Did you go yesterday?

   c. Who did you go with?

   d. Did you say a beach concert?

2. My brother is a reporter for a newspaper in Seattle.

   a. Did you say your father is a reporter?

   b. He works in Boston?

   c. Did you say your brother's a photographer?

   d. Is he a TV reporter?

3. My mother and I are going to Miami for a week in March.

   a. Did you say you're going to Maryland?

   b. You're going to Miami for a weekend?

   c. Did you say you and your brother are going to Miami?

   d. You're going in May?

CORRECTING INFORMATION

EXERCISE 4: Highlight the Correct Information

🎧 **A |** *Listen and repeat the sentences. Each sentence has incorrect information.*

1. There are 58 minutes in an hour.*
2. Miami is in Texas.
3. The president of the United States lives in the Pink House.
4. Water freezes at 10° (ten degrees) Centigrade.
5. Chicago is a small city.
6. Mexico is north of the United States.
7. April is the third month of the year.
8. There are 22 hours in a day.
9. The *Titanic* was a large bus.
10. Shakespeare was a famous Japanese writer.

> ***Natural English**
>
> Highlight the noun or adjective after *there is/are.*
>
> There's a BOOK on the table.
>
> There are TWELVE months in a year.

B | *PAIRS: Take turns reading a sentence and correcting the information. Remember to use your voice to highlight the correct information. Then check your answers on page 126.*

EXAMPLES:

STUDENT A: Paris is in ENGLAND.
STUDENT B: Excuse me, but Paris is in FRANCE.

STUDENT A: The weather's COLD at the equator.
STUDENT B: That's WRONG. The weather's HOT at the equator.

EXERCISE 5: Your Turn

A | *Write three sentences with incorrect information. Include information that your classmates will know is wrong. Your sentences can be about people or places.*

1. _____

2. _____

3. _____

B | *PAIRS: Take turns reading your sentences. Use your voice to highlight the correct information.*

STEP 4 EXTENDED PRACTICE

Accuracy Practice *Listen again to Exercise 1A on page 123. Then record each sentence in the exercise three times. Highlight a different word each time.*

Fluency Practice *Correct the sentences in Exercise 4A on page 125. Record your corrections. Follow the examples.*

EXAMPLES:

There are **60** minutes in an hour, not **58**.

Miami is in **FLORIDA**, not **TEXAS**.

Exercise 4B: 1. There are **60** minutes in an hour. **2.** Miami is in **Florida**. (**Dallas/Houston** is in Texas.) **3.** The president of the United States lives in the **White House**. **4.** Water freezes at 0° (**zero** degrees) Centigrade. **5.** Chicago is a **big** city. **6.** Mexico is **south** of the United States. (**Canada** is north of the United States.) **7.** April is the **fourth** month of the year. (**March** is the third month of the year.) **8.** There are **24** hours in a day. **9.** The *Titanic* was a large ship. **10.** Shakespeare was a famous **English** writer.

And, or, *and* can *are common weak words. They have short, unstressed pronunciations.*

And

In speaking, *and* is usually a weak word. It sounds like /ən/. Join *and* to the word before it.

Sometimes *and* is spelled '*n*': *Rock 'n' roll.*

Or

In speaking, *or* is a weak word. It sounds like /ər/. Join *or* to the word before it.

Can

Can is a weak word when a verb follows it. It sounds like /kən/. Join *can* to the words around it.

Can is a strong word in short answers: /kǽn/

Can you drive? Yes, I cán.

Can't

Can't is always a strong word: /kǽnt/.

I cán't come.   We cán't do it.

127

STEP 2 | FOCUSED PRACTICE

EXERCISE 1: Phrases with *and*

A | *Listen and repeat the phrases. They describe foods that often go together. Pronounce* **and** *as /ən/. Join it to the first word.*

1. bacon and eggs
2. bread and water
3. cake and ice cream

4. chips and dip
5. cookies and milk
6. fish and chips

7. surf and turf
8. turkey and stuffing
9. rice and beans

B | *Choose four phrases. Write them in the left column.*

Your Phrases

1. _____
2. _____
3. _____
4. _____

Your Partner's Phrases

1. _____
2. _____
3. _____
4. _____

C | *PAIRS: Listen to your partner's phrases. Write them in the right column.*

EXERCISE 2: Matching

A | *The foods in Exercise 1A are eaten by different groups of people or in different places. Use these foods to complete the sentences.*

1. For breakfast, it's _____*bacon and eggs*_____.

2. In the Caribbean, it's _____.

3. For dessert, it's _____.

4. At beach restaurants, it's _____.

5. For a children's snack, it's _____.

6. For Thanksgiving, it's _____.

7. At a party, it's _____.

8. In England, it's _____.

9. In prison, it was _____.

B | *GROUPS: Compare your answers (you can also check them on page 132). Then talk about foods that often go together in your country.*

EXERCISE 3: Phrases with *or*

A | *Listen and repeat the phrases. Pronounce* **or** *as /ər/. Join it to the first word.*

1. chocolate or vanilla
2. chicken or steak
3. coffee or tea
4. cook or clean up
5. hot or cold
6. left or right
7. March or April
8. married or single
9. milk or cream
10. north or south
11. off or on
12. one or two
13. right or wrong
14. Monday or Tuesday
15. stay in or go out

B | *Choose four phrases. Write them in the left column.*

Your Phrases	Your Partner's Phrases
1. _____	1. _____
2. _____	2. _____
3. _____	3. _____
4. _____	4. _____

C | *PAIRS: Listen to your partner's phrases. Write them in the right column.*

EXERCISE 4: Conversations

A | *Listen and repeat the conversations. When there are two choices, say the first choice with rising intonation. Say the second choice with falling intonation.*

1. **A:** Is my answer right or wrong?

   B: I think it's wrong.

2. **A:** Do I turn left or right?

   B: Left.

3. **A:** Do I go north or south?

   B: North.

4. **A:** Do you want coffee or tea?

   B: Coffee, please.

(continued)

5. A: Are you married or single?

   B: Single.

6. A: Do you want to stay in or go out?

   B: Let's go out.

7. A: Is the test on Monday or Tuesday?

   B: Monday.

8. A: Do you want to cook or clean up?

   B: I want to cook.

B | *Listen again. Draw intonation lines (⌣ or ⌢) over the words joined by* **or**.

EXERCISE 5: Sentences with *Can*

A | *Listen and repeat. Make* **can** *a weak word and join it to the pronoun. Stress the pronoun more than* **can**.

1. I can . . .	I can dance.
2. You can . . .	You can use my car this weekend.
3. He can . . .	He can swim.
4. She can . . .	She can speak three languages.
5. We can . . .	We can study together.
6. They can . . .	They can fix your computer.

> ### Natural English
>
> Use the weak pronunciation for *can*: /kən/. Your listeners will understand you better.
>
> If you pronounce *can* as /kæn/, your listeners may think you mean *can't*.

B | *PAIRS: Complete the sentences. Then take turns reading them aloud. Pronounce* **can** *as a weak word.*

1. I can _____.

2. You can _____.

3. He can _____.

4. She can _____.

5. We can _____.

6. They can _____.

ABILITIES

EXERCISE 6: Hearing *Can* and *Can't*

A | *Listen to the sentences. Complete the sentences with the words you hear:* **Can** *or* **can't**. *Check your answers with the class.*

1. I _____ swim.

2. You _____ drive.

3. He _____ play the piano.

4. She _____ play soccer.

5. We _____ help you with your homework.

6. They _____ play the drums.

7. I _____ dance, but I _____ swim.

8. I _____ speak Chinese, but I _____ speak German.

9. I _____ come on Saturday, but I _____ come on Sunday.

10. They _____ come early, but they _____ stay late.

B | *GROUPS: Choose a sentence. Complete it with* **can** *or* **can't**. *Your classmates will say, "Positive" if they hear* **can**. *They will say, "Negative" if they hear* **can't**.

EXERCISE 7: Your Turn

A | *Read the abilities and skills in the chart. Place a check (✓) in the middle column near the things that you can do.*

Abilities and Skills	I can . . .	_____ can . . . (My partner)
Music: play the guitar	☐	☐
play the piano	☐	☐
sing	☐	☐
Sports: golf	☐	☐
ski	☐	☐
swim	☐	☐
Other skills: cook	☐	☐
drive	☐	☐
speak _____ (language)	☐	☐

B | *PAIRS: Use the abilities and skills listed in the chart to ask your partner, "Can you _____ ?" Then check (✓) your partner's answers in the right column.*

C | *CLASS: Use information from the chart to write two sentences about your partner. Read the sentences to your classmates.*

1. _____

2. _____

STEP 4   EXTENDED PRACTICE

🎧🎤 **Accuracy Practice** *Listen again to Exercise 5A on page 130. After you listen, record the pronoun and* **can**. *Stress the pronoun more than* **can**. *Then record a complete sentence.*

🎤 **Fluency Practice** *Record sentences about yourself using* **can** *and/or* **can't**.

Exercise 2A: 1. bacon and eggs **2.** rice and beans **3.** cake and ice cream **4.** surf and turf **5.** cookies and milk **6.** turkey and stuffing **7.** chips and dip **8.** fish and chips **9.** bread and water

Contractions

STEP 1   PRESENTATION

A contraction is a short form of a word. Use contractions when you speak. They sound friendly.

1. **Contractions of *am*, *is*, *are***

   I'm (= I am) 25.   She's (= She is) tired.

   It's (= It is) raining.   You're (= You are) late.

   We're (= We are) early.   He's (= He is) a doctor.

2. **Contractions of *not***

   I don't (= do not) like scary movies.

   He isn't (= is not) here.

   I can't (= cannot) come today.

   They aren't (= are not) coming.

   There is no contraction of *am not*.

3. **Other Contractions**

   I'd (= I would) like a hamburger.

   I'll (= I will) bring your book tomorrow.

   I've (= I have) seen that movie.

   He's (= He has) been sick for two days.

EXERCISE 1: What You Hear

🎧 *Listen to each sentence. Do you hear a contraction or the full form of the verb? Circle the bold word or phrase you hear.*

1. The **teacher is not / teacher's not** here today.

2. I **did not / didn't** like that movie.

3. You **are not / aren't** eating your dinner.

4. I think **it is / it's** raining.

5. We **cannot / can't** go out tonight.

6. He **does not / doesn't** work very hard.

7. **They would / They'd** like to see you.

8. **I will / I'll** see you there.

EXERCISE 2: Conversations with Contractions

🎧 **A** | *Listen and repeat the conversations.*

1. **A:** Let's hurry. We'll be late.

   B: Don't worry. We've got time.

2. **A:** They aren't home yet.

   B: They're probably stuck in traffic.

3. **A:** I've heard she's a professional[1] skater.

   B: Really? I didn't know that.

4. **A:** I think you'll like this restaurant.

   B: I'm sure you're right.

5. **A:** We're leaving at 8:30.

   B: Don't worry. I won't forget.

6. **A:** She doesn't work here anymore.

   B: Do you have her phone number? I'd like to call her.

B | *Circle the contractions in each sentence.*

---

[1] professional: *someone who earns money by doing a sport that other people do just for fun*

EXERCISE 3: Words That Sound Alike

Listen and repeat the sentences. The underlined words are pronounced the same or almost the same.

1. <u>Nick'll</u> give a <u>nickel</u>.
2. <u>I'll</u> bring them <u>all</u>.
3. <u>He'll</u> climb the <u>hill</u>.
4. Mr. <u>Peep'll</u> meet <u>people</u>.
5. Your <u>price's</u> higher than their <u>prices</u>.
6. Mr. <u>Loak'll</u> take the <u>local</u> train.
7. <u>Some are</u> coming this <u>summer</u>.
8. <u>Rose's</u> near the <u>roses</u>.

EXERCISE 4: Listening for Contractions

A | Listen to the conversation. Complete the sentences with the contractions you hear. Then compare your answers with a partner.

KOJI: What'_____ you going to do this summer?

DAVOR: I'_____ got a job for June and July. Then I'_____ going to travel.

KOJI: Where'_____ you going? To Europe again?

DAVOR: No, I _____ afford¹ that. I'_____ going down south, to three new states.

KOJI: Three new states?

DAVOR: Louisiana, Mississippi, and Alabama. I'_____ like to visit all 50 states before

          I'_____ 30, and I _____ been to those states yet.

KOJI: That'_____ an interesting goal. How many states have you been to?

DAVOR: Twenty-three so far. I'_____ from California. We went to a national park every summer

          when I was a kid. So I'_____ been to almost all of the western states.

KOJI: It'_____ a pretty long drive to Louisiana. Are you going alone?

DAVOR: No, with my cousin. We'_____ share the driving.

B | PAIRS: Practice the conversation. Take turns.

---
¹ afford: *have enough money to buy or pay for something*

DREAMS

EXERCISE 5: Dreams and Goals

A | *Listen and repeat. Make sure you understand all the words and phrases.*

1. dreams for our future
2. careers
3. scientist

4. war
5. breathe
6. soldier

B | *PAIRS: Listen to the recording. Then read the sentences. Check (✓) whether each sentence is an example of a personal dream, a career dream, or a dream for a country or the world.*

Sentences	Personal Dream	Career Dream	Dream for a Country/World
1. I'd like to fall in love.*	____	____	____
2. I'd like everyone to have a place to live.	____	____	____
3. I'd like to be a doctor.	____	____	____
4. I'd like to have a large family.	____	____	____
5. I'd like everyone to have clean air to breathe.	____	____	____
6. I'd like to be a scientist.	____	____	____

*Natural English

When you use *I'd like* (for *I would like*), be sure to keep the /d/ short. Then say *like*. Don't separate *I'd* and *like*.

I'd like to fall in love.

I'd like to be a doctor.

EXERCISE 6: Your Turn

A | *First check (✓) the sentences that describe your personal goals. Then write your career goals.*

1. Personal Goals:

_____ I'd like to get married.

_____ I'd like to have a big family.

_____ I'd like to live in _____.
(city or country)

_____ I'd like to stay single.

_____ I'd like to travel to _____.
(city or country)

_____ I'd like to _____.

2. Career Goals:

I'd like to _____.

B | *PAIRS: Read your goals to your partner. Pronounce the contractions correctly.*

STEP 4 EXTENDED PRACTICE

Accuracy Practice *Listen again to Exercise 3 on page 135. Then record the sentences.*

Fluency Practice *Record sentences about your personal goals and career goals. Use the phrase* **I'd like***.*

STEP 1 PRESENTATION

Your English will be more understandable if you pronounce words together in groups (phrases).

About Word Groups

at **night**

We **need** to **bring** some **food**.

Call me at **9:00**.

A word group is a meaningful phrase. A word group has a word with strong stress, and it usually also has words with weak stress.

Don't for**get** to **bring** your **lunch** to the **picnic**.

OR

Don't for**get** to **bring** your **lunch** to the **picnic**.

You can make word groups in different ways, but don't put too many words into one group.

Join groups together this way: Pause briefly at the end of the first group. Then say the next group.

Common Word Groups

1. **Article + Noun**

   the **party**   a **picnic**

2. **Verb + Pronoun/Noun**

   call me   **bring** something

3. **Preposition + Noun**

   at **night**   for the **party**

STEP 2 FOCUSED PRACTICE

EXERCISE 1: Word Groups with Articles and Prepositions

A | *Listen and repeat the phrases. Group words together. Nouns have strong stress.*

1. in the **park**
2. by **bus**
3. at **noon**
4. on **Sunday**

5. in **class**
6. at **home**
7. to **work**
8. in an **hour**

9. for **lunch**
10. for my **birthday**
11. on the **weekend**
12. with a **friend**

B | *Choose four phrases. Write them in the left column.*

Your Phrases	Your Partner's Phrases
1. _____	1. _____
2. _____	2. _____
3. _____	3. _____
4. _____	4. _____

C | *PAIRS: Listen to your partner's phrases. Write them in the right column.*

EXERCISE 2: Word Groups with Verb + Pronoun

A | *Listen and repeat the sentences. Group words together. Verbs have strong stress.*

1. **Invite** them.
2. **Ask** her.
3. **Buy** it.
4. **Throw** it.

5. **Call** us.
6. **Tell** me.
7. **Bring** it.
8. **Open** it.

9. **Finish** it.
10. **Carry** it.
11. **Take** it.
12. **Surprise** her.

B | *Choose four sentences. Write them in the left column.*

Your Sentences	Your Partner's Sentences
1. _____	1. _____
2. _____	2. _____
3. _____	3. _____
4. _____	4. _____

C | *PAIRS: Listen to your partner's sentences. Write them in the right column.*

EXERCISE 3: Game: Chain Sentences

A | *Listen and repeat the phrases.*

Noun	Place	Time
1. **a.** the books	**b.** to the library	**c.** at 1:30
2. **a.** my laundry	**b.** to the basement	**c.** on Monday
3. **a.** the packages	**b.** to the cleaners	**c.** at 7:00
4. **a.** the car	**b.** to the post office	**c.** tomorrow
5. **a.** your mother	**b.** to the mechanic	**c.** at 3:00
6. **a.** my homework	**b.** to the teacher	**c.** in the morning
7. **a.** the boxes	**b.** to the doctor	**c.** on Thursday

B | *GROUPS: Work in groups of three. Make chain sentences.*

STUDENT A: Start the sentence with **Please take** and a noun from Exercise A.
STUDENT B: Repeat Student A's sentence and add a place.
STUDENT C: Repeat Student B's sentence and add a time.

EXAMPLE:

STUDENT A: Please take the books . . .

STUDENT B: Please take the books to the library . . .

STUDENT C: Please take the books to the library on Monday.

Then switch roles: Student C will start, Student A will add the place, and Student B will add the time.

EXERCISE 4: Word Groups in Stories

A | *Listen to the story. Notice how the word groups break the story into shorter, more meaningful parts. The word groups make the story easier to understand.*

1. My friends gave me a birthday party when I turned 25.

2. But I didn't know about it. It was a surprise party.

3. No one called me on my birthday.

4. So, I was feeling pretty sad when I drove home from work.

5. I thought nobody cared, nobody remembered.

6. I didn't want to go home. But I didn't have anywhere else to go.

7. When I got home, my house was dark.

8. I opened the door.

9. Suddenly, the lights came on.

10. People shouted, "Happy birthday!"

11. I was really surprised.

12. Everyone came: My friends and my family.

B | *PAIRS: Take turns asking and answering the questions about the story.*

1. What did the speaker think when no one called her on her birthday?
2. How did she feel when she was driving home from work?
3. What happened when she opened the door?
4. Who came to the party?

C | *Read the sentences in Part A. Be sure to group words together and join the groups smoothly. Take turns.*

PLANNING A PARTY

EXERCISE 5: The Surprise Picnic

🎧 **A** | *Listen to the conversation.*

TAKA: Melissa's birthday is this Friday.

AMIR: We should throw her a party.

TAKA: Our apartment's too small for a party.

AMIR: I know! We could have a picnic in the park.*

TAKA: Yeah. After class on Friday. We could invite the whole class.

AMIR: Let's surprise her. But what if she's busy after class?

TAKA: I'll find out from Lucas. They're always together.

AMIR: I'll find out about the weather on Friday.

> ***Natural English**
>
> Use *could* + verb to talk about a possibility. Stress the verb more than *could*.
>
> We *could háve* a picnic in the park.
>
> I *could bríng* a cake.

B | *PAIRS: Underline word groups in Part A. Your groups do not have to match the word groups on the recording. Then practice the conversation. Take turns.*

EXERCISE 6: Plans: Who's bringing what?

🎧 **A** | *Listen and repeat. Make sure you understand all the words.*

1. park
2. soccer practice
3. the north entrance
4. blankets
5. the cake
6. the deli

🎧 **B** | *Listen to the plans for Melissa's surprise birthday party.*

C | *Circle the correct word or phrase to complete each sentence. Then read a sentence to the class. Group words in phrases together.*

1. Melissa's friends are planning a (picnic / class party).

2. They are meeting (in class / at the park).

3. Lucas is bringing (Melissa / Nuri).

4. Sonia and Marko are bringing (blankets / napkins).

5. Ricardo is bringing the (food / cake).

6. Miss Adams is bringing (paper plates / drinks).

7. Nuri is going to get some (drinks / food) at the deli.

8. Felix is bringing (drinks / paper plates).

EXERCISE 7: Your Turn

A | *GROUPS: Plan a class party. Think about what you will need. You can use your own words or those from Exercise 6C. Write this information on a piece of paper.*

	Class Party
○	When: Friday at 7:00 P.M.
	Where: Room 219
	My classmates need to bring: Food, drinks, music

B | *GROUPS: Tell the class about your party. Group words into phrases. Then vote for the best plan.*

STEP 4 EXTENDED PRACTICE

🎧🎤 **Accuracy Practice** *Listen again to Exercise 4A on page 141. Then record the story.*

🎤 **Fluency Practice** *Record the plans you made in Exercise 7A. Group words together.*

26 Joining Final Sounds to Beginning Sounds

STEP 1 PRESENTATION

There are different ways to join words with final consonants to the next word.

1. Final Consonant + Beginning Vowel

an apartment   last April   arrive early

Join final consonants to beginning vowels clearly.

A final consonant before a vowel is easy to hear.

2. Final Consonant + Different Beginning Consonant

hard work   start now   work clothes

Keep the final consonant short.

Don't separate the two consonants with a vowel sound.

3. Final Consonant + Same Beginning Consonant

finish shopping   one night   plant trees

Say one long consonant. Don't say the consonant twice.

STEP 2 FOCUSED PRACTICE

EXERCISE 1: Joining Consonants to Vowels

A | *Listen and repeat the phrases and sentences. Join the consonant sound and vowel clearly.*

1. Clean up.	5. It's inexpensive.	9. an old address
2. Come in.	6. good experience[1]	10. an apartment
3. That's a good idea.	7. That's OK.	11. this evening
4. half an hour	8. an office	12. Leave early.

---

[1] good experience: *something good that happens to you or something good that you do*

B | *Choose four phrases or sentences from Part A. Write them in the left column.*

Your Words   **Your Partner's Words**

1. _____   1. _____

2. _____   2. _____

3. _____   3. _____

4. _____   4. _____

C | *PAIRS: Listen to your partner's phrases or sentences. Write them in the right column.*

EXERCISE 2: Joining Final Consonants to Different Consonants

A | *Listen and repeat the phrases. Keep the final consonant short. Then say the next word. Don't separate the two words.*

1. hard⁾ work   5. good⁾ book   9. childhood⁾ friend

2. large⁾ family   6. five⁾ children   10. sports⁾ team

3. good⁾ job   7. cold⁾ night   11. big⁾ city

4. bad⁾ storm   8. spring⁾ break¹   12. dark⁾ night

B | *Choose four phrases. Write them in the left column.*

Your Phrases   **Your Partner's Phrases**

1. _____   1. _____

2. _____   2. _____

3. _____   3. _____

4. _____   4. _____

C | *PAIRS: Listen to your partner's phrases. Write them in the right column.*

EXERCISE 3: Joining Final Consonants to the Same Consonant

A | *Listen and repeat. Don't say the consonant twice. Make one long consonant.*

1. this student   4. Stop playing.   7. one number   10. good day

2. big group   5. five volunteers²   8. Work quickly.   11. Come Monday.

3. work clothes   6. right time   9. Call later.   12. this city

---

¹ spring break: *a week of vacation from school in the spring*; ² volunteers: *people who give their time or money to help others*

B | *Choose four phrases or sentences from Part A. Write them in the left column.*

Your Words   **Your Partner's Words**

1. _____   1. _____

2. _____   2. _____

3. _____   3. _____

4. _____   4. _____

C | *PAIRS: Listen to your partner's phrases or sentences. Write them in the right column.*

EXERCISE 4: Joining Sounds in Compound Nouns

A | *Listen and repeat the compound nouns.*

1. drug'store   5. health' care

2. bike' path   6. homeowners

3. Web' site   7. team'work

4. bus stop   8. Red' Cross

B | *Listen. Complete each sentence with the compound noun from Part A that you hear. Then compare your answers with a partner.*

1. I volunteer to build homes for people in need. I share the work with other members

   of my team. _____ is very important.

2. The best part of volunteering to build a house is seeing the smiles on the faces of the

   new _____.

3. I volunteer online. Last month, I helped a _____ group in Kenya

   build a _____.

4. I gave money to the _____ after the earthquake in Haiti.

5. A busy street goes through my neighborhood. No buses stop here. We need the city

   to add a _____.

6. I ride a bicycle to work, and I don't feel safe riding on the street. I'd like the city

   to build a _____.

VOLUNTEERING

EXERCISE 5: Habitat for Humanity

A | *Listen and repeat. Make sure you understand all the words.*

1. individuals	**4.** apply	**7.** heat
2. simple	**5.** building materials	**8.** taxes
3. affordable	**6.** electricity	**9.** lends

B | *PAIRS: Listen to the recording. Then make sentences by matching the information in columns A and B. Take turns reading the sentences aloud.*

A

___c___ **1.** Habitat for Humanity

_____ **2.** The organization receives money

_____ **3.** Habitat builds

_____ **4.** The houses are

_____ **5.** Homeowners need to

_____ **6.** All of the houses

_____ **7.** Volunteers

_____ **8.** People of all ages

B

a. from companies and individuals.

b. simple, but well built.

c. is a volunteer organization.

d. pay for building materials and expenses.

e. don't have to know how to build a house.

f. houses for people who need them.

g. are affordable.

h. volunteer.

EXERCISE 6: Volunteering

A | *Listen to the conversation.*

ZHANG: What did you do on spring break?

NORA: I volunteered with Habitat for Humanity.

ZHANG: You built a house? Where?

NORA: Right here in Baltimore.*

ZHANG: What kind of work did you do?

NORA: I worked on the roof.

ZHANG: Did you finish the house?

NORA: No, but we finished the roof. I met the new owners. The husband worked with us.

ZHANG: What was it like?

NORA: It was very hard work. I've never felt so tired. The best part was meeting the new owner and his family. They were really happy.

ZHANG: Maybe I should volunteer next year. I know something about building houses. My father is a builder.

---

*Natural English

Add the word *right* to *here*, *now*, or *away* to make the meaning of a phrase stronger.

right here (exactly here)

right now (immediately)

right away (very soon)

B | *PAIRS: Practice the conversation in Part A. Take turns.*

C | *GROUPS: Answer the questions.*

1. Does Habitat for Humanity build homes in your country?
2. What kind of volunteer work do people in your country do?
3. Have you ever given money to a volunteer group? If so, which group?
4. Have you ever worked as a volunteer? If so, what did you do?

EXERCISE 7: Your Turn

A | *Read the information in the chart. Check (✓) the volunteer jobs that you could do. Then check (✓) the jobs you'd like to do.*

Volunteer Jobs	I Could Do This	I'd Like to Do This
Build a house for people who need it	☐	☐

Environmental volunteers:
     Plant trees
     Clean up parks and natural areas
	
	 ☐
	 ☐
		
		 ☐
		 ☐

Help animals	☐	☐

Online volunteering (E-volunteering):
     Teach an online course
     Make a Web site
	
	 ☐
	 ☐
		
		 ☐
		 ☐

Spend time with older people who are alone	☐	☐

Volunteer in schools:
     Coach a sports team
     Help children learn and study
     Help teachers
	
	 ☐
	 ☐
	 ☐
		
		 ☐
		 ☐
		 ☐

B | *PAIRS: Tell your partner about your chart.*

STEP 4 EXTENDED PRACTICE

Accuracy Practice *Listen again to Exercises 1A, 2A, and 3A on pages 144 and 145. Then record the phrases and sentences.*

Fluency Practice *Have you ever done volunteer work? What did you do? If you haven't volunteered, would you like to? Why or why not? Record your answers.*

Rising and Falling Intonation

PRESENTATION

Intonation is the music of your voice. Using intonation correctly will make your English easier to understand.

Intonation usually rises or falls after the strongest word in a sentence.

Do you LIKE him?

He's NICE.

1. Rising Intonation

Intonation often rises on *yes/no* questions.

Intonation also rises on words in a list. It usually falls at the end of the list.

Do you like SPORTS?

BASketball, BASEball and SOccer.

Use rising intonation to show you aren't sure.

Uhh, one liter is about one quart?

Use rising intonation to show you aren't finished speaking.

To get a driver's license, you have to be at least 16 years old. You have to pass a written test . . .

2. Falling Intonation

Intonation often falls after the strongest word in a sentence.

Intonation often falls in *wh-* questions (questions with *Who*, *What*, *Where*, etc.).

Use falling intonation to show you are sure.

Use falling intonation to show you're finished speaking.

I'm finished. Now it's your turn.

STEP 2 FOCUSED PRACTICE

EXERCISE 1: Hearing Different Intonations

Listen to the sentences and questions. Do they end with rising intonation or falling intonation? Check (✓) the correct column.

	⟋	⟍
1. Are you going out?		
2. Why do you look so angry?		
3. I'm from Puerto Rico.		
4. Your intonation is great!		
5. Does Jake ever sit down?		
6. Um, I think it costs five dollars.		

EXERCISE 2: Saying Different Intonations

A | *Listen to the conversations.*

1. **MARKO:** We're going to the park.

   SUSAN: When? Right now?

2. **JOSE:** John plays the guiTAR.

   ALICE: He also plays the piAno, vioLIN, and harMOnica.

3. **LEE:** She's from DALlas.

   MARIA: From DALLAS?

4. **ABDUL:** Do you want soup or a salad?

   LUCY: Soup.

5. **ANNA:** What did you do this weekend?

   CHANG: Nothing. I was sick.

B | *PAIRS: Practice the conversations. Follow the intonation lines.*

EXERCISE 3: One-Word Conversation

A | *Listen and repeat the conversation.*

FELIX: Hungry?

ANNA: Very.

FELIX: Sushi?

ANNA: No.

FELIX: Burgers?

ANNA: No.

FELIX: What?

ANNA: Pizza.

FELIX: Where? Tony's or Sal's?

ANNA: Tony's.

B | *Listen again. Add intonation lines (⌣ , ⌢) over the words.*

EXERCISE 4: Scrambled Conversations

A | *PAIRS: Order each set of questions and answers to make a conversation. Then add intonation lines (⌣ , ⌢) .*

1. _____ Not yet.

   _1_ Ready?

   _____ When?

   _____ Soon.

2. _____ A boy and a girl.

   _____ Married.

   _____ Children?

   _1_ Single?

3. _1_ Coffee?

   _____ No thanks.

   _____ Sure.

   _____ Milk?

4. _____ Thanks.

   _____ My sweater?

   _1_ Cold?

   _____ Very.

B | *PAIRS: Choose a conversation and read it to the class.*

EXERCISE 5: Matching

PAIRS: Match the sentences and answers. Then practice the conversations. Use correct stress and intonation.

Sentences	Answers
_d_ **1.** What are you STUdying?	**a.** TWO, please.
_____ **2.** I need some new SHOES.	**b.** To the GYM.
_____ **3.** How many do you WANT?	**c.** SURE.
_____ **4.** I went out with a new GUY.	**d.** ENGlish.
_____ **5.** Can you HELP me?	**e.** Let's go SHOPping.
_____ **6.** Where are you GOing?	**f.** INteresting.
_____ **7.** How was CLASS?	**g.** Did you have FUN?

DATING CUSTOMS

EXERCISE 6: Zoran's Ex-Girlfriend

A | *Listen to the conversation.*

DAN: What's up? I haven't seen you for a while. How is Ivana?

ZORAN: We broke up—about a month ago.

DAN: That's too bad.*

ZORAN: Not really. We weren't interested in the same things.

But we're still friends.

DAN: Are you seeing anyone else?

ZORAN: No. But I'm thinking about asking Ivana's friend out. What do you think?

DAN: Her friend? I don't know about that. Do you think that's a good idea?

> ***Natural English**
>
> When someone has a problem or bad news, you can say, "That's too bad," to show you're sorry.
>
> I didn't know you broke up.
>
> That's too bad.

B | *PAIRS: Practice the conversation. Follow the intonation lines. Then discuss this question: Do you think Zoran should date his ex-girlfriend's friend? Why or why not?*

EXERCISE 7: Your Turn

PAIRS: Ask and answer the questions. Take turns.

1. Do young people in your country date?
2. When do girls begin to date?
3. When do boys begin to date?
4. Do young people date for fun?
5. Do young people date to find a spouse?[1]
6. Do couples go out on dates alone or with a group of friends?
7. What do couples do on dates?

STEP 4 EXTENDED PRACTICE

Accuracy Practice *Listen again to Exercise 2A on page 152. Then record the conversations.*

Fluency Practice *Record the questions and your answers from Exercise 7.*

---
[1] spouse: *husband or wife*

Other Uses of Intonation

Use correct intonation on question words and **right?** *Intonation helps the listener know whether you are asking for a repetition, asking for information, or checking understanding.*

Asking Someone to Repeat

Use rising intonation with question words when you want the speaker to repeat.

Asking for Information

Use falling intonation on question words when you want information.

Checking Understanding

Use rising intonation on the word *right* when you want to check understanding.

EXERCISE 1: Hearing Intonation

A | *Read the conversations. Ali can answer Max's question in two ways: Answer a means that Max didn't hear what Ali said (or didn't hear everything). Answer b means that Max heard what Ali said and wants more information.*

1. **ALI:** I bought something.

   MAX: What?

   ALI: **a.** I said I bought something. **b.** A sweater.

2. **ALI:** I'm going to play soccer tomorrow.

   MAX: When?

   ALI: **a.** Tomorrow. I said tomorrow. **b.** In the morning, at 10 o'clock.

3. **ALI:** There's a party at school tonight.

   MAX: Where?

   ALI: **a.** At school. **b.** In the gym.

4. **ALI:** I met a new student today.

   MAX: Who?

   ALI: **a.** I said I met a new student. **b.** Maria Mendoza.

5. **ALI:** There's something on your face.

   MAX: What?

   ALI: **a.** There's something on your face. **b.** Maybe mustard. It's yellow.

B | *Listen to the first two lines of each conversation. Listen to Max's voice when he says the question word. How will Ali answer Max's question? Circle **a** or **b**.*

EXERCISE 2: Game: What?

A | *PAIRS: Practice using intonation to ask information questions.*

STUDENT A: Read one of the sentences on page 162 to Student B.

STUDENT B: Listen to Student A's sentence. Ask a one-word question: **What? Where?** or **When?** Use rising intonation if you want a repetition. Use falling intonation if you want more information.

STUDENT A: Listen carefully to the intonation Student B uses. Repeat your sentence or answer the question. Then read another sentence. When you finish your sentences, switch roles with Student B.

STUDENT B: Read the sentences on page 164. Listen as your teacher reads the examples.

EXAMPLES:

STUDENT A: Something great happened! **STUDENT A:** Something great happened!

STUDENT B: What? **STUDENT B:** What?

STUDENT A: The teacher canceled the test. **STUDENT A:** I said something great happened.

EXERCISE 3: Intonation and Feelings

A | *The intonation you use can help express your feelings. Listen to the conversations.*

_____ **1.** ROOMMATE: How are you?
YOU: Fine. I just got a job.

_____ **2.** ROOMMATE: What's up?
YOU: Not much. I got that job.

_____ **3.** ROOMMATE: How was your day?
YOU: Great! I got that job.

B | *Read the situations below. Then listen to Part A again. Write the letter of each situation next to the matching conversation in Part A.*

a. You don't want to talk. You just got a job that you don't really want.

b. You're angry. You don't think you should have to work, and you don't want the job.

c. You're very happy. You just got a great job, and you're excited.

EXERCISE 4: Right?

A | *Listen to the conversation.*

ALIYA: Hi, Marty. Thanks for inviting me to your party. Can you give me directions to your house?

MARTY: Sure.* You live on Leggett Road, right?

ALIYA: That's right.

MARTY: OK. Drive toward town on Leggett Road. Turn left before you cross the bridge. That's called—

ALIYA: Wait, wait! You're going too fast. I turn before the bridge, right?

MARTY: That's right. Turn on Broad Street. It's before the bridge. My house is the first one on the left, 210 Broad Street.

ALIYA: 210 Broad, right?

MARTY: That's right.

ALIYA: Thanks, Marty. The party starts at eight o'clock, right?

MARTY: That's right. See you tonight.

---

*Natural English

Use the word *sure* to say, "Of course," informally.

A: Can you give me directions?

B: Sure.

B | *PAIRS: Listen again and repeat the conversation in Part A.*

CHECKING INFORMATION

This is what you wanted, right?

PEPPERS 89¢

EXERCISE 5: Checking Information

A | *Listen and repeat. Make sure you understand all the words.*

1. slices   2. toast   3. olive oil   4. onions

B | *PAIRS: Complete a recipe for an easy sandwich.*

STUDENT A: Read the information in the chart on page 162 to Student B.

STUDENT B: Write what Student A says. If you want a repetition, ask, *What?*

Then read what you wrote to Student A and add, *Right?* Correct your information if it is wrong. Finally, switch roles. Read the information in the chart on page 164 to Student A. Follow the example.

EXAMPLE:

STUDENT A: Cut a loaf of bread into slices.

STUDENT B: _____ *What?* _____

STUDENT A: Cut a loaf of bread into slices.

STUDENT B: *You said, "Cut a loaf of bread into slices," right?*

STUDENT A: That's right.

EXERCISE 6: Your Turn

A | *Choose a classmate you don't know well. Write three things you know about that person on the lines below. Follow the example.*

EXAMPLE:

Your first name is spelled H-A-N-S.

1. _____

2. _____

3. _____

B | *PAIRS: Work with the classmate you wrote about. Read your sentences. Add **right?** to the end of each sentence. Your partner will tell you whether your information is correct or not. Follow the example.*

EXAMPLE:

STUDENT A: Your first name is spelled H-A-N-S, right?

STUDENT B: Yes, that's right.

STEP 4 EXTENDED PRACTICE

Accuracy Practice *Listen again to Exercise 4A on page 158. Then record the conversation with a partner, or by yourself, reading both parts.*

Fluency Practice

1. *In the chart, write directions to your home from school. You can use your own ideas or those from Exercise 4A on page 158.*

To My House from School	To My Partner's House from School
1.	1.
2.	2.
3.	3.
4.	4.
5.	5.

2. *PAIRS: Follow the steps below. Record the conversation that you have with your partner.*

STUDENT A: Read your directions to Student B.

STUDENT B: Write Student A's directions in the chart. Then read the directions aloud, adding the word **right?** Student A will tell you whether you wrote the directions correctly.

APPENDICES

1   FOR TEAM A PLAYERS / STUDENT A

UNIT 6

Exercise 5, page 30

1. What's the third month of the year?
2. What do you find in a dictionary?
3. What does a man wear under a jacket?
4. What's the opposite of *last*?
5. What's the past tense of *are*?
6. What's the opposite of *clean*?
7. What's the opposite of *finish*?
8. What's the opposite of *remember*?
9. What number comes after 33?

Answers:

1. March	4. first	7. start
2. words	5. were	8. forget
3. (a) shirt	6. dirty	9. 34

UNIT 8

Exercise 3, page 43

1. What's the opposite of *north*?
2. What day comes after Wednesday?
3. What's the name of the white things in your mouth?
4. What do you say when someone does something nice?
5. What street comes between Fourth Street and Sixth Street?
6. What number comes after 29?
7. What's a word for things you wear?
8. What can you do with a ball?
9. What's the plural of *that*?
10. What's the opposite of *everything*?

Answers:

1. south	6. 30
2. Thursday	7. clothing
3. teeth	8. throw (it)
4. Thanks / Thank you.	9. those
5. Fifth (Street)	10. nothing

UNIT 9

Exercise 7, page 51

1. What letter comes after *U*?
2. What is the opposite of *morning*?
3. What do many people drink in the morning?
4. What's the opposite of *noisy*?
5. What's another word for *persons*?
6. What's the opposite of *white*?
7. What's another word for a *male child*?
8. What's the opposite of *east*?
9. What number comes after 6?
10. What's the opposite of *slow*?
11. What month comes after January?

Answers:

1. V	5. people	9. 7
2. evening	6. black	10. fast / quick
3. coffee	7. boy	11. February
4. quiet	8. west	

Exercise 6B, page 113

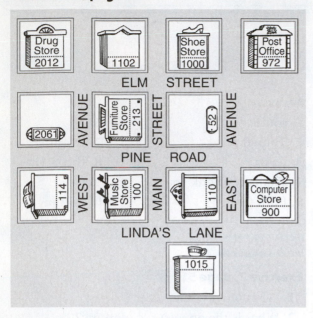

Ask your partner about the addresses on your map with blanks.

EXAMPLE: What's at _____*1102 Elm Street*_____?

Your partner will tell you the answer. Write the answer in the blank.

Exercise 2A, page 157

1. Something terrible happened.
2. I'll meet you this afternoon.
3. Let's go to the country.
4. There's something on your shirt.

Exercise 5B, page 159

1. Cut a loaf of bread into slices.
2. Toast the bread.
3. Put a little olive oil on each slice of bread.
4. Put a little salt and pepper on the bread.
5.
6.
7.
8.

UNIT 6

Exercise 5, page 30

1. What's a Ford™?
2. What's the name of a round shape?
3. What's the opposite of *south*?
4. What do people do at their jobs?
5. What animals fly?
6. What's the opposite of *after*?
7. What number comes after 3?
8. What's the opposite of *easy*?
9. What number comes after 29?

Answers:

1. (a) car	4. work	7. 4
2. (a) circle	5. birds	8. hard
3. north	6. before	9. 30

UNIT 8

Exercise 3, page 43

1. What's the name for the day you were born?
2. What's the opposite of *south*?
3. What number comes after 999 (nine hundred ninety-nine)?
4. What part of your face is under your nose?
5. What's a word for your mother's son?
6. What's the plural of *this*?
7. Where do you go to see a movie?
8. What's the opposite of *healthy*?
9. What's 1 + 2?
10. What is January?

Answers:

1. birthday	6. these
2. north	7. (a) theater
3. (one/a) thousand	8. unhealthy
4. mouth	9. 3
5. brother	10. (a) month (the first month)

UNIT 9

Exercise 7, page 51

1. What season is between fall and spring?
2. What's the opposite of *an answer*?
3. What do people speak?
4. What's a word for *a male parent*?
5. What's the opposite of *start*?
6. What do we call the front of the head?
7. What's the opposite of *unhappy*?
8. What number comes after 4?
9. What's the opposite of *always*?
10. What's the opposite of *after*?
11. What's the opposite of *small*?

Answers:

1. winter	7. happy
2. a question	8. 5
3. language(s)	9. never
4. father (papa, pop, pa)	10. before
5. finish / stop	11. big
6. face	

UNIT 20

Exercise 6B, page 113

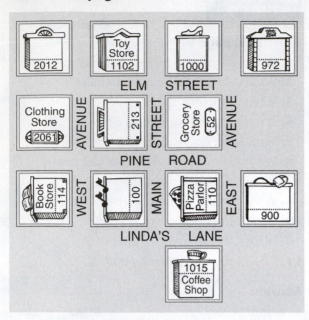

Ask your partner about the addresses on your map with blanks.

EXAMPLE: What's at _____ *2012 Elm Street* _____?

Your partner will tell you the answer. Write the answer in the blank.

UNIT 28

Exercise 2A, page 157

1. Something strange happened.

2. I have some good news.

3. Let's get together this weekend.

4. I met Felix on vacation.

Exercise 5B, page 159

1.	
2.	
3.	
4.	
5.	Cut up onions and tomatoes.
6.	Mix the onions and tomatoes together.
7.	Put some onions and tomatoes on each slice of bread.
8.	Put some cheese on top of the onions and tomatoes.

3   RECORDING AND SENDING A SOUND FILE

Windows XP Operating System

Recording

1. Plug in the microphone.

2. Open the START menu and click on the following: ALL PROGRAMS → ACCESSORIES → ENTERTAINMENT → SOUND RECORDER.

3. With the microphone plugged into the computer, click the red RECORD button and speak into the microphone. The recorder will record one minute of speech. Click the red RECORD button again to continue recording.

Saving and Compressing

4. Open the FILE menu and click SAVE AS. Compress the file if it is large: On the SAVE AS window, click the CHANGE button. In the SOUND SELECTION window, under FORMAT, select MPegLayer 3 (MP3). Close the SOUND SELECTION window. Name the file and save it.

Sending

5. The file can now be attached to an email and sent.

Windows VISTA and Windows 7 Operating System

Recording and Saving

1. Plug in the microphone.

2. Open the START menu and click on the following: ALL PROGRAMS → ACCESSORIES → SOUND RECORDER.

3. Click the red START RECORDING button and speak into the microphone.

4. Click the STOP RECORDING button when you finish. A SAVE box will appear. Name the file and save it.

Compressing and Sending

5. Right click on the saved sound file. SEND TO → COMPRESSED (ZIPPED)

6. Attach the compressed file to an email and send it.

MACINTOSH

Recording and Saving

1. Open an existing Sound Recording application on your Mac. If you do not have a Sound Recording application installed, download and install the free version of **Audacity**™ sound recorder (http://audacity.sourceforge.net/download/). It is very easy to use.

2. After installing **Audacity**™, open the application from your desktop and then use the recording tools to Record, Stop, Rewind, Pause, or Fast-forward.

3. To save the recorded file, click on the FILE menu and then click on EXPORT AS MP3.

4. Choose the location to save the file and then click on SAVE.

STUDENT AUDIO CD-ROM TRACKING GUIDE

The Student Audio CD-ROM has MP3 files for these Accuracy Practice exercises.